Blacks and Social Change

BLACKS AND SOCIAL CHANGE

Impact of the Civil Rights Movement in Southern Communities

JAMES W. BUTTON

Princeton University Press
Princeton, New Jersey

Published by Princeton University Press,
41 William Street, Princeton, New Jersey 08540
In the United Kingdom: Princeton University Press,
Guildford Surrey

Library of Congress Cataloging-in-Publication Data

Button, James W., 1942– Blacks and social
change : impact of the civil rights
movement in southern communities
/ James W. Button.
p. cm. Bibliography; p. Includes index.

ISBN 0-691-07795-9 (alk. paper)

1. Afro-Americans—Southern States—Politics and government.
2. Afro-Americans—Civil rights—Southern States.
3. Afro-Americans—Florida—Politics and government.
4. Afro-Americans—Civil rights—Florida.
5. Southern States—Politics and government—1951–
6. Southern States—Race relations.
7. Florida—Politics and government—1951–
8. Florida—Race relations.
9. Civil rights movements—Southern States.
10. Civil rights movements—Florida.
I. Title E185.92.B88 1989 305.8'96073'.075—dc19 88-39618 CIP

This book has been composed in Linotron Baskerville

Clothbound editions of Princeton University Press books
are printed on acid-free paper, and binding materials
are chosen for strength and durability. Paperbacks,
although satisfactory for personal collections,
are not usually suitable for library rebinding

Printed in the United States of America
by Princeton University Press
Princeton, New Jersey

Contents

Figures

TABLES

Preface

Some thirty years ago the black civil rights movement emerged as a social revolution that was to shake the South at its very foundation. The movement provided the ultimate test for American democracy: could and would the South provide greater equality for its black citizens who had been denied almost every opportunity for a decent life? This book is an attempt to answer that question. It is the story, and analysis, of the racial changes that have taken place in six fairly typical southern communities. In a larger sense, *Blacks and Social Change* is also about how well democracy works for the most disadvantaged, and to what extent the contradiction between American beliefs on equality and the reality of inequality has been resolved.

This book represents the culmination of a very long and arduous journey for me. Original plans for the study were first discussed in 1975, inspired by the earlier, groundbreaking works on the South by Donald Matthews and the late James Prothro (*Negroes and the New Southern Politics*) and by William Keech (*The Impact of Negro Voting*). The research design was bold and certainly ambitious, especially given the lack of significant funding. The first and most thorough investigations of these communities took place in the years 1976–1978 with substantial follow-up field work carried out in the early 1980s and again in the mid-1980s. Many additional hours were spent reading each edition of local newspapers from the late 1950s through the mid-1980s. Simply digesting the wealth of information on each community alone proved to be no small task; making sense of it all for *six* communities was sometimes overwhelming. I was convinced, however, that the process of social change could be understood well only if communities were examined fairly closely, over considerable time, and in a comparative context. I am still confident that this assumption is correct, and my only regret is that I was not able to spend more time in each community.

Nevertheless, this project, like any venture of such magnitude, would not have been possible without the assistance of a number of individuals. I owe a special debt of gratitude to my colleagues Larry

Berkson and Richard Scher, who participated in the important early stages of the study. Their help in developing the conceptual framework and in gathering data was invaluable. To Richard I am especially grateful for his friendship, encouragement, and support throughout the project. Other colleagues who willingly offered useful comments and criticisms at various stages of the research included Charles Bullock, David Colburn, Al Clubok, Peter Eisinger, Joe Feagin, David Garrow, Steve Sanderson, Bert Swanson, and Ken Wald. I wish to thank each of them for their suggestions and ideas.

A number of University of Florida students, both graduate and undergraduate, also played an important role in assisting with the field research during the initial phase. While participating in a class on community research, each of them gathered some data on particular cities in this study. This information sometimes proved to be of mixed quality and some of the work had to be replicated, but a good deal of the student research was extremely useful. Of particular value was the field work of Paige Parker, a doctoral student who labored with me in rural north Florida. His insights, dedication, and support were very helpful on a number of occasions. To all of these students, I am very grateful.

Although I received no major outside grants or funding for this research, I was fortunate to obtain some internal institutional support. Specifically, University College, the College of Liberal Arts and Sciences, and the Division of Sponsored Research all contributed funds for my travels at various times. Moreover, the university's librarians and staff were always generous with their time and assistance. In particular I would like to thank Steve Kerber and Elizabeth Alexander of the P. K. Yonge Library of Florida History, and Kay Haile and Debra Van Ausdale who so carefully typed the manuscript through several drafts. My gratitude is also extended to the University of Texas Press, which granted me permission to reprint material from my article "The Quest for Economic Equality: Factors Related to Black Employment in the South," *Social Science Quarterly* 62, no. 3 (September 1981). In addition, I am deeply appreciative of the work of my editors at Princeton University Press, Gail Ullman, Wendy Wong, and Ed Levy.

To the dozens of persons, both black and white, in each of these communities who contributed to this project, I am also extremely grateful. These people took time from their busy lives to share with me their thoughts and perceptions about complex and often sensitive issues. A number of them went out of their way to steer me toward valuable sources of information and, in some cases, to actually locate important records and documents for me. Although some of these people will disagree with my contentions, this book could not have been written without their help.

Finally, I am most deeply appreciative of the love and support given me by my wife, Barbara, and by my two sons, Matt and Adam. Through the many long years of research and writing, they always stood by me with encouragement and with an understanding of my moral commitment to this project. Thus it is to them that I dedicate this book, with the hope that it may add to our knowledge of how to create a more just society.

Abbreviations

CCC	Citizens Coordinating Committee
CDBG	Community Development Block Grant
CDC	Community Development Corporation
CETA	Comprehensive Employment and Training Act
CFAC	Community Fair Action Committee
CORE	Congress of Racial Equality
CTA	Citizens' Taxpayers Association
FBI	Federal Bureau of Investigation
HEW	Department of Health, Education, and Welfare
HRC	Human Relations Commission
HUD	Department of Housing and Urban Development
KKK	Ku Klux Klan
NAACP	National Association for the Advancement of Colored People
NASA	National Aeronautics and Space Administration
SCLC	Southern Christian Leadership Conference
SICA	Singer Island Civic Association
TIP	Titusville Improvement Program
WESTPAC	Westside Political Action Committee

BLACKS AND SOCIAL CHANGE

1

The Civil Rights Movement and Its Consequences

> The one word which better than any other describes the position of Negro Americans in the South from the 1890s until the outbreak of World War II is *powerless*. . . . Negroes were totally excluded from positions of decision making in all institutions. . . . All public facilities in the region, including city parks and playgrounds, theaters, hotels, and restaurants were rigidly segregated—as was, of course, the entire school system. The disenfranchisement of Negroes was virtually complete.
>
> —Everett Carll Ladd,
> *Negro Political Leadership in the South*, 1966

The civil rights movement in the South was considered one of America's most important periods of political and social readjustment in this century, and perhaps one of the most profound in the country's history. The movement represented the first major effort to gain greater equality for blacks since Reconstruction. Indeed, the primary assumption underlying the civil rights movement was that, once freed from overt intimidation and granted basic political rights, blacks would be able to translate those gains into political power and economic advancement. Political equality and the betterment of social and economic conditions for blacks were the foremost goals of the movement. Black political power was also seen as the fundamental precondition to advances in other aspects of life. "If Negroes could vote," claimed Martin Luther King, Jr., "there would be no more oppressive poverty directed against Negroes, our children would not be crippled by segregated schools, and the whole community might live together in harmony."[1]

Despite this generally accepted formula for racial change, there is still widespread debate about the effects of the civil rights movement on the lives of black southerners. A longtime scholar of southern politics, William Havard, wrote in the early 1970s that "any middle-aged southerner can attest to the fact that changes have taken place in race relations in the South within the period of his adult experience that would have been inconceivable to his father, let alone his grandfather."[2] In more specific terms, John Lewis, civil rights activist of the 1960s and later director of the Voter Education Project, contended that the black movement in the South has meant "not only the changes in the number of [black] people elected, in the breakdowns of barriers in public accommodations and desegregation, or in better jobs for blacks," but also "a new, recognized sense of black dignity and pride."[3] These sanguine accounts suggest that a number of significant gains have taken place in the quest of black Americans for political and economic equality.

Other analysts, however, have disputed these views concerning the impact of the black movement. A dozen years after passage of the 1965 Voting Rights Act, the *New York Times* claimed that "the full potential of black political power in Dixie remains unrealized" owing to a lack of black political experience, organization, motivation, and economic power.[4] Most noticeable has been the apparent lack of progress for blacks in the economic realm. Moreover, while Jim Crow may have died, subtle forms of racism continue to plague blacks. In the words of southern historian William Chafe, "inequality and discrimination still suffuse our social and economic system, buttressed by informal modes of social control even more powerful than the law."[5] The question remains as to what effects the civil rights movement has had for southern blacks, and specifically whether or not increased black political participation has resulted in significant improvements.

The purpose of this book is to assess the impact of that movement and the role of black political participation in local communities in the South. Much has been written about the rise and development of the civil rights movement.[6] The sit-ins and freedom rides, Martin Luther King, SCLC and CORE, Selma and Montgomery—all represent interesting symbols or tales of conflict in the struggle for change. Little attention, however, has been focused on the results of that movement in the lives of black southerners. Thus the emphasis here is on a neglected area of academic and public concern—the effects of black participation on the formation of local policies.[7] In the process of exploring this issue, several basic questions will be addressed: What was the nature of the civil rights movement at the local level in the South? How much political, social, and economic change took place? How did these changes occur? Most importantly, *why* did these transformations take place, and what was the impact of various black political activities? The answers to these questions, of course, go well beyond the black movement and have important implications for political and social change more generally in the United States.

Forms of Political Participation

In both its philosophical and practical aspects, the civil rights movement in the South was concerned with increasing the extent and quality of black participation in politics. Political involvement, especially electoral participation, is considered the most fundamental element in American democracy. Through such participation all other rights theoretically are protected and each citizen is granted a potential influence in the determination of governmental policy.[8] According to democratic theory, the political process serves as a conduit through which the needs of the people are communicated to the government, which in turn makes the key decisions as to how the benefits of society are to be distributed. Since public resources are scarce, the ability to participate in the process governing their distribution is of crucial importance. During the 1960s the black movement in the South raised anew the issue of whether political participation was an adequate instrument for alleviating serious inequities among American citizens.

What needs to be recognized about the civil rights movement, however, is not simply that it brought about greater political mobilization and increased participation of blacks. It should also be kept in mind that the forms of participation by blacks and other groups were in many cases new or used previously to only a minimal extent. For that reason, this study examines a broad range of strategies used and assesses their relative efficacy for bringing about increased equality for blacks in the political and economic sectors.

In terms of conventional strategies, the vote was long sought by blacks as the principal goal of the movement that culminated in the 1965 Voting Rights Act. Martin Luther King, Jr., as well as many other civil rights leaders, regarded the ballot as the most accessible and most potent weapon in the struggle for equality. Indeed the assumption was that voting rights would pave the way for all other changes, since the franchise is the normal method by which demands of citizens are fulfilled.[9] By electing blacks and moderate whites to office, it was expected that blacks could advance themselves through the public realm. Ideally, the vote would enable blacks to obtain important gains in a variety of areas, including education, employment, housing, and public services. Beyond this instrumental value, the ballot was seen as crucial in providing previously disenfranchised blacks with a sense of full citizenship and increased self-esteem. Yet despite these strong beliefs in the efficacy of the vote, some studies have indicated that electoral strategies are often indirect and uncertain mechanisms for bringing about change.[10]

Another orthodox political activity of blacks involved interest-group formation and action. The civil rights era marked the rise of a number of important black-led organizations, including CORE and SCLC. The NAACP, having been active in the legal realm for decades, increased its efforts and expanded its focus to include more basic economic issues. In addition, there were numerous local black groups that developed in response to particular community needs. Although the goals of these various organizations differed somewhat, most tended to stress fundamental political rights (especially voting) and economic improvements for blacks. Tactics varied as well, but the emphasis was usually on traditional forms of interest-group action, including lobbying public officials, petitioning, attending public meetings, and mobilizing the vote.[11]

Of great importance was the solicitation of federal assistance by blacks (and sometimes by moderate whites). With the passage of the civil rights acts of 1964 and 1965 and the social legislation of the Great Society, Washington assumed the position of a valuable ally for the black movement. Federal grant monies were increasingly available to communities, and many of the funds were earmarked for programs to benefit the poor. Washington was also able to force local governments to achieve more racial equality by threatening to cut off federal funds, by sending investigators into communities, by instituting lawsuits, and by various other means. Indeed, federal district courts, the primary enforcers of national law in the South, were often called upon to protect the rights of blacks in this period.[12] All told, the resources of the federal government were formidable, and attempts by blacks to utilize those resources as a counterforce to southern recalcitrance seems to have been crucial to the success of the movement.[13]

In addition to these conventional strategies, the civil rights movement developed and used a variety of unconventional political approaches for which it became widely known. Protest techniques, including peaceful demonstrations, sit-ins, boycotts, marches, and pickets, became a major addition to the arsenal of blacks and their leaders. Protest was not new to American politics, although the last major outbreak of demonstrations had been during the Depression days of the 1930s. The black movement, however, utilized protest extensively and, in some cases, rather ingeniously. As a result, protest emerged as a significant form of political participation in the United

States during the 1960s, and this development clearly affected the goals and strategies of other social movements of the period as well.[14]

While most Americans regard protest as an unorthodox and extreme kind of political action, they tend to consider peaceful demonstrations at least quasi-legitimate, since—theoretically—no personal injury or property damage results. In fact, peaceful demonstrations are legal under most circumstances. In any case, during the 1960s protest activity was increasingly seen as an effective technique for communicating policy preferences to those in power. Demonstrations not only exposed in dramatic fashion the injustices of society, but also imposed political or economic sanctions upon elites. In terms of the civil rights movement, protest was instrumental in desegregating public accommodations, although its usefulness appeared limited when applied to other areas of racial injustice.[15]

Yet the movement for black equality ultimately went beyond peaceful protests to more radical, unconventional activities like rioting and interracial violence. This shifting of tactics occurred as the movement began to encompass all classes of blacks, not just the middle and upper classes, and moved from trying to guarantee basic political rights to attempting to fulfill more difficult welfare and economic goals. These new demands on behalf of the masses of blacks were sometimes viewed as attempts to reformulate, rather than simply tinker with, basic American institutions, and developed as more militant black leaders appeared on the scene to challenge the conventional approaches to change of moderate blacks.[16]

Collective violence, especially riots, have been relatively common in American history. A number of minority groups have used violence to influence social change, and in turn the government has often resorted to the forcible repression of various groups; the use of violence by political outgroups, however, is illegal and is almost always considered outside the pale of legitimate political action. In general, Americans have tended to view mass violence as aberrant and unnecessary, contending that change occurs according to a routinized, stable process.[17] Nonetheless, during the 1960s blacks often supported and used violence as a form of collective political expression. The number and intensity of black riots alone—more than 329 important instances in some 257 cities between 1964 and 1968—clearly indicate their significance as a factor in the civil rights struggle.[18] How effective these radical approaches were, however, is a relatively unexplored question.

These were the major instruments of political change used by blacks during the civil rights movement. Undoubtedly other activities were employed as well, strategies especially developed or adopted because of local circumstances and goals; but very few were as well publicized or seem to have been as important as those we have just discussed. The critical question is, How significant was each of these forms of political participation and mobilization in effecting changes for blacks in the South?

Plural and Elite Views of Black Politics

The views of scholars who have assessed the question of black Americans and political participation are rather diverse and often conflicting. On the one hand there are those social scientists, most of whom are proponents of some variation of pluralist theory, who contend that political power is widely distributed in this country and that the political system is relatively open and responsive to a variety of demands. Pluralist theory tends to emphasize the utility of conventional political participation, especially electoral and interest-group efforts, in the process of political change.[19] Through peaceful negotiation, bargaining, and compromise, the pluralists argue, most demands of various competing groups are fulfilled, although in a rather slow, incremental manner. Electoral participation is considered the dominant feature of the political system, since it is the primary means by which most persons in power are selected and by which power is transferred from one group to another. Indeed, pluralist theory contends that the strategy of the vote has worked successfully for many groups in United States history and that blacks, too, have been able to expand their power recently through the electoral system.[20]

Pluralism clearly suggests a system that emphasizes stability, orderly and rational means of change, and avoidance of violence. Since existing institutions and conventional political strategies are felt to be adequate for advancing the interests of minorities, the resort to unconventional activities such as protest and violence is considered unnecessary and irrational. Pluralists contend that such forceful tactics are not only destabilizing but unproductive, and rarely result in any kind of meaningful societal change.

Support for these pluralist assumptions is provided by several studies of black participation in the South. Hugh Price, for example, reported in the mid-1950s that black voting in some Florida cities seemed to have resulted in better police protection and more public services, such as paved streets, playgrounds, and civic centers, for blacks.[21] In another study, Frederick Wirt investigated one predominantly black county in Mississippi in the late 1960s and suggested that conventional black political participation there had meant more black police, more paved roads and streetlights, less-prejudiced media attention, and some psychological benefits.[22] Huey Perry's somewhat later study of black electoral participation in Greene County, and Birmingham, Alabama, reported similar findings, including progress in public education and in the desegregation of public accommodations.[23]

The most systematic investigation of the benefits to be derived from black voting in the South has been William Keech's mid-1960s study entitled *The Impact of Negro Voting*.[24] Looking longitudinally and in depth at two southern cities, Durham, North Carolina, and Tuskegee, Alabama, Keech compared concomitant variation in black electoral participation with public- and private-sector payoffs for blacks. He concluded that increases in black voting were responsible for progress in the public sector, especially improved streets, water and sewage, recreation, and police and fire protection. Few changes, however, were reported in the private, non-governmental sector.

Perhaps the best evidence in support of pluralist assumptions is the dramatic increase in black elected officials in the South and their impact on the political system. Gains in black voter registration and turnout in the sixties resulted in substantial numbers of black southerners being elected to office, especially at the local level. In 1965 approximately 70 blacks held elected office in the eleven ex-Confederate states, but by 1974 this number had risen to 1,314, and by 1986 the total was 3,510.[25] Although data on the impact of these black officials are still somewhat sparse, these representatives seem to have been moderately effective in providing both material and symbolic rewards for their black constituents.[26] The tremendous increase both in the number of black elected officials and in their influence tends to confirm the pluralist contention of an open and responsive political system.

Because the pluralist perspective views power as relatively accessible to outgroups utilizing conventional means, unruly and disruptive tactics are considered unnecessary and usually unproductive. David Colby found, for example, that the distribution of federal antipoverty funds to Mississippi counties in the late 1960s and early 1970s was influenced more by black electoral power than by black protests and riots.[27] His explanation for this phenomenon was that elites generally respond in a positive manner only to tactics they see as normal and legitimate, such as electoral politics. Not only are most protests, and certainly riots, considered unconventional and illegitimate, but these disruptions often send no clear messages or demands to those in power. Furthermore, mass protest may so alienate other groups in society that it gives rise to intense resistance by countermovements.

Clearly, studies of the southern segregationist movement indicate that it emerged partly in response to black civil rights tactics.[28] Those in power may also respond negatively to unruly insurgents by attempting to control and punish them. Thus many cities reacted to the black riots of the 1960s with increased expenditures for police and riot controls.[29]

In contrast to pluralist theory, the theory of elitism characterizes the role of black political participation quite differently. Elite theorists view the American political system, and especially southern politics, as a relatively closed system in which power is concentrated in the hands of a few groups. These elite groups share a consensus about the basic norms of society, have decided the political rules of the game, and are in a position to enforce those rules and impose their values. Hence those in power are able to exclude all other less powerful groups from having any real influence over major political and economic decisions. Although electoral politics is the dominant mode of mass influence in the pluralist model, it serves no such function here. Electoral participation is controlled, limited, and structured by elites such that elections have little impact on public policy.[30]

The results of various studies lend credence to the elite view. In their comprehensive study of the early 1960s entitled *Negroes and the New Southern Politics*, Donald Matthews and James Prothro concluded that the benefits for blacks through the election process were few and that the idea of the vote as the key to racial equality was "political hyperbole."[31] They argued that the poverty of southern blacks often makes them economically dependent on whites, who are thereby able to control blacks politically. Other studies, too, have shown that fear of white social and economic coercion has reduced black voter turnout in some parts of the South.[32] Impoverishment has also meant that blacks lack the necessary leadership that usually comes from the middle class and is necessary for effective political organization. Moreover, institutional barriers, such as inadequate registration hours, lack of transportation to the polls, shortages of campaign finances, and especially the prevalence of at-large city elections and gerrymandered election districts, may also serve as significant impediments to the successful use of the ballot.[33]

Even when blacks are able to elect members of their own race to political office, these officials are often seriously constrained by a variety of factors. In a 1970s overview of black politics, Hanes Walton maintained that many black elected officials in the South lacked the economic means to improve conditions for their constituents. Walton contended that small-town black officials, in particular, were overburdened with such problems as a lack of industry, low tax rolls, and uncooperative whites.[34] In addition, black officeholders almost always constitute a small minority of elected officials, are often opposed by intransigent white officials, and are therefore unable to make unilateral decisions or change policy priorities. When black representatives cannot fulfill the high expectations of their black constituents, hopes are often dashed, leading to alienation and lack of continued support and participation by black citizens.[35]

Elite assumptions are also supported by the contention that political participation is not very effective because real power in American society resides in the private economic sector. Consequently, according to this thesis, blacks who pursue politics as a means of socioeconomic change are following an unproductive path. Keech, for example, found that black voting had little impact in the private realm, particularly in the areas of employment and housing.[36] Similarly, Chandler Davidson, in a study of black politics in Houston, reported that increased black electoral participation had not influenced economic institutions. In his words, "economic decisions which vitally affect blacks are beyond their control."[37]

Since powerless groups are generally precluded from achieving significant change through conventional political approaches, claim the more radical critics of elitism, such groups tend to develop unconventional strategies in the attempt to influence change.[38] Hence protest and even violence are seen by an outgroup as rational attempts to communicate dissatisfaction and to pursue collective interests when other political tactics have been tried and found wanting. Indeed, despite the pluralists' view of a pacific and orderly political system, American society has never been all that stable, and most social movements have been accompanied by some degree of violence and conflict. Thus from a more radical perspective, collective protest and violence may be considered normal, structured, and sometimes efficacious strategies employed by minority groups who are engaged in a struggle for political and economic power. Nonetheless those in power often respond to such demands by making only the most modest changes in the system consistent with maintaining stability and control.[39]

Previous research provides some evidence concerning the role of political protest and violence in the civil rights movement. In a study of how the important Voting Rights Act of 1965 reached enactment, David Garrow claimed that black protest activity was an effective instrument of change because it gained the support of larger sympathetic audiences around the nation.[40] In a book on the development of black insurgency, Doug McAdam also contended that civil rights protests were successful because they "nationalized" the issues, thus insuring federal intervention on behalf of blacks. McAdam found that insurgency yielded other positive by-products as well, including increased mobilization of blacks and the generation of outside financial support for the movement.[41] Additionally, several studies have reported that black demonstrations, such as sit-ins, marches, boycotts, and other such tactics, were principally responsible for the desegregation of public accommodations in the South.[42]

Even collective violence seemed to be an effective strategy at times. In an examination of the effects of black riots and other political activities on changes in the number of Mississippi welfare recipients during the 1960s, Colby found that such violence influenced the expansion of the number of welfare applicants. He explained that violence (as well as nonviolent protest) directly affected policy by influencing those aspects of policy that are "controllable" by the masses but are "uncontrollable" by public officials.[43] These findings supported the earlier conclusions of Frances Fox Piven and Richard Cloward who asserted that, at least in the North, the rise in the number of welfare recipients was a response to the black riots of the 1960s.[44] This claim has been confirmed by several subsequent studies.[45] Moreover, in a later work entitled *Poor People's Movements*, Piven and Cloward examined the southern civil rights movement (as well as three other lower-class movements) and the relative efficacy of several forms of political participation.[46] They claimed that mass insurgency, including violence, often produced policy changes favorable to blacks. "When government is unable to ignore the insurgents," concluded Piven and Cloward, "and is unwilling to risk the uncertain repercussions of the use of force, it will make efforts to conciliate and disarm the protestors."[47] Less disturbing forms of political behavior, such as electoral participation, were considered relatively ineffective strategies for the poor because such modes are structured and controlled by those in power. Other studies, too, have suggested that more militant and unruly tactics by powerless groups are often successful in achieving tangible, though typically short-term, political gains.[48]

As we have seen, plural and elite theories differ markedly in their positions of how open or closed the political system is. Proponents and critics of these two perspectives also disagree significantly on the relative efficacy of conventional and unconventional political strategies when such tactics are employed by comparatively powerless groups. Of course, these two conceptual frameworks are not the only ways in which one might generalize about the American political system or southern politics. Nonetheless, pluralism and elitism are rather commonly used theories that purport to explain power relationships in American society. Thus these two conceptualizations provide a general framework for the debate among social scientists as to the possible impact of the civil rights movement and the utility of various black political strategies.

Theories of Social Movements and Change

While pluralism and elitism help to explain the nature and structure of power in society, they offer less adequate explanations of social movements and change. Here sociologists have been able to provide theoretical frameworks that more completely and thoroughly account for the origins, development, and outcomes of social actions like the civil rights movement. Essentially there are two major sociological theories that purport to explain collective action and change: classical collective behavior theory and resource mobilization theory.

Classical collective behavior theory dominated sociological thinking about social movements until relatively recently.[49] Although there are several variations of this model, most collective behavior theorists accept the pluralist assumptions concerning the distribution of power. Thus they assume that all groups are capable of exercising influence through "normal," institutionalized means. Social movements, however, differ from normal behavior in that they arise in response to severe strains or disruptions within the system, such as urbanization and industrialization. Social strains tend to create tensions that, when severe enough, trigger social movements, and participation in such movements is therefore motivated by the need to manage or resolve psychological tensions produced by system strain. According to this model, movement participants are not engaged in "rational, self-interested political action."[50] Their departure from normal channels of political behavior is due, rather, to irrational and mainly emotional concerns. Social movements are therefore relatively spontaneous and disorganized and are not usually effective in promoting social change. In fact, collective behavior theorists claim social change is typically antecedent to social insurgency, in that it is the source of structural strain, which is a necessary precondition for movements.

Resource mobilization theory, a more recent development, differs markedly from the classical theory.[51] This model rests more on elite theories of power whereby groups in society differ a great deal in the influence they wield. Thus social movements are "not a form of irrational behavior but rather a tactical response [by the relatively powerless] to the harsh realities of a closed and coercive political system."[52]

Accordingly, movements are rational attempts to pursue political interests. Resource mobilization theory, as the name implies, claims that it is the amount of resources available to outgroups, not the level of discontent, that gives rise to social movements. It is assumed that a degree of discontent is ever present among outgroups in any society but that the resources necessary for a movement are not. Hence it is the ability of outgroups to organize and manage resources that determines whether a social movement emerges. These necessary resources vary but normally include organizations, leaders, money, labor, and communications systems. In providing such resources for poor and powerless groups, external groups with money and power, such as churches, philanthropic foundations, organized labor, liberal groups, and the federal government, assume importance. Finally, this model sees such collective actions as explicitly political rather than psychological phenomena, and contends that the degree to which social movements are conducive to social change often depends on the level of sustained outside support and the degree of resistance from those in power.

Although resource mobilization theory has gained widespread acceptance among sociologists, it has its critics and those who would modify it.[53] The chief criticism is that this theory overemphasizes the role of external resources and de-emphasizes the function of internal organization and resources in the generation of social movements. The claim here is that while outside groups are important, it is the "pre-existing social structures [that] provide the resources and organizations that are crucial to the initiation and spread of collective action."[54] External resources are thus seen as more "reactive" rather than "initiatory" in the movement process. Furthermore, outside groups may shift their responses to the movement over time, especially if that movement is perceived as a threat to outside interests. Rather than supporting insurgents, the government and other external groups may move to suppress and control them, thereby contributing to a movement's lack of success or demise.

In the light of recent studies, resource mobilization theory (with some modification) seems to provide the best general explanation of the rise and development of the southern civil rights movement. Briefly, proponents of this theory argue that since at least the 1930s broad social processes, including the increased urbanization of blacks, have improved the political opportunities for blacks to press their demands for change. In addition, external resources, especially those provided by the federal government and other elite groups, and the development of indigenous organizational strength, in black churches,

colleges, NAACP chapters, and other forms, has provided the conditions necessary for blacks to initiate and sustain a social movement. Moreover, the widespread legitimacy accorded the early goals of the movement served to reduce opposition to insurgency. Although other factors may also have been important in the emergence of the movement, it seems clear that the level of social strain experienced by blacks was not sufficient in itself to produce collective action. Resource mobilization theory, since it is a relatively recent development, needs further testing and refinement. More importantly, neither of these sociological theories deals to any great extent with the consequences, or political and social change, *resulting* from such movements. The focus of theoretical concern has been on the development or emergence of, but not the effects of, insurgency. As a result, we know very little about what patterns arise in the aftermath of social movements.

Not only is social change an understudied phenomenon, but there is confusion and a general lack of agreement as to even the meaning of the term. The concept of social change is clearly multidimensional, and attempts to define it have led to various classification schemes, developed along such lines as short-term versus long-run changes, material versus psychological/symbolic alterations, group-specific versus systemic outcomes, and political versus socioeconomic changes.[55] Most studies have been criticized for measuring change along only a single dimension and within a limited time frame. These approaches offer very inadequate answers to the important questions of whether social change really occurred, how much change was involved, and over what time period or at what rate it took place.

The Nature and Setting of This Study

The few studies of the impact of black political participation in the South have usually been somewhat limited and often marked by methodological problems. Perhaps the most serious deficiency has been the notable lack of empirical evidence to support basic contentions. This impressionistic quality has been most obvious in some of the earlier studies of Price, Ladd, Wirt, and Walton. Moreover, most scholarship has focused on just one mode of black political participation—usually the vote or elected officials. While these forms or goals of participation were very important aspects of the civil rights movement, such emphases are extremely narrow and seriously neglect other modes of political action that may have been significant in affecting policy. In a recent critique of the "civic culture" concept, Carole Pateman commented on this noticeable lack of assessment of unorthodox political activity:

> *The Civic Culture* and the empirical democratic theory of its period gave no hint that a "participation explosion" was imminent within the civic culture itself. Nor have empirical investigators paid attention to "protests and demonstrations." . . . Although unorthodox activities take widely differing forms, they are either ignored or dismissed as "undemocratic," . . . so defined as to be robbed of all political impact.[56]

Another weakness has been the rather limited scope of most studies. The geographical setting of most works has included just one or two cities or counties, with no clear rationale for such selected sites. Thus the settings have been too narrowly conceived to have broader theoretical implications. Finally, the time period of many studies has been too early, and the time frame too short, to capture long-term policy changes. Many investigations of the civil rights movement were undertaken in the 1960s, the period in which the movement reached its apex. Moreover, the time frame was often no more than a few years after the peak period of civil rights activity. Such limitations precluded any focus on possible changes in the South during the 1970s and 1980s, decades that may have been important in terms of furthering or consolidating gains resulting from black political activity.

Of all previous studies, however, perhaps the most thorough and systematic has been that of William Keech. His longitudinal investigation of the impact of the black vote in two carefully selected cities has received general acclaim and has often been quoted. Yet Keech's work suffers from many of the drawbacks mentioned above. His sample of cities is somewhat limited, he investigated only the political efficacy of voting, and the time frame of his study in the span of years before and during the period of greatest civil rights activity in the South. Furthermore, Keech did not measure his dependent variables (public- and private-sector benefits) with any degree of precision. To be able to infer successfully the degree of causality between independent and dependent variables, studies of this nature need to be more precise in the measurement of both black political participation and service levels for the black community. Finally, Keech's study failed to investigate simultaneous service changes in white subcommunities of these two cities. It may be that improvements of services in white areas were greater than such service alterations in black areas during the same time period. Hence investigating service changes in black neighborhoods alone may lead to erroneous conclusions concerning local political responsiveness to black participation.

The charting of changes in white neighborhoods allows a partial testing of the thesis that "natural growth and progress over time" is a sufficient dynamic to bring about improved services, and that this process best accounts for most service changes. Better known as the developmental/modernization perspective, this view contends that changes in public expenditures are a function of socioeconomic development.[57] Urbanization and industrialization create new needs, and government responds because of the increase in discretionary resources that arises from economic growth. If this developmental/modernization thesis is correct, then various black political activities should account for little change in services, and white and black neighborhoods should experience approximately the same rates of change over time. This assumes, of course, that clearly discriminatory policies regarding the distribution of public services are no longer operative—a questionable assumption in some communities, as will be seen. Where discriminatory public policies are still the norm, this thesis argues that white subcommunities will experience greater changes than black residential areas despite any special efforts by blacks.

This study hopes to avoid many of these methodological problems while building upon the preliminary and valuable work of Keech and others. For reasons of manageability, the focus is at the community level. Identifying and measuring differences, both in political participation and in policy effects, is easier in smaller and simpler political units than in large and more complex ones. The choice of a community emphasis tends to minimize extraneous factors that may unnecessarily complicate the study.[58] Furthermore, the South is not a heavily urbanized area; it is made up primarily of relatively small cities and towns, and the focus of the civil rights movement was on rural areas and smaller cities where, traditionally, blacks have been least politically aware and organized.[59] Investigation at the municipal level, however, will not preclude looking at county, state, and federal policies as they bear on communities.

This study explores six different communities over time to measure the impact of black political participation on public and private sector policies. Ideally, a study of this nature would involve a much larger sample of cities or counties and would utilize statistical methods to assess the relationship between variables. However, there is practically no detailed, easily accessible information available on either a county or city basis about the various kinds of public and private benefits blacks may have received as a result of political activity. The time, money, and personnel necessary to gather such information, even for one or two cities, are great and therefore preclude aggregate analysis.

Nevertheless, there are alternative methodological approaches that still allow valid causal inferences about these independent and dependent variables. First, this study explores each of the six communities over a period ranging from the late 1950s through the mid-1980s. This length of time—approximately two and one-half decades—seems adequate to assess possible changes, both short-term and longer-term, resulting from black participation. This time frame was also selected because it extends from a period in which there was no—or else very limited, or white-manipulated—black voting and other political activity to a period of much more substantial, and independent, levels of black political participation. Not only did almost all forms of black political action, especially voting, increase rather dramatically over these years, but black politics also gained a much greater degree of independence from white control in most communities.[60] This longitudinal emphasis enabled me to investigate the effects of changes in black participation over time, thereby allowing a look at the values of the dependent variables both before and after significant changes in the independent variables.

Secondly, by investigating more than one community, it was possible to explore the effects of certain contextual variables that may have influenced black politics and its impact. One seemingly important contextual factor is the relative size of the minority population. According to Matthews and Prothro, "as the proportion of Negroes in southern communities increases, so do the racial anxieties and fears of southern whites," and such white concerns often translate into repression of black political activity.[61] Keech indicated more precisely the influence of this demographic factor. He claimed that there is a linear relationship between the size of the black electorate (which by the late sixties was roughly equivalent to the relative size of the black population) and political gains, until a threshold point of white fear and resistance is met. At this point the electorate, or population, is between 30 and 50 percent black, and white opposition is greatest. When the black electorate moves beyond 50 percent of the voters, and a black majority is able to overcome any white resistance, a linear relationship occurs once again.[62] To explore the effects of this demographic variable, the six communities were selected along a continuum of black population size: two communities with relatively small black populations (5 to 25 percent); two communities with medium-sized proportions of black citizens (30 to 45 percent); and two majority-black communities.

Another contextual variable that the literature indicates may significantly affect black participation and its consequences is political culture.[63] Political culture means more than empirically discovered belief systems; it includes the traditions, history, and customs of a community that give order and meaning to the political process.[64] According to Matthews and Prothro, the components of political culture that especially seem to modify black politics in the South include the political style of white leaders in dealing with racial issues, the factional system peculiar to the community, the local electoral system, the relative homogeneity of the community, and the Civil War and Reconstruction experiences of the area. These factors are of varying importance and they may overlap to some degree, but such "situational variables pretty much determine whether or not the Negro community can organize for political ends."[65]

In order to explore differences in political culture among communities, the state of Florida was selected as being a manageable and accessible political unit for study. Florida is somewhat different from most other southern states in that it is generally more urbanized, faster growing in terms of population, more diversified economically, and more affluent in terms of per capita income. It also has a relatively small black population.[66] In the words of V. O. Key, the state has only "occasionally" given a "faintly tropical rebel yell,"[67] and no jurisdiction in the state was covered by the original 1965 Voting Rights Act. Yet for purposes of this study Florida is ideal because it contains in microcosm the broad range of political cultures or environments in which blacks are found throughout the South. The northern counties of the panhandle region, for example, are representative of the rural, agricultural Old South. With comparatively large numbers of blacks, this old plantation region, where in antebellum days cotton and slaves were mainstays of the economy, is still very much like its Deep South neighbors of Alabama and Georgia. In contrast, most of the southern counties of peninsular Florida are typical of the more urbanized, fast-growing New South. Virtually unsettled prior to the twentieth century, this region, particularly the coastal areas, is relatively cosmopolitan, affluent, and economically diversified. As one would expect, racial fears and anxieties have not been a major part of the white mentality in the New South area.[68]

This unique regional dichotomy in Florida allowed me to explore the influence of different political cultures on black politics. To do so, I also selected the six cities and towns according to the criterion of cultural distinctiveness. Specifically the communities were chosen to adhere to this Old South–New South dichotomy: three communities from the Old South, panhandle area and three communities from the

New South, peninsular region (see figure 1.1). Table 1.1 depicts the typology, as well as names and characteristics, of the communities. The 1970s demographic data shown in the table were the primary data upon which community selections were originally made. Beyond these contextual variables, a community was chosen only if local political events were reviewed adequately by a local press—a criterion that is sometimes difficult to fulfill in the rural Old South.

I also selected communities roughly "typical" of cities and towns within each specified category (i.e., low-percent black, Old South; medium-percent black, New South; etc.). To do this required some general knowledge of contemporary race relations and local politics across a wide range of Florida communities. Two major sources provided much of this general information. The first was a study directed by me in the mid-1970s of all black elected officials in Florida.[69] Representing some thirty-eight communities spanning every major region of the state, these black officials provided invaluable, current information not only about their own cities and towns but about other nearby communities as well. Several more historical investigations of race relations in a variety of Florida communities were a second major source. Most helpful among these studies was the excellent one carried out by Clubok, De Grove, and Farris in the early 1960s.[70] Also useful was Price's careful analysis of race relations in Florida in the forties and fifties.[71]

This choice of communities was not a random one, and therefore it is not possible to generalize the findings to other cities and towns directly. Moreover, this typology of communities is imperfect, since it does not allow for the variation of only one contextual variable at a time. This limitation makes it difficult to ascertain the independent effects of any single community characteristic. Nevertheless, by investigating each city intensively over time and comparing developmental sequences from one community or community grouping to another, I was able to reach some tentative conclusions about the singular effects of each contextual variable on the policy-making process. In addition, the use of multivariate analysis with statistical controls makes it possible to look more closely at the independent influence of particular factors (see appendix 1).

As already mentioned, the primary focus of this book is on various forms of black political participation and their effects on policy. The model in table 1.2 presents the general analytical framework. I investigated black voting, black elected officials, and black organizational efforts very closely. More unconventional political strategies, including black protest and violence, were also explored. The role of the federal

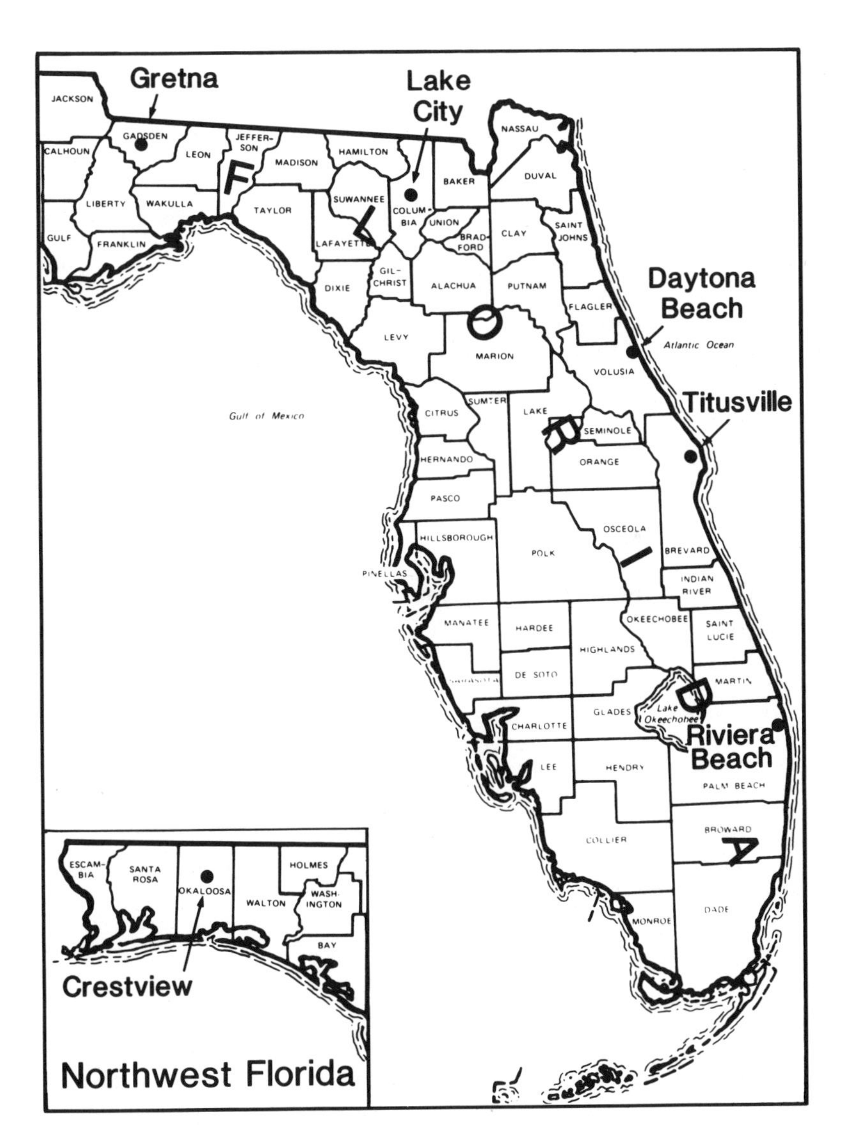

FIGURE 1.1
Map of Florida

TABLE 1.1
Typology and Characteristics of Communities

	Community Characteristics	*Old South*	*New South*
Low-Percentage Black (5–25%)		Crestview	Titusville
	Population (1970)	7,952	30,515
	% Population Change (1960–1970)	6.5%	376.1%
	% Black (1970)	17.8%	9.0%
	Per Capita Income (1969)	$2,194	$3,306
Medium-Percentage Black (30–45%)		Lake City	Daytona Beach
	Population (1970)	10,575	45,327
	% Population Change (1960–1970)	11.7%	21.2%
	% Black (1970)	31.5%	31.3%
	Per Capita Income (1969)	$2,547	$2,723
High-Percentage Black (over 50%)		Gretna	Riviera Beach
	Population (1970)	883	21,401
	% Population Change (1960–1970)	36.5%	64.0%
	% Black (1970)	80.0%	55.6%
	Per Capita Income (1969)	$1,469[a]	$2,605

SOURCE: U.S. Bureau of the Census, Census of Population: 1970, General Social and Economic Characteristics, Final Report PC (1)-C 11, Florida.

[a] This figure is for the county (Gadsden) since no such data were available for small communities.

government, in terms of both financial assistance and varieties of political pressure, was examined as well. In addition the strength and activities of the white countermovement, as a source of resistance to change, were also considered in this scheme (see appendix 1). While these political factors constituted the major independent variables, other potentially important sources of racial change were focused on to a lesser degree. Hence some attention was given to the role of white community leaders, both public and private; to the media, especially the local press; and to changes in other important community institu-

TABLE 1.2
Conceptual Model

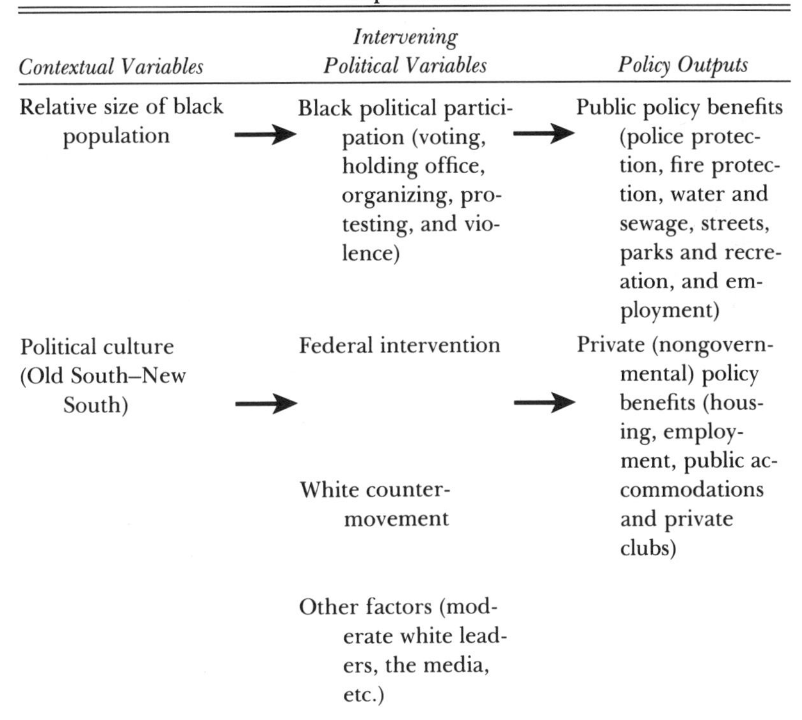

Contextual Variables	*Intervening Political Variables*	*Policy Outputs*
Relative size of black population →	Black political participation (voting, holding office, organizing, protesting, and violence) →	Public policy benefits (police protection, fire protection, water and sewage, streets, parks and recreation, and employment)
Political culture (Old South–New South) →	Federal intervention →	Private (nongovernmental) policy benefits (housing, employment, public accommodations and private clubs)
	White countermovement	
	Other factors (moderate white leaders, the media, etc.)	

tions, especially educational and economic institutions. Some of the literature suggests that these factors, too, may have been influential in fostering change.[72]

As for the policy impact of the civil rights movement, this study examines its effects on public and private policies for both black and white neighborhoods. Investigating and comparing policy changes in both types of racially distinctive neighborhoods enabled me to test the developmental/modernization hypothesis with regard to the process of change. In terms of public policies, six services were chosen for investigation: police protection, fire protection, water and sewage, streets, parks and recreation, and employment. These public services were selected for a variety of reasons. First, they represent city, not county or state, services. Thus education, health services, and welfare were not chosen, since they are dispensed primarily at the county level. In addition, studies have shown that these selected service areas have often been the focus of black allegations of discrimination.[73] Second, in any list of municipal services regarded as important, these will likely occupy prominent positions. This is especially true for blacks who, because they often cannot rely on personal resources to supply them with basic services, are more dependent on city government for the amenities of life. Finally, these public policy areas represent a range of kinds of services. Streets, water and sewage, and parks can be regarded as capital-intensive services. Law enforcement, fire protection, and employment, while not devoid of substantial capital investment (especially fire equipment), are better regarded as essentially human, or labor-intensive services. Recreation, while perhaps not as basic as the other areas, reflects the "quality of life" of a city, the extent to which it commits itself to services beyond those that are necessities.

In the private, nongovernmental realm, four general areas were selected for study: housing, including residential and apartment; employment; public accommodations, including restaurants, movie theaters, and motels; and private clubs. These four areas represent not only a variety of kinds of private-sector services, but also include indicators (especially housing and employment) of social and economic gains that most citizens value highly. These private areas have historically been policy arenas in which blacks have been most excluded. The civil rights movement, moreover, placed great emphasis upon breaking down barriers of discrimination in public accommodations and jobs. But knowledge of race relations in the South suggests that desegregation in the private realm has been the most difficult to achieve. As a result, one would expect to find that improved social and economic conditions for blacks have lagged behind changes in the public sector.[74]

In terms of methods of data gathering, this study employs multiple modes of analysis so as to corroborate the findings of any single approach.[75] These multiple approaches include: a thorough search of available public records and interviews with a sample of departmental personnel in order to chart public-service changes; lengthy interviews with white and black community informants in order to tap their perceptions concerning black political activity and its effects; interviews with the owners or managers of randomly selected businesses to gain information on desegregation and hiring practices in the private sector; and finally, a careful reading of local and regional newspapers (including the black press, whenever available) for the nearly three decades encompassed by this study. Appendix 1 presents further details of these approaches. It should be emphasized that these multiple modes of analysis not only offer a variety of sometimes rich sources of information, but also provide a cross-check on the reliability of the data generated by any single source.

Perhaps the most unique and informative of these approaches were the intensive interviews with community informants—public and private citizens, both black and white, who were familiar with the politics and race relations of the community over the period from the late 1950s or early 1960s to the time of this study. The average length of community residence of these knowledgeable citizens was twenty-seven years. Those interviewed were selected on a careful, systematic basis. Names were initially gathered from newspapers, public officials, and prominent private citizens. Before an individual was interviewed, however, he or she had to be nominated by at least two other persons. At the end of each interview, respondents were asked to nominate other community informants. By utilizing this "reputational approach," a substantial number of names of white and black citizens was gathered; yet only those mentioned at least twice were contacted for interviews. More than 80 percent of those nominated were actually interviewed in each city, and our interviewees for all six cities totaled 113 residents (58 whites and 55 blacks).

In terms of format, this book is divided into seven major chapters. Chapters 2 and 3 present a rather detailed analysis of the black civil rights movement in each of the six communities. Included here is a brief political and economic history of each community with an emphasis on the changing nature of race relations. Chapter 4 details changes in police and fire protection, including personnel and service delivery. In chapter 5, streets, and parks and recreation, which are more capital-intensive services, are reviewed, and factors related to changes are analyzed. The private realm, particularly the desegregation of public accommodations and black employment, is explored in chapter 6. The final chapter summarizes and theorizes about the nature and impact of the civil rights movement in southern communities and further analyzes the effects of various black political strategies. In a broader sense, I attempt to go beyond the black movement to discuss more generally its implications for theories of democracy and for theories of social movements and change in this country.

I hope that the questions and issues addressed in this book are not of academic significance alone. It would seem that these issues are of central importance to a better understanding of domestic politics in the United States over the last several decades. The ways in which southern blacks have begun to participate politically, the kinds of demands they have made, and the responses of the political and economic systems to those demands are crucial questions for all Americans to consider. But the answers to these questions go well beyond a more thorough comprehension of the civil rights movement and of the changed nature of race relations in the South. Ultimately such answers should help to increase our knowledge of power, control, and change in a democratic society, and of how effective a dispossessed minority can be in bringing about a transformation of power relationships.

2

The Old South and the Politics of Race

Florida has its own North and South, but its Northern area is strictly Southern. . . .

—Florida Federal Writers' Project,
Florida: A Guide to the Southernmost State

The Old South region of Florida is located in the long-settled, rural northern counties and is centered in the Apalachicola and Suwannee rivers area. As late as the turn of the century this area was Florida's black belt, with blacks composing a majority of the population in nine north Florida counties that contained one-half the total state population. During the antebellum period King Cotton and tobacco had reigned supreme in a plantation system supported by slave labor. Even as cotton (and later tobacco) production declined, and more whites moved in and many blacks departed, the Old South mentality remained, and blacks still made up a significant proportion of the citizenry.[1]

In Florida's northern counties elements of traditional society are dominant, much as they are in other parts of the Deep South. The area is rural and agricultural, with few urban centers; the people are relatively homogeneous, poor, and lacking in education. Demographically, the area is mostly stable (many of its residents grew up in the rural South and have remained) or is decreasing slightly in population. The number of blacks is moderately high in many of these counties, and the "southern way of life," including Civil War memories and the issue of race, is a central part of the subculture.[2]

While politics in the Old South tends to be highly personal, with local economic elites usually in control, race persists as a dominant political factor. As Key has explained, it is not that blacks are in the "forefront of debate," but "rather the presence of the Negro has created conditions under which the political process operates."[3] Thus the desire to keep the black man "in his place" has prevailed over all else, and there has been great resistance to racial change. Indeed, white supremacy organizations, especially the Ku Klux Klan, were active in the north Florida area and have remained so in some parts of the region. Following the 1954 *Brown* decision and up until the mid-1970s, most panhandle counties strongly supported segregationist candidates both for governor and for president.[4]

In this traditional setting blacks were, until quite recently, either political nonparticipants or completely manipulated in their participation by white politicians. Blacks were "parochial" subjects—the political system acted upon them but they could not act upon it.[5] Although the civil rights movement promised to liberate blacks politically, the movement was stymied to a large extent in most Old South communities. Racial change was usually slow and difficult to achieve, mostly because of white intransigency but also owing to a lack of black political experience and organization. Consequently the intervention of potent outside forces, usually in the form of the federal government or national civil rights organizations, or both, was necessary for real change to occur. In addition, greater economic independence for blacks was often a precondition to the success of the movement, as poor blacks were especially vulnerable to economic intimidation by whites.

This chapter presents an overview of each of the three Old South communities: Crestview, Lake City, and Gretna. After giving a brief history of each, I will focus on civil rights movement activities and their general impact in the community. In each case I will look at the nature of race relations, how and when black political activity developed, the role of outside forces and other major factors, and general changes in the living conditions of blacks. Because each of these communities has a dominant Old South political culture, certain similarities in racial conditions and the process of change should be apparent. But it is also important to keep in mind the differences in political development among the communities, especially those differences that seem attributable to the relative size of the black population. It has been suggested that the proportion of black residents is a significant contextual variable and should affect the nature of race relations and political change. Thus in each community analysis careful consideration has been given to the possible influence of the size of the black population, and the overviews themselves are presented in order of increasing proportion of black citizens: first, Crestview with a relatively small black population; second, Lake City, which is a little more than 30 percent black; and finally Gretna, a majority black community.

Crestview: Modest Change amid Poverty and Racism

Crestview is a small, quiet community like so many others in rural northwest Florida. Nearby Eglin Air Force Base and the military dominate the area as they have since World War II, but the lumber industry and agriculture are still the way of life for many. Religion pervades this traditional setting; the community boasts some thirty-four churches. The Okaloosa County seat is located here, as is the Robert L. F. Sikes Library, a majestic Georgian-style structure honoring the area's longtime and influential congressman. But the library contrasts sharply with the pressing poverty which plagues the city. Since 1950, people and economic prosperity have shifted southward in the county to the "miracle strip" along the beautiful Gulf Coast, leaving Crestview with a stagnant population and little industry. With a relatively passive and small black populace—always less than 20 percent of the total population—race relations have rarely been an important issue. In the words of one longtime white resident: "The coloreds here are small in numbers. They're more like an ethnic group . . . a Chinese or Oriental family. They just blend in."[6]

Historically, Crestview was an outgrowth of the railroad era, having been born when the L&N railroad was completed across the Florida panhandle in 1883. In the late 1800s lumber was the chief source of income, followed by turpentine, cattle, cotton, and fisheries. Blacks were brought in from other areas in the Southeast to provide the bulk of the labor force. Life was poor and harsh for most of these laborers. As one historian wrote: "The turpentine camps were run with the same authority as that assumed by the captain of a ship at sea. . . . Negroes who caused trouble frequently disappeared never to be seen again."[7]

Crestview's development was slow, primarily because until the early 1900s most of the land area was owned by either the federal government or the railroad. But in 1916 the city was incorporated, and a year later it became the county seat, despite the fact that it had no paved streets and its population numbered only some four hundred. Through the next several decades Crestview experienced slow but steady growth. By 1950 its population totaled 5,003, of which 10.5 percent were black. Much of this growth was due to the development of Eglin Air Force Base in the 1930s and its rapid expansion after World War II. Before long, this military base—spreading over more than 724 square miles and parts of three counties—was one of the largest air bases in the world.[8]

Through the 1950s relations between blacks and whites in Crestview conformed closely to the traditional Old South pattern. Schools were completely segregated, as were all public accommodations and the city's Okaloosa Memorial Hospital, built in 1956. Local restaurants, if they served blacks at all, usually did so through the back door.[9] The local weekly newspaper, the *Okaloosa News-Journal*, referred to blacks as "coloreds" or "Negroes" and included them in the news only occasionally in a separate short section in the back on black school activities or social news.

Following the *Brown* decision of 1954, the local newspaper editorialized that "neither our Southern businesses, churches, schools, nor society in general are yet ready to embrace a true mixture of the races."[10] The editorial went on to state that racial change must be "gradual," that people must want it first, and that laws cannot force it. The county superintendent of schools was even more critical of the court's decision, claiming that the problem of ending segregation was an educational one that could not be legislated "down peoples' throats."[11] Many white citizens of Crestview also responded negatively to the idea of integration. When a rumor was circulated in the fall of 1957 that black students would attempt to desegregate the all-white high school, an angry crowd of more than one hundred whites converged on the school grounds to block the attempt. However, no black students showed up.[12]

Crestview's black population, poor and numbering only 526 in 1950, was segregated in the southwest portion of the city, an area which some whites called "niggertown." Many blacks worked for whites, performing menial jobs. Local politics had always been monopolized by whites and few age-eligible blacks were registered to vote (the countywide black registration rate was 21.3 percent in 1950). There were stories that prior to the late 1940s whites often turned back blacks who attempted to register or vote. In addition, the Ku Klux Klan was said to have been moderately active in the area in the past, and this group surfaced briefly again in the early 1950s to burn a cross in front of the county courthouse.[13]

With the growth of the nearby air base, however, race relations began to change. Black soldiers and their families stationed at Eglin, many of whom were from northern states, insisted on being allowed to register and vote locally.[14] As a result, any remaining barriers to black voter registration were quietly removed, and by 1960 the county registration rate for blacks reached almost 45 percent—a figure somewhat above the state average of 39 percent for blacks. Blacks in the military also began to challenge the segregation of public accommodations. As early as 1953 a black air force officer was arrested for occupying a seat reserved for whites on a bus in Crestview. When the case came to court it achieved a great deal of local notoriety; the accused officer's lawyers were the first black attorneys to appear in court in Okaloosa County history.[15]

Not much integration occurred, however, until after the passage of the federal 1964 Civil Rights Act. Black soldiers then began to enter public establishments more frequently to test them and force them to desegregate. These soldiers were accustomed to racial integration at the military base and expected surrounding accommodations to be accessible to them as well.[16] According to one black former air force officer, there was a prevalent feeling among blacks in the military that "they weren't going to fight overseas for their country and not be allowed to enter places here."[17] Taking their lead from the military, some younger blacks in the city joined in the process of integrating local establishments. Many white businessmen, not wanting to lose military clientele, acceded rather quickly and easily to the black demands for integration.

Racial desegregation of schools began to take place in the early 1960s as well, and was ultimately accomplished without major incident and without the impetus of a court suit. This was unusual; in most Florida counties the school integration process was begun only when black parents filed a desegregation suit.[18] Okaloosa County, however, with its relatively small black population (only 6.4 percent and 12.9 percent of the county and Crestview populations, respectively, in 1960), found the transition to integrated schools to be a relatively smooth one. Again, the military was an important motivating force initially. Prior to the 1954 *Brown* decision Eglin Elementary School, located on the air base but run by the county, was commanded by federal executive order to desegregate because it was part of a military installation. As a result of this order, the school was turned over to the federal government and became the first school in the state to integrate. This ultimately encouraged the desegregation process to begin elsewhere in the county, though further federal pressure was necessary.[19] With the Department of HEW threatening to cut off funds for local schools, the county instituted a "freedom of choice" plan in 1965.[20] By 1967 all of Crestview's public schools were integrated, with the exception of all-black Carver Hill School where white parents refused to enroll their children.[21] Moreover, no private schools emerged during this period to offer segregated education for whites. With school integration proceeding more easily and rapidly than in other areas, the Okaloosa County school system was chosen by regional school administrators in 1967 as a model for other counties.[22]

Blacks in Crestview were also able to achieve some significant political gains during the sixties. Although the proportion of the city's adult blacks registered to vote was estimated to be more than 40 percent in 1960 (compared with a white registration rate estimated at 54 percent),[23] black registrants totaled less than 10 percent of Crestview's registered voters because of the relatively small black population. Nevertheless, black political rewards were disproportionate to their electoral strength. In 1961 the city hired a black policeman, Crestview's first black public employee. The appointment was requested by the local Okaloosa County Negro Civic Club and by other black residents who wanted better law enforcement. The newly hired policeman patrolled mainly the black residential area and could arrest only blacks, but few other north Florida cities had any black police at this time.[24] In addition, the city council allocated small amounts of funds in the early 1960s for long-sought improvements in Fairview Park, located in the black area, and to the Okaloosa Negro Civic Club for improved recreation programs for blacks.[25] And despite the negative view most of the city fathers had toward federal aid, the council sought out and received several federal grants during the 1960s for low-rent housing projects, with a moderate number of units earmarked for the black area.[26]

The most important black political achievement, however, was the election of a black man, Samuel Allen, to the city council in 1968. This was a significant accomplishment in light of the fact that there were estimated to be only sixteen black elected officials in the entire state, and none in northwest Florida, at the time.[27] Moreover, the five-member Crestview council and mayor were all elected at-large (though three council members had to live in specific districts), a system that meant any victorious minority candidate had to garner a large number of white votes. Allen, a middle-aged junior high school mathematics teacher, initially ran for the city council in 1966 and was the first of his race to seek local office in Crestview. The Okaloosa Negro Civic Club conducted a voter registration drive prior to the 1966 election, but Allen was defeated in a runoff election with the incumbent; he carried only the majority-black precinct.[28] But in 1968 he ran again, pledging to help develop a street-paving and sewage program, increased recreation facilities, and improved housing. Allen was victorious this time in the runoff, defeating the white incumbent to whom he had lost in 1966 and carrying one of two all-white precincts. In

1970 when Allen sought reelection to the council, he won without a runoff and carried all precincts by substantial margins.[29]

Despite their political gains in the 1960s, blacks in Crestview continued to be neglected for several reasons. The racially conservative attitudes of whites dominated the political life of the city. Robert Sikes, the popular congressman from Crestview since 1940, vehemently criticized every attempt at racial change, from school desegregation to the national civil rights bills.[30] Editorials in the *Okaloosa News-Journal* strongly opposed the 1964 civil rights bill, arguing that it would bring "totalitarianism to the U.S., allowing radicals to upset America through legal revolutionary tactics."[31] The local Jaycees prepared a campaign to point out the grave dangers to constitutional government embodied in this bill.[32] And in the November 1968 election, racist candidate George Wallace carried the county and the city by an almost two-to-one margin in his bid for the U.S. presidency.[33]

Pressing poverty also tended to undermine any attempts at progress. One-third of all Crestview families had incomes below the poverty level in 1960, and the city budget of approximately $240,000 for 1960–1961 was less than the city expenditures for 1954.[34] An editorial in the local newspaper lamented the low level of public services and the inability to attract new residents and businesses, claiming that "dirt-filled streets without curbs and gutters, leading to miniature sand storms when a brisk breeze blows, are not the mark of a progressive city."[35]

Amid this environment of staunch conservatism and poverty, blacks often fared none too well. As of 1966, approximately 70 percent of the streets were unpaved in the predominantly black area (compared with an estimated figure of 50 percent unpaved streets in the white areas). Sidewalks and streetlights were nonexistent in the black section, and the black park was poorly maintained. Black housing in 1966 was the worst in the city by far, with 45 percent of the units estimated to be deteriorating or dilapidated. The substandard housing rate for whites was a considerably lower figure of 17 percent.[36]

The 1960s brought little improvement in public services for blacks. Despite black voter support in a successful city referendum on a $2 million bond issue in 1965 for improvements in water, sewage, and street paving, the southwest area was consistently shortchanged in services.[37] Moreover, Crestview's assessment program for street paving required homeowners to pay two-thirds of the costs of paving. Because most blacks could not afford to pay such assessments, their streets often remained unpaved.[38] By the late 1960s the housing authority was being criticized as well for lack of progress in clearing blighted housing and in replacing it with low-rent public housing. Although there were at least three times as many eligible housing applicants as there were public units available, white landlords successfully opposed the construction of additional low-rent units because they feared it would endanger their housing rental business.[39] Federal antipoverty aid, which might have helped poor blacks, was criticized by Crestview politicians as "unneeded," "wasteful," "too costly," and another step toward "socialism." Consequently, such aid was late in coming to the city and most of the programs were meagerly funded.[40]

Blacks were often shortchanged in public education as well. The all-black Carver Hill School had been sorely neglected for years, and in 1966 it was the only public school in the city which was not fully accredited.[41] Moreover, the burden of transition to integrated schools fell almost completely on blacks. Black students and some black teachers were sent to formerly all-white schools, but no white students or teachers would enroll or work in the formerly all-black school. Because of this situation, and despite the pleas of black parents who identified closely with Carver Hill, the black school was ordered by local school officials to close in 1969.[42] (It was reopened a few years later as an all-city kindergarten center.) During the school integration process a number of black students reportedly dropped out of school altogether because the transition was just too great. This cost had been anticipated by some federal authorities; in the words of one HEW official who visited Okaloosa County in the late 1960s, the Department of HEW had "written off this generation of blacks" in the thrust for complete and total integration immediately.[43]

Slow Progress Continues

During the 1970s modest improvements in race relations continued in Crestview, however, and the federal government and the military were still important forces contributing to these changes. But another factor was now at work: a moderate increase in the political activity of blacks. Prior to the 1970s no national black political organization had established itself locally either in the city or the county. The Okaloosa County Negro Civic Club had been somewhat active on behalf of black interests in the 1960s; to a lesser extent, so had several small social organizations of black women.[44] But in 1972 a state official of the NAACP spoke at a black rally in Fort Walton Beach, a fast-growing city on the Gulf some thirty miles south of Crestview, and he helped to set up the area's first NAACP chapter.[45]

A year later a branch of the NAACP was begun by a military officer in Crestview. One of the expressed purposes of the organization was to bring the black community together, and over the next two years the local branch was fairly active in black voter registration, youth organizing, and school desegregation issues.[46] In addition, the county NAACP chapter was instrumental in bringing a successful federal district court suit against the county sheriff, a native of Crestview, for refusing to employ any black deputies. The sheriff was found guilty of racial discrimination and ordered to hire two black police officers immediately.[47] No doubt this was a major victory for local blacks and the NAACP, since the county sheriff in most parts of the Old South has tremendous power and authority, both substantive and symbolic. In 1976 the NAACP (Fort Walton Beach chapter) assisted in the filing of another successful federal court suit, this time against Eglin Air Base for alleged racial discrimination in the hiring and promotion of its civilian work force. While this suit was not finally settled until 1981, its ultimate impact for area blacks was considerably greater than the court decision against the sheriff. In the Eglin case blacks won an estimated $2 million consent judgment in which the air force agreed to hire and promote more blacks under federal court supervision.[48]

Locally, Councilman Allen won reelection again in 1973, running unopposed this time, and he began to press more actively for improvements in sewage, street paving, and recreation for blacks.[49] The city responded with $25,000 for an addition to the building at Fairview Park and began to seek federal grants for other service improvements in the black area.[50] There were also some symbolic changes. In February 1973 the mayor proclaimed Negro History Week for the first time, and the local newspaper editorial cited the accomplishments of blacks in Crestview. In 1974 a black girl was declared runner-up among eighteen girls for Miss Crestview High School, and a black teacher was named "citizen of the month" by the local chamber of commerce. Later in the decade the city council accepted the recommendation of the street renaming committee to name three streets in honor of area citizens, one of whom was a black (General Chappie James). In addition, black citizens were appointed to seats on most of the city's advisory boards.[51]

A few blacks asserted their political demands more forcibly through protests, most of which occurred over racial incidents in the schools or with police in the early 1970s. In one instance the school board proposed to change the name of formerly black Carver Hill School, but black protests successfully quashed this proposal.[52] In other organized actions before the city council, blacks complained about a proposed zoning change and property assessments for street paving.[53] All of these protests were relatively small, not well organized, and few of them achieved their limited goals. "Few blacks come to the city meetings to complain," claimed Councilman Allen, ". . . and usually not until a crisis emerges. Blacks just don't protest enough. Many have learned to live with dirt streets and poor recreation."[54]

Eglin Air Force Base continued to exert a progressive influence in the city. Some of the best employment opportunities for both blacks and whites were found at the military base, which provided jobs for 3,800 civilians by the mid-1970s. In fact, 40 percent of total employment in Okaloosa County was estimated to be related to military activity in 1975.[55] Moreover, military retirees increasingly settled in the relatively inexpensive Crestview area and began to challenge the traditional leadership and values in the community. As already mentioned, black military officers and retirees helped to found and develop the first NAACP chapter in the city. In addition, the first serious black political candidate to oppose Councilman Allen—Samuel Hayes, a retired military officer—defeated Allen in his second bid for office in 1977.[56] What little integration in housing there was in Crestview by the late 1970s was due primarily to the purchase of homes by black ex-military personnel in middle-class residential areas that were previously all white.[57]

By the mid-1970s federal aid to the city began to play a very important role in improving public services and housing for blacks. In 1976 Crestview received its first Community Development Block Grant funds totaling $100,000; by 1979 the city had its third such grant and the annual amount had risen to $372,000. The vast majority of this federal money was targeted for the predominantly black area for rehabilitation of houses, street paving and drainage, and demolition of irreparable houses.[58] At the same time the city also secured a federal section 8 housing grant to subsidize the rent payments of low-income persons, and a large public works grant ($535,000) for street paving. In 1980 Crestview was awarded a $2.3 million HUD grant for a 73-unit housing project, 43 units of which were targeted for low-income families.[59] In addition, the city employed twelve CETA program workers, three of whom were black, among its 109 full-time employees.[60]

Even with this federal aid, black progress was usually slow and often difficult. Arch-conservatism and anti-black views were still the prevailing sentiments in the white community. When George Wallace challenged again for the presidency in 1972 and 1976, the local newspaper favored him and he swept Crestview in the presidential preference primaries by more than two-to-one margins in both years.[61] City fathers, moreover, were often reluctant to spend nontargeted funds in the black area. In 1973, for instance, the council allocated the majority of both its federal revenue sharing and its new $1 million revenue bond monies for the construction of a new city hall complex, a recreation center far from the black area, and the new Sikes Library. Although Councilman Allen objected to these spending priorities, arguing that these were nonessential projects and that certain areas of the city still lacked basic services, it was to no avail.[62] Increasingly blacks were forced to compete with poor whites for improvements in city services. The substantial number of poor whites in the southeast section, second only to the adjacent black area in level of poverty, began to voice their complaints about lack of sewage, drainage, and street paving. As a result, by 1974 the city was targeting many of its service projects for this area rather than for the predominantly black southwest section.[63]

The late 1970s brought even further deterioration in black-white relations in Crestview. In 1976–1977 three local white women were beaten and one of them was sexually assaulted by black men. Not long after these attacks a cross was burned in the middle of a dirt road in the heart of the black section, and store managers reported a huge increase in the sales of handguns. More flaming crosses were found near city-limit signs a year later.[64] In July 1978 racial antagonism surfaced on a much larger scale when forty to fifty robed and hooded Ku Klux Klansmen marched down some of the main city streets. The Klan had been active earlier in the 1970s in Pensacola,[65] a larger city some fifty miles southwest of Crestview, but no KKK activities had been reported in Okaloosa County in several decades. On this occasion the Klan, made up primarily of outsiders from various parts of north Florida, paraded to the city's Confederate Memorial marker and raised an American flag. Somewhat later in July, Klan members received permission from the city council to fly a Confederate flag as well over the memorial marker. In mid-August KKK leaders attempted to donate an American and Confederate flag to the council directly, and proclaimed that the Klan's three basic goals were to "preserve the white race, the Constitution, and to block Communism." When the city council unanimously refused to accept the flags, several Klansmen raised both flags over city hall in protest and camped the night there to make sure the flags were not taken down.[66]

Although most blacks reacted with restraint, generally ignoring the racist statements and displays of the KKK,[67] and the Klan's activities soon died out, some Klan complaints struck a sympathetic note among a number of whites. Several letters to the editor of the *Okaloosa News-Journal* applauded the Klan and what it was doing to protect the rights of whites, particularly in the areas of education and employment.[68]

Editorials in the local newspaper in the latter 1970s also railed against busing and affirmative action programs as "racist" in reverse, and as an infringement of individual rights by the federal government.[69]

City officials, too, showed little concern for Crestview's black citizens. The city council, for example, decided to resurface several streets although many roads, particularly in the black area, were still unpaved. Public attention increasingly shifted, moreover, to the needs of the growing senior citizenry, especially in public housing and recreation.[70] Fairview Park was more and more neglected, and in 1980 one white councilman suggested that the city "bulldoze down" the black park after results of a recent fire inspection showed the main building to be unsafe and dangerous for public use.[71] In addition, black employees made up only 7 percent of all full-time city personnel in 1977 despite federal grant and affirmative action requirements.[72] Even most of the menial, low-paying city jobs, traditionally filled by blacks in most cities, went to whites. As one well-informed black resident put it: "This city has tried to keep blacks from having jobs so whites can have them. We didn't even have a black garbageman until the mid-1970s."[73]

Some Setbacks in the 1980s

By the early 1980s it was clear that political power and economic prosperity had shifted to the Gulf Coast portion of the county, leaving Crestview relatively poor and isolated. Blacks in particular continued to suffer the ill effects of economic hardship, as 51 percent of black families had incomes below the official poverty level (the proportion of white families with poverty-level incomes was only 14 percent).[74] The proposed 1980 neighborhood strategy area for Community Development Block Grant funds was made up of predominantly poor blacks, 68 percent of whom lived in substandard housing and almost all of whom lived in areas that lacked paved streets and sidewalks.[75] Black educational achievement was low as well. According to the results of the state's first functional-literacy test, reported in 1978, the black failure rate among Crestview High School juniors was high, with only 26 percent passing the math portion (the passing rate for white students was 75 percent).[76]

Blacks, moreover, had been politically disorganized and weak since the late 1970s. The local NAACP chapter, due to a lack of strong leadership and consistent local support, rarely met and was no longer considered an effective political organization. Factionalism, particularly between the Allen and Hayes camps, had split the black community.[77] In addition, black voter registration remained low. The last official count of city voters in the mid-1970s had shown the black registration rate to be only 40 percent and lagging 13 percentage points behind that of whites.[78] The black community did manage, however, to hold on to its lone seat on the city council with Hayes winning reelection in 1981 and 1983. Two years later, however, blacks ousted Hayes for his inability to deliver more street paving and decent recreational facilities, replacing him with Mamie Jolly, a retired schoolteacher and a more outspoken advocate of black interests.[79]

Black-white antagonisms continued to hamper black progress as well. The rapes of three white women by blacks early in 1980 created another wave of outrage among white citizens and prompted the city council to hire two more policemen.[80] Later that year a black female employee of the city housing program filed a discrimination complaint with the Department of HUD alleging that a promised promotion was given to someone else. After filing the complaint, she was promptly fired by the city.[81] Many whites continued to perceive local blacks as basically lazy and not worthy of a decent job. "Not many coloreds are employed at city hall today because most just don't want to work," claimed one public official.[82] Some whites suggested that the main reason blacks refused to work was because they had become overly dependent on income from welfare.[83] Indeed the 1980 census indicated that 38 percent of the city's black households received public assistance income other than Social Security.[84]

The loss of federal funds struck perhaps the most serious blow to black aspirations in the 1980s. Although it applied yearly, the city received no Community Development Block Grant funds between 1981 and 1986. Such grants for small cities had become increasingly scarce and competitive as a result of federal cutbacks in the program. In requesting $500,000 to $1.5 million annually in CDBG monies, the city had hoped to carry out much-needed street paving and housing improvements, primarily in black neighborhoods. Federal revenue sharing, providing Crestview with more than $100,000 each year, was also reduced and finally terminated in 1986. Revenue sharing had been used for library maintenance and recreation, and its loss was partly responsible for the city's decision to turn the recreation program over to local private organizations and to provide only limited maintenance of municipal parks.[85] In addition, black city employment dropped to less than six percent in 1986 (although blacks made up almost 20 percent of the city's population by then), in part because of the demise of the federal CETA program and the decreased emphasis on affirmative action.[86] While the city compensated to some degree for this loss in revenue with an increase of two mills in its property tax rate and the annexation of more than one thousand acres of developing residential land, blacks suffered disproportionately from the withdrawal of federal support.[87]

Yet despite dire poverty and persistent white racism, blacks in Crestview made moderate progress over these two and one-half decades. Racial desegregation of the schools began relatively early and went smoothly, as did the integration of most public accommodations. The city appointed a black policeman and elected a black councilman sooner than most other communities in north Florida, and public services in the black area improved slowly. Indeed, racial change was generally greater than one might have predicted given the relatively small, passive black population. But this small population was a key ingredient to black success, for it meant that racial transformations rarely threatened white political and economic dominance, and therefore did not arouse increased white resistance. Nevertheless the impetus to change came only partly from local blacks. The military and Eglin Air Base, and the federal government through laws, court decisions, and grants, were essential in ameliorating racial conditions in Crestview. These outside institutions proved vital in helping to loosen the yoke of racism and poverty which had thwarted most black progress prior to the 1960s.

Lake City: The Struggle for Black Political Independence

The second of the Old South communities is Lake City. Often referred to as the "New Gateway to Florida," Lake City is located sixty miles west of Jacksonville and just south of the Georgia border at the point where several major federal and state highways converge. It is the Columbia County seat and largest city in this rural county, yet it has a small-town atmosphere with unquestioned scenic beauty—rolling hills, pinewood forests, and numerous lakes. The county's developing industry, productive farm lands, and commercial advantages have marked the area as rich in potential economic and population growth.[88] Moreover, the city boasts a sense of southern gentility; indeed, a long-time sign on a highway leading into the city proclaimed it as "friendly and progressive."

But Lake City's natural beauty, relative prosperity, and claim to civility belie the blatant racism and poverty which have afflicted the sizable black population in the northern part of the city. In fact, Lake City was one of the last communities in north Florida to racially integrate its major institutions. Olustee Park with its Confederate monument, located in the center of the city, and the annual reenactment of the Battle of Olustee, a Civil War clash in which the Yankees were defeated and driven off Florida soil, still have a special meaning for most white Lake Citians.[89] As one city official described racial attitudes here: "This is an old redneck area. . . . Blacks are considered subservient. The typical attitude here is 'if they're black, to hell with them.' "[90]

Columbia County was originally established in 1832, but little development took place until after the Indians were driven from the area in the Seminole War of 1835. Lake City, whose original name was Alligator, was settled mostly by small farmers. As cotton growing expanded, however, more black slaves were brought in, and by 1860 the population of the city (and the county) was almost 50 percent black. At that time cotton was, of course, the dominant cash crop, but tobacco, vegetables, and livestock were important and profitable as well.[91]

Following the Civil War, many newly freed blacks began to take part in local politics, and with the help of white Republicans and carpetbaggers from the North, several blacks were elected to local office. This generated a great deal of antagonism among most whites, who feared any development of political power for "illiterate Negroes." As part of this white reaction, the Ku Klux Klan became very active in the county after the Civil War, and intimidation and violence against blacks and sympathetic white Republicans were common. In fact, Klan members in north Florida, particularly in Lake City, were "about as violent as Klansmen anywhere" in the postwar period.[92] One Republican state senator from Columbia County was warned by the KKK in 1871 to resign if he wanted to live. He defied the warning; in later Congressional testimony he described eight killings (seven blacks and one white Republican legislator) in the county since 1868, and numerous whippings, house burnings, and other acts of terrorism by the Klan. Approximately two to three hundred blacks reportedly fled the county to escape the violence, and whites soon reasserted their total control of local politics.[93]

This early white terrorism of blacks seemed to set the tone of future race relations in Lake City. The proportion of blacks in the population, always totaling between one-third and one-half of the city's populace, served to engender strong white fear and resistance. And the fear was not only of black political power, but of black economic power (particularly landownership at first) and ultimately of black men possibly "taking advantage of white women."[94] In addition, somewhat later the city developed a reputation as a "frontier town" replete with gambling, prostitution, bootlegging, and white vigilantism.[95] Such an atmosphere was conducive to continued Klan activity and white suppression of blacks. As late as the 1970s, a number of local blacks could still vividly recall past instances of KKK lynchings and beatings of blacks who tried to vote or in some way to defy white control.[96]

An Uphill Battle

By 1950 blacks made up one-third of the city's 7,571 residents, but were segregated in the northeast section, cordoned off from white Lake City by railroad tracks. Most blacks were very poor and worked as menial laborers for whites. All services, including schools, restaurants, motels, and public recreation facilities, were completely segregated racially and most remained so through the 1960s. When black freedom riders passed through the city in the early 1960s, the signs indicating segregation in the bus station were removed and the riders were served, but once the freedom riders left to continue their journey, the signs were replaced.[97]

From the period of Reconstruction up until the late 1940s, very few blacks had been allowed to register and vote in Lake City. By the early 1950s, however, white politicians, experiencing greater competition among whites for public office, began to openly encourage and organize black registration. Manipulation of the potentially large black vote was seen as an important means of either obtaining or retaining control of political power. Hence by 1959 fully 54 percent of black adults were registered (compared with a white registration rate of 85 percent) and blacks composed 22 percent of the total registered vote.[98]

Various techniques were used by whites to turn out the black vote. According to one significant study, part of which focused on voter manipulation in Lake City in the late 1950s and early 1960s:

> Taxis are hired to take Negroes to the polls, and city-owned cars have been used on occasion for the same purpose. The police and the sheriff's deputies openly campaign. Many of the credit groceries in the Negro section of the town are tied to the manipulative camp in the town, and these are used to remind the Negro patrons of their civic duty to vote and, most important, for whom to vote.[99]

For blacks who required a greater incentive to vote, whiskey and direct cash payoffs were also readily available at election time. By using these manipulative techniques, it was estimated that white politicians and their agents controlled about 75 percent of the black vote, and much of this control continued through the early 1970s.[100]

Payoffs for the sizable black vote, however, were very modest. A few streets were paved in the black section, two black policemen were put on the force to patrol the black area, and several blacks were hired for unskilled citywork.[101] Yet by the early 1960s approximately 90 percent of the streets in the black area were still unpaved, drainage and sewage services were sparse, and there were still no city recreational facilities in the northeast section. Although blacks mounted a drive in 1961 for funds to construct a swimming pool for black residents (whites had their own segregated pool at Youngs Park), the drive failed to produce sufficient funds or support from city hall, and a pool was never built.[102]

White elites continued to control Lake City politics throughout the 1960s. Despite the increasing impact of the civil rights movement in other parts of the Old South, black attempts at gaining independent political power in Lake City were doomed to failure. In 1964, for example, a popular seventy-four-year-old black tinsmith ran for a city commission seat, the first black to challenge for city office since Reconstruction. Although the commission elections were by precinct and the black candidate ran in majority-black precinct ten, the tinsmith was still narrowly defeated by the white incumbent. A year later the city commission requested and received a favorable vote from the state legislature to alter its commission election system from precinct to at-large, thereby virtually eliminating any chance of a black being elected in the future.[103]

Black challenges in the 1960s to segregation in the schools were not very successful either. Black public education had always been separate and unequal; in fact, all-black Richardson High School had never been fully accredited until the mid-1960s.[104] As a result of a suit filed by black parents in 1964, the federal district court in Jacksonville ordered school desegregation to begin in Lake City in 1965. However, a "freedom of choice" plan brought only token integration, since it meant in practice that black students could go to formerly all-white schools if space was available and if they could arrange their own transportation. A great deal of federal pressure from HEW and the federal courts was required before substantial school desegregation finally occurred in the 1970–1971 school year.[105]

The removal of racial barriers in public accommodations also faced considerable white resistance. Even after the passage of the 1964 Civil Rights Act, few blacks were willing to risk physical abuse, verbal insults, or the loss of their jobs by attempting to integrate facilities. Alyce Caesar, a well-educated black leader and an economically independent mortician, successfully desegregated a few restaurants by taking small groups of black students into several whites-only establishments. On another occasion several young blacks challenged segregated seating at the local movie theater. This confrontation enraged some whites and resulted in a minor race riot with several persons suffering injuries. Such violent conflict moved the mayor to appoint a biracial committee, with two blacks on it, and to push for integration in the theater and several other public places. More importantly, these direct challenges by black youths captured the attention of older blacks, who, for the first time, began quietly to question white hegemony. Yet few public facilities were completely integrated and little change occurred in the 1960s.[106]

Throughout this period whites in Lake City continued to be deeply hostile toward blacks. In the presidential elections of 1964 and 1968, two advocates of racial segregation, Goldwater and Wallace, carried the city and the county respectively by large margins.[107] Editorials in the local weekly newspaper, the *Lake City Reporter*, railed against the national civil rights bills and the civil rights demonstrators, claiming that "the [blacks] should realize that they must earn respect and do things for themselves before demanding of others. At the same time, as a free nation, one must be allowed to associate with whom he pleases."[108] The local newspaper believed that the civil rights movement was infiltrated by Communists, and strongly supported the jailing of demonstrators. The KKK held several well-publicized rallies during this period, and one such meeting in 1963 attracted more than two thousand persons.[109] In addition a local barber, an outspoken racist and former Klan member, was elected five times during the fifties and sixties to the state legislature.[110]

This history of extreme white racism, coupled with physical and economic intimidation of blacks, effectively suppressed most black attempts at political change. Lake City's black middle class, small in numbers and still quite economically dependent upon whites, was unable to organize the black community to bargain with the white political structure. Even schoolteachers, the largest segment of the black middle class, felt vulnerable to reprisals by local whites. Furthermore, potential black leaders, such as talented young blacks who left Lake City to acquire skills elsewhere, seldom returned due to the repressive atmosphere and lack of job opportunities.[111] As one white leader described it: "Blacks are factionalized and therefore not very influential, . . . they have no real leadership. They're only important at election time, and then they only vote for a price."[112]

But even with a sizable and effective black middle class, the political organization of the masses of poor and undereducated blacks would have been very difficult. As late as 1969, almost 60 percent of the black population had annual incomes below the federal poverty level (the comparable figure for whites in Lake City was 12.5 percent), and the black per capita income of $1,303 was only 42 percent of white income. Moreover, while the majority of white adults (twenty-five years and older) had graduated from high school, only 27 percent of blacks had done so, and the median number of school years completed by blacks was less than eight years.[113] Yet despite the presence of these inopportune conditions, the rumblings of political change began to occur by the middle of the next decade.

Protest for Change

In an early 1960s study of black voting and its consequences in Lake City and five other small Florida communities, it was argued that the transformation from a manipulated situation to an independent-bargaining one for blacks was difficult to achieve. The study contended, however, that the street-demonstration technique might help to effect such a transformation by bringing the black middle and lower classes together and by avoiding the manipulative strategies of whites.[114] Clearly the challenges to segregation in public accommodations and the movie theater riot of the 1960s suggested this. Such a recipe for change proved to be prophetic for Lake City blacks.

In November 1974 the first organized demonstration took place, as black discontent with poor living conditions and the slow pace of change began to boil over. Some fifty blacks, many of them teenagers, led by a black man from nearby Gainesville and a nascent SCLC organization, gathered in front of the county courthouse to protest police brutality, lack of black employment opportunities, and the lack of paved streets in the northeast section. The next night a large black crowd showed up at the county school-board meeting to protest the reinstatement of a white bus driver who had been suspended for allegedly choking a black girl. Several black leaders, including some from outside the county, used the incident as an occasion to charge the school board with racial discrimination in a number of policy areas.[115]

These initial demonstrations were harbingers of events to come throughout the latter 1970s, as blacks increasingly protested the discriminatory policies of city and county governments, the school board, and other local institutions. Several black leaders from outside the city were instrumental in providing expertise, helping to train local leaders, and challenging the white power structure without fear of reprisal. On occasion charismatic outside leaders were able to focus attention on particularly salient issues, thereby helping to mobilize large numbers of previously quiescent blacks. In January of 1975, for example, Reverend Ralph Abernathy, a national civil rights leader and president of the SCLC, spoke at a large black rally and denounced city officials for the lack of paved streets, the existence of outdoor toilets, and excessive brutality by police.[116] Abernathy appeared at another meeting of some 350 blacks in late March. At that time he helped organize a large protest march in which an outdoor toilet was carried and placed on the steps of city hall in symbolic protest of inadequate sewage facilities in black neighborhoods.[117]

Along with the development of local black leaders and political organizations like SCLC and the NAACP, forces in the white community supportive of racial change also began to emerge. In 1974 the longtime mayor resigned and a reform mayor, sympathetic to the plight of the city's blacks, was elected a year later. He immediately appointed a new biracial committee to improve communications between blacks and whites; the previous committee, lacking any substantive powers, had proven ineffective and was long defunct. In addition, he encouraged the seeking of federal funds to help alleviate the "horrible conditions" in the black section, and advocated changing the city election system to precinct elections in order to favor black political aspirations.[118] Two developments, the election of several city commissioners who were politically less conservative and the transformation to a city-manager form of government in 1977, encouraged more professionalism in local government and somewhat more sensitivity to black demands.[119] Also of importance was the liberal, activist county administrator who was instrumental in securing the first major federal grants (community development, rent subsidy, and day-care) used in north Lake City, and in prodding city officials to seek federal monies.[120]

In terms of creating a greater awareness and concern for the plight of blacks, the local newspaper, the *Lake City Reporter*, began to play a significant role by the mid-1970s. Previous to this, the newspaper had generally ignored the black community or taken a conservative stance on major racial issues. But in 1968 the newspaper became a Monday-through-Friday daily, and in the early 1970s it was purchased by the New York Times Company. As a result, the *Lake City Reporter* began to assume a more national scope and a more liberal perspective on race relations. Black poverty in north Lake City was reported much more thoroughly, and in 1975–1976 editorials began to strongly criticize city officials for the "disgrace" of having numerous "dilapidated shacks" and a heavy predominance of unpaved streets in the northeast section.[121]

Despite these emerging factors and increased black politicization, racial change was slow and difficult. The general attitude of most city commissioners toward blacks was still that "they want all they can get for nothing, and they don't pay taxes and don't want to work."[122] The commission was unwilling to allocate major increases in city funds for the black section and was reluctant to pursue federal funds out of fear of federal intervention in local affairs. City officials also opposed black attempts at insuring black representation on the council, voting four to one against a 1976 proposal to change the election system to precinct voting.[123] Due to threats from organized criminal elements, the city's reform mayor resigned in 1976 and the liberal county administrator departed two years later.[124] The biracial committee, with only advisory powers, began to atrophy by 1977 due to "dwindling interest" and its inability to accomplish much.[125] Moreover, the *Lake City Reporter*, now considered by many whites to be a "Yankee" newspaper, came under considerable attack for its muckraking articles and liberal editorials.[126]

Nevertheless, some black political progress did take place in the late 1970s, but usually not without outside assistance. A lawsuit to change the city's election system to precinct elections, a major focus of black efforts since 1975, was finally filed by the NAACP in federal district court in October 1977. On three occasions (1967, 1971, and 1975) black candidates had challenged under the at-large system for a seat on the city commission, but all had been defeated.[127] There was ample legal precedent supporting the NAACP claim that the at-large system was unconstitutional because it denied minorities the realistic opportunity of election. As a result, city officials began to compromise. They agreed to have another referendum on the issue (a previous citywide referendum to change the election system had been narrowly defeated in 1976). With open support from city officials who feared having a federal judge reorder their election process, the referendum was approved in all voting districts in June 1978. In precinct elections held later that summer, a black candidate, Samuel Thompson, a semiretired former veteran's hospital employee, was elected to the commission from majority-black precinct ten, and another black candidate narrowly lost in adjacent precinct twelve where blacks numbered more than 40 percent of registered voters. Thompson thus became the first black elected Lake City official since Reconstruction.[128]

Pressure from local blacks was also instrumental in getting blacks appointed to important city boards and in blocking attempts at rezoning for a new concrete plant and a liquor store in the northeast section.[129] Yet major changes, such as improvements in city services for blacks, required substantial outside help. In 1978 the NAACP filed suit again in federal court, this time alleging discrimination in the distribution of public services. A year later a black complaint, charging that the city spent far more money for services in the white areas than in the black section, was lodged with the U.S. Treasury Department's Office of Revenue Sharing. After conducting an investigation, the Office of Revenue Sharing determined in 1981 that Lake City had violated the racial discrimination provisions of the 1972 Revenue Sharing Act, and threatened a cutoff of federal funds if the city did not begin to remedy the violations. City officials refused to admit guilt to any violation, arguing that the federal government's allegations were not completely correct and that the city was already doing much to remedy the situation. Nonetheless, in the wake of rising legal fees and out of fear of losing federal funds, city officials entered into a negotiated compliance agreement, both with the Office of Revenue Sharing and with the federal court, whereby $1.7 million (primarily federal grant monies) would be spent over the next eight years to improve streets, drainage, water, sewers, and recreational services for blacks.[130]

In 1979 a racial crisis shook the school system, and this crisis marked a major challenge to, and finally a watershed in, race relations in Lake City. Since the substantial school desegregation of the early 1970s, black teachers and parents had complained to the school board on a number of occasions about alleged discriminatory school practices, but to no avail. Most of the complaints dealt with alleged discrimination in the hiring and firing of black teachers or administrators and with the discriminatory punishment of black students.[131] However, blacks became outraged in March 1979 when the school board expelled a black tenth-grade boy for allegedly exposing himself to a white girl. Blacks argued that the black student was denied due process at the expulsion hearing. More importantly, they maintained that the action exemplified the racist attitudes of the all-white school board, arguing that if the boy were white and the girl black, the boy would never have been expelled. Angry black youths began to boycott school to protest the expulsion, and interracial fighting occurred in some of the schools. Within a few days parental encouragement of the boycott resulted in approximately 95 percent of black students staying home, and more than three hundred black citizens met nightly to discuss what should be done.[132]

To deal with the expulsion case and other discriminatory issues in the schools, concerned blacks organized a group called the Community Fair Action Committee (CFAC). The committee called off the student boycott, feeling that black students would suffer most if it continued, and aired a variety of grievances before the school board. Most board members resented the black boycotts and felt that the expressed grievances were not legitimate. The only major action by the board was to hire five security officers to help maintain peace in the schools.[133] But CFAC was not to be deterred. The school expulsion case was appealed to federal court, where a favorable ruling reduced the length of the expulsion.[134] In the meantime, CFAC and the local SCLC organized three protest marches, each involving several hundred blacks, to demonstrate to the city the intensity of their feelings concerning discriminatory school-board policies.[135]

Although the student boycotts and protest marches surrounding the expulsion case had no immediately visible policy effects, they were important in further politicizing and mobilizing young blacks. The crisis also produced some capable, local black leaders who were more willing to challenge the white power structure. CFAC continued as a viable local organization, carrying out voter registration drives and neighborhood forums with elected officials in order to raise black "voter consciousness."[136] The door-to-door voter registration campaigns were quite successful, adding some 245 blacks to the voter rolls in less than a year and raising the black proportion of city registrants to a record level of almost 32 percent.[137] CFAC also proved adept at organizing the black vote for elections, endorsing three white candidates who were victorious in county elections and helping President Carter carry the county in the 1980 presidential election.[138]

Clearly the black electorate had become a major independent factor, no longer easily manipulated by whites. As the president of CFAC put it: "The politician who comes in [to the black area] with cheap liquor and ten-dollar bills is not going to make it anymore."[139] CFAC was successful in monitoring city commission and school board meetings, often raising issues and making demands to improve services for blacks. When this strategy proved unsuccessful, the committee would often appeal to the courts or to the federal government. As an example, in 1980, following a complaint brought by CFAC, HEW's Office of Civil Rights charged the school board with racial discrimination in the employment of administrators, and threatened to terminate some $2 million in federal education funds.[140]

A Continuous Fight

Though CFAC and several other black organizations had effectively raised black political consciousness and confidence, racial change in Lake City in the early 1980s still proved difficult. Most school board members and some city officials continued to be insensitive to racial issues and, at times, totally intransigent. Alleged discrimination in the hiring of black school administrators and in the expulsion of black students was still an issue.[141] Moreover, despite deplorable housing conditions in the northern section (which one local state senator, after touring the area, claimed were the worst in north Florida), city officials consistently refused to condemn the housing or to actively pursue public housing.[142] City services for blacks had improved only marginally by 1980, and more than 42 percent of blacks were still mired in poverty. The city's only black elected official, a political moderate who was generally respected by both the black and white communities, found serving on the commission to be frustrating. In Thompson's words: "We get along well [on the commission] until I talk about discrimination. Blacks don't ask for much, and we've got lots of dirt roads, ditches, and weeds to cut. But the city doesn't want to do much. They seem to have a priority list, and we're low on it."[143]

The attitudes of many white Lake Citians were still less than sympathetic toward blacks. Moderate black candidates, running in at-large election systems for both the county commission and the school board in the late 1970s, failed to attract enough white votes to win election.[144] Moreover, despite a number of complaints from blacks, the logo adopted by the city in 1981 pictured a Confederate flag and two Confederate soldiers. For many blacks the logo clearly suggested "a return to the old southern ways."[145] So too did a sizable Ku Klux Klan rally held near Lake City in September 1981. The last previous KKK rally in 1977 had been relatively small, but this gathering attracted more than two hundred people, most of them Lake City residents. The rally had been well advertized; handbills had been given out in local stores. The "Imperial Wizard" of the KKK's Invisible Empire was there, speaking out against racial integration and affirmative action, and warning whites to arm themselves in preparation for the race riots that he predicted would occur after President Reagan's welfare cuts took effect. Although the local NAACP and *Lake City Reporter* editorials strongly opposed allowing the KKK rally to take place in the city, arguing it would pull the community apart racially, few white leaders publicly condemned the gathering.[146]

By 1982, however, black political fortunes began to change, primarily as a result of their own electoral and organizational challenges. In city elections in that year, Glenel Bowden, black activist and president of the local NAACP, defeated Thompson for the tenth-precinct seat on the council. Bowden, an organizer of CFAC, had emerged as the foremost leader in the black community. Outspoken and assertive compared to Thompson, Bowden also proved adept at negotiating and working effectively with the white councilmen and mayor.[147] In the same year, blacks helped to elect their first black county commissioner, Ron Williams. A relatively young businessman, Williams was another new black leader who was skilled at representing black interests without unduly offending whites. Indeed, Williams, having been appointed to a vacant seat on the commission in 1981, was able to win office in an at-large system, defeating three white opponents and attracting a number of white votes.[148] By 1986, blacks were also able to capture their first seat on the school board, but only after the NAACP had filed a federal court suit which resulted in a change to district elections for the board.[149]

While these electoral victories were significant and marked a real change in local politics, blacks actively pressed for improvements in other areas as well. In education, both CFAC and the NAACP registered numerous complaints with the school board and the federal Office of Civil Rights concerning alleged racial discrimination in teacher hiring, student discipline, and ability grouping. Many of these complaints had little impact on the recalcitrant board, and the federal government under the Reagan Administration, demanding more stringent proof of discrimination, dismissed most of the charges as well.[150] Yet when the school board refused to act on an NAACP complaint about the lack of black speakers at the annual high school baccalaureate program, the NAACP held a separate program for black students.[151] The NAACP achieved more success, however, in the area of employment. Challenging alleged discrimination in hiring in several local businesses and county government offices, the civil rights organization was able to increase black employment in several instances. Black groups also played an important role in bringing about the renovation of the Richardson High School gym, located in the heart of the black section, for use as a recreational facility. The formerly black high school had been closed since 1973 as a result of integration and had deteriorated to the point of resembling a bombed-out shell.[152]

Nonetheless the most significant changes for black Lake Citians in the 1980s were the direct result of the city compliance agreement with the federal government. While there was initial fear that city officials might evade full compliance, especially with federal dollars beginning to disappear, this fear proved to be unjustified. The federal government, in the form of both the courts and the Office of Revenue Sharing, provided oversight of the agreement, and the city's black official and the NAACP applied consistent local pressure for compliance. As a result, city officials actively sought CDBG and other federal funds, and by 1986, nearly $1.5 million had been spent and another $1 million allocated for minority neighborhood improvements. These dollar amounts represented more than twice the total of funds ordered by the compliance agreement and many of the infrastructure projects were completed two to three years ahead of schedule.[153]

Yet in general, the black quest for increased political power and change in Lake City has been strongly resisted by many white leaders who perceive this quest as a threat to white dominance. Despite this resistance, by the late 1970s black politics had clearly made the transition from white manipulation and control to an independent, bargaining form of power. There is little doubt that this transformation took place late in the civil rights era and was more difficult to achieve in Lake City than in most other Old South communities. Most significantly, little change would have taken place without direct black confrontations with whites and without the assistance of various "intervening" forces, including outside leaders, the federal government, and the courts. Nonetheless, black political independence and power remain fragile. The lack of a sizable middle class, the need for more educated and experienced leaders, and pressing poverty are political and economic liabilities that continue to plague the black community. And, as always, there is the lingering white racism which pervades the city like a night in fog.

Gretna: The Emergence of Black Political Power

Gretna is the last Old South community we will examine, and in many ways it resembles hundreds of other small southern towns.[154] A flashing yellow light cautions motorists to slow down as they pass through on U.S. 90. At one end of town is a grocery–gas station with a small post office attached. At the other end is an abandoned mini-shopping center with numerous broken windows. In between are less than a dozen scattered businesses—some struggling, some failed, none prosperous. Many of the homes are weather-beaten shacks along dirt roads. It hardly seems like the setting for a black revolt, yet the Florida panhandle community of Gretna experienced a political revolution of sorts. Between 1970 and 1972 the predominantly black population of this mile-square rural community of some nine hundred inhabitants took complete control of the formerly all-white town government. So sudden and sweeping were the changes in Gretna that it soon became a symbol of black political power in north Florida.

Gretna is located just south of the Georgia border in rural Gadsden County, which is approximately 60 percent black. Until recently black participation in political affairs had been nonexistent, except for a brief period during Reconstruction when two blacks were elected to the state legislature.[155] As late as 1950 only one percent of eligible black voters in the county were registered; by 1960 this figure had risen to just three percent. Yet between 1964 and 1966 a very dramatic increase in black politicization took place as the proportion of the county's black electorate expanded from 14 to 40 percent, and by 1972 the registration rate of blacks reached just over 50 percent (compared to a fairly consistent white registration rate of 61 to 64 percent). Increased black political awareness was inspired largely by federal government support of black aspirations and intense activity by national civil rights organizations, especially CORE, SCLC, and the NAACP.

Concurrent with these outside governmental and civil rights pressures was the rapid decline during the 1960s of the plantation economy based on shade tobacco.[156] Even in times of prosperity, the wealth generated by the tobacco industry had never been evenly distributed. In the mid-1960s the county ranked in the bottom 10 percent of United States counties in extent and severity of poverty, family resources, educational achievement, functional illiteracy, and sufficiency of housing.[157] In 1976, after the virtual disappearance of tobacco, 27 percent of blacks in the county's labor force were unemployed and the income of a majority of Gretna's residents was below the poverty level.[158] Yet the decline of this plantation economy gave blacks the economic independence which is often a prerequisite to political mobilization.

Early Isolation

Gadsden County, including Gretna, were largely unaffected by the civil rights movement in the 1950s and early 1960s. The *Brown* decision provoked no mention in the local newspaper. The schools and most other institutions remained totally segregated. A local White Citizen's Council, formed in 1956, denounced integration as a violation of the word of God and saw the NAACP as a tool of the Communist party.[159] As late as 1958 only seven blacks were registered to vote, although more than ten thousand blacks lived in the county in 1950. Two United States Civil Rights Commission reports, one in 1959 and the other in 1961, indicated that physical and economic reprisals by whites—and threats of such—had prevented black citizens from registering in the county. Indeed, even black ministers and teachers reportedly had "deep fear" and some of them had been "warned against voting."[160] Despite extensive civil rights activity in Tallahassee, less than thirty miles to the east, in 1957 and 1960, no visible black political mobilization was evident in Gadsden County.

The outside intervention of CORE in 1963, however, sparked a rise in political awareness among blacks in the county, although not yet in Gretna to any great degree. Reflecting the general shift in the southern civil rights movement from direct confrontation to voter registration, CORE concentrated on voter education and registration in rural areas, including north Florida.[161] CORE activities proved initially to be quite successful in Gadsden County. Between October 1963 and April 1964 some 975 black voters were added to the registration rolls, and on one day alone, August 3, 1964, more than four hundred blacks were registered.[162]

But CORE activists, laboring under conditions as repressive as they were in Mississippi, faced arrest and sometimes even violence.[163] A CORE field representative in the area charged that local police attempted to intimidate her and potential black voters by following her constantly, parking outside black churches during voter registration rallies, and taking automobile license numbers.[164] The more subtle forms of intimidation gave way to violent action at times. In December 1964 the CORE offices in Quincy were burned, and in other incidents registration workers were harassed and physically beaten.[165] Despite concentrated efforts, CORE was able to raise the black share of registered voters to only 40 percent by 1966. Blacks who attempted to gain political office in Quincy, the county seat, and elsewhere in the county met with lopsided defeats.[166] One black, eventually elected to office in Gretna, suggested that many of the older blacks were unable to conceive of one of their own holding political power; their feeling seemed to be that local government, having traditionally been a matter of exclusive white control, was not a black concern.[167]

Concurrent with the voter registration drives spearheaded by CORE was pressure from the national government for integration in public accommodations and schools. Following the signing of the Civil Rights Act of 1964 by President Johnson, many Quincy businesses closed early whenever black residents tested segregation; but most establishments began to integrate not long thereafter. Due to federal pressure, a few black students began in 1966 to register at previously all-white schools under a "freedom of choice" plan, but not one white student applied at any all-black schools. Further school desegregation did not take place until 1970, and only then under the pressure and compulsion of a federal district court order.[168]

In the late 1960s, still unable to gain direct access to the decision-making sphere, blacks became increasingly dissatisfied with the slow rate of progress, and their frustration and discontent began to surface. In May 1970 an electrical substation in Quincy was bombed. A week later a bomb was found at the county courthouse, and a few days later another bomb was located at a local farm-tractor dealer. Two black men later confessed, stating, "We wanted to give the big man some trouble."[169] The bomb incidents were only a prelude. On a Saturday night in October 1970, a black Quincy policeman shot a crippled black man when he allegedly attempted to evade arrest in a local bar. The city of Quincy exploded with a black riot. The police chief urged the governor to call out the National Guard; and highway patrolmen, a Leon County riot squad, and area police units were used to control the violence. At least sixteen white-owned stores were damaged by the rioting and twenty-two blacks were arrested. The following evening approximately one hundred young blacks attempted to march to the Quincy jail but were dispersed without incident. Three fires were reported in the county.[170] In Gretna, whites feared for their property, and a volunteer group armed with shotguns stood watch for nearly a week at the new all-white private school in nearby Mt. Pleasant.[171]

The Quincy riot proved to be a watershed in race relations in the county. As a Gretna black man, later an elected public official, expressed it: "The riot opened the eyes of lots of whites. They couldn't control blacks as well afterwards. They couldn't just do things to blacks just because they were white."[172] One of the immediate effects of the riot was the revitalization of the Quincy-based chapter of the NAACP. In the weeks following the riot the NAACP planned new voter registration drives and demanded that more blacks be hired by local businesses and government, that access to voter registration books be facilitated, and that treatment of black prisoners at the county jail be improved.[173] Assisted by other outside groups, especially the SCLC, the NAACP organized marches and boycotts in Quincy over the next few months in support of their demands. Even with the intense CORE activity of previous years, Gadsden County had never experienced such organized mass protest. One march in downtown Quincy in February 1971 attracted some six hundred blacks who walked four abreast and chanted "soul power."[174]

The protests in Quincy seemed to have a contagious effect in the county. Early in 1971 black junior high students in nearby Havana initiated a march to protest school assignments due to desegregation. Sheriff's deputies broke up the demonstration with tear gas, and in reaction Havana blacks boycotted local stores to force increased black hiring.[175] Two weeks later a black man was shot during an argument in Midway, a rural community between Quincy and Tallahassee. Local blacks began throwing rocks through the windows of the store where the shooting occurred, and twenty-one were arrested. Several hundred more protesting blacks gathered outside the county jail in Quincy, where those arrested were brought. On the same day, a ten-year-old black child was killed at the train crossing in Gretna. A protest involving some fifty blacks developed out of what was felt to be an inexcusable delay on the part of the ambulance crew in getting the still-breathing child to a hospital.[176]

The riot and the later direct-action tactics did produce some significant results. In terms of symbolic changes, the *Gadsden County Times*, the local white-owned newspaper, eliminated its segregated black news section and substituted the word "black" for the previously used term "Negro." Substantively, more blacks were hired by local businesses and government, including several deputies in the sheriff's department. The voter rolls were opened on a daily basis and the registration office was moved to a public building that was more accessible.[177] Within this volatile context, black voter registration began to climb again, increasing by over one-third in the year following the Quincy riot. Despite an electorate that was 50 percent black in 1972, attempts by blacks to gain electoral office in Quincy and on the county level met with defeat. Yet an underlying feeling had emerged among blacks that change would come as a result of direct political power rather than through negotiations with the white community. As one Quincy black put it: "It's just a matter of time until the blacks here learn how to turn their numbers into voting power. That's what all the whites in this town are really afraid of."[178]

Awakening and Participation

While Quincy was the focal point of most of the political activity that engulfed Gadsden County in the early 1970s, fundamental changes were also starting to take place in Gretna, located just six miles west of Quincy. The town was originally developed in the late 1800s when a railroad first penetrated this area; turpentine was the main industry, but there was also a cotton gin and sawmill by 1900. Gretna was incorporated in 1909, but its government fell dormant in the 1920s with the decline of the turpentine business and the stress of the Depression. It was not reactivated until the late 1940s in order to take advantage of the cigarette tax then available to municipalities.

Whites dominated the town's affairs from the start.[179] The cigarette tax was used to pay back a loan obtained by the white residents in the late 1950s to build a municipal water system, the major portion of which was confined to the white section of town.[180] Despite a population that was 80 percent black by 1970, blacks had never held or even run for public office.

But blacks in Gretna were not immune to the political activism sweeping the county. Following the Quincy riot in the fall of 1970, blacks boycotted two Gretna stores as a result of the alleged mistreatment of blacks. In one instance a black child was said to have been struck by a white store owner after the black child scuffled with the store-owner's son. The other instance involved the beating of a black man, described as mentally unstable but harmless, after he had been found in the bedroom of a white female store owner. The boycotts drove both store owners from business, demonstrating the potential of the town's blacks for united political action.[181]

Although some Gretna blacks had participated in county, state, and national elections in the past, they charged that Gretna whites had maintained a "secret government." Blacks had been unaware that separate registration with the town clerk was necessary to be eligible to vote in town elections.[182] Gretna's registration books were kept in a store owned by a white resident, and no blacks were listed. In January 1971 a member of the NAACP, who resided in Gretna, attempted to attend a meeting of the town council but was asked to leave. He reported the incident at the next meeting of the NAACP in Quincy and a committee was formed to investigate the issue. Upon discovery of the separate registration process, an appeal was made to the Florida House Committee on Elections, and the registration books were moved to the town hall.[183] The Quincy NAACP then spearheaded a massive effort to get Gretna blacks on the books for the upcoming 1971 election by canvassing the town, knocking on every door and driving people to the town hall to register. They were spurred on by the white mayor's assertion that local blacks were simply "too lazy" to register. One hundred and eighty-six black voters were registered for town elections in 1971, giving blacks a two-to-one electoral margin.[184]

In meetings sponsored by the NAACP, Gretna blacks decided to contest the two available town council positions as well as that of town clerk (elected officials included the mayor, five council members, and a town clerk). NAACP leaders decided that whites should retain control of the mayor's office for the time being. However, Earnest Barkley, a Florida A&M student who had organized an SCLC chapter in Gretna, decided to seek the office of mayor, and the NAACP threw its support behind him. On election day the NAACP, in cooperation with Gretna blacks, launched a "get-out-the-vote campaign" by stationing people at every street corner and providing rides to the polls. Black candidates were successful in all contests, including the mayor's race, and when the three remaining council seats became available the following December, they were captured by blacks as well.[185] Thus within the period of a year, Gretna had gone from an all-white town government to one that was totally black.

The assertion of black electoral power in the early 1970s was due in part to the increased economic independence of blacks. The most effective means of preventing black voting, at least in the recent past, had been threats of economic sanctions, especially the loss of jobs and housing. However, with the decline of tobacco as a cash crop, most blacks in Gretna were no longer dependent upon local whites for employment. According to a 1974 survey, 88 percent of the employed town residents commuted over five miles to work, with many working at the state hospital in Chattahoochee, eleven miles away.[186] Another study in 1977 indicated that almost 80 percent of employed Gretna blacks owned their own homes.[187]

In the first years following the black political takeover, relations between the white and black communities in Gretna were strained. One of the main issues in the political campaigns was the inadequacy of public services for blacks, especially water, sewage, and street paving. Black town officials felt that the former white leaders were now jealous of black attempts at town improvements, and resistance from whites was apparent.[188] In 1975, for example, black officials attempted to annex some surrounding land in order to accommodate a proposed sewage treatment plant and to attract industry for future growth. White landowners, whose lands and property taxes would be affected by annexation, filed suit to block the action on the grounds that the annexation procedure had been improper. Annexation was eventually successful, nearly doubling the town's population and qualifying the town for a greater share of federal revenue sharing funds.[189]

Another area of dispute centered around Gretna's attempt to obtain an independent police force. Gretna in the past had relied on the county sheriff's department for police protection. Members of the black community, however, felt that sheriff's deputies neglected black residents when they sought assistance. White residents considered the protection offered by the sheriff as adequate, especially considering the prospect of a black policeman enforcing the law—or as one white town official put it, of "some hired Negro who might shoot someone."[190] The sheriff's department was successful in blocking an attempt to obtain funds through the Federal Law Enforcement Assistance Administration, claiming that the sheriff's deputy residing in Gretna provided adequate protection. Gretna was ultimately able in

1978 to piece together a racially mixed police force of eight men by obtaining surplus equipment through the county and state, and paying salaries in part through CETA funds.[191]

The biggest complaint of Gretna's white residents, however, was their exclusion from the official decision making in the town's government. Few whites ever attended town meetings, preferring private meetings with black leaders when issues of importance emerged. Whites attempted to gain seats on the council through election, but were always opposed by a black candidate and defeated. "Every time we try to run someone, they run a black against us," complained one white candidate. "It is all right to run it [the town government]," he continued, "but they ought to listen to whites, too."[192] Charges of reverse discrimination were denied by black leaders, who contended that if whites would actively campaign in the black community and take an interest in town affairs they would be elected. This argument was apparently confirmed in the December 1977 election when a nineteen-year old white college student, one of the few whites to attend town council meetings, defeated a black challenger for a seat on the council.[193] Nonetheless this was the last white to win public office in Gretna, as the town's affairs became increasingly dominated by blacks.

Yet not all of the difficulties experienced by the black officeholders were due to conflict with whites. Black officials in Gretna were very young (their average age after the first election was twenty-four years) and politically inexperienced. Mayor Barkley, in particular, developed personal and political problems that plagued both him and the town. Just prior to the 1973 town election he was charged with adultery with a fifteen-year-old girl in Decatur County, Georgia, where he taught secondary school. He went on to win reelection as mayor, but he was forced to resign his teaching position after pleading no contest to the charges, and his Florida teaching credentials were suspended as a result.[194] Yet more serious difficulties lay ahead. In September 1974 the Gadsden County grand jury indicted Barkley on three counts of grand larceny and misconduct in his official capacity as mayor. Earlier the grand jury had issued a presentment concerning the town itself, charging poor bookkeeping procedures and lack of appropriate approval of official actions. The indictment against Barkley stated that he used an American Express credit card issued to the town to obtain personal items, including a diamond ring, a wedding ring, a Masonic ring, and a suit of clothes. Governor Askew suspended Barkley from office and appointed a black councilman as his replacement. Barkley pleaded no contest to the charges, and in early 1975 was sentenced to nine months in the county jail with three years probation.[195]

Despite these problems, Gretna made significant progress after blacks assumed political power. The town's treasury, limited in the past to the state cigarette-tax rebate and water fees, was bolstered by the newly available federal revenue sharing funds, which totaled more than $100,000 in 1972. Gretna became eligible for the funds when it levied its first real-estate tax of three mills. Whereas previously the town employed only a part-time maintenance man for the water system, the black administrations were able to establish a town hall, hire a town administrator plus clerks and a secretary, and employ a full-time maintenance crew of four men. Elected officials began drawing salaries ranging from $315 per month for the mayor to $125 per month for councilmen.[196] Most importantly, Gretna officials, with the assistance of professional consultants, began to pursue federal and state grants, and they proved to be very successful. By the late 1970s the town had obtained funds for a self-help housing program, a day-care center, a pilot solar-energy program, a sewer system and treatment plant, street paving, an upgrading of the water system, and small police and fire departments manned primarily by black CETA trainees. By 1981 Gretna had completed construction of a large, multipurpose municipal complex, with most of the money coming from a $320,000 federal grant.[197]

Some whites in the area began to refer pejoratively to Gretna as the "federal government's town," and they claimed that much of the outside funding was being wasted or used inefficiently.[198] In fact, federal funds were crucial to the town; in its 1977–1978 budget of almost half a million dollars, for example, approximately 85 percent of the revenues came from the federal government.[199] But most of the money helped to provide public services that few of the town's blacks had previously enjoyed. Thus in less than a decade of black hegemony, dramatic changes occurred in this small, poverty-stricken town, and in 1978 the *Gadsden County Times* praised Gretna and claimed that it was "at the forefront of the progress taking place in Gadsden County."[200]

Trying Times in the 1980s

Although the political revolution in Gretna achieved prominence and a degree of success, problems continued to trouble the town. The emergence of factionalism among blacks sometimes served to divert energies from the town's affairs. The main division in the black community developed between those who supported and those who opposed Mayor Barkley, but the basis of the dispute seemed to rest on familial considerations, not ideological differences. When Barkley returned from prison, ran for mayor once again in 1977 and was elected, the factional differences intensified.[201] Members of the town council openly criticized Barkley on several occasions between 1978 and 1980 for alleged illegal purchases and unaccounted travel funds. A county grand jury investigation in 1980 of the alleged spending improprieties found "no probable cause" of criminal conduct by Barkley but called for a state ethics commission investigation of what it termed "inappropriate conduct."[202] In 1979 the council supported a referendum on a town charter amendment to weaken the powers of the mayor, but the charter proposal was defeated at the polls.[203] These political conflicts jeopardized federal funding at times, and town meetings often degenerated into wild shouting matches.[204] Yet such factional competition decreased substantially by the mid-1980s as Barkley built a consensus on the town council, and most political opposition to the mayor faded.

A more severe problem continuing to plague Gretna blacks was that of economic deprivation. During the decade following the black political takeover, the number of whites declined as whites either died or moved out of town. By 1980 only 11.6 percent of the population was white (compared with 20 percent white in 1970). What remained was a very poor black population. Almost half of all black families were below the poverty level and approximately 26 percent were unemployed.[205] In the area of education, results of the statewide functional literacy test in 1977 indicated that Gadsden County students were the most poorly educated in the state, and black Gretna students tended to score lower on achievement tests than students elsewhere in the county. One reason for the low scores was the fact that more than twelve hundred whites had fled to all-white private schools, leaving the public schools with an enrollment which was approximately 90 percent black (97 percent in Gretna) by the early 1980s and therefore virtually segregated once again. In the mid-seventies a federal court order had been necessary to modify school district practices of grouping children by race rather than ability within schools, and of bypassing qualified black teachers and administrators in favor of whites.[206]

Pressing poverty also seriously hampered local government efforts to improve conditions. The tax base remained so low (only an estimated 20 percent of homeowners were eligible to pay local taxes) that local property tax receipts barely met the necessary expenses to maintain the new municipal complex. Many blacks could not afford to pay their user fees for the new water and sewage systems and for garbage collection, and as a result the town ran annual deficits due to the loss of such fees.[207] Serious deficiencies in the water system, which town officials claimed they could not afford to correct, threatened the health of local residents and resulted in a court suit brought by the Florida Department of Environmental Regulation. Only with state and some federal aid was the town able to improve this vital service.[208]

Finally, federal funds, which had been a panacea for Gretna, began to dry up in the late 1970s. Although it had been successful in the past in securing CDBG funds, the town received none of the increasingly scarce and competitive small-city grants from 1979 through 1985. This marked a serious loss, since basic infrastructure improvements and desperately needed housing rehabilitation were almost totally dependent on such federal funds.[209] In addition the federally funded, self-help housing project, which was expected to construct twenty-two homes for low-income persons, resulted in only eleven new houses because few blacks could afford them or qualify for the loans. The pilot solar-energy program for the houses was dropped altogether because of the projected maintenance expenses. And federally paid CETA employees, who made up the majority of the town's work force at one time, were all withdrawn in 1979 due to inadequate recruitment procedures and to the fact the town could not afford to hire many of these employees permanently.[210] As a result of various personnel problems and the loss of CETA, the town's police force was dismantled altogether in 1982.[211]

Despite its problems and general lack of resources, Gretna was able to achieve some notable successes in the 1980s. Federal funds enabled the town to build a new health clinic and a fifty-one-unit housing complex for farmworkers, and to develop a small park. The new health clinic was particularly important since the town had a number of homes with no indoor plumbing, and public sanitation had created a number of health problems.[212] A degree of community spirit and pride continued to inspire many of the town's citizens, even in the face of crushing poverty, and resulted in several cleanup and self-help projects. One of the most significant of these community efforts was known as Project Hope, funded by the state in 1986. This project helped uneducated local residents earn the equivalent of a high school degree and provided useful seminars on such tasks as personal budgeting, buying nutritious foods, fixing one's house, and participating in civic affairs.[213]

Certainly the most grandiose and potentially far-reaching community project, however, is a currently planned $9 million industrial park for Gretna. Seen as the economic boon the town so desperately needs, the 120-acre park should attract businesses (two have already committed to it) and provide an estimated 160 new jobs. The park has the strong support of the mayor, and the nearby Florida A&M School of

Business and Industry has provided the important technical expertise. By late 1986, town officials had taken a loan to purchase the land and had garnered more than $700,000 in federal and state grants for park development. While the project is long-term oriented and economically risky in a town so poor in resources, its success is also crucial to Gretna's economic future.[214]

In spite of the electoral success of blacks in Gretna, the black political revolution has not yet been fully exported to other nearby communities or to county government. Only in Quincy have blacks been somewhat effective, but much of this success has been due to an appeal to the federal courts that resulted in the conversion to a district from an at-large election system. This change resulted in the election of two blacks to Quincy's five-member commission in 1975, and two years later one of those elected blacks was named mayor by vote of the city commission.[215] However, even with black registration comprising 45 percent of the county's registered voters, attempts to gain black representation on the county commission and county school board were generally unsuccessful until the 1980s. Suits were filed in federal district court to have county commission and school-board seats contested by district, but the suits were initially denied.[216] Blacks were able to elect one minority member to the school board in 1978, but in 1980 with county registration of blacks outnumbering that of whites and with eight black candidates contending for seven different county offices, not one black was able to win office.[217] The high voter turnout among whites seemed to indicate a strong, lingering fear of a black political takeover that whites felt might "bring to office the anger of past grievances."[218] In 1982, however, with black registrants clearly in the majority and aggressively seeking to elect minority members to office, blacks finally won a majority of seats on the school board. Two years later, the federal courts ruled that school-board elections must be by district, and in a 1986 referendum, county voters approved district elections for county commission seats.[219] Thus blacks gained political power in the county only very slowly and with much difficulty.

Although the black political transformation in Gretna has had its limitations, it does suggest that the mobilization of blacks has been so extensive and pervasive that it has deeply altered even some of the most rural, poverty-stricken areas of the Old South. These are the communities where whites have been most intransigent in their racial attitudes and blacks most oppressed, and where political change was considered all but impossible. Yet it is clear that the black quest for political dominance in such a hostile climate could not have been achieved without the intervention of civil rights forces from outside and without a well-organized black electoral majority that was relatively independent of whites economically. This political control resulted in much-improved public services in Gretna. But it may be that the greatest benefit in the long run for blacks here was a new pride, a sense of community, and for the first time, a greater feeling of control over their own destiny. One black elected official stated that being in office "made me more aware of government and want to know more about government . . . and my kids are going to know more about government when they grow up. I now realize that government can work for people. I didn't used to believe this, but my attitude has changed."[220]

Nevertheless even a successful political mobilization can take an economically disadvantaged group only so far in the struggle for equality. The economic dependence on the plantation economy of tobacco is gone but the residue of poverty, racism, and the lack of education and opportunities remains. The intervention of the federal government, an important factor in Gretna's revitalization in the 1970s, has begun to fade from the scene. Thus the specter arises that Gretna's black officials might soon be governing a virtual "ghost town."

SUMMARY

It is hoped that these brief contemporary histories provide a general understanding of race relations and recent black politics in each of the Old South communities. By way of summary, figure 2.1 presents a time-line of major political events for Crestview, Lake City, and Gretna from 1960 to 1985. Clearly the civil rights movement was delayed in developing in the Old South. Indeed, there was little significant organizational or independent electoral activity by blacks prior to the 1970s. Desegregation of public accommodations occurred only after the passage of the 1964 Civil Rights Act, and there was only token desegregation in the public schools before the early 1970s. Thus racial change was slow and difficult, thwarted primarily by white racism. Political inexperience and pressing poverty also served to maintain blacks in a "parochial" status until relatively recently.

Similarities in the patterns of black subjugation were matched by common patterns in the development of black political activism in the Old South. The intervention of an external political force was absolutely necessary in order for blacks to challenge seriously local white hegemony. Most often this outside force consisted of the federal government (including the courts) and/or national civil rights organizations such as the NAACP. Increased economic independence for blacks

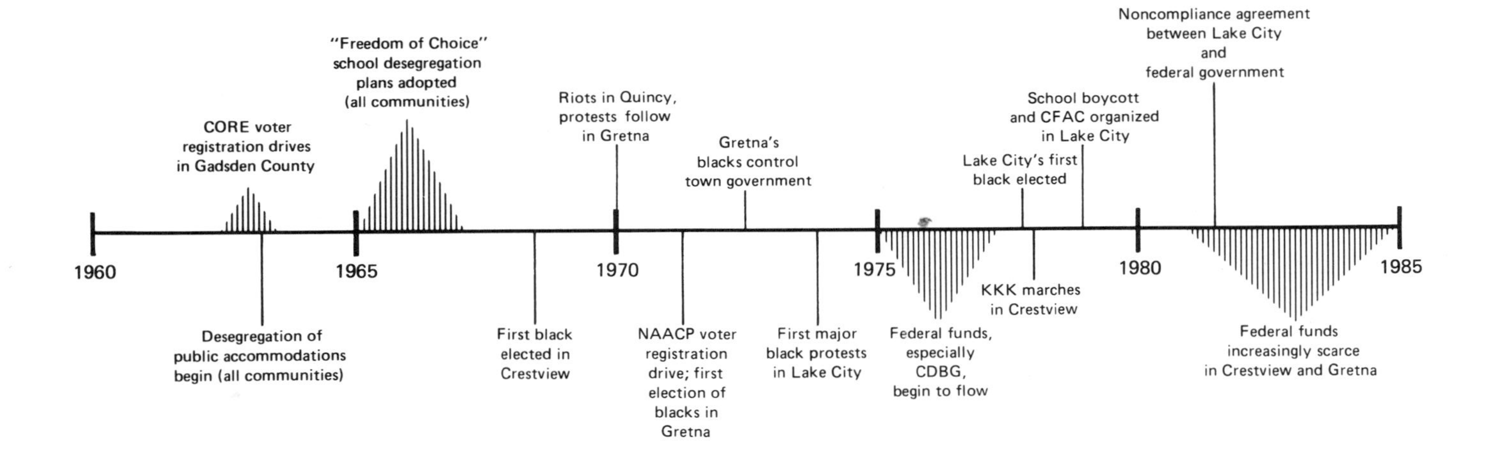

FIGURE 2.1

Time-Line of Important Political Events for Blacks in Old South Communities

also proved to be an important factor wherever poor rural blacks were vulnerable to economic sanctions by whites. The emergence of at least some moderate whites who aligned themselves with the interests of blacks was usually essential to the black movement as well. Finally, protests by blacks were common in each of these Old South communities and seemed crucial to the mobilization of blacks and the reduction of white control over the process of change.

These similarities among Old South communities, however, should not obscure some basic differences in the nature of race relations and change. Some of these differences seem attributable to the relative size of the black population. In Crestview, for example, racial conflict was rare and yet change was moderate, due in part to a small black citizenry that rarely threatened whites. In contrast, Lake City's sizable black population tended to make whites fearful of potential racial challenges and thus more protective of their power and resources. As a result, change for blacks in Lake City was exceedingly slow and difficult. Gretna, however, with a clear black majority, was able to redefine local politics and priorities, but only after overcoming a history of complete white control that was endemic to the Old South.

3

The New South and Political Change

> "While the state [Florida] has a relatively large number of Negroes, the whites of the newly settled areas do not seem to be governed by a Negrophobia to the same extent as the long settled agricultural areas of the Old South."
>
> —V. O. Key, Jr.
> *Southern Politics*

Unlike the rural, traditional Old South counties of north Florida, the state's New South areas were relatively unsettled before the early part of this century. The absence of a plantation economy and a slave past meant not only a smaller black population, but a white citizenry relatively unencumbered by racial fear. This fact, plus the diversity of south Florida's population, with many immigrants from the Northeast and Midwest settling along the coasts, tended to moderate racial hostility. The New South, as an ideal type, is near the opposite end of the continuum of modernization from traditional Old South society. New South communities are typically more urbanized, with growing populations that are relatively affluent and cosmopolitan. The economy of the New South is diverse and relatively prosperous; most of its cities experienced dramatic economic and demographic changes following World War II. Indeed many of those communities "eagerly embraced the economic growth of the postwar period, actively soliciting new industry and northern immigrants."[1]

These major economic and population changes have tended to focus attention in the New South on issues other than race, including jobs, housing, education, transportation, and the environment. Moreover, traditional racial fears of southern whites have been ameliorated by the large-scale immigration of people with more moderate racial attitudes. As a result, white supremacy groups, although surfacing occasionally, have proved relatively weak and increasingly have become extinct in many cities of the New South. The heavy economic dependence on tourism also provided a general moderating influence.[2] Finally, rapid economic and population growth encouraged both the development of more pluralistic political and economic elites and the emphasis on "professionalism" (especially in the form of city managers and trained bureaucrats) in local government.[3] Hence in the New South there has generally prevailed a "politics of economics" rather than one of race.[4]

In this nontraditional setting, blacks have "gone far toward rejecting the submission and passivity long expected of them; they are likely to be highly organized and participant" politically.[5] With a reservoir of educated, middle-class leaders and a certain degree of economic independence from whites, blacks began to organize, vote, and even compete for political office relatively early. Indeed, the civil rights movement found fertile ground in the New South. Challenges to segregation in public accommodations and in the schools took place sooner here than elsewhere, and racial change in general occurred earlier and more easily than in most Old South communities. As a result the intervention of outside political forces, such as the federal government, was not so important, though federal aid did prove helpful in providing more equitable public services for blacks. Nevertheless the New South was not immune to racial conflict and even at times to violence as the rapid pace of change produced turmoil. Yet such instances of open conflict were more the exception than the norm, and the politics of moderation dominated in most racial matters.

This chapter follows the format of the previous chapter, presenting overviews of each of the New South communities: Titusville, Daytona Beach, and Riviera Beach. In each summary the emphasis is on the civil rights movement and its general consequences. Although there are certain similarities in the political development of these New South cities, it is also clear that the processes of modernization associated with urbanization and economic development were not always sufficient in themselves to change racial conditions. Thus other factors were usually influential in the process of political and social change. One of these important factors is the size of the black population, and attention is devoted to this contextual variable and its possible effects. As in the last chapter, community analyses are presented in order of the relative proportion of blacks in the populace: first, Titusville, with a small number of blacks; second, Daytona Beach, which has a moderate-sized black population; and finally, Riviera Beach, where blacks make up the majority of citizens. Because these New South cities are somewhat larger and more complex than the Old South communities, the overviews that follow are necessarily longer and more detailed.

Titusville: Race Relations Transformed by the Space Age

Prior to the 1950s, Titusville was just another small, sleepy community on the Florida east coast, surrounded by citrus groves and recognized for its fishing and recreational activities. However, the development of the Cape Canaveral Air Force Station and the Kennedy Space Center resulted in the rapid growth and almost complete transformation of the area. Indeed, between 1950 and 1970, Brevard County, of which Titusville is the county seat, was the fastest-growing county in the U.S.[6] This tremendous influx of outsiders (primarily well-educated, nonsoutherners) had an impact on every facet of life, including race relations. Furthermore, the relatively small black population in the area and the historical absence of a plantation economy tended to ameliorate the conflict generated by the black civil rights movement of the sixties and seventies.

Titusville was not settled until after the Civil War when, in 1867, Colonel Henry Titus arrived and built a major hotel, thereby insuring that the area would be a travel stop along the Indian River near the coast. The city was slow in developing, however, and was not officially incorporated until 1886. Even then Titusville had only an estimated four hundred residents, with a dozen or so blacks. Early economic activities centered around a large fishing industry and the citrus groves, which were some of the first producing groves in the country. With the extension of railroad lines through Titusville in 1893, the city's population began to grow, including the black community. Many blacks worked on the railroad, and they settled just south of the downtown area and west of the railroad tracks in an area known as "Colored Town."[7] Even today most blacks in Titusville live in this section of the city.

Despite the emergence of a modest tourist industry by the early 1900s, the development of Titusville was relatively slow until recent times. In 1920 the city's population numbered only 1,361, and as late as 1950 the population had increased to only 2,604. Although the nonwhite proportion of the population was 31.9 percent in 1950, the substantial in-migration of whites during the development of the missile industry reduced this proportion. By 1960 blacks made up only 22.4 percent of the city's 6,410 residents, and by 1970 Titusville's population had increased to a little more than 30,000, with blacks constituting no more than 9 percent. The presence of a relatively small proportion of black residents tended to reduce racial friction. As a longtime white businessman put it: "Our black population is small and thus less of a threat. This makes a difference. We've never had many of the problems other communities have faced."[8]

Although the racial history of Titusville and Brevard County was relatively calm and uneventful, a shocking incident occurred in 1951 which clearly affected race relations for some time thereafter. On Christmas night of that year a bomb blast ripped through the home of Harry T. Moore, a Florida NAACP leader living in Mims (a small community just north of Titusville). The blast killed both Moore and his wife, and the deaths gained national notoriety. Moore had been an active crusader for black rights throughout the state, helping to organize NAACP chapters, advancing educational opportunities for blacks, and encouraging blacks to register and vote. Both he and his wife had lost teaching jobs because of his activities, but the major motivation for the killings seemed to have been Moore's campaign to prosecute a Lake County sheriff for shooting two blacks arrested in a 1949 rape case. Though the FBI investigated the Moore murders, and some evidence did suggest that Ku Klux Klan members were involved, the brutal slayings were never solved.[9]

The deaths of Moore and his wife left an indelible mark on the minds of many in the Titusville area. Almost thirty years later the longtime editor of the local newspaper wrote: "It was one of the most sensational and tragic stories I ever covered. [The murders] rank high as one of Brevard's most tragic moments."[10] Blacks in particular were affected by this act of racial violence. The majority of black citizens interviewed in the late 1970s still had vivid memories of Moore's slaying and its effects. As one black claimed: "After the Harry T. Moore killing, there was a real fear of participation and it didn't let up until the late 1960s."[11] County voter registration figures tended to support this claim. Partially due to Moore's efforts, the 1950 black registration rate in Brevard County was 51 percent, one of the highest levels among the sixty-seven Florida counties.[12] Yet not long after his death the registration rate for Brevard blacks began to plummet, totaling only 33 percent in 1956 and rising to 50 percent or better only once (in 1964) during the next fourteen years.

But the Moore murders proved to be the most negative chapter in Titusville's recent racial past. Indeed, race relations in the 1950s were moderately good by southern standards. After the Supreme Court's 1954 school desegregation decision, for example, the *Titusville Star-Advocate*, the local newspaper, editorialized that the decision was now the law of the land and urged states to accept it and comply peacefully.[13] In the same year, the newspaper endorsed Leroy Collins, a political moderate, for governor against the conservative encumbent,

Charley Johns. One reason for the endorsement was that Collins had cosponsored a bill in the state legislature to unmask the Ku Klux Klan, while Johns had voted against the bill. Collins carried the city's vote in the gubernatorial election a week later.[14]

As a result of the early development of Cape Canaveral and the inmigration of nonsoutherners, the city government began to professionalize and evinced greater concern for blacks. It adopted a city-manager form of government in 1947, and in the early 1950s began to enlarge the police and fire departments with full-time, trained personnel. The first black policeman was hired in 1952, long before most Florida communities initially integrated their police forces. And in 1953, when relatively few streets in Titusville were paved, the city government reported that it had recently "opened and shelled several streets in the colored section."[15] Yet as in almost all southern communities in the 1950s and early 1960s, Titusville's schools, public accommodations, and city facilities remained racially segregated.

Slow, Steady Change

In most parts of the New South the early and mid-1960s were a time of significant racial progress. To some degree this held true in Titusville, although the city's relatively small, poor black population was a factor that mitigated against rapid racial change. Another factor limiting progress was the partial carryover in Titusville of a rural, traditional past. As a white mayor expressed it: "Through the early 1960s the city council was composed of an old-line group of people—rural, southern, here all their lives, and some of whom still carried Civil War memories. Blacks did not receive their fair share of services because they were considered second-, even third-class, citizens."[16]

Despite these moderating influences, changes in race relations did begin to take place in the early 1960s. The city manager and other officials took note of the poor housing conditions in the black area and began to solicit federal money for public housing. By January 1963, the first fifty-four low-rent housing units, thirty-six of which were for blacks, were completed and more were being planned.[17] In addition, the city voted a special allocation of funds to improve Sylvan Park, located in the black neighborhood, and made plans (which were never carried out) to construct a separate library for blacks.[18] Several blacks, moreover, were appointed in 1961 to the subcommittee on housing of the city's Citizens Advisory Committee. Two years later, in the wake of racial demonstrations over integration, the mayor appointed a special biracial committee of twenty-two persons, eleven of whom were black, to discuss and make suggestions regarding racial issues.[19]

Many of these changes were at least partly the result of the political activities of increasingly well organized black groups. The local Negro Civic and Voter's League was particularly active in the early and mid-1960s, carrying out voter registration drives, monitoring local officials, and pushing for the appointment of blacks to city boards and committees. The league seemed to be successful in increasing black voter registration and securing more black appointees, especially to the important planning and zoning commission and to the local housing authority.[20] The activities of the county NAACP chapter were also instrumental in bringing about the development of the biracial committee and in pressing for a fair school integration plan.[21] Additionally other smaller, black community groups encouraged voter registration and conducted fund-raising campaigns to improve recreational opportunities for blacks.[22] Finally, several demonstrations and organized challenges to segregated public accommodations were carried out by the Negro Voter's League and the NAACP, and some of these challenges took place even prior to the 1964 Civil Rights Act.[23]

The process of desegregating the public schools also occurred relatively early and easily in Brevard County. In 1961 black parents petitioned the school board to integrate. Though their petition was denied, the parents filed suit in federal district court later that year. By 1964 the federal court ordered the school board to draw up integration plans, which it promptly did, and a modified "freedom of choice" plan went into effect in the fall of 1964.[24] It was 1968, however, before all schools in Titusville were desegregated. As usual, the formerly black schools were closed in the process, because of declining enrollments. Nevertheless, Brevard County schools were some of the first in the state to desegregate,[25] and this transformation generated considerably less conflict here than it did in most other counties.

Several factors, in addition to black political activities, were significant in encouraging racial moderation and change in the 1960s. Most important by far was the tremendous growth of nearby Cape Kennedy and the resulting influx of new residents who worked there and at the high-technology industries that began to spring up in the area. Annexations to Titusville city boundaries alone added almost 23,000 people to its population during the 1960s, and it was estimated that by 1968 more than 40 percent of city employees were affiliated in some way with the aerospace industry. Most of the new residents were engineers, skilled technicians, and civil service employees from outside the South; they were more affluent and better educated than the national norm.[26] These new Titusville citizens and the industries at the Cape promoted a good-government "ethos," and encouraged voter registration, improved city services, and racially integrated facilities.[27] As one black expressed it: "Racial changes came about because of changes in the community due to the Cape. You can't live in a space age and still treat people in antiquated ways. We have better human relations now because there are more people in the community who care about *all* the people."[28]

The local media, especially the newspaper, also appear to have played an important role in setting a tone of moderation in race relations. The *Titusville Star-Advocate*'s coverage of local race-related incidents was relatively thorough and fair by the mid-1960s. "Blacks here have generally had good access to the newspaper editor and the media," claimed one longtime public official.[29] Needless to say, this kind of newspaper coverage and access for blacks was rare among southern, small city presses in the 1960s. Editorials in the *Star-Advocate*, however, were critical of black demonstrations and violence, and particularly of the 1964 Civil Rights Act, calling it a "cover-up for a giant instrument of federal control."[30] The newspaper urged a nonviolent, gradualist approach to the solution of racial problems, but consistently endorsed the ideal of equality under law for all people.[31] Later in the decade the *Star-Advocate* assumed a more supportive posture toward local blacks, advocating a federal urban renewal program and improved services, and applauding black organizational efforts and progress in race relations.[32]

Yet despite such improvements in racial matters, a thread of racism continued to run through the city's social fabric. The Ku Klux Klan, although not historically active in the area, held several small rallies in Titusville and north Brevard County in 1966–1967.[33] On several occasions flaming crosses were found in the black section, and in other instances the Klan attempted to thwart the integration of public accommodations and residential areas by openly threatening or confronting black residents.[34] In perhaps the most publicized incident, KKK youths, armed with a leaded billyclub and a blackjack with the words "nigger getter" embossed on them in gold letters, scuffled with several black teenagers at a Mr. Donut store in May 1969. Nine youths were arrested as a result of this melee.[35]

These blatant acts of racism were clearly not the norm in Titusville. Nonetheless, more subtle forms of discrimination were evident, especially in the low level of black employment in the public and private sectors, the lack of city services in the black section, and the lack of real integration in the schools (some high school classes, for example, were still segregated).[36] Evidence of this conservative, and sometimes racist, strain was also apparent in the results of the 1968 presidential election. North Brevard County and Titusville electors voted overwhelmingly for Nixon and Wallace, with these two candidates combined outpolling Hubert Humphrey by a margin of almost three to one.[37]

Yet increased black demands, and sometimes militancy, inadvertently helped to precipitate some of this white backlash in the late 1960s. By 1966 blacks were claiming disillusionment with the slow rate of progress, and some black leaders stated that their power was waning as their nonviolent methods of achieving racial equality proved less than successful.[38] Henceforth blacks asserted their demands more forcefully, sometimes through confrontational tactics, and occasionally these tactics resulted in violence. One of the major demands was the formulation of a commission on human relations to replace the defunct biracial committee. In 1967, with local race relations in turmoil and riots raging in cities across the country, some 150 blacks, led by the NAACP, met with the mayor and city manager. With a NAACP leader admonishing that "we intend to wage war for equal opportunity," the city soon established the Human Relations Commission (HRC) to improve communications between races and to investigate and suggest solutions to racial problems.[39]

Although the formulation of an active HRC probably helped to reduce racial friction, blacks continued to press their demands and to confront various forms of racial discrimination. The NAACP charged in 1967, for example, that the city was discriminating in its hiring and promotion practices, since most black employees were in the public works department and only 6 percent of responsible city positions were held by blacks. The city responded by hiring more black police and firemen and by eventually appointing a black superintendent of sanitation, the first black to head a city administrative post.[40] Blacks also claimed in 1968 that minority youths were being excluded from Sandrift, a youth-owned and -operated recreation center, and that black teenagers were often treated in a discriminatory manner at the local theater. While an HRC investigation helped to integrate Sandrift peacefully, confrontations at the movie theater resulted in racial violence and no easy solution.[41]

Black demands and racial animosity resulting from desegregation of the schools proved to be irreconcilable as well, and violence flared frequently following racial incidents at Titusville High School.[42] In perhaps the worst such incident, more than a dozen persons were injured in September 1968 when racial fighting broke out at a football game after the opposing school's band began playing "Dixie."[43] But the most intense racial violence in recent Titusville history took place in 1971 in response primarily to alleged police brutality. In the first disturbance, on the Fourth of July weekend, some two hundred black youths pelted police and motorists with rocks and other objects following the arrests of several black youths in the aftermath of a fight in the ghetto area. Police reinforcements were brought in from the sheriff's department and from other nearby cities, ten motorists were injured, and property damage totaled $3,500.[44] Several blacks blamed excessive use of force by the police in the arrests, and the city manager admitted that "past treatment by police and school authorities" of black youths was a major underlying factor in the disturbance.[45] Later that same year, a drive-in store was firebombed and angry blacks protested outside the police department after a black youth was arrested on charges of robbing the store's owner. Again blacks and the HRC, which investigated the arrest, claimed the young black was unjustifiably beaten by police at the time of his arrest.[46] The black suspect was later found innocent of the charge.

No doubt these black-white confrontations fueled a growing white resentment toward civil rights protest and violence. This white backlash helped explain the large 1968 and 1972 city votes for presidential candidates Nixon and Wallace, the approval in 1968 by the city council of a law-and-order ordinance giving the mayor the power to declare a civil emergency, and the city's purchase of $5,600 worth of riot gear for the police in 1971.[47] And yet several very positive benefits for blacks resulted from these racial conflicts. The city's conservative chief of police, long criticized for his insensitivity to blacks, was fired in the aftermath of the violence and replaced by a more moderate chief. Moreover, Titusville's blacks became better organized than previously and seemed to develop a new pride and a greater sense of the efficacy of political participation. As the local newspaper, in summarizing black progress, put it in 1968: "The new attitude [of blacks] reflects a newly felt position of equality in the community. . . . [Black] residents feel progress . . . can be measured in gaining a voice in city affairs, if not yet gaining the full benefits of their white counterparts."[48] Several blacks also claimed that the protest and violence helped to improve conditions in the city and schools for blacks because "it got their [whites'] attention—it shocked them, and it showed them we were not kidding, that we were serious."[49]

Working within the System

With the exception of the violence early in the decade, the 1970s proved to be relatively free of racial turmoil for Titusville. Blacks continued to press their political demands but tended to use more moderate tactics. This shift in strategy was due in part to the new realities confronting local blacks. By 1970 the black population totaled only 9 percent of the city's growing populace and only an estimated 5 percent of the city's registered voters. Thus blacks lacked the political power, at least in terms of numbers, to effect major change. But blacks did have several viable political organizations, political leaders who had gained experience during the 1960s, and a growing reservoir of well-educated, middle-class black residents (and moderate whites as well) who had been attracted to the city by the space center. These seemed to be the necessary ingredients for working within the system to bring about racial change.

Another reason for the shift in tactics by blacks was that many of the issues of the 1970s were different from those of the 1960s. By this time most of the blatant forms of discrimination had been overcome; what remained were the more subtle, institutionalized in some cases, and intractable kinds of discrimination. Whereas blacks had been able to desegregate relatively easily almost all public accommodations in the city, some facilities were still resistant to change. One of these was the ABC Liquor Lounge, well known for its discriminatory treatment of blacks. While several blacks openly challenged this racial practice, it required the threat of a lawsuit in 1971 before the lounge would allow blacks to enter.[50] In another set of cases, a black minister was refused space in a local trailer park and two whites who associated with blacks were evicted from their lots in another trailer park. Although the HRC gave assistance to these individuals, the refusal and evictions were not overturned.[51] Finally, in a case of institutionalized discrimination, plans to build a $250,000 black-owned shopping center in the black community collapsed in 1973 because no bank in the county would back the developers. The banks claimed the proposal was too risky, and an application for federal money through the Small Business Administration failed as well.[52]

As a clear signal of their intent to work peacefully through the system, blacks ran two candidates for the city council in the early 1970s. However, black efforts failed here as well, reflecting the impotency of the small black vote but also the unwillingness of most whites to support black candidates. In 1968, black voters had helped defeat a major city referendum on urban renewal and street paving,[53] and in 1970 they were very supportive of James Foster, a member of the Negro Civic and Voter's League and the first black to seek a city council seat. Although Titusville council elections were at-large (with three of five council members having to reside in geographical districts), blacks were encouraged by the victory in the mid-1960s of a black council candidate in the nearby city of Melbourne.[54] Nevertheless, Foster went down to defeat in the runoff election, capturing only precinct thirty-five (wherein most blacks resided) among the city's thirteen precincts.[55] In 1972 another black, Robert Manning, competed for the same council seat. Like Foster, Manning was in the field of educational administration (both had master's degrees) and was a respected black leader who had served as vice-president of the HRC for three years. Although Manning attracted a number of white votes in addition to carrying the thirty-fifth precinct, he also was defeated, but narrowly, in a runoff election.[56]

The greatest political successes of blacks came through the relatively quiet lobbying and self-help efforts of their middle-class leaders and community organizations. While the NAACP and the Negro Civic and Voter's League had been moderately effective during the 1960s, these organizations were relatively inactive by the early seventies. The HRC, too, was less effective because of lack of support from the city council.[57] However, a number of other black community groups soon developed. Foremost among these new organizations was the Concerned Citizens of Titusville, heir apparent to the Negro Civic and Voter's League, which was active in mobilizing the black vote and in pressuring city hall to improve services in the black area.[58] Also of importance by the latter 1970s were two other middle-class groups, Citizens Backers and the Progressive Action Society. While Citizens Backers was composed of younger, more aggressive, professional blacks, both groups sought to establish a dialogue with city councilmen and administrators as a way of improving conditions for blacks.[59] As the president of the Progressive Action Society put it in emphasizing a strategy of moderation: "You can't *demand* changes, not as a small minority. You have to work through the system to accomplish real change."[60] The society was especially effective in getting blacks appointed to important city boards, in pressing for federal grants, and in improving youth recreation and housing for blacks.[61]

Some of these organizations were criticized, however, for behaving too much "like a bunch of Uncle Toms," for being too moderate, and for being out of touch with poor blacks. In addition, having a variety of political groups led to increased division and fragmentation in the black community, and to some confusion over which ideology and strategies to follow.[62] Moreover, conditions in the black section were still relatively poor in the 1970s. Approximately one-half of the streets were still unpaved, drainage was lacking, sidewalks and streetlights were sparse, and there was a high level of citizen dissatisfaction with recreation services.[63] According to the 1970 census, only 32 percent of adult blacks had completed high school, while more than 75 percent of whites in Titusville had done so. Black income was also relatively low; per capita earnings for blacks were reported to be $1,822, approximately 50 percent of the comparable income figure for whites.[64]

Yet blacks had a number of valuable allies among whites both in the community and in city hall. White professionals, attracted by the employment opportunities at the Cape in the 1960s, began to win election to the city council, and in 1974 the city hired a moderately liberal and politically influential city manager. These whites proved to be sympathetic to black needs, and began to push to improve city services and employment for blacks. Although providing services to the newly annexed areas drained city coffers, and major cutbacks at the Cape in the early 1970s reduced local tax revenues,[65] city officials still sought funds for improvement in the black section. The major source of such funds proved to be the federal government.

During the 1960s federal dollars had been used to construct some 255 units of low-rent public housing in Titusville (with approximately one-third of these located in the black area), and had supported a Section 235 housing program which assisted minorities in purchasing their own homes. This latter program encouraged the desegregation of some residential areas and for this reason was strongly opposed by a number of whites.[66] In 1969 Titusville garnered a $1.2 million HUD grant, called Project Betterment, to provide public service improvements and housing rehabilitation in the deteriorating downtown area. Though this grant area was predominantly poor white and located just north of South Street and the black section, Project Betterment helped to provide the city's first neighborhood social service center.[67] After a good deal of black protest, this social service center was finally moved in 1975 to the predominantly black section.[68]

By far the most important federal program to affect blacks was the Titusville Improvement Program (TIP), funded by a Community Development Block Grant of almost $1 million a year. Begun in 1975, this program was concentrated almost entirely in the black section and provided paved streets, sewers, sidewalks, recreation facilities, and housing rehabilitation. TIP was awarded annually to the city through the mid-1980s, and along with some federal revenue sharing and city funds, TIP monies had by 1979 provided for the paving or improvement of more than five miles of streets, the rehabilitaton of fifty homes, and other basic services for the South Street target area.[69] In addition to TIP, federal funds supported some twenty-five CETA employees a year for the city (approximately 25 percent of whom were black) and a Section 8 rent subsidy program for more than one hundred low-income families.[70] In accordance with federal regulations, the city also established an affirmative action program in 1974 to improve minority hiring.[71]

Despite the steady progress of Titusville's black community during the 1970s, some remnants of racism remained. A *Star-Advocate* editorial in 1977 deplored the fact that "destructive racial attacks still take place in Titusville in the third quarter of the 20th century," and cited the still common occurrence of passing whites yelling "nigger" at blacks crossing streets.[72] Friction between black youths and the police remained an issue in the early 1980s, but such conflicts leading to racial unrest were much less common than a decade earlier.[73] The schools continued to be a focal point for racial issues through the mid-1980s, with blacks complaining about the low number of black teachers and administrators, prejudicial discipline, and racism in sports programs. (All the head coaches in the high schools, for example, were still white.)[74] The more subtle aspects of racism were made apparent in a 1979 HEW report that listed the Brevard County school district as one of the top one hundred districts in the nation in terms of both the rate of suspension of minority students and their placement in special-education classes. In Titusville high schools, for example, blacks made up only 11 percent of the total student enrollment but constituted 30 percent of all suspensions from school and almost 50 percent of the students in special-education programs.[75]

Yet serious racial confrontations were relatively rare in Titusville by the 1980s, and the moderate progress of the previous decade continued. The schools were beginning to respond more positively to the problems of integration by revising curriculum, developing black history courses, and providing in-service programs for teachers that emphasized communication and human relations skills.[76] By 1981 eight percent of the principals in the county's schools, and 19 percent of the assistant principals, were black and there were efforts to recruit even more minority administrators. In 1985, moreover, a black was appointed provost of the local branch of Brevard Community College.[77] The major drawbacks to further progress seemed to be the lack of a large, local pool of certified black administrators from which to select and the increased competition for administrative positions from well-qualified white females.[78]

Black employment at city hall had also improved somewhat by the early 1980s, primarily because of a progressive affirmative action program and an activist city manager. The police department initiated a special training program to attract minorities who did not meet the regular entrance requirements, and the city began a released-time educational program to upgrade the skills of its minority employees. When federal funds for the CETA program were cut, the city absorbed these employees into its regular work force. In spite of the efforts to recruit and promote blacks, however, a number of qualified minorities refused to apply for or stay in city jobs because of the considerably higher wages offered them at nearby Kennedy Space Center (the center had experienced a renaissance in the late 1970s as a result of the shuttle space program).[79] In addition to city employment, there were one or more blacks on every citizen board or commission of the city by 1980.

Yet blacks continued to fare poorly in local electoral politics. Despite several voter registration drives by a rejuvenated NAACP organization and a special county program to enlist volunteers to register voters, black voter registration remained low. By the mid-1980s blacks totaled only 7 percent of registered city voters and the black registration rate lagged some 17 percent behind that of whites.[80] Well-qualified black candidates continued to vie for office, however. In 1982 two professional blacks, one a NASA employee and the other a former high school principal, competed for positions on the city council and school board respectively. Both candidates lost, despite conducting well-financed campaigns and attracting a modest share of white votes.[81] These defeats prompted the NAACP to urge adoption of single-member district elections, arguing that this would provide blacks with a greater opportunity to be elected. A 1985 city referendum on district elections, however, was narrowly defeated by Republicans and by a growing number of retirees who wielded significant power.[82]

While success in the electoral arena proved illusory, racial change, albeit modest to be sure, was evident in the private sector. More professional and managerial positions were being filled by blacks, and increasingly middle-class blacks were moving into white residential areas with little adverse reaction from whites. The Titusville Jaycees had several black members, as did the chamber of commerce, and by 1981 the formerly all-white Rotary Club had its first black Rotarian.[83] These changes benefited mainly middle-class blacks, however, as economic conditions for most other blacks remained grim. According to the 1980 census, black annual incomes still averaged only half that of whites and almost 50 percent of blacks lived on incomes at or below the poverty level.[84] Yet the racial and political atmosphere had clearly improved. As a longtime black leader, who was often critical of city officials, put it in 1981: "Race harmony is better here than almost anyplace around. I can get an ear in city hall and at the county commission anytime I want. It's as close to a community of togetherness as I can imagine."[85]

Given their small proportion of the population, blacks in Titusville experienced more progress in the last several decades than one would have predicted. As in the case of Crestview, the small black population left whites feeling relatively unthreatened and therefore less resistant to racial change. Yet other factors were important too. Despite the impotence of their small numbers at the polls, blacks proved to be politically well organized by the mid-1960s and a growing black middle class provided a reservoir of capable leaders. Black political strategies, moreover, were generally shrewd and effective, with confrontational tactics utilized to challenge the blatant racism of the 1960s and moderate, accommodating strategies designed to deal with the more subtle issues of the mid-1970s and 1980s. In addition, vital support for black progress was often provided by a relatively professionalized city government, a moderately liberal city manager in the 1970s, and the local newspaper. City government support was especially crucial in securing the large federal grants to improve black services. But the most important catalyst to racial progress was the development and growth of the space center and the concomitant influx of well-educated, racially moderate outsiders. Within a decade, this significant economic development transformed Titusville from a small, backwater southern community into a populous, industrialized New South city.

Daytona Beach: Progressive Race Relations in the Tourist City

Daytona Beach, the second New South city, has essentially been a tourist haven for much of this century. Located on the Atlantic seaboard not far north of Titusville, the city has an equable climate, a natural beauty, and a twenty-three-mile beach (called by some "The World's Most Famous"), all of which have enabled it to become a well-known winter and summer resort. Daytona's renowned Speedway also attracts many auto-racing enthusiasts on various weekends of the year, and during their spring vacations thousands of college youths make their annual pilgrimage to this city of sun and sand.[86]

Although blacks make up more than 30 percent of the population and represent a potential threat to white dominance, race relations in Daytona Beach have been quite progressive. Indeed, blacks here have established a history of political activism and community change which is unparalleled in all but a few Florida cities.[87] A number of factors help to account for this remarkable record of black achievement, but foremost among them have been a sizable black middle class, a number of tolerant and often helpful whites, and the existence of a black college that has provided both an ideology of political action and a reservoir of leaders with liaisons to the white power structure.

Like Titusville, Daytona did not begin to develop until after the Civil War, when settlers arrived to take part in the propagation of the large orange groves of the area. Development was slow, and although the city was incorporated in 1876, it was the arrival of the railroad a decade later which began to spur settlement. The "big freeze" of 1894–1895, however, destroyed many of the orange groves and led to a greater dependence on resorts and tourism as the major businesses. This new venture was given added impetus when, at the turn of the century and with the development of the automobile, road racing came to Daytona. The long, smooth beach with hard-packed sand was ideal for racing, and many early land-speed records were set here.[88]

The first blacks in Daytona came as freedmen after the Civil War and worked as laborers for whites in the building of the city, the planting of crops, and somewhat later, the construction of the railroad. They settled in the downtown, mainland section just west of the railroad, an area which is still predominantly black. No doubt the most significant event in this early period was the arrival of Mary McLeod Bethune, a black educator, who established a school for black girls in 1904. The school was based on Booker T. Washington's concept of education, emphasizing domestic, vocational, and religious training. Though small and poor at its beginning, it gained a good reputation and was increasingly supported by financial contributions from churches and white philanthropists. In the 1920s, Bethune's school merged with Cookman Institute of Jacksonville, establishing itself as a coeducational but still predominantly black institution, and the name was later changed to Bethune-Cookman College.[89]

Mary Bethune was more than an inspirational educator; she was a respected political leader who later gained national recognition. Early on, despite some threats from the Ku Klux Klan, she taught her students to vote. In fact, black Daytonans were relatively active politically as early as the late 1800s, even electing a local black barber to the city council in 1896.[90] But Daytona's sizable black population (52 percent of the city's 3,082 residents in 1910) was poor and generally illiterate, and when a local political machine developed in the early twentieth century, it quickly gained control of the large but vulnerable black electorate. Indeed, a few black leaders served as a conduit between the black community and machine officials. These black leaders sold the black vote and several reportedly got wealthy doing so. As one white public official recalled: "There used to be stories about bagging black votes with a couple of dollars and a half-pint of whiskey. Blacks didn't even know who they were voting for."[91]

Early Black Challenges

As machine rule began to fade by mid-century, manipulation of the black vote began to give way as well. Much of Daytona's black populace, often led by faculty members (and sometimes by students) of Bethune-Cookman, started to become increasingly assertive of its basic rights. In the first significant challenge to white boss-rule, George Engram, an independent black businessman, ran in 1948 for the zone three city-commission seat (the city had five commissioners each elected within a zone or district). A majority of adult blacks were registered to vote by the late 1940s, and Engram was supported by the Daytona Beach Citizens League, a recently formed black political organization headed by the president of Bethune-Cookman. Despite KKK threats to burn a cross in front of Engram's home, and other attempts to intimidate black voters, Engram placed second among five candidates in the primary election. In the general election, the machine rallied its forces and Engram was defeated.[92]

But black Daytonans were not dismayed by this early defeat. Indeed the Engram candidacy seemed to stimulate further black organization and challenges to racial segregation. As in almost all southern communities, public and private facilities were completely separate and usually unequal. According to a local historian: "There was an understanding that each race would occupy its own area and keep out of the other. The early taxi driver would carry passengers of his own race—not both."[93] The peninsula area (including the beaches), located across the Halifax River from the larger mainland portion of the city, was the exclusive domain of whites, and blacks were allowed there only during daylight hours to perform menial labor for whites. But in the late 1940s the West Side Business and Professional Men's Association, a middle-class black organization developed in 1948, asked the city to allow blacks to use Peabody Auditorium, a city-owned facility located on the peninsula. The city commission refused the request, arguing that blacks had their own separate auditorium on the mainland. With this response, the West Side Business Association and the local NAACP filed suit in federal district court in 1949, and eventually Peabody Auditorium was desegregated.[94]

The segregation of other public facilities was challenged soon after and thus Daytona Beach began to integrate long before most other southern communities. With pressure again from the black business association, by 1955—a full year before the U.S. Supreme Court banned segregation on city buses—the city bus system began to employ blacks as drivers and integrated bus seating arrangements.[95] Even the public beaches began to be integrated slowly in the 1950s, though not without a prolonged struggle. Blacks had had their own separate beach (Bethune Beach) for several years, thanks to Mary Bethune and black businessmen who had developed it, but in the early 1950s they began to petition for use of the public beaches on the peninsula. The petitions were to no avail; partly to protect the tourist trade, many whites strongly objected to any black invasion of what were whites-only beaches. But blacks were persistent, and a few of them, usually led by Bethune-Cookman faculty and students, began swimming at the city beach. They were often harassed by whites and tourists, or asked to leave by city police, but eventually the city relented and began to open the beaches to blacks.[96]

Additional black political organizations were developed in the 1950s and began to seek improved public services for blacks. Early on blacks protested cuts in city funds promised for a new recreation center.[97] Somewhat later an antislum committee made up of black citizens inspected homes in the ghetto area and made a report urging the city to take immediate steps to eliminate the housing blight. Partly as a result of this report, Daytona Beach entered the public housing market early and was able to achieve improvements in black slum housing by 1960.[98] In the private area, Mary Bethune helped set up the Citizen's Welfare League in 1951 to foster the cause of black workers, and in 1956 the league organized a strike of black laundry workers to protest low wages and poor treatment on the job.[99]

The reaction of white Daytonans to the black demands of the 1950s was mixed, but most whites seemed to sympathize with many of the goals of the black organizations. Even the 1954 Supreme Court school-desegregation decision evoked a primarily favorable response. The local newspaper, the *Daytona Beach Evening News*, editorialized that the ruling was "inevitable" and it was "for the best interests for all concerned."[100] Moreover the county (Volusia) superintendent of schools claimed the Court's rulings on desegregation were "done in the best possible way" and that school integration posed no special problems for the area.[101] A few whites even assisted in breaking down the barriers of racial exclusion. A number of white ministers, for example, joined ranks with black ministers in 1956 to found the Halifax Area Ministerial Association. This organization of some forty ministers was one of the first interracial ministerial groups in the South, and it soon played a valuable role in promoting integration.[102] On the other hand, a relatively small number of whites were active in opposing any mixing of the races. Perhaps most vocal among these whites were approximately one hundred residents who in 1956 organized the Halifax Citizens Council, a group pledged to maintain segregation by lawful means. Though the council's greatest fear was neighborhood integration, it also opposed other forms of racial mixing, but was not very successful.[103]

By the early 1960s blacks in Daytona Beach were among the first in the state to confront segregation in the private sector. Initial action was taken against stores with segregated lunch counters, and the first sit-ins were staged in the early 1960s at Woolworth's and Walgreen's Drug by twelve students from Bethune-Cookman. The students were refused service, but the next day the NAACP began an economic boycott of four downtown stores which refused lunch service to blacks. The boycott lasted several months and, although a number of blacks disregarded the NAACP action, the four stores began serving persons of all races by the end of the summer.[104] In 1963 more extensive demonstrations against segregation in restaurants and in the downtown movie theater took place. More than one hundred blacks (plus a few whites), most of them Bethune-Cookman or high school students, conducted sit-ins and picketed a number of establishments for a full week. The NAACP and several white leaders intervened to halt the demonstrations after black youths clashed with whites, but subsequent negotiations led to the desegregation of some fifteen restaurants.[105] Due to these early demonstrations and the resulting integration, the passage of the 1964 Civil Rights Act led to little fanfare in Daytona, and court suits (or more typically, threatened court suits) soon opened almost all public accommodations to blacks.[106]

Black Daytonans continued to forge progress in the public sphere as well. In the early 1960s they challenged segregation of a local state park, the Halifax Hospital, the city's golf course, seating in the baseball park, the police department, and county grand juries. In each case a greater degree of racial integration was ultimately achieved through a variety of approaches. Desegregation of the city's hospital required federal (HEW) pressure, while the decision to allow blacks on grand juries was the result of a circuit court suit.[107] Political pressure and activity by several black organizations were instrumental in the integration process and were also important in encouraging the city to reactivate the Interracial Advisory Committee in 1960.[108] This committee, originally established in 1955 but long dormant, was one of the first of its kind in any Florida city. It consisted of twelve whites and twelve blacks who advised the city commission on racial issues. The committee's first recommendation was to desegregate the municipal golf course, and this was approved unanimously by the city commission in 1961. Though the committee proved helpful initially in airing desegregation issues and preserving racial harmony, it had only advisory powers and was unwilling to deal with the most controversial issues.[109]

Attempts to desegregate Volusia County schools were also begun early and proceeded relatively smoothly. The NAACP first filed a federal district court suit in June 1960 on behalf of thirty-nine Daytona Beach residents, two of whom were white. The school board filed a countersuit contending that the petitioners had not exhausted all remedies under state law, but the board also began to admit blacks to elementary schools the next year.[110] In 1962 the U.S. District Court ordered the desegregation of Volusia County schools, and two years later gave final approval to the school board's "freedom of choice" plan. The plan was one of the first in Florida to be approved by federal court, and it allowed blacks to apply for admission to any grade level at any school through junior college. By 1965, more than 157 black students had applied and been reassigned to formerly all-white schools.[111]

Yet not all political efforts by blacks were successful. The achievement of elected city office was still an unattained goal, and in 1960 two black candidates sought city commission seats. While blacks made up 31 percent of the city's 37,395 residents, they were only 18 percent of Daytona's registered voters; the black registration rate lagged behind the white rate by approximately 20 percent. But the black candidates competed for office in zones three and four, where blacks made up approximately one third of the registered voters.[112] George Engram, who first challenged for office in 1948, was the zone three candidate, and Charles Cherry, an administrator at Bethune-Cookman and an outspoken NAACP leader, vied for the zone four seat. Both blacks made it to runoff elections but were defeated, as voting reflected racial divisions.[113] An editorial in the local newspaper analyzed the election results in zones three and four: "These were contests beset by the racial issue. . . . The people, faced with a moment of decision on a great change in human relations, decided they were not ready to make that change."[114]

Following these political defeats in 1960, blacks did not contend for city office for several years. In 1964, however, a newly formed black organization, the Citizens' Taxpayers Association (CTA), petitioned successfully for election to recall the zone three city commissioner. The CTA claimed that the commissioner, a proponent of an unpopular urban renewal program, was ineffective in providing public services for blacks. In the recall election, votes again were cast along racial lines and the recall failed.[115]

The next year the city commission, responding to a circuit court ruling that its election zones were seriously malapportioned, voted to form six approximately equal population zones, with at-large elections. Citywide voting for each commission seat and for mayor usually increases the difficulty of electing a minority member to office. But city officials claimed that the new election system was instituted to attract better-qualified candidates and to make it more difficult to build a political machine.[116] In 1965, however, in the first election under the citywide voting system, a black candidate named James Huger was able to win election to a commission seat. Huger, business manager at Bethune-Cookman and a political moderate who supported urban renewal, carried the predominantly black precincts and a surprising number of white precincts to win the election.[117] Huger's victory was the first by a black in contemporary Daytona history and was evidence that a number of whites were now willing to support a moderate black for office.

One of the issues in both the 1964 recall election and the 1965 general election was the recently initiated urban renewal program. With planning having begun in 1963, the $5.7 million federal program was designed by city officials to improve basic services in the blighted ghetto area. Nonetheless, the Citizens' Taxpayers Association and other blacks strongly opposed urban renewal because of the lack of black participation and because it often resulted in blacks being removed from their homes without receiving relocation assistance. Taking the issue to federal court, the CTA attempted several times to obtain an injunction to halt the program, but all attempts failed. Despite this opposition, urban renewal achieved substantial improvements in sewage, drainage, street paving, and housing for blacks over the next decade.[118] In fact a majority of both white and black citizens, interviewed in the late 1970s, expressed the belief that urban renewal had contributed more than any other factor to the progress in services in black neighborhoods.

Frustration and Turbulence in the 1970s

Clearly Daytona Beach had made remarkable progress in racial integration and improved public services by the mid-1960s. Indeed, according to an early 1960s random survey of black and white citizen attitudes in Daytona and two other Florida communities, the community satisfaction rate of black Daytonans was much higher than for blacks in either of the other two cities. The survey's authors attributed this high level of satisfaction to the fact that almost 50 percent of Daytona's blacks had moved there from smaller, rural communities and Daytona's high level of services compared favorably with those found in most smaller communities. Moreover, the tourist trade in Daytona Beach offered blacks steady employment opportunities rarely found in other cities. Blacks also evaluated Daytona's race relations very favorably. When asked what were the best three things about Daytona Beach as a place to live, surveyed blacks ranked "friendly people, good race relations" second only to climate.[119]

While a number of black organizations and astute leaders were crucial in forging racial progress in the 1950s and early 1960s, several other factors were important as well. The local newspaper in particular was significant in supporting blacks' rights and demands. Early on the *Daytona Beach Evening News* (and the morning equivalent, the *News-Journal*) gave thorough coverage to national and local civil rights events. Beginning in the late 1950s the editorial page of the *Evening News* carried the syndicated columns of Ralph McGill, one of the symbols of southern white liberalism. Its own editorials strongly supported school integration and the 1960 and 1964 civil rights bills.[120] As early as 1960, the *Evening News* endorsed a black candidate for city office and decried the "blight of slums" which plagued the black neighborhoods.[121] Although the influence of the local press is difficult to evaluate, it was a constant prod for racial integration and the achievement of individual dignity. In the words of one longtime white resident (echoed by several other community informants): "The local newspaper has been a public conscience on racial issues. The 'rednecks' resent it, but the paper has consistently advocated the cause of blacks."[122]

A moderate degree of white support of black aspirations was also important to racial progress. A sizable proportion of Daytona's white population had recently migrated from states outside the South and most seemed supportive of integration and improved race relations.[123] Huger's victory as a black candidate in 1965, for example, was due largely to white votes, and pro-civil rights presidential candidates Lyndon Johnson (1964) and Hubert Humphrey (1968) carried Daytona Beach by sizable margins against conservative opponents.[124] Moreover, there was little of the stringent white resistance to integration found in other communities. A relatively small number of whites continued to actively oppose residential neighborhood integration, but militant groups like the Ku Klux Klan found little fertile ground for development in east Volusia County.[125]

White public officials and even some businessmen often proved helpful to the black movement too. Besides establishing an interracial advisory committee in 1960, the city commission had begun to appoint black members to important city boards dealing with planning, charter revision, urban renewal, and civil service.[126] In addition, Daytona's progressive city manager appointed a black as his administrative assistant in 1964, thus giving blacks their first administrative post in the city and making Daytona the first city in Florida to hire a black general administrator.[127] Several white businessmen, often sensitive to factors affecting the tourist trade, also played important roles in promoting moderate racial change. They felt the need to keep the city calm, thereby maintaining the image of a friendly place to visit. As always, Bethune-Cookman College served as a vital conduit between white and black leaders, encouraging cooperation and mutual respect. As a white businessman put it: "Bethune-Cookman has been a focal point for blacks and whites to meet, and has provided strong black leadership. Many whites in this community are proud of the college and many contribute to it financially."[128]

These various factors continued to be supportive of racial change, but by the latter 1960s, after the rapid pace of the 1950s and early 1960s, black progress slowed, and a period of consolidation of previous gains seemed to set in. James Huger, the lone black city commissioner, was reelected to office in 1967 and again in 1969, and he proved moderately effective in improving services and protecting the rights of blacks.[129] However, the black chaplain at Bethune-Cookman, a candidate for two different county offices (school board and county council), failed in three consecutive bids.[130] The massive urban renewal program continued slowly to upgrade housing and public services in the black area despite some charges of corruption and criticisms for black evictions.[131] Other smaller federal programs such as Head Start, Legal Services, and Community Action were also initiated in Daytona by 1965–1966.[132] In terms of school desegregation, progress was slow as well, with ten of twenty-four city schools still totally segregated or with only token integration (less than 10 percent white or black) in 1969. Later that year a federal district court ordered Volusia County to complete its school desegregation, including desegregation of the faculty, by early 1970.[133]

Black attempts at further racial improvements in Daytona Beach were not always successful. By the latter 1960s the desegregation of most public and private establishments was completed and the primary goal shifted to improved welfare and employment for blacks. This goal proved much more elusive. In 1969, for example, the NAACP organized a bus boycott to protest against poor bus service and the recent dismissal of ten bus drivers for complaining about work conditions. Bus service, operated by a private firm, eventually went out of business, but black attempts to set up their own city bus system, or have the city take over the existing service, failed.[134] Early in 1970, black garbagemen carried out a lengthy strike for better working conditions and bargaining rights, and a year later the SCLC organized a march to Cape Kennedy to protest against low wages for motel maids,[135] and yet little changed.

Although protests had been relatively successful in desegregating facilities, they were much less effective in improving economic conditions for blacks. As of 1970, almost half of the city's black employed adults worked as service or private household workers for low wages. Forty-four percent of blacks had incomes below the official poverty line while only 15 percent of whites in Daytona were classified as poverty-stricken. In terms of education, 64 percent of white adults had a high school degree but only 34 percent of blacks had graduated from secondary school.[136] Frustrated with the slow pace of change and with lingering poverty, some blacks began to turn to more militant approaches.

Black frustration soon erupted in violence, and the focus of the first disturbances was the schools. Many black high school youths were bitter over the school desegregation plan which called for several concessions by blacks, including the closing or modification of some formerly black schools.[137] Several rock- and bottle-throwing incidents after football games in the fall of 1970 raised racial tensions, and a fight between white and black youths on Halloween escalated the tension. Soon after, racial violence broke out at Mainland High School and blacks began a boycott of classes. Within a few days the violence had shifted from the schools to the community, inspired by the shooting and wounding of a black youth by a white whose service station had been the target of rock throwers. The resulting weekend of racial strife saw at least ten stores heavily damaged by firebombs, and several police cars were hit by snipers. A subsequent protest march and sit-in at city hall by approximately 150 blacks culminated in 19 arrests and numerous charges of police brutality.[138]

The organizer of the school boycott and protest march was the militant Citizens Coordinating Committee (CCC), established in 1969 as an umbrella organization for several black action groups. Claiming to represent the economic interests of poor blacks, the CCC soon became the extremist group in a militant-moderate split between Daytona's black leaders. The CCC labeled Bethune-Cookman a "bastion of Tomism," and accused it of being essentially a middle-class school whose students cared little about poverty-stricken blacks. The CCC was widely viewed by white leaders, however, as the instigator of unnecessary and illegitimate black violence.[139]

For their part, black leaders tended to agree upon the basic grievances underlying the violence. These grievances, in addition to the process of school desegregation, included police brutality, job discrimination, urban renewal, and the lack of black employees in several city departments.[140] To deal with these grievances the CCC recommended the formation of a Daytona Beach Area Community Relations Council, and white leaders agreed. The Interracial Advisory Board, set up in 1960, rarely met any more and was considered ineffective. The new council, composed of forty-four members representing almost every interest group in the city, helped to smooth racial animosity and reported some progress in rectifying black grievances.[141]

But not all whites were so conciliatory, and feelings of alienation and backlash soon developed in reaction to the black violence. The city commission refused to respond quickly or positively to most of the black demands. Evidence of a backlash was also reflected in the results of city elections in the fall of 1971. James Huger, the lone black commissioner, ran for mayor in hopes of creating more "community togetherness," and Charles Cherry, now president of the CCC, competed for the zone six seat vacated by Huger. With renewed black violence occurring again just before the election, both black candidates were defeated, and racism was clearly a factor in the outcome.[142] For the first time since 1965 blacks had no representative in elected city or county office.

Before long, however, the forces of moderation among whites and blacks began to reassert themselves. Indeed, the black violence had probably made moderate black leaders more credible in the white community. By 1972 the NAACP vigorously renewed its claim to leadership in the black community, challenging alleged discrimination in employment (public and private), in the media, in the public school system, at Daytona Beach Community College, and at Halifax Hospital. Progress was slow, partly because of the subtle nature of many of the issues, but also because of lack of a programmatic agenda and consistent follow-through on issues by the NAACP.[143] Nevertheless, one notable NAACP success was an out-of-court settlement of a class-action suit against Halifax Hospital for alleged discrimination in the firing of three black employees. The settlement resulted in the hospital board agreeing to a monetary adjustment for the former employees, the hiring of a black administrator, and the establishment of an affirmative-action plan.[144] In the electoral arena, moderate blacks soon regained office. Huger won election to the Volusia County Council in 1972 (the first black to do so), and in 1973 a Bethune-Cookman professor gained election to the zone six seat Huger had held on the city commission.[145]

Moderation and Progress Once Again

After the violence and extremist politics of the early 1970s, the remainder of the decade and the early 1980s proved to be a period of political moderation for most of Daytona's black community. The NAACP continued to challenge various forms of discrimination, particularly in the school system. Although the city's schools were relatively well integrated by 1971, the NAACP claimed there was still racial discrimination evident in the hiring and promotion of black teachers, administrators, and coaches, and in the selection of student homecoming courts. Indeed, in 1975 more than one hundred black students walked out of classes at Seabreeze High School because they were not allowed to participate fully in choosing the homecoming king and queen, and in 1983 approximately 150 black youths staged a sit-in at the same school to protest alleged discrimination in discipline and other minority grievances. Due to persistent pressure and threatened legal action from the NAACP, some progress was made. Seabreeze High School appointed a black administrator, opened all service clubs to blacks, and gave black students more of a voice in electing student leaders. By 1980, fifteen percent of the county's school principals were black and in 1983 a black was appointed principal of a Daytona high school, although there were still no black head-coaches in the high schools.[146]

Not all NAACP efforts were successful, however. Six black housekeepers at Halifax Hospital, fired in 1976 for criticizing new work procedures, were not reinstated despite NAACP support and a general strike of other hospital housekeepers.[147] NAACP attempts to register a goal of five thousand new black voters in 1977 also ended in failure, with the drive netting only a few more than one hundred registrants.[148] By mid-1977 the local chapter was in disarray with only 244 members (it once had a high of 750 members) and few funds. Its fundamental problem seemed to be a lack of appeal among younger blacks, who had not experienced the blatant racism their elders had and could not therefore appreciate the civil rights record of the NAACP. Loss of support among middle-class blacks also hurt; economically secure blacks tended to feel that they had achieved success on their own and that other blacks could do the same thing. But the organization also suffered from conflicts among its leaders and from a "crisis-orientation" which made organizational continuity difficult.[149]

Despite problems in the NAACP, black Daytonans experienced a good deal of success in several areas. The electoral arena in particular recorded dramatic progress. Through the latter 1970s blacks maintained their zone six seat on the city commission while Huger won reelection to the county council in 1974 and was voted its chairman.[150] In 1979 the Community Coalition for Progress, a small, newly organized group of young professional blacks, staged a voter registration drive which added more than seven hundred blacks to the rolls. Members of the new coalition were critical of citywide elections, arguing that this election system deprived blacks of additional representation on the city commission. With the increased registrants, blacks made up almost 27 percent of the city's total, and this black proportion represented the highest in recent city history. In the 1979 fall elections blacks mobilized their sizable vote, ran three black candidates, and helped elect all three to commission seats. For the first time in Daytona history the city had more than one black on its city commission (now three of seven). Perhaps of even greater importance, however, was the indication that race was not a major issue in the election, as the black candidates all received significant support from most of the white precincts.[151]

Major progress was also made in improving black neighborhoods and employment through federal funds and initiatives. The most important federal program was the Community Development Block Grant program begun in 1975 and totaling more than $10 million through 1984. As an extension of urban renewal, Community Development emphasized capital projects in predominantly black areas, including improvements in sidewalks, street paving, social services, water and sewage, recreation, and housing. With James Huger taking over as director of the program, and with a mostly black citizens advisory board, Community Development funds through the early 1980s were used in three predominantly black, low-income neighborhoods.[152] Federal revenue sharing monies, some $1 million a year beginning in 1974, were also used for capital improvements, with black areas receiving approximately one-half of the funded projects.[153] In addition, the federal Office of Revenue Sharing, acting on an NAACP complaint, investigated the city's minority employment record in 1976. It found the city in noncompliance with federal employment guidelines and threatened termination of federal funds. Reacting to federal pressure, Daytona implemented its affirmative action plan more aggressively and the city's minority employment figures began to improve markedly.[154]

Other Washington-funded programs were moderately important as well, including the Volusia County Community Action Agency, CETA (with more than one hundred employees in 1978), low-rent public housing, and summer jobs for youths.[155] The significance of all these federal programs cannot be overemphasized. In the words of one black leader, which were reiterated by several other well-informed blacks and whites: "The biggest change over the last twenty years has been an upgrading of the black community beginning with urban renewal in the early 1960s. Blacks used to have dirt streets, few streetlights, and poor housing, but federal funds have really helped to improve these conditions."[156]

By the early 1980s the politics of moderation was still dominant and black progress continued. The school board had its first black member (the president of Bethune-Cookman), and the *Evening News* editorialized that "inside the schools black and white teachers and administrators work harmoniously side by side in ways that would have seemed impossible ten short years ago."[157] The editorial also claimed that successful integration of the schools had helped to foster improved race relations in the community. Blacks continued their electoral success, too, helping to reelect two of the three black city commissioners in 1981.[158] A revitalized NAACP, assisted by black churches, carried out several voter registration drives in 1982–1983, concentrating primarily on younger blacks. As a result, black voter registration remained relatively high, and blacks were able to maintain their two seats on the city commission through the mid-1980s.[159] Moreover the black commissioners, most of whom were political moderates, proved adept at working with white city commissioners and encouraging the city to hire more blacks. They were also able to have more blacks appointed to the numerous citizen advisory boards; by the early 1980s black citizens held 35 percent of board positions, with one or more blacks on most major committees.[160]

Black employment had also improved by the early 1980s, but primarily in the public sector. In city hall, blacks made up 24 percent of the work force (up from 16.6 percent in 1976), and increased numbers were now holding supervisory positions.[161] Even with the elimination of the federal CETA program and local budget cuts, the city was able to absorb most CETA workers (primarily blacks) as permanent employees.[162] This improvement in the city's minority employment record was due primarily to active implementation of the affirmative action plan, but also to the hiring of a progressive city manager committed to equal employment opportunities. The city manager was primarily responsible for the establishment in 1982 of a special student youth program, which spent approximately fifty thousand a year in federal revenue sharing monies to hire thirty to forty high school students from low-income families (primarily black) for part-time city jobs. This program not only provided employment for poor black youths, partially replacing CETA, but it also placed these employees in highly visible jobs in an attempt to provide role models for other minority youths.[163] In addition, the recruitment of several new black police and the promotions of other black officers were particularly important, as they helped to undercut renewed criticisms of the police for a lack of black officers (especially in high-level positions) and for lack of attention to crime problems in minority neighborhoods.[164]

Yet progress in employment was much less apparent in the private sector. With little industry, the city continued to be dominated by tourist-oriented businesses that offered primarily menial, low-paying jobs to blacks. Thus the 1979 per capita income of blacks was still relatively low ($3,264 compared to a comparable figure for whites of $7,186), and the black poverty rate remained high at 39 percent.[165] Black-owned businesses that had thrived in the 1950s and 1960s were faltering due to increased competition from large retail stores and other disadvantages. The NAACP, moreover, claimed that a number of local employers were still not making an effort to hire blacks or to place blacks in management-level positions.[166]

In light of these serious economic inequities, black leaders in Daytona increasingly focused attention in the 1980s on improved opportunities for blacks in the private sector. The NAACP surveyed areawide businesses and threatened to boycott those that were not providing blacks with a fair share of jobs.[167] The city government, moreover, at the urging of its black commissioners and the NAACP, approved an ordinance in 1984 with the goal of achieving a 10-percent bidding preference for minority firms on city construction projects. This minority preference program, which applied also to firms owned by women, was similar to one passed by the county in the same year, and both programs, after early appraisal, appeared to be moderately successful for blacks.[168] With CDBG funds, the city also began a $150,000 per year low-interest loan program for minority businesses. In addition, black leaders organized a nonprofit Community Development Corporation with state funds to help secure loans and provide a variety of services to local minority businesses.[169] And finally, a coalition of black businessmen formed a separate chamber of commerce in 1985 to promote minority businesses and attempt to bring in more industry in order to provide additional jobs for blacks.[170]

While these activities focused on the economic plight of Daytona's relatively poor blacks, middle-class blacks began to enjoy a marked increase in social and economic opportunities. Perhaps the best indicator of the improved status of a number of the city's more prosperous blacks was their ability to buy or rent homes in most of the traditionally white residential areas without major problems. By 1981 seventy percent of the city's voter precincts (compared with only 37 percent in 1960) had ten or more registered blacks voters and therefore residents, and only the peninsula area remained exclusively white.[171] This fact was also vivid testimony to the improved quality of race relations in the city. So, too, was the increased acceptance of blacks into the Rotary, Kiwanis, Elks, and other local civic clubs.[172] Daytona's racial atmosphere, moreover, seemed to spawn prominent black leaders who were recognized statewide and even nationally. Charles Cherry, local NAACP leader and former city commission candidate, had become president of the state NAACP organization, while Joseph Hatchett, local attorney and former urban renewal adviser, became Florida's first black supreme court justice. Finally, Sylvester Murray, Daytona's first black city administrator back in 1964, had become in 1980 city manager of Cincinnati, one of the nation's largest cities.[173]

Clearly, remarkable progress in race relations was achieved in Daytona Beach. Once the local machine declined and blacks were more politically free and independent, the city began to desegregate public, then private, establishments. Always keeping both conventional and unconventional political pressure on the white power structure, Daytona's blacks gained integration earlier and more completely than most other southern communities. Surprisingly, the fact that blacks numbered more than 30 percent of the city's population and were potentially a threat to white dominance did not hamper racial change. Several factors served both to diminish white resistance and to fuel the forces of progress. One such factor was a relatively enlightened white population; many of Daytona's whites came from outside the South, and were generally supportive of black goals and aspirations. Many white leaders, particularly city administrators, but a number of businessmen as well, were sympathetic to the plight of blacks and were committed to the politics of "fair play."[174] Another factor, and one which perhaps helped to ameliorate white racial attitudes, was the local, liberal newspaper. In addition, federal funds (and political pressure at times) served to provide the much-needed revenue necessary for major public-service improvements in the black neighborhoods. But the most important factor was the well-educated, black middle class and black leadership associated with Bethune-Cookman College. From the students and faculty involved in the early sit-in demonstrations to many of the black elected and appointed officials who later participated in Daytona's government, Bethune-Cookman provided a reservoir of talent and leadership and an ideology of political and social action that were vital to racial progress. Indeed the legacy of Mary McLeod Bethune, with its emphasis upon education, hard work, and political activism, was instrumental in helping Daytona to achieve one of the most progressive records in race relations in the state.

Riviera Beach: Racial Conflict in Suburbia

Riviera Beach, the last of the New South cities, was once a small, quiet suburban town supported mainly by commercial fishing and tourism. It is now a satellite community in the midst of a sprawling, bustling metropolitan area which includes Miami, Fort Lauderdale, and West Palm Beach. When the city's black population expanded dramatically during the 1950s and 1960s, racial conflict and competition for political power with the formerly dominant white community soon became the central issue. With few remnants of a slave past and with a number of middle-class leaders, the black community was able to mobilize its new majority and ultimately wrest political control from whites in 1971. Black hegemony resulted in markedly improved city services for blacks, but it also infuriated many whites, who soon retaliated with improved organization and determination. The black community, meanwhile, had begun to suffer from a sense of complacency and from internal divisions. What has occurred since has been a continuing and often bitter struggle for power between two racial groups with approximately equal political resources and an equal commitment to gaining control.

Unlike recent events in the city, the early development of Riviera Beach was relatively gradual and unspectacular. The settlement of the community was closely related to the development of Palm Beach County, which, because of an inadequate harbor and hostile Indians, did not attract many white settlers until after the Civil War. Growth of the area was limited until the 1890s, when railroad magnate Henry Flagler began to develop the Palm Beaches as a resort area. It was 1893 when the name "Riviera" was first adopted (the community was formerly known as Oak Lawn) because of the area's similarity to the Riviera in Europe. Unofficially, the community was also known as Conch Town, a name derived from the many commercial fishermen from the Bahamas, called "conchs," who fished the ocean waters off Riviera. Fishing remained an important commercial and tourist activity in the area, and eventually many of the conchs settled on the mainland, ultimately becoming a significant political force in the city.[175]

A number of the early settlers in Riviera were blacks, all freepersons by this time. Some were laborers who helped in the construction of the railroad and the early resort hotels in the late 1800s, but other blacks bought land and operated their own small farms. These black settlers were an integral part of the community, and by the mid-1890s they had established their own churches and a school. Not long after the turn of the century several black subdivisions were established on the west side of town (west of the Old Dixie Highway and the adjacent Florida East Coast Railroad), an area which has remained predominantly black.[176]

The promise of an early and rapid development of Riviera Beach never materialized. The collapse of the land boom in south Florida and the onset of the Depression, coupled with a destructive hurricane in 1928, served to dash all hopes for growth and prosperity. In 1922, when the town was finally incorporated, its population numbered only about two thousand. Over the next two decades the town actually lost some population, and other residents of Palm Beach County increasingly looked upon Riviera as a backward community. In 1940, however, the town purchased a beautiful beach on Singer Island, located just off the mainland. This purchase encouraged the growth of tourism and eventually led to the annexation of the south end of Singer Island, a wealthy white resort area. These developments brought increased population and some industrial growth to Riviera, and by 1960 its population numbered more than thirteen thousand.[177]

Political Success Comes Early

The 1950s and 1960s marked a period of dramatic change in the racial composition of Riviera Beach. From 1950 to 1970 the proportion of blacks in the population increased from 23 percent to 56 percent, as more than ten thousand blacks moved into the city. Much of this inmigration was from neighboring cities, especially West Palm Beach, where many lower-middle-class blacks were unable to obtain decent housing.[178] Real estate developers evidently saw Riviera Beach as an area where they could build and sell homes to moderately well-to-do blacks, and thus the city eventually became a black dormitory community with 64 percent of the nonwhite population owning their homes in 1960.[179] "The first time I saw neat, well-kept lawns with children of the 'wrong color' was in Riviera Beach," claimed a social scientist who studied the city in the early 1960s.[180]

As the black population began to increase in the early 1950s, so too did black political activity. Few blacks had registered or voted prior to this period. In Palm Beach County, transplanted Republicans were beginning to threaten incumbent Democrats in local government, and neither the Republicans nor the local conservative Democrats were eager to increase the registration of blacks, who generally voted "liberal" in primaries and Democratic in general elections. Yet the county was hardly a stronghold of white supremacy,[181] and Riviera Beach soon had the most politically active black community in the area. In 1952, in the wake of a dispute over water rate increases in a west-side housing development, Riviera blacks organized a local voters' league. The predecessor to the league, the Inlet City Progressive League, had been organized in 1944, and it and several smaller organizations merged to form the voter's league. The league raised black political consciousness and was instrumental in getting blacks registered to vote. Before long, blacks were registered at almost the same rate as whites and constituted 35 percent of the voting population. The voters' league also encouraged its members to attend city council meetings and make recommendations, and Riviera soon began to employ its first blacks (other than menial laborers) in city hall and to construct a swimming pool for the west side. In addition, with the support of the league, the first black candidate for elected city office emerged in 1956.[182]

This initial attempt at gaining local office failed, however, as black candidate F. Malcolm Cunningham, a lawyer and a president of the voters' league, lost in a runoff election in the city's at-large system. Riviera's white population, which outnumbered black registrants by a two-to-one margin, turned out in large numbers to defeat Cunningham.[183] At the same time, fear and harassment served to intimidate many black voters. In Cunningham's words: "In 1956, some of my closest friends, teachers and some of the old heads got afraid. In 1956 there were two or three crosses burned in the Negro community. Rumors spread. A lot of Negroes became frightened. There was strong feeling against my running."[184] The conchs, moreover, still dominated local politics, and despite black organizational activity, they were able to manipulate some black voters.[185]

But attempts by blacks to achieve more political power were not to be denied. The voters' league continued to make requests of the city council for integration of public facilities and for improvements in recreational facilities, police protection, and streets. As in other southern communities, Riviera's services for blacks were very poor and all institutions were totally segregated; in fact, blacks were routinely arrested if they dared to venture across the railroad tracks into the white section after dark.[186] While the council agreed that several of the requests for public service improvements were justified, it claimed that no additional revenue was available for such projects. Nevertheless the council did hire a few more black public employees, including a black recreation director for the west side, and appointed two blacks to the eight-member city planning board.[187] But the black population was increasing rapidly (43 percent of the city's population in 1960), and 60 percent of the eligible black population was registered to vote by 1961. More importantly, blacks had become an independent political force no longer susceptible to manipulative techniques.[188]

In 1962 Cunningham challenged again for a council seat and this time he was successful. Even though whites composed 68 percent of the registered voters, only 38 percent turned out in the runoff election, compared to the turnout rate for blacks of 61 percent. The victory, however, was due not only to Cunningham's power to deliver a bloc vote among blacks (95 percent voted for him), but also to his ability to cut into the white vote (18 percent voted for the black candidate). In the 1956 election there were no whites involved in Cunningham's campaign; now Cunningham had a number of whites working for him in the white neighborhoods. His victory was unprecedented: he was believed to be the first black to win a city-council seat in a racially-mixed Florida community in modern times.[189]

Cunningham's election and effective bloc voting by blacks, which soon became an important factor in determining the outcome of several all-white election races as well, brought some concessions for Riviera's blacks. Many city facilities were soon desegregated, and modest improvements were made in fire protection, parks, and sewer services.[190] In 1966 the city council approved a $3.9 million bond issue to be used for a major street paving and drainage program, but the bond issue was narrowly defeated in a freeholder's election as whites turned out in large numbers to vote solidly against the issue. Finding an alternative way to fund a less extensive street program, the council voted to use cigarette taxes and special assessments to repay the bond issues.[191] At the time, approximately 60 percent of the west-side streets were without paving while only an estimated 20 percent of the streets on the east side, which was predominantly white, remained unpaved.

Racial integration of public accommodations began relatively early and proceeded smoothly in most of the urban areas of the county, including Riviera Beach. In the late 1950s and early 1960s, blacks conducted peaceful sit-ins at lunch counters and restaurants in Miami and West Palm Beach, and soon afterward many establishments in the area began to serve blacks. Riviera's public beaches, however, were more difficult to desegregate, and only after more extensive demonstrations and numerous meetings with city officials was this accomplished. No doubt the relatively liberal atmosphere of the Miami metropolitan area was conducive to early integration, and the local newspaper with the largest circulation in Riviera, the *Palm Beach Post*, was supportive of the goals of the civil rights movement.[192] Of greatest importance, however, was the fact that Riviera's blacks were well organized by now and, buoyed by their initial electoral success, were willing to challenge segregation in a variety of institutions.

As in the case of public accommodations, the desegregation of public schools was also initiated relatively early. The first desegregation court suits in Palm Beach County were filed in the mid-1950s by a local black attorney, and black students began attending formerly all-white schools by the early 1960s. Schools in Riviera Beach were among the first to begin desegregation. In 1963, when Riviera's all-black Lincoln High School opened for classes while still in an unfinished state of construction, some black parents organized a student boycott. In the same year several blacks picketed school-board meetings to protest the denial of admission of blacks to Palm Beach Junior College. While these challenges hastened the pace of integration and improvements in black schools in Riviera, desegregation in other county schools lagged behind.[193]

Despite their increasing numbers and early political successes, blacks discovered that substantial racial change in Riviera was slow and difficult. Though blacks constituted almost one-half the population by the latter 1960s, whites continued to dominate the political scene. The conchs were being replaced in positions of power by wealthy whites from Singer Island. But the results for blacks were essentially the same. After Cunningham's initial electoral victory in 1962, other black candidates challenged for council seats on three occasions between 1964 and 1966 and all went down to defeat. Only popular incumbent Cunningham, drawing larger proportions of the white vote each time, was able to triumph in two reelection bids. Finally, in 1967 the lone black on the five-member council was joined by Bobbie Brooks, a black engineer at nearby Pratt and Whitney, who eked out a victory in a close runoff election.[194]

City services for blacks remained relatively poor, however. Most streets were still unpaved and the west side was woefully lacking in sidewalks, drainage, trash collection, and streetlights. Few blacks were employed in city hall except for those in menial positions in the public works department. There were no minority firefighters, and although 26 percent of the police force was black, patrolling was completely segregated, with black police limited to duty in west-side neighborhoods.[195] The prevailing rationale for this service deprivation was best expressed by a black informant: "Blacks were seen as 'inferior,' as 'secondary citizens.' The feeling was, 'Give 'em a bone and they'll be satisfied.' Also many whites felt blacks didn't pay enough taxes to merit the services."[196]

Racial Violence to Political Control

By the late 1960s, Riviera's blacks were extremely disgruntled with the lack of progress in west-side neighborhoods. In a bitter unleashing of frustration and anger, blacks rioted en masse on July 31, 1967 following an incident of alleged police brutality in the arrest of two black men. More than four hundred blacks, almost all Riviera residents, burned a manufacturing plant and a lumberyard warehouse, threw rocks and bottles at police, and detonated several Molotov cocktails before sheriff's deputies and state troopers could quell the violence. Forty-six blacks were arrested, and property damage was estimated at $350,000.[197] In a summer in which racial riots swept U.S. cities from coast to coast, the outburst in Riviera Beach was considered one of the most serious in any city of its size.[198]

A black investigating committee charged that the major causes of the riot were general slum conditions, inadequate recreation facilities, and the prevalence of "shoddy businesses." Other blacks cited police brutality and injustice in the local courts.[199] Riviera's mayor, on the other hand, denied that the police had used undue force in the arrests or during the riot,[200] and a *Palm Beach Post* editorial deplored the riot, calling it "mob action" and suggesting that it would only break down racial harmony and "good will" which had existed for years.[201]

The riot clearly increased racial animosity among many whites. As one white city official put it: "The riot lost support for blacks, even among normally sympathetic Jews. Rioting is not an acceptable strategy to most people."[202] This white backlash was most evident in the form of immediate electoral reprisal. In 1968–1969 four black candidates, including incumbent Bobbie Brooks, competed against whites for city council seats and all four were defeated as whites turned out in relatively large numbers. Malcolm Cunningham, who had resigned his council seat to run for the state legislature from the area, was also beaten by a large margin.[203] For the first time since 1962 blacks had no elected representatives in the city.

Some whites retaliated even more forcefully against blacks. Minority youths complained of increased harassment by whites on parts of the city beach, while a small group of whites formed a National Caucasian Organization to "force the government, under Caucasian pressure, to let our schools alone" and to maintain a segregated society.[204] In fact, as late as 1968 the all-black schools in Riviera remained in poor condition and completely segregated, since no white students chose to attend them under a "freedom of choice" plan. (A number of black students, however, did attend the formerly all-white schools.)[205]

Despite this backlash, the riot proved to be politically efficacious for blacks in several ways. "The rioting was probably justified," observed one white city official. "Whites simply wouldn't acknowledge blacks in the 1960s, and the violence gained their attention."[206] In addition to drawing attention, the violence was instrumental in black mobilization efforts. "The riot was a catalyst to change. . . . It rallied the black community together," claimed a black citizen.[207] In the wake of the outburst, several black neighborhood organizations developed and pushed for improved public services, more jobs, and increased voter registration.[208] Foremost among these groups was the Imperial Men's Club led by vocal black activist, Herman McCray. McCray's confrontational tactics and constant berating of the city council tended to polarize the community racially, but these same strategies also rallied blacks. West-side voter registration increased noticeably and blacks began to challenge inequities with direct action.[209] Reflecting McCray's approach, blacks protested at council meetings for improved garbage collection, and when rents were suddenly raised at a large west-side apartment complex in 1969, 125 blacks banded together to carry out a successful rent strike. In another instance, blacks picketed and eventually closed a local gas station, claiming blacks were mistreated by the white manager of the station.[210] Direct action was also employed in school issues, as black students carried out large-scale boycotts of classes in protest of a 1970 desegregation plan that called upon blacks to bear the burden of school integration.[211]

The mobilization of blacks following the riot was soon reflected at the polls as well. By 1970 blacks constituted the majority (56 percent) of Riviera's population and were estimated at slightly less than one-half of the registered voters. Most west-side residents, moreover, were relatively independent of local whites; a large majority owned their homes and many were employed outside the city.[212] Median annual family income for blacks was relatively high ($6,745), while only 26 percent of black persons had incomes below the federal poverty level.[213] Thus most blacks were free from potential political manipulation by whites. When two black candidates sought council seats in 1970, west-side voters wielded their newly developed political power, turning out in large numbers to elect both candidates.[214]

While these election victories lifted the confidence of blacks, racial violence at a local high school in early 1971 seemed to increase black anger and awareness of racial inequities. In its first year of complete desegregation through court order, formerly white Suncoast High School erupted in several days of student rioting as black students complained of mistreatment by whites. Blacks were especially critical of school administrators who they claimed would not listen to them, but they also condemned the all-white makeup of various school organizations, the failure to arrange for a black history week, and the small number of black teachers. White students complained of the increased "militancy" of blacks and claimed they were harassed at times by minority students. On one occasion when the school violence spilled over to a nearby shopping center, the police intervened with force, provoking an outcry of "police brutality" once again among blacks.[215]

At a large black rally in the midst of the violence, activist McCray asserted: "Black people in this city have taken abuse from the white community for so long that they have grown accustomed to it."[216] The school riots tended to further mobilize the black community, and McCray urged greater black voter participation in order to elect more of their people to office and thereby rectify racial injustices. One month later in 1971 two black candidates did vie for city council seats in an election in which the major issue was clearly which race would control city government. Some 70 percent of the registered voters turned out in the hotly contested election as one of the blacks was able to gain a narrow victory in a runoff.[217] Riviera Beach thus became the first racially mixed city in Florida with a majority of blacks (three-to-two) on its governing body.

With blacks in political control, changes in city services and employment began to occur almost immediately. In one of its first and most significant moves, the council fired the white police chief and appointed a black, Boone Darden—a former police officer from West Palm Beach—to succeed him. Darden soon promoted several blacks as well as whites and discontinued the practice of segregated police patrols in racially distinctive areas.[218] In other key high-level appointments blacks replaced whites as city attorney, city clerk, and superintendent of refuse collection. This last position was filled by McCray, who began to improve trash pickup on the west side. The council also allocated more money for water and sewage, and ultimately for street paving, with disproportionate amounts going for west-side improvements. By 1972 the city had constructed two new fire stations, one of which was located in the black community.[219] Finally, in the area of housing, the majority black council boosted the development of a long-stalled public housing project for blacks, and passed a local fair-housing ordinance to buttress federal law and help prevent racial discrimination in the sale or rental of homes.[220]

Even before the 1971 election, white fears of a black political takeover in Riviera had begun to crystallize. During the election campaign several black candidates were threatened and harassed, and whites published a newsletter, described as a racial "fear" letter, trying to scare whites into voting. After the election many whites claimed that the black councilmen were dangerous "radicals," and they contributed some $2,500 to challenge the 1971 defeat of a white council member. The court challenge was successful and the election overturned on the grounds that some illegally registered voters had taken part in the balloting, but nonetheless the black councilman was reappointed to finish out his term. Amidst fear of a "second Reconstruction," several whites, including a councilman, resigned their city positions and were soon replaced by blacks. Rumors of a white exodus from the city proved ultimately to be exaggerated, but white home buyers tended to stay away from the community. Some Singer Island residents even attempted to de-annex their residential area from Riviera Beach, but this move failed.[221]

Although whites' fears of the negative consequences of black rule proved largely unfounded, the black majority on the council did abuse its power at times. Whites were sometimes shortchanged in city services as an attempt was made to improve services on the west-side as rapidly as possible. Moreover, in an effort to fill a number of city jobs with blacks, some of those hired were, in the words of one black city official, "not as competent as they should have been."[222] On occasion, white employees were dismissed unfairly. In the most blatant example of this, the black council, all of whom were returned to office in another racially divisive election in 1972, demoted the white elected city clerk and appointed a black replacement.[223] Even the *Palm Beach Post*, which had endorsed the black incumbents for reelection, criticized this move, claiming it displayed "shocking bigotry" by the black officials.[224] Ultimately the decision was reversed by a circuit court order, but the reinstated white clerk resigned in disgust.[225]

Racial Antagonism Continues

Black political control in Riviera continued for several years, but whites soon challenged black dominance. Several white political organizations developed and began to utilize both the court and election systems to thwart black power. Among these organizations, the Singer Island Civic Association (SICA) proved to be the most effective. By running white candidates against black incumbents, and by getting white voters out in large numbers, these organizations were able to elect three white councilmen in 1973–1974 and thereby regain a majority on the council.[226] But blacks soon retaliated, registering enough west-side citizens to give them a majority (52 percent) of potential voters and then electing two blacks to the council and winning the mayorship in 1975–1976. Voting preferences in city elections were still clearly along racial lines.[227] Thus racial conflict persisted through the 1970s as whites and blacks alternated control of city hall.

Without continuous hegemony, blacks found it difficult to carry out many of the changes they desired. Even though whites were a minority of the city's population, they were still able to slow and sometimes impede black progress. Singer Island residents, for example, strongly advocated changing the city election system to geographical districts in order to guarantee whites some representation in city government. This proposal was narrowly approved with widespread white support in a city referendum, and while it maintained at-large voting, it called for four councilpersons to be residents of defined districts.[228] In addition, whites on the city's housing authority were able to limit the development of public housing, a tactic designed to discourage more blacks from settling in Riviera. In the area of city employment, whites held 185 of 295 full-time positions as late as 1977. Lack of black applicants and poor performance by minorities on the civil service exam were major reasons for the lack of more blacks in city jobs. But also of importance was the failure to implement fully the city's affirmative action plan, a program opposed by many whites, including the chairman (a white) of the civil service board.[229] Finally, Riviera blacks usually found little support outside the city.[230] Most of Palm Beach County was more conservative than Riviera, with retirees and Republicans making up greater proportions of the population. Blacks, on the other hand, constituted only 18 percent of the county's residents in 1970 and began to experience increased competition from the growing Cuban population later in the decade.

But black progress was also hindered by corruption and conflict within the black community. In 1975, one of Riviera's black councilmen was charged and tried for allegedly failing to report a campaign contribution. The councilman claimed the charge was politically and racially inspired, and he was ultimately acquitted in circuit court. He was fired, however, from his city job in West Palm Beach, and the charge and trial tended to diminish the reputation of blacks in local government.[231] In a more serious scandal, in 1977 the black chair of the city's housing authority was asked by the council to resign for a variety of wrongdoings, including nepotism, ignoring federal (HUD) guidelines, and hiring and protecting a fugitive felon. Two other employees of the authority were convicted of taking "kickbacks" from contractors while constructing low-income housing.[232] This scandal, besides setting back public housing progress in Riviera, clearly reinforced whites' claims that blacks were not competent or trustworthy enough to run city government.

In addition to corruption, factionalism and conflicts among blacks were also more prevalent in the latter seventies and early eighties. Black council members began to disagree openly with one another on occasion, and they frequently criticized black appointees, including the popular chief of police, Darden, and the black city manager. Moreover, black candidates of somewhat differing ideologies began to oppose each other in council races. On one occasion, two opposing blacks split the minority vote in a predominantly black district, thus enabling a third candidate, a white, to make the runoff election in the district—although a black ultimately won.[233]

Despite white opposition and increased lack of unity among blacks, steady progress in services for the west side continued. In 1974 the council approved a $3.5 million street-improvement program, and although poorer blacks protested the assessment of property owners for part of the cost, most streets on the west side were paved by 1979.[234] More important was the garnering of federal funds, and the majority black council and mayor proved to be very successful in obtaining federal grants to improve services. In 1975, for example, the city joined eighteen other municipalities and Palm Beach County in gaining funds from the Community Development Block Grant program, most of which in Riviera were used for west-side street improvements and housing rehabilitation. By the mid-1980s CDBG funds for the city totaled more than $5 million.[235] In addition, after lobbying by black mayor Bobbie Brooks, the city was awarded a $3.9 million federal Economic Development Administration grant for a new municipal complex. Completed in 1978, the modern complex included a library, fire and police departments, and council and administrative offices.[236] Federal revenue sharing, totaling more than five hundred thousand dollars annually, was used primarily for maintaining the current level of services (especially in the police department), while by 1979 CETA provided to the city thirty-nine employees, most of whom were black, and considerably more summer jobs for impoverished youths.[237] Finally, in a period of reduced federal funds, the city was awarded in the 1980s several HUD grants for housing, with the largest being a $3.6 million grant for a 520-unit complex on the west-side.[238]

Even into the early 1980s, however, racial conflict continued as the dominant theme in Riviera Beach politics. During the previous decade the black population increased by almost six thousand, while the number of white residents declined slightly. Thus by 1980 blacks constituted 67 percent of the city's population and some 54 percent of its registered voters.[239] Suncoast High School continued to provide a barometer of the city's racial situation as a number of white students transferred to other schools in the county, leaving Suncoast more than 80 percent black and in relatively poor condition by mid-decade.[240] While voting by race continued as the norm, whites turned out in large numbers in the 1979 elections, winning two council seats over black incumbents and regaining control of city government. Whites added another seat in the 1980 elections and commanded a four-to-one majority on the council.[241] The high turnout at the polls reflected whites' feelings that they were being shortchanged on city services by an insensitive black-controlled government. Such feelings were particularly prevalent among wealthy Singer Island residents who paid an estimated 60 percent of local taxes, and the Singer Island Civic Association with more than eleven hundred members was instrumental in mobilizing the white vote.[242]

In a manner reminiscent of the first black council of a decade earlier, the new white government moved immediately to appease white voters. Despite an outcry from blacks, the council passed a big increase in water and sewer rates. In addition, the white council fired the black city manager (but hired his assistant, a black, to replace him) and attempted to replace the black chief of police, Boone Darden. The chief, however, rallied enough support to force the council to rehire him. In the area of housing, the white government moved to protect Singer Island residents by reducing the living-unit density there, and refused to approve any low- or moderate-income housing projects for the mainland. The intent of the latter decision was to curb black population growth in the city, thus reducing black political power.[243]

For their part, blacks in Riviera tended to be factionalized and somewhat apathetic. As one black expressed it in the late 1970s: "Black political power has fragmented and stagnated. There's no leadership on the council, and there's too much animosity among blacks. And many have lost confidence in those they elected to office."[244] Clearly blacks were not voting as frequently anymore, and their effective bloc voting of the past was giving way to voting patterns that reflected the emerging ideological divisions within the black community. West-side residents, however, rallied their forces in 1981, pulled together by black ministers and others who helped form the Westside Political Action Committee (WESTPAC). Candidates backed by WESTPAC ousted two white incumbents, enabling blacks to recapture a majority on the city council. WESTPAC influence continued for several years, as blacks built a substantial four-to-one majority on the council and still held the mayor's post. At the same time, the power of SICA began to wane, thus allowing blacks to consolidate their power in local government.[245] But black political success and stability proved to be relatively short-lived.

In the most shocking incident of political corruption in Riviera history, Police Chief Darden was indicted in 1983 for accepting a bribe from a Mafia loan shark. He had been caught in the midst of an FBI investigation of organized crime in the county. Darden was convicted and sentenced to six years in federal prison.[246] The incident not only embarrassed many blacks but confirmed for many whites their contention that blacks could not be trusted in positions of power and responsibility. Turbulence in city politics, however, had only just begun. Darden's successor as chief of police, a black former-FBI official, became overly involved in city hall political conflicts and was ultimately fired in 1986 by a majority vote of the council. This firing caused the resurfacing of splinter groups in the black community. Seeing their political opportunity, many whites joined with moderate blacks to target the council for a recall election. In the meantime, two council members resigned, another died in office, and the FBI began a second investigation of alleged corruption in city hall. Although the recall election was called off as a result of a court decision, in early 1987 recall proponents ran candidates against a majority of the council and the longtime mayor and were victorious. Shortly thereafter, the city manager was fired, completing the ouster of most of the top-level officials in the city.[247]

While corruption and political instability brought about tremendous upheaval in Riviera Beach, perhaps the greatest casualty of this turmoil has been long-term economic development. The emphasis of the 1980s for the city's black leaders was minority employment and expanded economic opportunities. In 1983, for example, the city council adopted a bonus-density ordinance which allowed Singer Island developers more units and floors for their condominium projects if they hired more black contractors and workers. Although the ordinance was strongly opposed by Singer Islanders, it proved to be modestly successful in increasing jobs for blacks.[248] Of greater importance in the long run, however, were the planned commercial and residential development of the large lakefront area and the attempts to bring in more industry to the city. Both ventures, city officials thought, would significantly fuel economic growth and provide long-term employment oportunities for blacks. Because of political instability in the city, however, industrialists have become leery of investing in future development. This instability, along with Riviera's reputation as an "all-black, crime-ridden town," have seriously jeopardized attempts at economic revitalization.[249]

While blacks may not have realized the great expectations that were created when they took political control in the early 1970s, they succeeded in bringing about vast changes in Riviera's public sector. Increasingly large in numbers and relatively well-to-do economically, blacks organized politically quite early. With high voter registration rates, the west side had elected a black to city office by 1962 and the blatant barriers of segregation began to crumble. But substantial economic and political change came slowly. The white community, first through the conchs and then buttressed by wealthy Singer Island residents, proved intransigent and given primarily to a policy of "tokenism." Nevertheless, a major riot in 1967 and later violence in the schools served to mobilize blacks further, enabling them to elect a majority on the city council and thereby control local government. Significant improvements in city services for west-side residents took place soon after. But whites, still numerous and well organized, counterattacked, and the 1970s and early 1980s proved to be a time of tremendous political strife between blacks and whites. Lack of continuous political control, coupled with corruption and increasing internal divisions, stymied black progress. Yet political change continued, due partly to black determination and partly to the increased flow of federal dollars. As in the case of Gretna, one important contribution political power has made to blacks in Riviera has been greater confidence and racial pride. As Riviera's black mayor claimed: "We showed that blacks are as good as whites in public office, and we have eliminated the feeling that whites run everything and blacks aren't going to get anything."[250]

Summary

These profiles of three cities indicate that the nature and pace of racial change was quite different in the New South than it was in the Old South. With no direct history of plantations and slavery, and with a relatively diverse and growing white population, the New South was less preoccupied with the issue of race. Instead, economic growth and demographic change have dominated the recent political agendas of these cities. Moreover, New South blacks, along with moderate whites, have been able to forge significant political changes in a brief period of time. Figure 3.1 presents a time-line summary of major political events for blacks in each of the New South cities from 1950 to 1985.

Beginning in the 1940s and early to mid-1950s, blacks in Daytona and Riviera Beach began to organize politically, challenge blatant racial inequalities, and even vie for elective office. Titusville, with a relatively small black population and some lingering features of the Old South, lagged behind somewhat until the economic transformations of Cape Canaveral and the Kennedy Space Center took hold in the early 1960s. From that point on, however, all three New South cities experienced similar black demands and racial changes. In the late 1950s and early 1960s, for example, blacks demonstrated to desegregate the schools and public accommodations. By mid-decade, Riviera and Daytona Beach had each elected its first black to local office. Racial violence shook each of these communities in the late sixties and early seventies, as blacks, seemingly frustrated with the slow pace of change, asserted their demands more aggressively. Despite a temporary white backlash in response to these upheavals, blacks achieved greater organization and continued to press peacefully for the fulfillment of more formidable economic and social goals. In addition to their own ample organizational and leadership resources, blacks enjoyed valuable support from liberal and moderate whites, especially those in public office, business, and the media. Intervention by the federal government, however, was not as crucial to black progress as in the Old South, yet federal programs often provided an impetus to public service and other changes.

Although similarities in the political and racial development of these New South cities are apparent, there were also some variations from one community to another. Many of these variations were due, at least in part, to the relative size of the black population. Titusville, for example, with a small black citizenry, was unable to elect a black to local public office. Nonetheless fairly substantial changes took place there, owing partly to the lack of vigorous resistance from whites, who perceived blacks as little or no threat. In Daytona, on the other hand, the black population was sizable enough to create tension and fear among many whites. Yet surprisingly, many of these traditional racial fears were attenuated by growth of the moderate white citizenry, by the well-educated, middle-class black leadership, and by the presence of a respected black college which often served to forge a unity between the two races. As a result, racial progress in Daytona was greater than demographic factors alone would have predicted. Of the three cities, Riviera Beach experienced the greatest racial antagonisms. Although its black population was large enough to seize political control and cre-

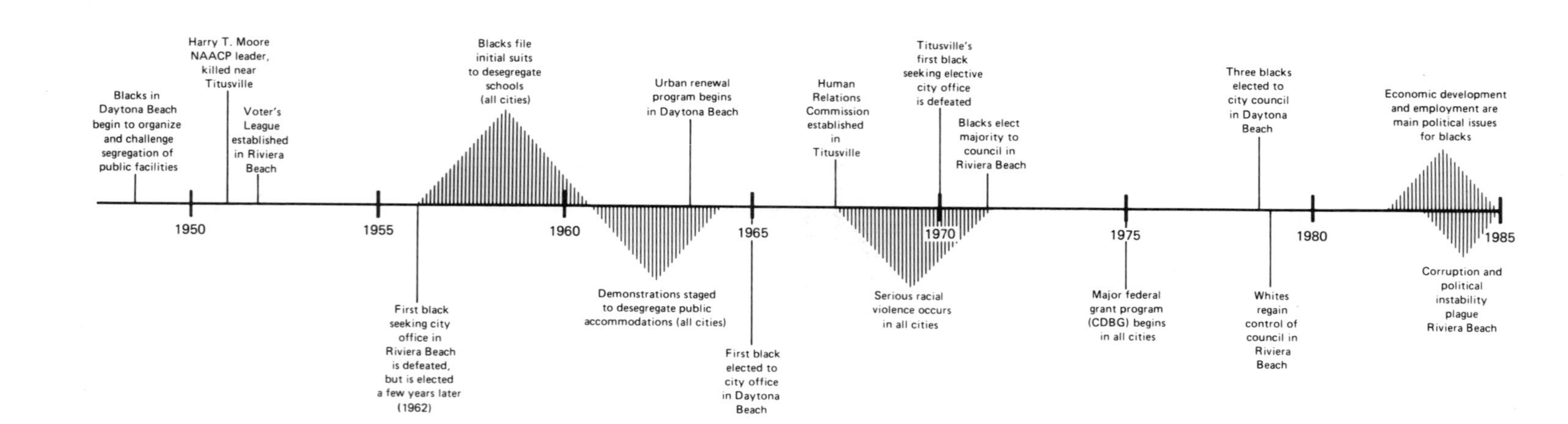

FIGURE 3.1

Time-Line of Significant Political Events for Blacks in New South Cities

ate significant changes, the sizable and conservative white community counterorganized and, taking advantage of divisions within the black community, actively frustrated racial progress. Thus in these New South cities, the size of the black citizenry alone was not as important a contextual variable as it was in the Old South. This is not to argue that minority population size was insignificant in the New South, but rather to suggest that its influence was often moderated by other factors.

4

Black Political Participation and Changes in Police and Fire Protection

> "The police department used to be small and dominated by a 'southern mentality,' and they treated the coloreds very poorly."
> —White city councilman, Titusville

> "Whites put fire hydrants mainly in their neighborhood and few in the black areas . . . and small water lines to black hydrants made them useless."
> —Black town councilman, Gretna

While the nature and evolution of the civil rights movement varied from Old to New South, the fundamental goals of the movement were the same almost everywhere. The ultimate goal, of course, was complete equality for black citizens. Achievement of equality, however, required that blacks first gain basic political rights, and that these rights then be translated into public power. It was assumed that such power would enable blacks first to improve their political condition and then to ameliorate their economic and social plight. Whether this is the process by which blacks can fulfill their ultimate goal is still uncertain. It is clear, however, that the civil rights movement enabled blacks to gain a greater, and more permanent, share of political power than they had ever enjoyed previously. What blacks did with this power, and whether they were able to wield it successfully to secure greater public resources, are part of the untold story of the movement.

One of the more immediate political goals of blacks was the improvement of local protective services. Police protection and the reduction of police brutality were always a high priority, but improved fire service and the increased employment of black firefighters were also considered important. However, few conclusive studies have been made of the effects of increased black political involvement on changes in protective services. Fire protection in particular has not been a widely researched urban issue, since it is often perceived as a purely "technical" matter and therefore of little relevance to social science.

Yet the human-safety services are the most important services offered by most municipalities. Indeed, most cities spend more on police and fire protection combined than on any other urban service (except when education is part of the municipal budget). Black neighborhoods, more so than most white areas, have a significant need for protective services. It is well known that poverty-stricken black areas with a good deal of dilapidated housing suffer disproportionately from high rates of crime and fire.[1] Moreover, there has long been a racial double standard in law enforcement (and fire protection to a lesser extent), while blacks have often endured a disproportionate amount of police brutality.[2]

Historically the local policeman in the South was not only a significant symbol of political authority, but the very personification of "white supremacy." His duties and powers went well beyond those necessary for the maintenance of civic order; he was given extralegal authority to enforce a whole set of social customs associated with white supremacy. Accordingly police brutality toward blacks, often in the form of corporal punishment and sometimes even resulting in destruction of life, was seen not only as a way to prevent crime but, more importantly, as a method of keeping blacks in their place. Moreover, some police in the South were known to conspire and sometimes even to actively participate in white mob violence against blacks. Typically, southern policemen shared experiences and attitudes that supported their playing these roles. They were usually poor whites with little formal education or professional police training, and their social heritage had taught them to hate blacks. This negative view of most blacks, together with the fear of entering high-crime areas in which much of the population disliked the police, served to discourage any police protection for many black neighborhoods.[3]

The historical legacy of police brutality and a double standard of justice instilled deep-seated fears and hatred of the police in many blacks. Although there was not the same level of hostility toward firefighters, many southern blacks tended to perceive fire protection as inadequate at best and sometimes discriminatory.[4] Hence one of the foremost goals of increased black politicization was the reduction of police brutality and the improvement of protective public services.

Several studies in the 1950s and 1960s of black political participation in the South have suggested that black voting often resulted in a decline in police violence against blacks.[5] Moreover, the reduction in officially sanctioned brutality served to gain black votes with little monetary cost to the white community. Even the psychic cost for whites seemed modest; such reforms appealed to the white middle-class sense of "fair play and impartiality."[6] Black political mobilization and the election of blacks to local office also tended to result in an increase in the number of black police and firemen, although black police were usually assigned responsibilities only in minority neighborhoods. This reflected the feeling of many white officials that law enforcement would be improved with black police patrolling black areas. In addition, because white police were often fearful of entering black areas, many of them welcomed the idea of black officers' assuming that responsibility. By the 1970s, moreover, federal affirmative action programs were designed and implemented in order to encourage increased hiring of blacks in many areas, including police and fire departments.[7]

Other studies, however, have suggested a different view of the effects of black politics. Davidson, in his study of Houston, noted little decline in police brutality toward blacks and only marginal progress in police-force hiring of blacks during the 1960s. He concluded that there was little connection between black political pressure and improved benefits in these areas.[8] Similarly a report of the United States Commission on Civil Rights, based on a 1967 survey of seven major metropolitan areas, claimed that "barriers to equal opportunity for minority group members are greater in police and fire departments than in any other area of state and local government," and stated that employment progress was slowest in southern cities.[9] The report mentioned that the major barriers to minority hiring were lack of effective recruitment, unequal treatment on the job, harassment by fellow workers, and lack of promotion of minorities. The use of competitive civil service exams, required by most police and fire departments by the 1960s, embodied certain practices and procedures which also hindered employment opportunities for blacks.[10] Fire departments were slow to integrate racially because white firemen who were on duty tended to resist sharing the living quarters of fire stations with blacks.[11] Finally, the black fear and hatred of the police, feelings which permeate many minority neighborhoods, often served to discourage blacks from even applying to join the police force.[12]

Thus the literature provides no clear consensus as to the impact of black political mobilization on public-safety services. This chapter will trace major changes in police and fire protection for blacks in these six communities over the two-and-one-half decades from 1960 to 1985. The attempt will be made to assess the role that various political factors, especially black participation, may have played in producing these changes. Finally, the status of protective services for blacks more recently, especially the employment of blacks in these areas, will be explored and analyzed in some detail.

Fire Services in the Early 1960s

In each of the Florida communities, well-informed citizens of both races evaluated fire protection for blacks as the most effective of the six basic municipal services investigated in this study. This evaluation held true both for 1960 and for the latter 1970s. The only exception was Gretna, which was perceived as having a relatively low level of public services generally. In addition, these same informed residents rated fire protection as the urban service that, since 1960, had been distributed most equally to blacks and whites. Black leaders and black organizations, moreover, generally placed little emphasis on improved fire protection during this period. As will be seen, more objective indicators support these contentions that fire service for blacks was adequate, and yet still reveal certain patterns of racial discrimination, particularly in the employment practices of fire departments.

In 1960 the firefighting forces in almost all these communities were small and usually consisted of all-volunteer firemen (table 4.1). Only Crestview and Daytona Beach had full-time, paid firefighters and only Daytona Beach had a sizable force (sixty-one firemen). There were no black firefighters, either volunteers or professional personnel, in any of the communities. By 1965 all of the communities except Gretna had a full-time, paid firefighting staff, but the departments were still limited in size, poorly trained, and all white. Of course, these municipalities were quite small in the early 1960s—only Daytona Beach had a population of more than fifteen thousand—and therefore did not often require a sizable, professional fire force.

Crestview's fire department was typical of what was to be found in the other communities during this period. The city had three paid firemen, one of whom worked part-time as a policeman, and all of whom doubled as jailers and radio operators. The major equipment consisted of two fire trucks, one of 1940 vintage, and the department was housed in two small rooms of the centrally located city hall building. The limited manpower meant that only one fireman was on duty

TABLE 4.1

Numbers and Percentages of Black Firefighters, 1960–1985

	Ratios and Percentages of Blacks in Fire Department						
Communities	*1960*	*1965*	*1970*	*1975*	*1980*	*1985*	*% Point Change (1960–85)*
Crestview	(0/3) 0%	(0/6) 0%	(0/7) 0%	(0/10) 0%	(0/10) 0%	(0/11) 0%	0
Lake City	(0/13) 0[a]	(0/7) 0	(3/16) 19	(6/28) 21	(5/27) 19	(6/22) 27	+27
Gretna	(0/12) 0[a]	(0/12) 0[a]	(7/14) 50[a]	(7/14) 50[a]	(11/14) 79[a]	(9/12) 75[a]	+75
Titusville	(0/6) 0[a]	(0/34) 0	(1/38) 3	(3/44) 7	(3/45) 7	(2/57) 4	+4
Daytona Beach	(0/61) 0	(0/80) 0	(0/80) 0	(6/90) 7	(8/92) 9	(11/106) 10	+10
Riviera Beach	(0/30) 0[a]	(0/13) 0	(2/29) 7	(7/49) 14	(2/49) 4	(14/52) 27	+27

SOURCES: Local newspapers, public records, interviews with local firemen and public officials, and federal EEO-4 forms.

[a] All-volunteer firefighting force.

at all times. However, the volunteer force of some ten to fifteen men (all white) served as an important part of the city's fire defenses.[13]

The absence of black firemen was part of the historical legacy of the South and reflected the principle that blacks should not be given positions of public responsibility, even on a low level.[14] For many whites there was the assumption that blacks were simply not competent enough to handle such jobs. "Too many colored people are not efficient in rescue and firefighting," claimed a longtime white businessman in Lake City. "I don't think coloreds are as capable and as efficient as whites."[15] In the case of many white firemen, there was the obvious fear and reluctance to work with blacks. No doubt this historical legacy and resistance from white firemen served to discourage potential black applicants from even attempting to join regular or volunteer fire forces.

The volunteer fire groups functioned as informal social clubs as much as actual firefighting forces. These groups, which included wives who were often organized as auxiliaries for fund-raising activities, did a good deal of socializing off the job. These informal social networks reinforced the racially exclusionary practices of the all-white volunteer groups. In addition, the volunteer forces were made up mostly of lower-middle-class whites, who tended to perceive blacks in very negative terms. Furthermore black leaders and groups made little or no attempt to integrate fire forces in the early 1960s, partly because desegregation of fire houses was seen as an almost impossible task and partly because black resources were focused elsewhere at the local level—primarily in mobilizing an effective black vote and in attempting to desegregate public accommodations and schools.

Although there were no black firemen in these communities through the mid-1960s, there was little evidence suggesting any general reluctance by white firefighters to enter black areas to douse fires. In fact, informed citizens retrospectively rated fire protection as the *least* racially discriminatory of all basic urban services. Yet it is clear that certain physical and institutional factors served subtly to reduce the effectiveness of fire services for predominantly black areas (and even for some predominantly white areas). This was particularly the case in the relatively poor, Old South communities. For example, railroad trains, whose tracks were often a zone of demarcation between black and white neighborhoods, sometimes blocked the accessibility of fire engines to black areas during critical periods when fires were raging. This was the situation, at least during the 1960s, in two of the six communities: Crestview and Riviera Beach. So important was this issue in Riviera Beach that when the first black was elected to the city council in 1962, his initial attempt at change was to push for creation of a fire substation on the west side (the black area) of the railroad tracks so that trains could no longer impede fire department responses; the city's only firehouse was located on the predominantly white, east side of the tracks.[16]

The relatively low level of other municipal services for blacks also contributed to reducing the effectiveness of fire protection. The large number of unpaved roads, the lack of street signs, and inadequate streetlighting were all occasional impediments to rapid fire-service responses, especially in the Old South communities. Unpaved streets and poor drainage were serious hazards when heavy summer rains turned low areas into virtual quagmires, completely washing out some streets. And in 1960 black neighborhoods in Crestview, Lake City, and Gretna averaged less than 10 percent of their streets paved. Fewer and relatively smaller water lines, and a lack of fire hydrants, also plagued blacks in the Old South. Gretna, for example, had a water system composed of six-inch lines in the white area but only one- and two-inch lines in the rest of the majority-black town. Not only were these small lines inadequate for fire hydrants, but only three of the town's seven hydrants were located in the black areas.[17] Lake City's blacks, too, seriously lacked those services so essential to adequate fire protection. As late as 1976 the Community Development Block Grant target area in northeast Lake City contained a predominantly black population of which almost 50 percent were without water service and lacked fire hydrants.[18]

Perhaps the most important institutional factor which affected fire protection for blacks was the poor quality of housing. At least one study has shown that the least productive fire services are generally found in cities with high rates of deteriorated housing.[19] As depicted in table 4.2, nonwhite (primarily black) housing was very poor in 1960 and fire insurance rates were reportedly high in the black areas. Again, this was especially the case in the Old South communities. The vast majority of nonwhite homes in both Crestview and Lake City were reported to be deteriorating or dilapidated, and the black homes in Gretna were estimated to be in a similar deplorable condition.[20] Many of these houses were old, wooden structures with gas space-heaters and outdated, overloaded electrical circuits, all conditions which helped produce a high rate of fires. As a Lake City fireman put it: "The northeast section [predominantly black] is the hardest place to fight fires because the wooden shacks burn right up."[21] In Gretna, several residents claimed that once a dilapidated home caught fire, it was

TABLE 4.2

Characteristics of Housing

Communities	1960				1970				1980			
	% of Occupied Units Sound with All Plumbing Facilities		% of Occupied Units Deteriorating or Dilapidated[d]		% of Occupied Units with All Plumbing Facilities		Median Value of Owner-Occupied Units		% of Occupied Units with All Plumbing Facilities		Median Value of Owner-Occupied Units	
	White	*Non-White*	*White*	*Non-White*	*White*	*Black*	*All Units*	*Black Units*	*White*	*Black*	*White*	*Black*
Crestview	60[a]	16	36[a]	70	96[a]	75	$ 8,600	$ 5,000	99	97	$23,200	$18,500
Lake City	75[a]	14	21[a]	67	95[a]	53	10,400	5,500	99	89	30,800	14,700
Gretna	39[b,c]	—	47[b,c]	—	92	36	7,000[b]	5,000[b]	88	76	15,900[c]	—
Titusville	86[a]	31	10[a]	55	99	90	16,700	10,900	100	99	42,400	31,400
Daytona Beach	87	51	9	40	98	96	13,600	10,500	99	99	38,600	25,100
Riviera Beach	93	66	5	23	97	97	14,100	11,600	99	99	43,300	34,600

SOURCES: 1. U.S. Bureau of the Census, U.S. Census of Housing: 1960, Vol. 1, States and Small Areas, Florida, Final Report HC(1)–11, 1962, pp. 46, 52, 60, 68, 82, 118, 119, 122, 124, 125.

2. U.S. Bureau of the Census, Census of Housing: 1970, General Housing Characteristics, Final Report HC(1)–A11, Florida, 1971, pp. 46, 47, 49, 50, 58–64, 66–73, 87, 95, 100.

3. 1980 Census of Housing, Vol. 1, Characteristics of Housing Units, Chapter A, General Housing Characteristics, Part II, August 1982, pp. 87, 89, 94, 96, 229, 327, 332, 385.

4. Census of Population and Housing, 1980: Summary Tape File 3A (Florida) [Machine/Readable Data File]/Prepared by Bureau of the Census, 1982.

[a] Includes vacant, as well as occupied, units.

[b] County figures; data for town not available.

[c] Data are for all units; figures for Whites and Non-Whites are unavailable.

[d] These data no longer available after 1960.

gone, and the only thing the fire force could do was "save the chimney" and attempt to prevent the fire from spreading.[22]

Police Protection in the Early 1960s

Few city services evoke more criticism or stronger feelings from blacks than does police protection. Not only do the police provide a very significant and visible service, but the police officer has become a symbol of white authority, and sometimes oppression, for many blacks. Thus improvement in police services was given a high priority by most blacks. Informed citizens in the six communities, moreover, ranked the police third in a list of six services in terms of inequality in delivery over the years since 1960. As we shall see, more objective indicators also depict clear discrimination against blacks in the provision of police services and show only moderate improvement over time.

As in the case of fire protection, police departments in 1960 were relatively small and unprofessional (table 4.3). Only Daytona Beach had more than two dozen full-time police officers, and its sizable force was geared primarily to deal with the avalanche of tourists who descended on the city annually. Gretna, the smallest of the communities, had no local police force but depended on the county sheriff to send out a deputy in time of need. Lake City's force was probably typical of the quality of police departments at the time, at least in the Old South and in Titusville. Of the sixteen men on the force in 1960, six of them were reportedly illiterate and most others did not have a high school education. Uniforms were nonexistent. Data on arrests were unavailable because no permanent records or files were kept. Similarly, most policemen gained their positions not because of their personal qualifications but because of their political connections.[23]

All of the police departments except Crestview's had one or more black policemen by 1960. (Crestview hired its first black in 1961.) Both the numbers and the proportions of black police, however, were relatively low; only Lake City and Riviera Beach employed blacks in more than 10 percent of the positions on their forces (table 4.3). All three New South cities had one or more black police officers in 1960, as these cities had broken the racial barrier in their police departments somewhat earlier than had the Old South. In most communities the first black policeman was hired sometime in the 1950s in order to provide a greater degree of law enforcement for the black neighborhoods. This was partly a response to growing pressure from black citizens and groups for greater police protection, but it was also a response to the anxiety of white policemen who often feared entering

TABLE 4.3

Numbers and Percentages of Black Police, 1960–1985

	Ratios and Percentages of Blacks in Police Department						
Communities	*1960*	*1965*	*1970*	*1975*	*1980*	*1985*	*% Point Change (1960–85)*
Crestview	(0/5) 0%	(1/7) 14%	(1/9) 11%	(2/12) 17%	(2/15) 13%	(1/15) 7%	+7
Lake City	(2/16) 13	(4/22) 18	(4/21) 19	(6/32) 19	(4/30) 13	(4/23) 17	+4
Gretna	—[a]	—[a]	—[a]	—[a]	(4/5) 80	—[a]	—[a]
Titusville	(1/14) 7	(2/19) 11	(1/38) 3	(1/43) 2	(2/45) 4	(3/58) 5	−2
Daytona Beach	(6/78) 8	(1/87) 1	(2/100) 2	(10/154) 7	(26/170) 15	(24/199) 12	+4
Riviera Beach	(4/23) 17	(11/42) 26	(8/43) 19	(11/62) 18	(19/64) 30	(23/74) 31	+14

SOURCES: Local newspapers, public records, interviews with local police and public officials, and federal EEO-4 forms.

[a] Gretna had no police force of its own until 1977. Its police protection was provided by the Gadsden County Sheriff's Department, which employed four white deputies in 1960. The Gretna police force was discontinued in 1982, after which the Sheriff's Department once again provided service.

black neighborhoods and welcomed the employment of a black or two to fulfill this role.

Yet in some of these communities the hiring of a minority policeman was a way to further manipulate and control blacks politically. In Lake City and Daytona Beach, for example, several black police were put on the forces relatively early as a way of offering visible public rewards for blacks' votes. But the black police were often used as agents of white leaders, helping to mobilize the black electorate and generally serving to pacify black neighborhoods.[24] "Black police have been good at keeping peace with the blacks," claimed a Lake City public official.[25]

The first black police were clearly treated as second-class officers. In each community they patrolled only the black sections, never any predominantly white areas, and they could arrest only blacks, not whites. They patrolled either on foot or, if extra vehicles were available, in segregated police cars. In the police station, black patrolmen had to use separate bathrooms, locker facilities, drinking fountains, and office areas. In the words of a black leader in Daytona Beach, "Black policemen originally wore only half a badge."[26] So deeply ingrained were these norms that when several black groups and black police in Daytona requested the integration of police restroom and locker facilities in 1960, the city commission refused, even though several other public facilities in the city had been desegregated. Moreover, two black Daytona police who were active in challenging segregation in the department were dismissed from the force soon after.[27]

Police service for black neighborhoods was typically minimal in this period. "Police were there for the protection of whites," claimed a long-time Daytona news reporter.[28] They usually responded passively (if at all) to demands or reported crimes in black areas. According to one white resident of Crestview, "The police used to ignore nigger fights and rarely would go into nigger areas."[29] Sometimes the police would refuse to answer calls from black neighborhoods because of their fear of abuse from resentful or distrustful blacks. The hiring of black police did provide more law enforcement for blacks, but the black police alone were never able to provide the same level of protection for blacks as white police provided for most whites. With the low proportion of black police relative to the proportion of blacks in each community, it is clear that the minority sections were underpatrolled compared to white areas. Moreover, most predominantly black areas had *higher* reported crime rates than most white areas and thus had a *greater* need for police protection. Furthermore, black police were sometimes viewed by blacks as "Uncle Toms" and were resented as much as, or even more than, white law enforcement officers.[30] Even if they were not seen as "Toms," black police were generally more middle class than most other blacks and thus were often unsympathetic to the problems of lower-class blacks.

Not only was police protection traditionally minimal for blacks, but police brutality toward blacks had been an issue at one time or another in each of these communities. A number of black citizens still had vivid memories of such brutality. Several Lake City blacks recalled a dramatic incident in the mid-1940s when the mayor, assisted by the police, publicly horsewhipped a group of blacks, including several women.[31] By the late 1950s and early 1960s, however, such blatant and commonplace instances of police brutality were increasingly rare. No doubt black votes and the first stirrings of political organization served to curb the most flagrant acts of police hostility. But in some communities public officials saw the cessation of police brutality and the fair and friendly treatment of blacks by the police as acts of benevolence or "services" rendered to blacks. The provision of such "services," along with the public toleration of what whites considered victimless "impulse freedoms" (gambling, prostitution, rackets, and moonshine) in the black community, were used as techniques to manipulate the black vote. These manipulative strategies were not very costly and were certainly less expensive than offering other public services to blacks. Moreover, such techniques did not normally offend white voters and were a relatively easy way to attempt to insure important black political support.[32]

Progress in Protective Services

Traditionally, fire departments have been the most resistant of all municipal departments to hiring blacks, and this proved to be the case in these communities as well. Black firemen were not employed in any of these municipalities until the late 1960s. By 1970 all the communities except Crestview and Daytona Beach had broken the racial barrier and hired their first black firefighters (see table 4.1). It was not until 1975 that Daytona employed a black in its department; Crestview had no black fireman until 1979, and then only briefly. Promotions of black firefighters, too, have been slow to occur and relatively rare. As late as 1980 only Riviera Beach and Lake City had blacks in supervisory positions (a single lieutenant in each city). Somewhat greater progress took place in the early 1980s, however, as Titusville and Daytona promoted one black each; Riviera and Lake City added one and three high-level blacks respectively, and Gretna appointed a black fire chief to direct its volunteer force.

Although the employment of blacks was an important step in dismantling discriminatory barriers in fire departments, it may not have had as great an effect on the quality of fire service provided to the black community as changes in several other areas. One was the location of new fire stations and substations. As previously mentioned, railroad lines were an occasional barrier to rapid fire-service responses in two of the communities. In Riviera Beach this situation had been an issue for many years. In 1972, however, just a little more than a year after the election of a black majority to the council, the city built two new fire stations, one of which was on the west side of the railroad line within the black area.[33] In Crestview, too, fire-department access to black homes had at times been blocked by trains. The city's acquisition in 1975 of a small substation near the black area substantially reduced this problem, and in 1978 the city completed construction of a highway overpass of the railroad lines.[34]

All of the communities experienced improvements in black housing and street paving during the 1960s and 1970s (see table 4.2), advancements that reduced fire risks and helped to provide easier access for fire vehicles. Federally subsidized housing, more common in New South cities, offered better-quality housing for a number of poor blacks. Daytona Beach, in particular, was successful in securing such federal grants, and its sizable urban renewal program in the 1960s and early 1970s was instrumental in the improvement of blighted housing. Of greatest importance, however, was the federal Community Development Block Grant program initiated in 1974. By 1977 all of the communities had obtained CDBGs which were utilized to a great extent for housing rehabilitation in poor black sections. In the Old South communities, however, a much greater proportion of the CDBG money obtained was used for street paving in black neighborhoods, sewage and water systems, and fire hydrants. In the New South, these basic services had already been provided for most black residents.

Progress in police services for blacks was also relatively moderate and slow in the 1960s and early 1970s. By 1975 the number of personnel in the police departments in each of the communities had doubled or more, and increases in employment of black police had generally kept pace with this growth (see table 4.3). However, the proportion of blacks remained about the same as it had been in the early 1960s. Only Gretna, with a police department of almost all black officers, first established in 1977, showed a dramatic increase in black police late in the decade, but Gretna's department was dismantled because of a lack of funds in the early 1980s. Surprisingly, the more racially progressive New South communities made only modest proportional gains (with the exception of Titusville, which showed a slight decrease), and even then only by the late 1970s. The qualifications for police in New South cities had been relatively high, especially with respect to formal education. This factor, along with the keen competition for well-qualified blacks from the growing private sector, made it difficult to recruit and retain black police.

In terms of promotions and supervisory positions for blacks, the changes since 1960 have also been rather modest. No black policeman was ranked above patrolman in 1960 in any of the communities. As late as 1976, only Riviera Beach, with a black police chief and two black captains, had any blacks above the rank of sergeant; and only Lake City had black sergeants (two). Crestview, Titusville, and Lake City each had a black policeman who had been on the force for ten years or more, and each had been passed over several times for promotion. By 1980 each of these cities, plus Daytona, had a black sergeant, but only Lake City had promoted a black to a higher level (lieutenant). Gretna, of course, had a black chief by this time. Although blacks failed promotional exams at disproportionately high rates and some black officers left for higher-paying jobs elsewhere, a major reason for the lack of promotions was the lingering fear, expressed by both black and white police, of having blacks supervise whites.[35] This fear was especially evident in the Old South, where by 1985 blacks held a police supervisory position in only one community (Lake City), while New South cities showed some increase in promotions of blacks.

Somewhat greater progress was achieved in other aspects of police service, however. In terms of patrolling patterns, by the late 1960s and certainly by the early 1970s white officers were routinely working in some black neighborhoods and police cars, as well as departmental facilities, were often integrated. By the early 1970s, black police were usually allowed to patrol white neighborhoods and arrest white citizens. Yet in the Old South, a black policeman would commonly have to call in a white officer before arresting a white, and in most communities black police were still used primarily to patrol black areas, the assumption being that minority officers could relate better than white police to residents of black neighborhoods. In addition, many white police officers were still reluctant to enter black sections. In Titusville, for example, a white policeman would not respond alone to a call from a predominantly black area, and an ambulance or rescue vehicle would typically not go into these areas without a police escort.[36]

By the early 1970s, police departments were generally more sensitive to crime problems and poor police relations in black neighborhoods. This sensitivity was especially apparent in the New South. Titusville and Riviera Beach, for example, increased police patrols in high-crime ghetto areas.[37] Two cities, Daytona Beach and Titusville developed police-community relations programs, consisting of either "rap sessions" between blacks and the police or public-relations ventures by police into the schools or minority neighborhoods. But these innovations were typically short-lived and only moderately successful.[38] Somewhat more effective were the police-cadet and explorer programs developed in these two cities. Such programs helped to initiate and recruit youths, some of them black, into police work.[39] Perhaps because of these programs, as well as the increased police awareness of minority problems and greater professionalism, the reported incidents of alleged police brutality toward blacks had declined in most communities by the latter 1970s.

The "Politics" of Protective Services

Which political factors, if any, help to account for these changes over time in fire and police protection for blacks? A good indication is provided by multivariate analysis of political and contextual variables and their relationship to the level of black involvement in the protective services. The path model presented in chapter 1 (and explained further in appendix 1) suggests the relationships among these variables. The major dependent variables are the percentages of black uniformed fire and police personnel, and the proportion of blacks among those in higher ranks (supervisory and administrative positions) in each department.[40] As suggested above, the hiring and promotion of blacks were important policy goals of the movement. Another significant goal was the reduction in police brutality, and indicators of the incidence of such brutality allow the analysis of this phenomenon as well.[41] A longitudinal approach, which looks at these data at six evenly spaced time intervals between 1960 and 1985, permits a time-series analysis and enhances the possibility of suggesting causal relationships.

Figures 4.1 and 4.2 present the path models for the percentages of blacks in the fire and police departments. Also shown are models for the proportion of blacks in higher-level positions in each department. The coefficients are normalized regression coefficients, or beta weights, and depict the magnitudes of the statistically significant relationships. Statistically insignificant variables have been omitted in each model.

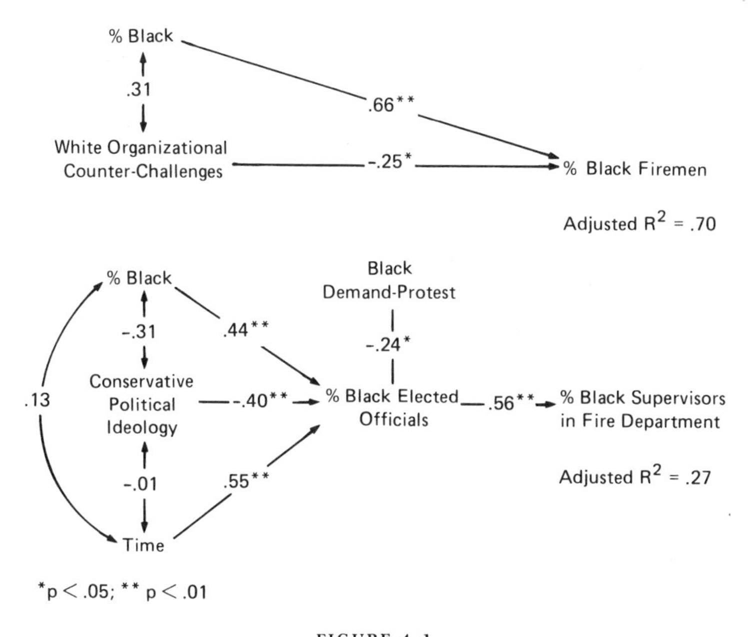

FIGURE 4.1
Path Models of Black Employment in Fire Departments (1960–1985)

The results clearly indicate that *black elected officials have had the most important direct and positive influence on the proportions of black personnel in these departments.*[42] This is especially the case for police rather than fire departments, and the effect on the percentages of blacks is generally greater in higher-level positions than at the lower levels.[43] Only for black firefighters were black officials not a statistically significant factor. Moreover, the models are able to explain a high proportion of the variation—an average of 70 percent in three of the four models—in black employment. While black resources (the percentage of blacks in the population), political culture (the degree of voting in a conservative manner), and the passage of time were also significant variables in most of these models, the influence of these factors was indirect and predictable in most cases. That is, these independent variables usually affected the number of black police and firefighters, but only through their impact on the proportion of black elected officials. Furthermore, separate analyses for Old South and New South communities indicate that black council members and mayors were significant factors in both settings, especially for police departments. Even when looking at *changes* from one five-year time period to another in the proportions of black employment (rather than at a cross-section of six different

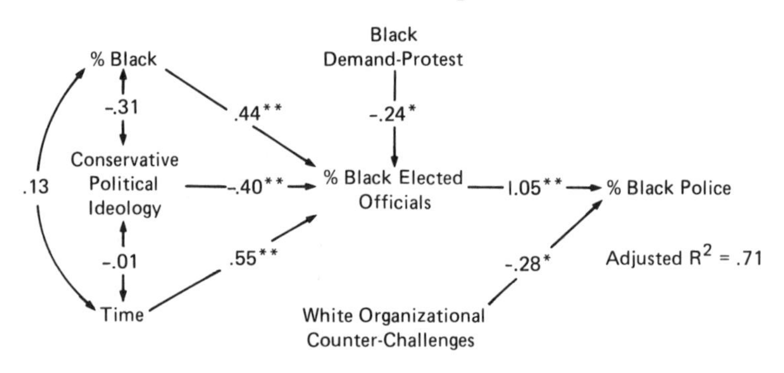

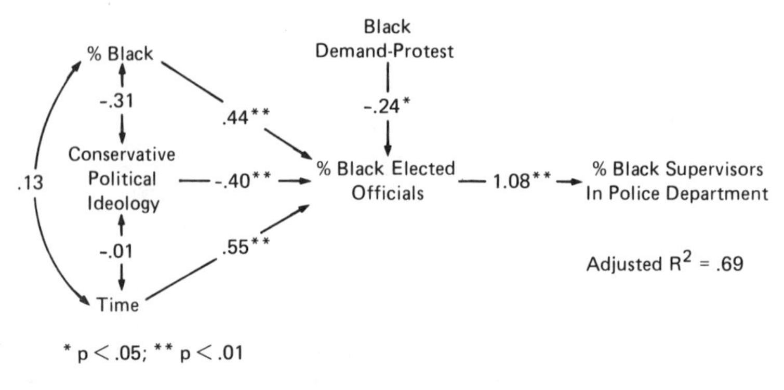

FIGURE 4.2
Path Models of Black Employment in Police Departments (1960–1985)

time periods), black elected officials continue to assume the position of most influential variable in each model. Only when black office-holders constituted less than a majority on the council were they not always a significant factor in promoting employment for blacks, although this was more evident for fire than police departments.

These findings are not surprising. Most black elected officials admitted to prodding city hall to employ more blacks and to trying to improve the protective services for blacks, and the focus of most such political pressure was on the police departments. An excellent illustration of this process was in Riviera Beach, where in 1971 the newly elected black majority council began to push for greater equality in city jobs. With this impetus from black councilmen, Riviera Beach hired several black firemen, a black police chief, and six additional black police between 1971 and 1975. One of the first actions of the new chief was to integrate patrols and to increase police protection in the black areas.[44]

In general, black officials in most of the communities provided useful liaisons with black neighborhoods and actively encouraged minorities to apply for jobs with the city. Black councilmen especially solicited potential applicants for police and firefighter positions, since these were the departments most clearly lacking in minorities. By the latter 1970s, blacks in office also pushed for increased promotions in these departments, arguing that blacks in supervisory positions were still too scarce and that such promotions would help keep newly hired blacks on the force and lure others to apply. Such input and internal pressure often persuaded city governments to give greater priority to the hiring and promotion of blacks.[45]

One other variable was shown to have a direct but much more modest influence on black police and firefighter employment. This variable was counter-challenges to black demands by white organizations, and its impact, as predicted, was in a negative direction. Thus in several communities organizations of whites developed or surfaced to oppose the black quest for improved services and employment. Such organizations ranged in ideological orientation from the extremist KKK to the moderate Singer Island Civic Association, but each of them sought in various ways to suppress black political demands. Of particular concern to many of these counter-organizations was the preferential treatment they believed black job candidates received at the expense of whites, and such organizations often acted to limit city hirings of blacks.

Somewhat surprising was the indication in three of the four path models that black demand-protest had an indirect and negative effect on employment. The explanation for this is that the more protest there was, the less likely blacks were to be elected to office, and vice versa, so that these two forms of black political activity did not usually occur simultaneously. Thus the 1960s was generally a time of protest and direct confrontation, with few blacks elected to local office. By the decade of the seventies, however, when more blacks were working within the political system and through their elected representatives, protest was increasingly rare.

Although the path analysis shows that demand-protest alone did not have a significant direct impact on black police and fire personnel, further analysis suggests that at times black protest and even collective violence were politically efficacious. As we have seen, protests often served to enhance the mobilization of blacks. Indeed the correlation between the number of protests and the number of political organizations is quite high (r = .65). Ultimately, such mobilization was sometimes useful in promoting black candidates for local office. In fact, if the number of black protests is "lagged" by five years (that is, correlated with the percentage of black officials in the subsequent five-year span) so as to capture better its long-term effects, it is positively associated to a moderate degree (r = .31) with the percentage of black elected officials.

However such unconventional political activities seemed to have largely one-time, and rather short-term effects on public policy. Thus all six communities had one or more black protests, and four communities had full-scale riots, in which criticisms of the police (and to a lesser degree the fire service) were voiced. In every situation except one (a minor protest in Crestview), the protests and violence were followed by changes in police or fire services to meet black demands. This response was stronger in the New South, and more common in the case of the police services, since police brutality or lack of black police were stated grievances in every major collective outburst. Typically, in the aftermaths of these disturbances, more black police were hired or promoted and police generally were more restrained both in response to black violence and in their day-to-day dealings with minority citizens. In Titusville, as reported above, a racially insensitive police chief was fired following the city's most intense interracial violence, and in Daytona and Volusia County several black officers were promoted to positions of greater responsibility as a result of serious black rioting and protests.[46] However, almost all such outbursts of blacks occurred within the relatively brief period from the mid-1960s to the early 1970s—very few took place before or after this time—and though their impact was immediate, it was short-lived. This helps to explain why the path analyses, measuring developments over a twenty-five-year period, show no significant direct effects for demand-protest or riots.

Another surprise in the results of the path models was the indication that the federal government had no appreciable impact, either through grants or affirmative action requirements, on black employment in the protective services. As required by federal law, most of the communities had an affirmative action plan, at least in form, by 1977, and they filed minority employment progress reports annually (EEO-4 forms). These plans seemed to encourage minority employment by setting forth goals and timetables for minority hiring and by calling for a reassessment of hiring and recruitment procedures. This process helped to open up city employment to a number of previously excluded groups, especially blacks. Nevertheless, only a few of the communities fully implemented their affirmative action plans, and this lack of implementation was particularly apparent in the Old South.[47] Many public officials saw affirmative action as an unnecessary federal intrusion into local affairs and thought that, in any case, there was little chance the federal government would enforce these plans. As one high-level official in Lake City put it: "This city doesn't want anyone telling them what to do, and we realize the 'Feds' can't enforce an affirmative action plan anyway. They aren't going to bother with a small city like this."[48]

Federal grant programs, too, had a relatively insignificant effect on the hiring and promotion of black police and firefighters. Only the CETA program seemed to have an impact, but this program was effective for only a few short years in the late 1970s. Nonetheless, CETA helped to make it financially possible for some cities with tight budgets to hire minorities. With a small, poverty-stricken population, Gretna was unable to employ full-time professional police or firefighting forces. But with the help of federal CETA funds, the town established its own predominantly black police department in 1977 and hired five fire-department trainees (four of them black) in 1979.[49] By the early 1980s, however, CETA was one of the casualties of the Reagan administration and was discontinued in all of these communities. Perhaps of greater importance than CETA for black fire protection in general was the federally subsidized Community Development Block Grant program. By the mid-1970s each of the communities had obtained these sizable block grants (Daytona Beach had also obtained the earlier urban-renewal version), and substantial proportions of the grants were utilized for the rehabilitation of substandard, fire-prone minority housing.

Other factors, though not specifically included in the path analysis, seemed to contribute to some degree to black penetration into the police and fire departments. One such factor was support from sympathetic white leaders in city government. The mayor of Daytona Beach, for example, appointed a special committee in 1970 to investigate the needs of the disadvantaged, and the committee suggested that the major obstacles to minority employment generally were racial discrimination and "culturally oriented" entrance exams.[50] With the urging of the city manager and the fire chief, the city in 1974 revised its civil service entrance exams to help remove cultural bias, and marked improvement in minority scores on the firefighter's exam was noted immediately.[51] At the same time, minority recruitment efforts were stepped up, including contacts with black organizations and ministers, newspaper ads, classes on test-taking, and the use of black recruiters.[52]

Similarly, in Titusville a liberal city manager was instrumental in encouraging black employment in the fire and police departments, while in Lake City a moderately sympathetic white mayor, and later the city manager, played analagous roles, though less effectively.

Beyond black employment per se, increased professionalism and the addition of more modern equipment, a result of the general trend toward modernization in these communities, also seemed to improve protective services for blacks as well as whites. By the mid-1970s, for example, state law required prospective police and firefighters to undergo 200 to 360 hours of combined classroom and practical instruction, and then to pass a standardized exam before being certified. The state also required all applicants to have at least a high school diploma or its equivalent. In addition, most departments in New South cities required a two-year college degree (or demonstrable progress toward one), an extensive background screening, and a variety of psychological and physical exams. These general requirements, while sometimes representing increased barriers to black employment, no doubt raised the competency level of personnel in all police and fire departments, and the outcome was a vast improvement over the all-volunteer and semi-professional forces of the early 1960s. In addition, by the 1970s police departments began to toughen their discipline for misconduct and to create more restrictions on the kinds of discretionary actions permitted by police officers. No doubt these changes were a result of the growing public (especially minority) dissatisfaction with police behavior, but the expansion of citizen rights to sue police departments for alleged misconduct was also a factor. General evidence suggests that such organizational changes, clearly more common in the New South, helped to improve police-black relations.[53]

The purchase of more modern equipment, especially communications technology, also tended to increase the quality of protective services, particularly in the Old South communities where existing equipment was often inadequate or outdated. Gretna, though it is an extreme case, illustrates this point. The town's only major fire apparatus was a World War II gas tanker which had been remodeled to carry water. The tanker was not very dependable, often arriving last at local fires after the equipment of other, nearby forces.[54] In 1979, with the old tanker in "total disrepair," the Gretna Council voted to purchase a new, modern $66,000 fire truck.[55]

What effects did improvements in police protection have on police brutality toward blacks? As we have seen, the reduction of such brutality was a major objective of the civil rights movement.[56] Figure 4.3 presents a path model showing the statistically significant variables related to the reported incidents of police brutality. As mentioned pre-

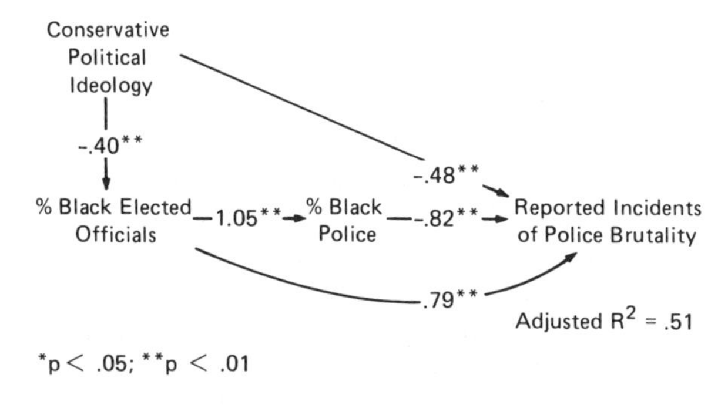

FIGURE 4.3
Path Model of Reported Incidents of Police Brutality of Blacks (1960–1985)

viously, incidents had declined by the late 1970s and early 1980s. Several factors were important in helping to bring about the reduction in brutality, but foremost among them was the increase in the percentage of black police. *The greater the proportion of blacks in the police department, the fewer the number of reported incidents of police mistreatment of blacks.* This finding clearly indicates that the hiring of more black police has an important direct influence on departmental policy and relations toward the minority community.

Somewhat surprisingly, the model indicates that black elected officials had a significant direct and positive effect on the number of incidents of police brutality. Perhaps having a greater percentage of blacks in office served to encourage black citizens to report such incidents. Yet it should be noted that the indirect influence of black officials was actually greater, through hiring and promotion of black police, and that the total effects (direct plus indirect effects) were relatively small but negative. Thus black mayors, councilpersons, and even perhaps administrators had some influence on police behavior toward black citizens. With blacks in power, the police could no longer assume an environment of white supremacy in which they could treat blacks in any manner they chose. By broadening the scope of political sanctions that could be used to discipline police, black officials added a note of caution to police interactions with blacks.[57]

Status of Police and Fire Protection in the 1980s

By the late 1960s, as has been shown, most of the fire and police departments in these communities were employing blacks, and other important changes were occurring as well to improve protective services for blacks. Yet by 1985 the proportion of black police and firemen in almost all of the departments was still surprisingly low. In not one of the departments had blacks gained proportional equality, and blacks had still not achieved parity with most white residents in police and fire protection. While increased hiring and promotion of black police and firefighters do not always translate directly into better services for the black community, they do indicate a correction in the traditional patterns of discrimination in employment and produce a more equitable distribution of the higher-paying jobs in local government. Moreover as blacks comprise an increasingly large proportion of these departments, they generally become "less isolated and more influential in shaping the values and culture" of the departments.[58] Racist language and actions, for example, typically are reduced simply because there are too many black employees around to hear and notice them. Thus increasing the number of black police and firemen can and usually does alter the internal organizational climate, and this in turn tends to improve services to, and interactions with, black citizens.

The employment of the first black policeman and fireman was a psychologically significant event, for it broke through long-existing practices of discrimination. Most police and fire chiefs claimed that after this watershed it was easier to hire other blacks. But the black employment figures for most of the departments showed little change, if any, over the period from 1970 to 1985 (see tables 4.1 and 4.3). Why was this the case, especially given the fact that initial barriers of discrimination had been removed a decade before, or earlier, in most departments?

A major reason was that relatively few blacks applied for jobs as police or firefighters. Job qualifications, which often were institutionally discriminatory, deterred a number of blacks. As mentioned, many departments (especially in the New South cities) required a two-year college degree, or work toward such a degree. Additionally, all of the communities' firefighter and police applicants were required to take and pass a general aptitude or civil service exam. These requirements often proved a special hardship for many black applicants, who generally had less formal education than whites. In Riviera Beach, for example, where black education level is relatively high, it was estimated that the black failure rate on the city's civil service exam was 30 to 35 percent greater than it was for whites. This situation often created, according to the city's personnel director, an attitude of "fear of exams and failure" among blacks, and of the prospective black employees as many as 50 percent dropped out of the application process before taking the exam.[59]

Another job qualification for firefighters and police in most of the cities was the demonstration of sound, moral character. This was a potentially discriminatory requirement for blacks, especially in the case of Lake City, where an applicant had to prove that he had no prior criminal record. Most departments, however, evaluated character or personality in more subjective ways, such as written responses on application forms or through an oral interview with a fire or police officer, usually the chief. The interviewers were always white, and the grounds for dismissing a candidate for lack of "good character" were vague indeed. For applicants for all sworn officer positions, Daytona Beach carried out a background check that included inquiries into any activity in "associations, organizations or movements." This practice was declared potentially racially discriminatory by the U.S. Office of Revenue Sharing.[60]

Another major deterrent to black applicants was the relatively low pay for firefighters and police. In 1978 beginning annual salaries for firefighters ranged from a little more than $6,000 in Crestview to $10,031 in Riviera Beach, with the New South cities averaging approximately $2,000 more than the Old South communities (Gretna still had an all-volunteer force which received no salary). Police entry-level salaries in 1978 ranged from $6,500 annually in Crestview to $11,019 annually in Riviera, compared with a national average of $11,472.[61] Even in Riviera Beach, where firefighters' entrance salaries were closest to the national norm of $11,078, firemen ranked low in pay compared with other municipal employees whose jobs involved equal or lesser skills, hazards, or responsibilities. These firemen also ranked lower than firefighters in other comparable municipalities nearby.[62] This comparative salary situation has made it very difficult in all of these communities to attract employees, especially qualified blacks. "No well-educated black wants to be a policeman or fireman. . . . He can get a much better paying job in the private sector," claimed a black official in Riviera Beach.[63]

In addition to receiving poor pay, beginning firemen must usually pay the expense of mandatory training courses to be taken at a regional training center or a community college. This is a financial burden for many blacks. Low salaries have also resulted in high turnover rates for the protective services, especially among blacks. Many police and firemen, both black and white, leave for better paying jobs in other cities or in private businesses. This is especially true in the New South cities, where the employment opportunities are the greatest. Riviera Beach, again, is a good illustration. Between 1965 and 1975, this city experienced a 55 percent turnover among its firefighters, and by the late seventies the rate was almost 20 percent a year, with the turnover rate among blacks even higher. Many of these firemen took jobs with other nearby suburban fire departments, particularly West Palm Beach, which paid salaries that were as much as $55 a week higher than Riviera Beach.[64] Titusville also has had problems keeping its black firemen and police. In early 1981 two of its three black firefighters resigned, with one of them taking a job at the nearby Space Center and allegedly doubling his city salary.[65]

Lack of promotion of black firemen and police has also discouraged black applicants and increased the black turnover rate within departments. Of the five cities studied that had professional fire departments, only Lake City and Riviera Beach had promoted black firefighters prior to the 1980s. The promotion record for police departments has been somewhat better: each community had promoted at least one black to the rank of sergeant by 1980. But many blacks still believe that there is little opportunity for advancement and higher pay in these services. And like many of the entrance requirements, the criteria for promotion are often a form of institutional discrimination against blacks. To be considered for promotion, all the departments require the passing of an objective written exam dealing with the technical aspects of the job. As in the case of entrance exams, black firemen and police tend to fail promotion exams more frequently than do whites. In addition, protective service personnel seeking promotion must complete a certain level of education beyond high school and must achieve credits for taking a specified number of advanced technical courses. Again, although some cities offer a small salary or partial tuition assistance as a financial incentive, the firefighters and police themselves must pay the expense of these advanced courses and blacks tend to feel more of an economic burden here than do most whites.

Longevity in the department is another criterion for promotion, with two to five years of service required, depending on the department and the rank one is seeking. Since black firemen and police have a higher turnover rate than whites, few blacks fulfill the necessary service requirement to even seek promotion. Finally, promotion requires the approval of the fire or police chief and city manager, based on their subjective evaluations through interviews or simply from on-the-job observations. In the smaller and less professional Old South communities, the mayor and elected council must also approve. Some black leaders and service personnel feel this requirement is too discretionary and political, and tend to favor white, "good-ol'-boy" types and to work against the promotion of blacks. In some cities black elected officials and the employee unions have made progress in objectifying and routinizing the more subjective requirements for promotion.[66]

Other major reasons why blacks in disproportionate numbers either leave or do not apply for firefighting and police positions are the codes of behavior and work discipline required. Reviews of personnel records and interviews show that blacks, to a greater degree than whites, quit or are fired for reasons of tardiness, absences from the job without leave, failure to adhere to the dress code, poor work records, or criminal offenses. The Daytona Beach Fire Department was typical in this regard. The first black fireman, hired by the department in 1967, was fired on the first day of training for a hair-code violation when he refused to shave his beard; firemen were required to be clean-shaven so that they could correctly operate their breathing apparatus. Between 1975, when the department hired six blacks, and 1977, two black firemen were fired for criminal convictions, another was fired for "conduct unbecoming a fireman" (he was allegedly carrying a concealed weapon), and one other quit after being reprimanded for an unauthorized six-day absence. Two more black firefighters resigned, one because of transportation problems in getting to work and the other because he felt "too pressured" during training. A number of whites were also fired or left the department for similar reasons during this period, but the rate for blacks was greater.[67]

The discipline required in fire and police departments was a problem for a number of blacks. In Crestview, after several years of searching, the force hired its first black firefighter in 1979. According to the fire chief, however, he proved to be "lackadaisical and lazy. . . . All he wanted was to sleep. He didn't want to work and clean up, but just fight fires."[68] The man left the department within six months without saying why or where he was going. The fire chief in Riviera Beach claimed similar problems. As he expressed it: "Many blacks lack discipline. Few work hard enough to pass the exam, and they want all the weekends off . . . but you only get one in three off."[69] Some black leaders and elected officials echoed these sentiments. As the black councilman in one Old South city put it: "Some blacks leave city jobs because they simply get tired of the regimen."[70] It seems that blacks entering the system often experienced a form of culture shock.

Other police and firemen (mainly blacks, but also some whites) contended that it was not so much poor black job performance as lingering white racism that drove blacks from the forces and discouraged others from applying. Although by the mid-1970s the presence of black firemen and police was established in all the communities except Crestview, and there seemed generally to be a good working relationship between the races, nonetheless, in Lake City police patrols were still racially segregated in the late 1970s, and black and white firemen and police in all the communities did not usually mix socially after working hours. A few whites exhibited common and sometimes crude forms of racial prejudice, and expressed various stereotypes about blacks, such as that they are "lazy," "smelly," "clannish," "rowdy," and "talk different." Although actual contact with black firefighters and police often modified these attitudes, a few whites continued to reflect antagonistic feelings toward blacks. Several even transferred to other substations or departments to avoid having to work with blacks. For their part, many blacks became uncomfortable at the least and often felt outrightly rejected by the racist sentiment. Said one black Lake City employee: "I felt ill-at-ease at first. I was the only black on the shift. I sensed the informal resentment and disparagement by the others."[71]

Police departments, in particular, still faced problems resulting from blacks' traditional fear of police authority. One important reason for the sparse number of black police applicants was the continued racial polarization of society, which made a black law-enforcement officer's position nearly untenable. As a black former deputy sheriff in Daytona explained it: "His [the black policeman's] white colleagues bring their traditional racism to bear, while his black brothers and sisters see him as a powerless and rankless tool for the establishment."[72] In addition to the strong black resentment of black police, many blacks, of course, still had a deeply ingrained hatred of the police in general. According to a Titusville black leader: "Many blacks are just not interested in being a policeman. 'Police' is still a dirty word for most blacks."[73] This traditionally unpopular image of the police continued to be a powerful deterrent to black applicants through the mid-1980s.[74]

Apart from white racism, negative feelings toward black police and firemen arose because of what whites perceived as "reverse discrimination" brought about mainly by affirmative action requirements. Some whites felt that blacks were being given preferential treatment, both in the hiring and promotion process and on the job. In Daytona Beach, for instance, there was the belief—and indeed, some evidence—that the first blacks hired by the fire department scored below the minimum for acceptance on the civil service exam. As part of the city's affirmative action program, the "rule of three" was in effect, whereby the final three applicants for a city job had to include the black applicant scoring highest on the civil service exam, regardless of the number of whites who may have achieved higher scores.[75] This rule and similar procedures for promotion were challenged in court by aggrieved whites in both Daytona and Riviera Beach.[76] In addition, there was the contention that some blacks who had reported to work late had received little or no disciplinary action.[77] Furthermore, some whites viewed the federal CETA program, under which blacks were hired in several of the departments, a "handout" program in which unqualified minorities gained jobs. These feelings of reverse discrimination by whites increased their resentment toward blacks and negatively affected race relations within several departments.

Another factor that contributed to the relatively low level of hiring of black personnel in the late seventies and eighties was a change in the emphasis of affirmative action programs. The original commitment of federal affirmative action, especially in the South, was to blacks. But by the late 1970s, federal and state requirements, as well as the policies of local governments, had begun to shift toward assisting other groups with a history of employment discrimination. Women, Hispanics, and Vietnam veterans were increasingly favored and employed in police and fire departments, and many males, both black and white, became disgruntled over the increased competition from these other minorities.[78] In addition to modifications in affirmative action, local budget constraints and the discontinuation of the public service CETA program in 1981 resulted in some reductions in the number of black employees, especially in the poorer Old South communities.

Finally, there seemed to be a general recognition among many blacks and whites that blatant discriminatory barriers to public employment had been removed in most of these communities, and now it was up to blacks to take the initiative in seeking municipal jobs. As a result, the black community exerted less political pressure to persuade police and fire departments to actively seek out and hire minorities. "The lack of black firemen and policemen is not a widely discussed issue anymore," said one black leader in Titusville. "There are just not many qualified blacks who want these jobs. And there are no obvious barriers to blacks getting these jobs."[79] A black councilman in one of the Old South communities echoed these sentiments: "Black city employment has not improved, but I can't blame the department heads. There's a lack of interest and concern by blacks in the work force and that's the major problem."[80]

Clearly the increased employment of blacks in these departments was an important goal. Yet the proportion of black firemen and police is only one general indicator of the level of protective services afforded black areas, and it is not always one of the best. The condition of streets, the quality of housing, and the level of poverty in these areas are other important variables affecting these services. Although in the 1970s improvements in these areas were made in all of the communities, in 1985 a significant degree of economic disparity between white and black citizens remained, and translated itself into the greater vulnerability of most blacks to fires and crime. Firemen claimed that both the higher rate of false alarms and the poor directions to fires that often still came from the black community reduced the response times of the departments. In addition, there was still in black areas, less crime prevention, less maintenance and departmental inspection of homes (which must be requested by homeowners), and greater carelessness leading to fires. Despite consistent improvement over the decades since 1960, poor housing was still a prominent feature of black neighborhoods, especially in the Old South (see table 4.2), and continued to create serious fire hazards. In 1979 in Lake City, for example, the state fire marshal's report on housing in the black area cited numerous safety violations, labeling the homes "firetraps,"[81] and every winter there were still cases of blacks dying in "shacks" which "go up in flames in a matter of minutes."[82] The loss in the 1980s of federal CDBGs for housing rehabilitation in Crestview and Gretna significantly reduced the chances for improved minority housing in those cities. Moreover, police patrols in most black areas were still not commensurate with the levels of crime found in these neighborhoods, and there continued to be a double standard when it came to law enforcement for blacks. According to a black leader in Titusville: "Police even today don't come into 'colored town' as much as other areas, whether it's stray dogs or black drunks."[83] Similarly, a Daytona black claimed: "Police still leave drugs to the niggers. They don't care about blacks."[84]

Summary

One of the immediate goals of the southern civil rights movement was the improvement of protective services, particularly police protection, for blacks. While fire services have probably been more equally shared than most other municipal services, blacks have long suffered both from a lack of law enforcement and from an undue amount of police brutality. The results of this study indicate that moderate improvements, both in employment and in service availability, did occur in both police and fire protection and that the increased politicization of blacks was an important factor in bringing about these changes.

Prior to the 1960s, fire protection in small cities and towns was provided by all-volunteer groups which were often ill-equipped. Police departments, too, were relatively small and unprofessional. While blacks were not allowed to join these all-volunteer fire forces, most police departments hired their first black officer sometime during the 1950s. However, these black police were clearly treated as second-class officers, patrolling only black neighborhoods and arresting only black citizens. This reluctance to hire blacks reflected not only the southern legacy of refusing to give blacks responsible jobs, but also the white fear of working with blacks (and in the case of fire departments somewhat later, the even greater fear of having to sleep in the same quarters with blacks). The provision of fire services was not blatantly discriminatory, but the lack of other basic public services (paved streets, streetlighting, water lines, and fire hydrants) as well as poor housing and certain institutional factors, often served to impede fire protection for blacks, especially in Old South communities. In contrast, police protection for blacks was clearly discriminatory; black neighborhoods were seriously underpatrolled and police brutality was an important and widespread issue.

Beginning in the 1960s and extending into the 1970s, changes took place that improved both fire and police protection for blacks. More street paving, improved water service, housing rehabilitation programs, increased professionalization of departments, and the construction of substations in or near black areas all served to enhance fire service. By the early 1970s, moreover, most fire departments had hired their first blacks. This was a major breakthrough, since these departments were typically the most resistant of city services to black employment. As for police departments, the proportion of black officers and numbers of black promotions increased only moderately, even in the more progressive New South cities. Nevertheless, by the early 1970s police patrols were usually integrated and black officers were allowed to arrest white citizens. The New South communities tended to develop police–community-relations programs and increased patrolling in the high-crime black neighborhoods. In addition, incidents of police brutality toward blacks declined in most municipalities. Although improvements in black employment or protective services were usually greatest in majority-black communities, cities with medium and low percentages of blacks typically experienced few differences in the level of service improvements. These findings tend to support Keech's claims of a curvilinear relationship between the relative size of the black population and gains in public services.

None of these changes in protective services occurred quickly or easily. Several political forces, particularly increased political activity by blacks, were instrumental in affecting changes in black employment. Most important by far were the increased percentages of black elected officials, who were very effective in encouraging the hiring and promotion of black police and firefighters. At the same time, white counter-organizations served to depress black employment, often contending that preferential treatment for black applicants was unfair to whites. Unconventional political activity in the form of black protests and violence had no long-term direct effect on the protective services, but sometimes helped mobilize blacks, and so led indirectly to increased election of blacks to office. The direct effects of protest and violence were immediate and often positive but short-term. The federal government, surprisingly, had no long-term impact on black employment either, though CETA and CDBG helped in the latter 1970s to improve both employment and housing for blacks. Other factors that seemed to play an important role in improving protective services included support from various white leaders (especially public officials), increased professionalism in city government, and the addition of more modern equipment.

Despite gains in black protective services and employment in the 1960s and early 1970s, such progress slowed by the late 1970s and early 1980s. This slowdown was most notable in the hiring and retention of black firefighters and police, since relatively fewer blacks applied for such positions and the turnover rate among blacks was high. This slowing of earlier gains in black employment came about because of a variety of factors, including some institutionally discriminatory application requirements, relatively low pay, better job opportunities in the private sector, few promotional opportunities, strict codes of behavior and discipline requirements, lingering white racism, and negative feelings toward blacks in most departments in response to alleged reverse discrimination. In addition, the emphases of affirmative action programs were modified to include other minorities, and federal cutbacks in CETA and local budget constraints reduced black employment in general. Moreover, black officials and organizations, having seen blatant forms of discrimination in public employment removed, applied less political pressure on protective services.

In areas other than employment, fire and police service for blacks continued to improve to some degree through the mid-1980s, as departments increased both their professionalism and their acquisition of more modern equipment. With overt discriminatory practices and police brutality much reduced, and with blacks now emphasizing political tactics other than organized protests and violence, police and firefighter relations with black citizens have tended to ease. Yet while significant progress has been made in the protective services in the last several decades, largely because of the civil rights movement, blacks have still not achieved employment or service equality with most whites.

5

Other Public Services and The Politicization of Blacks: Streets and Recreation

> Street paving is particularly poor for blacks, and street maintenance as well. Many whites just feel they don't need to give blacks as much.
> —Black official, Crestview

> Recreation is probably one of the most important public services for blacks, since a large number of black youths, unemployed and out of high-crime areas, are kept off the streets by this.
> —Black official, Daytona Beach

Although police and fire protection are life-preserving services that assume a high priority in most communities, other municipal services are valued highly. One of these services is streets. In a survey conducted in sixty-four communities across the United States, road conditions and maintenance ranked eighth in a list of twenty-five major problem areas mentioned most frequently by residents and leaders.[1] Streets provide a functional service as well as an aesthetic feature for most neighborhoods. Another significant public service is parks and recreation. Americans are very conscious of this public good, as it provides not only an improvement in the quality of life but, as in the case of streets and drainage, often affects property values and even health conditions.

Blacks in particular have been highly sensitive to the provision of good-quality streets and recreation. In a 1970s survey of citizen priorities in seven major cities, Floyd Fowler found that blacks ranked street conditions fourth and parks and recreation sixth on a list of ten service areas. Blacks were also much more concerned than whites about improvements in streets, parks, and recreation.[2] In addition, according to the *Report of the National Advisory Commission on Civil Disorders* (1968), inadequate recreational facilities and programs were major concerns of blacks in communities that experienced race riots in the 1960s. The only grievances ranking ahead of recreation were police practices, unemployment, housing, and education.[3]

For blacks in the South, streets have traditionally been a major issue at the local level. Street paving and maintenance often ended at the boundary of the black section of town; such service discrimination was a visible reminder of the inferior status of blacks. In the classic 1971 federal court case involving Shaw, Mississippi, nearly 98 percent of the town's houses without paved streets were occupied by blacks.[4] The black neighborhood lacked most other municipal services as well, and thus Shaw's black section became the archetype of what it was like to live "on the wrong side of the tracks" in a southern community.

Parks and recreation have also long been sources of deep dissatisfaction for southern blacks. Parks, playgrounds, beaches, and other public recreational facilities were usually closed completely to blacks, and often no separate facilities, or only very inferior ones, were offered them. In the words of sociologist Gunnar Myrdal, who investigated southern recreational services in the early 1940s: "Southern whites are unconcerned about how Negroes use their leisure time, as long as they are kept out of the whites' parks and beaches. Recreation involves 'social' relationships, and, therefore, southern whites are strongly opposed to mixed recreation."[5] Myrdal also claimed that many blacks felt that "great damage" was done to black youths by the lack of recreational outlets and that providing such services should be a high priority for local minority organizations.[6] In fact, poor blacks often had a greater need for public recreational facilities than most whites, who could better afford commercial entertainment or transportation to state parks, lakes, and ocean beaches.

For this reason another short-term goal of the civil rights movement was the improvement of basic municipal services for blacks, and among these services the condition of streets, parks, and recreation were often foremost. Yet the role of political participation in improving these services is still an unresolved issue. Studies in the 1970s of the distribution of local street quality in Houston and Oakland concluded that politics was not an important factor and that distribution could best be attributed to institutionalized decision rules.[7] These rules were based on an "extremely complex mixture of benefits, cost, and scheduling considerations."[8] Investigations of city park and recreational services offer more mixed findings, but few studies showed any consistent pattern of discrimination against poor, politically powerless, or non-Anglo neighborhoods.[9] Indeed, Robert Lineberry's careful analysis of both the location and quality of parks in San Antonio in the mid-1970s produced rather typical results. Lineberry found that parks were distributed according to what he characterized as "unpatterned inequalities," and that neither class, race, or political power offered much explanation.[10]

Several studies in the South, however, have found racial inequities in service distributions and have suggested that political participation can sometimes be important in changing the bureaucratic rules that affect the distribution of street and recreational services. These studies claimed that black voting in particular was instrumental in gaining improved services for blacks.[11] Paving a few streets was a favorite way for white politicians to "pay off" blacks for their electoral support. But even here political influence could be limited by local rules and procedures for street paving and maintenance. Keech reported, for example, that in Durham, North Carolina, city rules stipulated that citizens had to pay for their own street paving. As a result, getting one's street paved depended less on political influence than on one's socioeconomic status and on one's ability to persuade neighbors that they too should help pay.[12]

The black vote apparently played a role in improving recreational facilities for blacks as well. Bond-issue elections in particular were a "crucial channel of influence" for blacks because they posed a clear referendum on recreation and other projects.[13] But integration of parks was considerably more difficult to achieve than a fair distribution of parkland, and here black voting was not very effective. Desegregation of facilities was often accomplished only by the prospect of court litigation or by the threat of mass protest.[14]

Although these studies are suggestive, very little is known about the impact of the southern civil rights movement on basic municipal services. This chapter will investigate the distribution and quality of street and recreation services over time in the six communities, showing the extent to which these services have changed for blacks since 1960. Black employment in these city departments, a general indicator of racial equity, will also be explored. Most importantly, an attempt will be made to ascertain what role various political factors, especially black political participation, may have played in these service changes.

From Dusty Roads to Paved Streets

In the late 1950s and early 1960s, conditions of streets in the black sections of the six communities were deplorable. This was especially true for both blacks and whites in the poorer Old South communities. In Crestview, a city councilman wrote a letter to the local newspaper editor in 1960 complaining that "this city is full of sand streets being washed away with every rain. We work feverishly to repair this damage and are swamped with calls to 'do something with the ditch in front of my house.' "[15] The city, however, lacked the revenue to buy the heavy equipment necessary to refill washed-out roads. As a result of this condition and the lack of storm drainage, store owners in Crestview reportedly erected barricades in front of their doors and used mops and brooms to prevent heavy rains from invading their stores.[16] For blacks, the poor quality of the streets was felt even more keenly. As a black elected official in Gretna recalled: "There were terrible living conditions here when I was growing up. When it rained, I couldn't even get to my trailer home because the dirt roads were washed out or flooded."[17] Even the grading of dirt streets in black areas was haphazard or nonexistent.

Among well-informed citizens, poor roads were mentioned by both blacks and whites as the most serious municipal service issue faced by most of these communities over the period from the late 1950s to the mid-1970s. But poor roads usually denoted a variety of other conditions, each of which affected access to an area to some degree, and which taken together could seriously worsen living conditions. Areas which lacked street paving were often deficient in drainage, sidewalks, streetlights, and street signs, conditions that tended to hamper responses of emergency vehicles, especially fire and police services. During the rainy season, standing water on unpaved streets with no drainage was a potential health hazard.[18] Thus poor street conditions, along with a lack of other services associated with streets, not only resulted in substandard living conditions but also threatened the life and property of residents. Finally, the lack of such basic services tended to retard a community's growth and discourage new and beneficial commercial development.

Specifically what was the condition of streets in each of these communities, especially in the black neighborhoods, and to what extent did these conditions improve over the twenty-five year period between 1960 and 1985? Street paving is an excellent quantitative indicator of street services and one that is attainable relatively easily. Table 5.1 summarizes the data on street paving in both black and white areas for each of the six communities over these years.[19] The data indicate that the proportion of streets paved in the black subcommunities was very low in 1960 (the average was an estimated 20 percent), but that the proportion improved moderately in all cities by 1970 (to an average of 34 percent) and rather dramatically by 1985 (up to 81 percent). Thus an estimated 80 percent of the black population in these cities

TABLE 5.1

Percentage of Streets Paved in Black and White Subcommunities (1960–1985)

	1960		*1970*		*1980*		*1985*		*Percentage Absolute Change (1960–85)*[a]		*Percentage Relative Change (1960–85)*[b]
Communities	Black	White	Black	White	Black	White	Black	White	Black	White	
Crestview	12%	38%	30%	54%	52%	70%	65%	85%	53%	47%	−6
Lake City	10	50	20	70	44	87	75	90	65	40	−25
Gretna	0	20	53	0	51	40	51	40	51	20	−31
Titusville	10	92	40	80	97	91	99	98	89	6	−83
Daytona Beach	50	97	70	99	99	100	99	100	49	3	−46
Riviera Beach	37	85	40	90	98	100	99	100	62	15	−47

SOURCES: Data on street paving in 1960 were not available in official public records. Therefore the 1960 figures are estimates based on newspaper reports, interviews with longtime departmental officials, and later public records. Data for the later years were retrieved from newspaper reports, departmental records, federal grant applications, engineering studies, and in one case, our own windshield survey.

[a] The percentage of absolute change is computed by subtracting the percentage of streets paved in 1960 from the 1985 percentage.

[b] The percentage of relative change is derived by subtracting the absolute change figure for the black subcommunity from the comparable figure for the white subcommunity. A negative change indicates that increases in street paving for blacks has been greater than that for whites and that racial disparities have declined.

lived in areas without paved streets in 1960, but by 1985 only about 20 percent of blacks still lived in areas that lacked paving.

In predominantly white areas in these communities, the average proportion of streets paved was always greater than it was for black areas. In 1960, paving in white areas was estimated at 64 percent, and this increased moderately to 71 percent in 1970 and to 86 percent by 1985. Only Titusville experienced a modest decline in the proportion of streets paved in 1970 and 1980 because of its large-scale annexations of adjacent territory, some of which was underdeveloped. In terms of absolute changes over this time period, however, it is clear that street paving occurred more frequently (proportionately) in black than in white subcommunities, especially during the 1970s and early 1980s. Hence the relative change figures, which compare absolute change rates over the twenty-five-year period for blacks and whites, indicate that the differences in street paving between black and white areas have narrowed in all communities.

The results in table 5.1 also show differences according to the typology of communities. Most rates of absolute change in street paving for blacks, and certainly relative change rates, were greater in the New South than in the Old South. The more affluent New South cities could more easily fund infrastructure improvements. But part of this difference may also have been because in the New South a high proportion (an estimated 91 percent) of streets in the white areas had already been paved by 1960, so paving resources could be allocated more easily to the black neighborhoods without detracting notably from white sections. On the other hand, in poorer Old South communities only an estimated 36 percent of streets were paved in the white areas in 1960. Thus in the Old South the street-service needs of many whites were almost as great as those of blacks, and while absolute change rates still favored blacks, relative improvements in streets in black areas were much lower here than in the New South.

In terms of the size of the black population in these communities, there were only minor differences in rates of street paving between 1960 and 1985. In apparent support of Keech's hypothesis, the medium-proportion black cities (Lake City and Daytona Beach), where whites may have felt most threatened, showed somewhat lower absolute change rates for blacks up to 1980 than did either the low- or high-proportion black communities. But Lake City carried out a great deal of paving in black sections in the early 1980s with federal grant monies, and in Daytona a relatively high proportion of streets in black areas were already paved by 1960, thus artificially limiting potential change rates. Also contrary to Keech's findings, absolute and relative changes in street paving were somewhat less, on average, in the two majority-black communities (Gretna and Riviera Beach) than in the two cities with relatively small black populations (Crestview and Titusville).

While street paving for blacks had improved markedly in each of these communities by 1985, unpaved roads were still a major problem in the Old South. Almost 40 percent of the streets in the black neighborhoods of these cities were still unpaved, and road conditions were generally very poor. In Crestview, heavy rains periodically washed away many of the unpaved streets, making them impassable and creating high maintenance costs. In one three-month period alone in 1979, Crestview's public works department hauled 942 loads of dirt to fill in washed-out roads, many of which were in the predominantly black section, and the costs of street maintenance were estimated at $100,000 per year.[20]

New South cities, in contrast, had paved almost all their streets in both the black and white areas by 1980. Although a few black areas in these cities still lacked adequate drainage, sidewalks, or streetlights, the most important street-service issue was now the resurfacing and maintenance of paved streets. Even on this issue, however, officials in the New South generally remained more sensitive to the needs and demands of the black community. In Daytona Beach, for example, street resurfacing had become the major emphasis of the streets division of the public works department by the late 1970s. Between 1979 and 1981, thirteen miles of streets were resurfaced, with 37 percent of the resurfacing done in predominately black areas, a percentage somewhat higher than the proportion of blacks in the population. Daytona officials were obviously concerned that such street resurfacing be allocated equitably, and a public works department memo delineated the plans for such resurfacing not just by street and geographical area but by racial area as well.[21] Officials in other New South cities also proved to be sensitive to these racial issues. As a high-level white official in Titusville commented in 1981: "There are still some black complaints about open ditches and unpaved streets. These conditions are a special symbol to blacks, and they must be alleviated."[22]

Although significant progress in street paving for blacks was made over this time period, it is important to inquire as to *why* these streets were so poorly paved and maintained until relatively recently. The answer to this question is not as simple as it may seem. Surely racial discrimination was one factor, and the results of interviews with knowledgeable citizens indicated that this was an important factor. A black official in Crestview claimed, for example, that street grading, paving, and maintenance were very poor for blacks because "many whites just feel that they don't need to give blacks as much."[23] Blacks had always been considered second-class citizens and the neglect of streets in black areas was just one more vivid reminder of this historical legacy.

Yet there were other reasons for this neglect of streets in the black sections. Because poor blacks were viewed as paying relatively small proportions of local taxes, public officials and others generally deemed blacks less worthy to receive city services. A 1960 *Daytona Beach Evening News* editorial, citing major problems in the predominantly black area, stated this popular belief forthrightly: "It [the black area] has slums from which come practically no tax money. So [it] can't claim a share of the city budget to meet the area's needs."[24] This argument ignores the reality of indirect taxes and the generally regressive nature of local taxation, and thus exaggerates the claim that blacks pay practically no taxes. Nonetheless, this view was widely believed. Another explanation for the different levels of street paving had to do with the financing of this service. Most of these communities had street assessment plans whereby property owners petitioned to have their streets paved and were then assessed a portion (usually 25 to 50 percent) of the costs of paving, while the city paid the balance. This plan was used to help cities finance the expenses of such major capital improvements. But poor blacks were often unable to afford the street assessment; therefore they failed to petition and their streets remained unpaved. Private developers sometimes paved streets and included that expense in the costs of the housing development. However, since little or no private development took place in blighted black neighborhoods, roads in these sections remained undeveloped by private interests.

Whatever the reasons for the relatively poor condition of streets in black neighborhoods, many whites tended to perceive the inequality more in economic than in racial terms. "Blacks were just too poor to apply for street paving on the assessment program, so their streets were not paved as much—it's really more of an economic problem," claimed a white Crestview businessman.[25] In Lake City, a white public official put it more bluntly: "One of the problems with the colored section is they want something for nothing. Most whites paid for a portion of the expense of the road in front of their house, so why can't blacks do the same?"[26] Thus the traditional justifications for discrimination in basic public services still held sway, particularly in the Old South. Since blacks were so poor and paid virtually no taxes, it was felt they were not entitled to receive more services than whites cared to give them or than they were able to pay for directly. Hence whatever local services were provided to blacks were considered by whites to be the result of their own beneficence, and blacks had no right to demand more.[27] No doubt some whites continue to cling to this traditional explanation for the lower quality of services to blacks.

Parks and Recreation: Modest Shift toward Greater Equality

Like streets, city parks and public recreation in general were in relatively poor condition and undeveloped in 1960, especially in the Old South. Objective data confirm this assessment. Neighborhood park acreage, for example, is a relatively valid and easily obtainable indicator of recreation distribution.[28] Table 5.2 presents a summary of municipal park acreage for black and white neighborhoods for each of the communities. As shown in the table, none of the poorer Old South communities had developed public parks by 1960, while all three New South cities had parks in both the white and black areas. These parks, however, were completely segregated by race, and in proportion to population size, black neighborhoods usually had fewer acres of parkland than white neighborhoods.

Public parks and recreation programs were slow to develop in the relatively small, impoverished Old South communities. Typically, the only parks in 1960, if there were any at all, were privately owned and developed. In Crestview, for example, the Okaloosa County Negro Civic Club purchased land in the early 1950s to develop a park in the black section. Originally referred to as the "Colored Recreation Grounds," the park, later named Fairview, was slowly developed by the Negro Civic Club, which raised the necessary money through private donations, club dues, fund-raising activities, and rental fees charged for use of the park by outside black groups. The city government began to pay thirty dollars a month to help with the operational expenses of this park, and eventually it was deeded to the city so that it could continue to receive this vital public assistance.[29] Whites, too, often developed private parks in the Old South.

However, most blacks in the Old South had no formal recreational activities or parks prior to the 1960s. Most black youths (and adults as well) had to seek their own recreation. "Blacks were expected to keep to their own side of town, which meant swimming in an old water hole or playing basketball with an old hoop nailed onto a tree," claimed one black Lake Citian.[30] While white youths sometimes followed a similar course, they usually were able to supply greater variation and quality in their recreation. According to a white businessman in Crestview,

TABLE 5.2

Municipal Park Acreage for Black and White Subcommunities (1960–1985)

	1960		*1970*		*1980*		*1985*		*Absolute Change (1960–85)*[b]		*Relative Change (1960–85)*[c]
Communities[a]	Black	White	Black	White	Black	White	Black	White	Black	White	
Crestview	0	0	3.17	3.15	2.93	4.22	2.93	4.22	2.93	4.22	+1.29
Lake City	0	0	0.60	0.97	0.88	3.30	2.19	3.30	2.19	3.30	+1.11
Gretna	0	0	0	0	4.70	0	9.96	0	9.96	0	−9.96
Titusville	1.39	0.32	0.72	1.97	1.42	2.10	1.42	2.10	0.03	1.78	+1.75
Daytona Beach	1.61	2.38	1.33	2.96	1.36	2.66	1.36	2.66	−0.25	0.28	+0.53
Riviera Beach	0.88	1.58	1.48	3.52	1.81	2.67	1.81	2.67	0.93	1.09	+0.16

SOURCES: Newspaper reports, municipal records, interviews with departmental officials, and city Comprehensive Plans.

[a] Park acreage controls for size of population (number of acres per 1,000 persons) and is of developed neighborhood parks; it does not include school playgrounds, mini-parks (less than one acre), or community-wide recreational facilities which are accessible to all citizens.

[b] The absolute change is computed by subtracting the park acreage in 1960 from the 1985 acreage figures.

[c] The relative change is derived by subtracting the absolute change figure for the black subcommunity from the comparable figure for the white subcommunity. A negative change indicates that increases in park acreage for blacks have been greater than that for whites.

"Whites always could provide more of their own recreation than could blacks. Whites had more access to state parks and to the Gulf."[31]

While all three New South cities had public parks by 1960, those in the black neighborhoods were usually relatively small and poorly maintained. In Riviera Beach, where there was only one small park in the black section, black groups in the early 1960s consistently appealed to the city council to construct more recreational facilities. The council ignored such requests, claiming no funds were available.[32] Even racially progressive Daytona Beach, with two city parks dating back to the 1930s in the black neighborhoods, did not always maintain its recreational facilities well. In 1949, for example, the two swimming pools in the black parks were closed temporarily because they did not meet the sanitation standards required by the State Health Department.[33] The black parks, moreover, were typically last in the city's list of recreational development priorities.[34] Thus it was not surprising that in an early 1960s' survey of citizen attitudes in Daytona concerning health, police, and recreational facilities, only in the provision of recreation did blacks express markedly more dissatisfaction than whites.[35]

Unlike more basic public services such as police protection, water and sewage, and streets, recreation was not perceived by most well-informed citizens as an essential service or as a particularly salient political issue. Consequently, during the 1960s and 1970s, municipal parks and recreation programs for blacks showed only modest improvements. Although black park acreage increased absolutely in all the communities except Daytona Beach, park acreage in the white areas increased even more rapidly, even when controlling for population increases (see table 5.2). Hence relative increases in public parks from 1960 to 1985 favored whites in every community except Gretna.

In terms of community groupings, black neighborhoods in the Old South gained more parks than did those in the New South even controlling for Gretna. However, this surprising finding was due partly to the fact that there were no public parks in the Old South communities in 1960, so that the development of even some recreational areas was a substantial increase. Also, the New South cities typically had more community-wide parks (not counted in table 5.2) and municipal beaches than the Old South. The size of the black population also seemed to make some difference. In support of Keech's contentions, it was found that the majority-black communities experienced the greatest overall increases in parkland, while the medium-proportion black cities achieved the smallest absolute and relative gains.

Crestview again illustrates the modest changes in parks and recreation for black areas compared to white neighborhoods. During the

1960s the Crestview City Council, under some pressure from the black community, allocated several small grants, ranging from $230 to $1,000, for improvements of Fairview Park. At the same time the council budgeted $6,000 to purchase land for the development of a sizable park (20.6 acres) for whites.[36] In the 1970s the council continued to allocate modest amounts of funds for needed renovations and improvements in Fairview. By contrast, it funded a new recreation center for whites and allocated $150,000 toward the construction of the Sikes Library.[37] While the new recreation center and library were ostensibly for the use of everyone in the city, they were located far from the black section and were therefore inaccessible to most blacks.

Only in Gretna did increases in park acreage for blacks outstrip that for whites during these decades. Even in Gretna, however, such changes occurred only after blacks assumed political control in the early 1970s. At that point, the town's black officials purchased six acres of land to be developed as a park in the black area. But with poverty plaguing the town, no park development occurred until the acquisition of a federal grant in 1979.[38] Whites in Gretna received no public parks, but a number of white families belonged to a private, segregated country club located just outside of town.

Distribution and amount of park acreage is, of course, only one indicator of the level of park and recreation services. The quality of public parks, although difficult to measure, is another indicator. Several sources of data clearly suggest that park quality improved markedly in black neighborhoods in the New, but not the Old, South. Though park acreage for blacks did not change significantly in the New South cities from 1960 to 1985, qualitative changes did take place. In Titusville, Sylvan Park in the black section was redeveloped at a cost of $198,000 in 1973, and a tennis court was added later in the decade. These improvements were financed primarily through federal HUD grants.[39] Black parks in Daytona Beach also underwent extensive renovations. The Campbell Street Community Center was rebuilt in the latter 1970s at an estimated cost of $300,000, giving blacks one of the best-equipped recreation centers in the city. Besides improved recreational facilities, a black-history library, free legal services, a cultural center, and two vocational programs were added to the Campbell Street center. In the early 1980s the Cypress Street Park, the other major recreational area for blacks, also underwent extensive rehabilitation. These renovations were all funded primarily by federal grants.[40]

In contrast, few qualitative changes were made in Old South community parks. The conditions there continued to be similar to those in other small southern cities. As reported in a study by E. Franklin Frazier in 1940, "the dominant white group in these areas simply pay little or no attention to the recreational needs of Negroes."[41] The few improvements that did take place were primarily the result of self-help efforts by blacks. In Lake City, blacks had no developed recreational area until 1964, when several black businessmen, teachers, and ministers pooled their resources to purchase a ten-acre park site. Further donations by blacks were used to fence the park (called Annie Mattox) and to develop a baseball field. Efforts to raise enough funds to construct a swimming pool at the park failed. In 1970 blacks deeded two acres of Annie Mattox to the city in hopes of obtaining public support for improvements to the park. The city did install some playground equipment and picnic shelters, but made no other improvements and provided little park maintenance. Nonetheless, blacks obtained federal grants beginning in 1972 for a manpower training program at the park, and grant funds helped provide maintenance. Later in the decade blacks were able to upgrade Annie Mattox by selling two acres of the original tract and using the money to help construct a basketball court, a tennis court, and a small recreation building.[42]

Desegregation of Recreational Facilities

While the development and improvement of black-only parks and recreation programs were important to many black citizens, perhaps an even more significant issue in the 1960s and 1970s was the desegregation of white recreational facilities. Not only were segregated parks a vivid reminder to blacks of their second-class status, but the usually larger and well-developed white parks offered better recreational opportunities for blacks. Nowhere was such desegregation a potentially more explosive issue than at the municipal beaches in the New South. Whites tended to view the beach as a recreational area that "historically and traditionally had been used exclusively by white people."[43] For blacks to come into this area would represent a major break with established norms. But whites also feared the possible threat to tourism, since the presence of blacks on the beach might lead to conflict with white visitors and frighten other tourists away. For cities like Daytona Beach, where tourism was an important component of the local economy, such desegregation was seen as having potentially dire economic consequences.[44]

Integration of the public beaches was therefore a slow and often difficult process. In Daytona, for example, the threat of court suits by blacks and the intervention of the Interracial Advisory Committee had been instrumental in the early 1960s in desegregating the municipal golf course and seating at the city baseball park. But the interracial committee was fearful of even discussing the beach issue. Blacks, too, recognized the seriousness of trying to desegregate the beach, and realized that conflict there might result in greater economic hardships for blacks. Whites, moreover, often harassed blacks who attempted to use the beach, and city police usually assumed a laissez-faire attitude that tended to encourage white hecklers. Yet black Daytonans persisted in going to the beach on occasion and, led by Bethune-Cookman faculty and students, continued to challenge segregation. Whites, aware of the legal right of blacks to use a public recreation area and fearful of planned black demonstrations that might erupt into violence, slowly began to relent and eventually allowed blacks greater access to the beach.[45]

Another recreational issue that often created intense conflict between the races was desegregation of municipal swimming pools. Whites generally opposed the integration of any facility that brought about greater racial mixing of youths. In addition, many whites believed that allowing blacks to use public pools would somehow "contaminate" the pools, making them undesirable for use by anyone else. Hence whites strongly resisted the desegregation of municipal pools, and most communities that enjoyed such facilities had either a segregated pool in the white section or racially separate pools in white and black neighborhoods. As one would expect, the process of desegregating these pools began earlier and proceeded more smoothly in the New South than it did in the Old South. Of course, some Old South communities such as Gretna were simply too poverty-stricken to even consider the construction of a public pool.

Where municipal pools were available in the Old South, the mere thought of desegregation quickly heightened racial anxieties among whites. The case of Lake City clearly illustrates this point. Since the late 1950s, white Lake Citians had enjoyed a swimming pool at Youngs Park originally constructed by the Lions Club but deeded to the city in the 1960s. The pool was for whites only, and blacks were severely harassed and sometimes threatened if they dared venture near the pool. Blacks attempted to raise enough funds to build their own pool, and to avoid the issue of integrating the white pool, the county offered matching funds to encourage the effort. The fund drive by poor blacks failed, however. Throughout the 1960s and early 1970s the city repeatedly raised and then dashed hopes for a pool in the black area. Often the subject of whites' campaign promises, the pool was seen as a way to placate blacks, but city fathers were never willing to invest the large amount of money required to build it.[46] Only after years of criticism and persistence from blacks did whites begin to allow them to use the Youngs Park pool in the mid-1970s. Even then whites sought to discourage black access by limiting pool use to instructional periods only. When this subterfuge failed and blacks continued using the pool, the city decided to close the pool altogether, arguing that maintenance costs were too great. It was the mid-1980s before the city, with the help of a state grant, constructed an Olympic-size pool in a centrally located area. Even then there was some talk at first about the "water turning another color" if blacks used the pool, but before long both races began swimming at the facility.[47]

Although desegregation of municipal pools was achieved more easily in New South cities, racial fears concerning this issue were present there as well. Early on, Daytona Beach and Riviera Beach built swimming pools in the black neighborhoods, a strategy designed to keep blacks off the beach and away from pools in the white areas. This strategy was generally successful, but by the early 1960s blacks began to clamor for integrated recreational facilities, including pools. The same black demands were heard in Titusville, too, where the only city pool was for whites only. Because of black insistence upon recognition of their legal right, plus white fear of possible black demonstrations, Daytona Beach and Titusville passed city ordinances in the mid-1960s allowing integration of public facilities, including parks. Even then desegregation of city pools was slow, since blacks and whites usually preferred to swim in their own neighborhoods. Where blacks did venture to swim in nearby, formerly white pools, racial conflicts sometimes occurred, and some whites fled to the beach or to private pools. Whites, on the other hand, very rarely sought to swim in pools in black neighborhoods.[48]

Parks and Recreation in the 1980s

By the early 1980s, the quantity and quality of parkland had clearly improved for blacks over what it had been in the 1960s, but parks for whites had, in most cases, been expanded and improved more rapidly. This disparity was especially apparent in the Old South, where black parks and recreational programs continued to be sadly neglected in favor of facilities and programs in white neighborhoods. Gretna, of course, was an exception, since black political control there gave blacks unchallenged opportunities to develop recreation. In Crestview and Lake City, where blacks had little political clout, parks in the black areas remained in relatively poor condition. Crestview's city leaders, for example, still tended to see Fairview as "the black park," and little city money was allocated to it for development or maintenance. As a result of Fairview's increasing deterioration, almost all recreational programs were scheduled for the park and baseball fields in white neighborhoods.[49] This action encouraged segregated recreation and, according to Crestview's black councilman, "it reinforced the idea that Fairview is for blacks only and keeps it [the park] in bad shape."[50] In 1982 the city, partly due to an increasingly tight budget, turned over all recreation programs to private groups (a local black church was granted control over recreation at Fairview) but agreed to maintain all parks. By mid-decade, however, poor maintenance of the parks was an important political issue, and Fairview continued to be in the worst condition of all the city's recreational sites.[51]

In the New South, parks in black neighborhoods were also in less than adequate condition in the early 1980s, more because of high rates of vandalism than lack of city maintenance or funds. Indeed, vandalism was a major problem in most black areas of every community, and because of it park and recreational facilities often suffered high rates of destruction and property loss. In addition, black parks in the New South reported higher usage rates than did most other parks, since whites enjoyed a greater variety of recreational outlets. This heavy use also furthered early deterioration of facilities in black neighborhoods. Thus an amount of maintenance equal to that afforded white parks was not enough to keep most black parks in adequate condition. Exclaimed the director of recreation in Riviera Beach, "The high rate of vandalism makes it useless and expensive to keep repairing facilities on the west side [the black area]."[52]

As city budgets became tighter in the late 1970s and early 1980s, some cities reduced expenditures for park maintenance and recreation programs, and blacks in particular often suffered as a result. In Titusville, cutbacks in the recreation budget brought about the temporary closing of those parks with high maintenance costs, the major one of which was Sylvan Park Center in the black area. This closing sparked angry protests and complaints from a few blacks who charged racial discrimination, and eventually the center was reopened.[53] Riviera Beach, too, experienced budget constraints that resulted in the closing for two years of the city's only swimming pool, located in the black section, and in the reduction of summer program offerings.[54] Reductions in the federal CETA program also meant less park maintenance and fewer recreation programs in some cities.[55] Lake City, for example, closed Annie Mattox Park in 1981 when private-sector CETA cuts forced layoffs of the park's black staff.

By the mid-1980s the Old South still lagged behind the New South, and parks and many recreation programs remained almost completely segregated in Old South communities. In 1979 Lake City developed the modern and spacious Southside Recreation Center, whose location approximately four miles from the black northern section made it inaccessible to most blacks. City officials claimed they could not find available vacant land for the park closer to the minority area.[56] The investigation of Lake City by the federal Office of Revenue Sharing reported that the imposition of fees for all recreation courses (the average fee was sixteen dollars) had a probable "discriminatory effect of excluding a disproportionate number of black residents" due to the high black poverty rate.[57] Moreover, the lower quantity and quality of recreational facilities in the black section, and the poor maintenance of those facilities, tended to discourage whites from participating in programs there.[58]

In the New South, parks and recreation were considerably more integrated. Transportation and recreation fees were barriers to blacks in these communities as well, but greater efforts were made to reduce these obstacles. Titusville's recreation department charged lower fees for special programs in economically disadvantaged areas, and the city refurbished a sizable community-wide park located not far from the black section. This renovated park attracted a racially mixed population from various parts of the city.[59] Yet tradition and perhaps lingering racial fears kept swimming pools and municipal beaches largely segregated.

Black Employment in Public Works and Recreation

The employment of blacks in public service jobs is another measure of racial equity at the local level. Such employment not only provides a valuable source of income for blacks, but also confers a degree of status or prestige not found in the low-paying, menial jobs usually held by blacks. Municipalities, however, have traditionally employed blacks in the most menial positions, with little possibility of advancement to higher-paying, more prestigious posts.[60]

Findings for the streets division of public works adhere closely to this traditional norm (table 5.3). In 1960, blacks made up the majority of laborers in the streets division of each of the communities except Crestview, performing jobs that in all cases were the lowest-paying and most menial. There were no blacks in any city in administrative or supervisory positions, all of which were occupied by whites. Moreover,

TABLE 5.3
Black Employment in Public Works (Streets Division) and Recreation (1960–1985)

	Percentages of Blacks Employed									
Communities	*1960*		*1970*		*1980*		*1985*		*% Point Changes (1960–85)*	
Crestview	0[a]	—[b,c]	0[a]	—[b,c]	0[a]	33[b]	11[a]	—[b,c]	+11[a]	—[b]
Lake City	60	—[c]	60	17	60	30	50	50	−10	+50
Gretna	50	—[c]	60	—[c]	100	100	100	100	+50	+100
Titusville	50	0	50	20	61	30	63	20	+13	+20
Daytona Beach	60	44	60	35	45	33	40	25	−20	−19
Riviera Beach	60	10	60	29	82	75	100	78	+40	+68

SOURCES: Local Newspapers, public records, interviews with public personnel and officials, and federal EEO-4 forms.

[a] Percentage of blacks among all employees in the Streets Division of the Department of Public Works.

[b] Percentage of blacks among all employees in the Department of Recreation.

[c] City had no public recreation program.

blacks were usually not allowed to operate the trucks and heavy equipment used in street paving and maintenance. Apologists for this policy suggested that blacks had little education and little opportunity to learn about heavy equipment, and that such work was generally viewed as "too tedious," "too big," and "too complex" for blacks.[61] Another, probably more valid rationale was that no matter how menial the job, it was important to most whites to feel that they were at least one notch above blacks in job status, and control of the operation of heavy equipment provided this psychological advantage.

In recreation departments blacks fared somewhat better. None of the Old South communities had public recreation in the early 1960s, but in most of the New South cities blacks were employed in recreation by this period. In Daytona Beach black employees made up fully one-third of the department as early as the late 1950s. Blacks employed in recreation, however, were almost always assigned to parks in black areas, and white recreational employees worked primarily in the white neighborhoods. All top-level administrators were white, although Daytona Beach and Riviera Beach had black recreation supervisors in the black parks.[62]

By 1985 most communities had experienced only modest changes in employment in their street departments. The majority or near majority of the personnel in these divisions were still black, again except for Crestview, where poor whites competed with poor blacks for all jobs and whites traditionally held almost all public service positions. Most blacks in the streets divisions continued to be employed in the lowest-paying service or maintenance positions. Although two New South cities, Titusville and Daytona Beach, had promoted blacks into supervisory positions, and Riviera Beach had several black administrators by 1980, only Gretna among the Old South communities had any blacks above the lowest ranks.[63] Even when such promotions were made, black supervisors and foremen tended to oversee mostly blacks, not whites. Blacks were, however, more commonly found operating heavy equipment by this time.

Blacks made somewhat greater gains in recreational employment. In every city, blacks achieved an employment level of 30 percent or more by 1980, and in the majority-black communities of Gretna and Riviera Beach they comprised a large majority in the recreation departments.[64] Many of these gains, especially in the New South, were due to a sizable CETA program in the late 1970s. But in most of the communities there had been a modest commitment even beyond CETA to hire and promote blacks in recreation. By 1980, each community had one or more black supervisors, and Gretna and Riviera Beach had black recreation department directors. Nonetheless, blacks employed in recreation were still found primarily in minority neighborhood parks and tended to supervise members of their own race. According to Daytona's director of recreation, park employee assignments were designated along racial lines because "black kids pay no attention to white supervisors or to rules established by whites."[65] Similarly, and in accordance with tradition, only white lifeguards were assigned to the mostly white municipal beaches.

The "Politics" of Service Changes

It is clear that streets, parks, and recreation for blacks have improved in some measure in all communities since 1960. The number of paved streets in particular increased significantly, while changes in parks and recreation—especially the integration of facilities—came slower. Black employment in all these departments improved as well, but more modestly in public works than in recreation. It is important to determine which political factors helped to account for these personnel changes and improvements in service.[66] As in the case of protective services, multivariate and path analysis are used to indicate the relative influence of political and contextual variables.

Looking first at black employment, figures 5.1 and 5.2 present

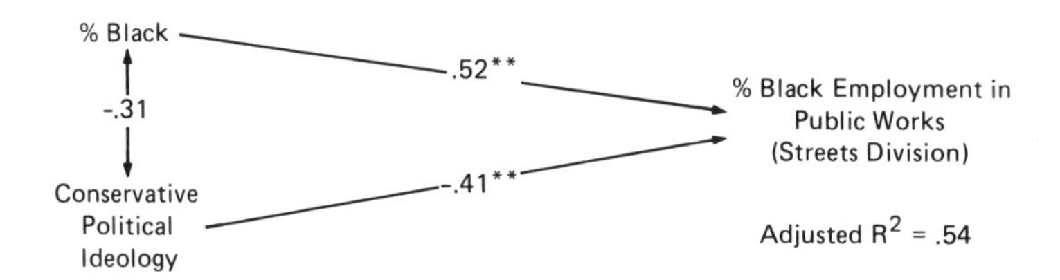

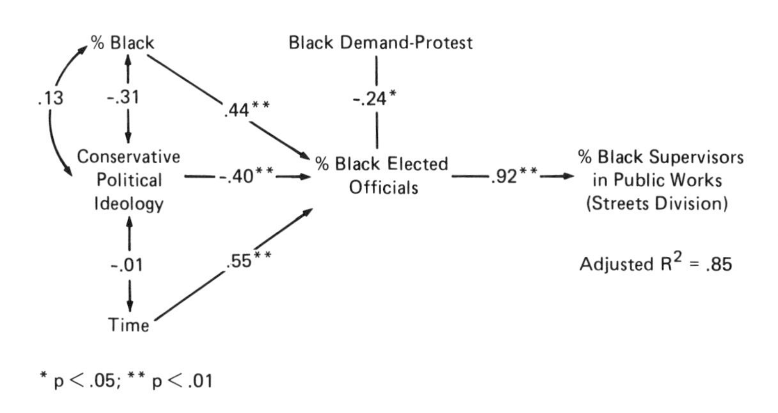

* $p < .05$; ** $p < .01$

FIGURE 5.1
Path Models of Black Employment in Public Works Departments (1960–1985)

regression models of the statistically significant variables explaining the proportions of blacks among all employees as well as among supervisors or those in higher ranks. *The percentage of black elected officials clearly has the most significant direct and positive influence in most of the models.*[67] Only for black employment in public works is the percentage of black officials not a significant factor, but as we have seen, blacks have traditionally been given the most menial and low-paying jobs in these departments. As a result, such jobs were not among those public positions most sought after by blacks. Blacks valued recreational employment and supervisory positions much more highly, and here black elected officials played an influential role. These results are similar to those found for black employment in fire and police departments, and confirm that black council members and mayors are very important in boosting not only the hiring but also the promotion of blacks. Such promotions and hirings at higher levels are particularly crucial to economic and social progress for blacks.

While the path models explain a high proportion of the variation in

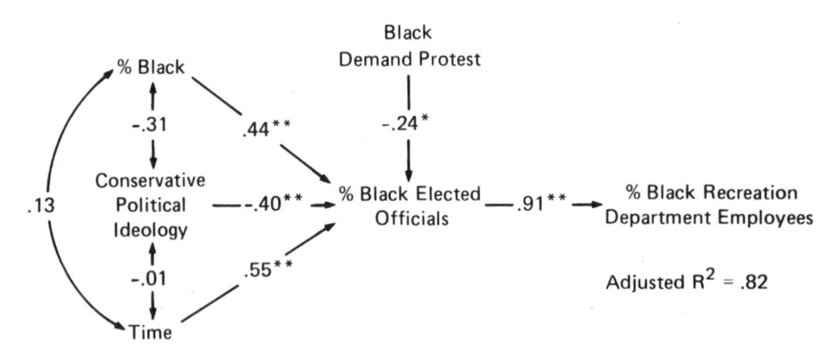

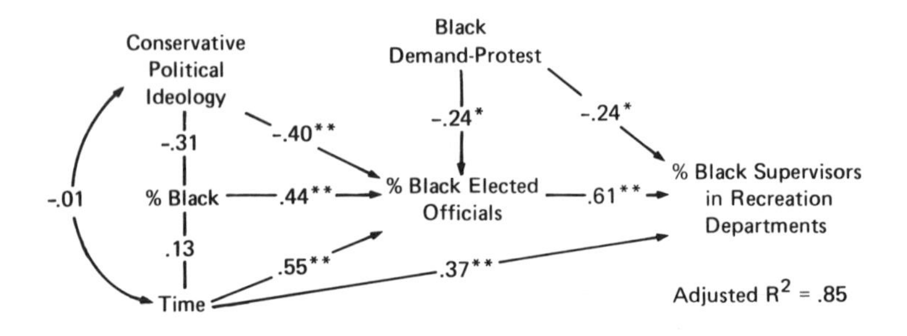

FIGURE 5.2
Path Models of Black Employment in Recreation Departments (1960–1985)

black employment (more than 80 percent in all but one model), few other political or contextual variables were significant. A more conservative political culture had an indirect (and occasionally direct) but always negative impact on black employment, suggesting that public jobs were more difficult to achieve in the conservative Old South than they were in the New South. Furthermore, the passage of time or "progress," as it might be termed, was also significantly and usually positively related to levels of employment. But the greatest influence of "progress" was normally indirect, through the increased election of blacks to local office. The final contextual variable of some importance was black resources, in the form of the black percentage of the population, but its influence, too, was mostly indirect and positive, through black officials.

The only other black political activity of significance in the path models was demand-protest. Typically, the relation of this variable to black employment, as in the case of the protective services, was indirect and negative. Its influence appears to have been one of depressing the percentage of elected black officials. However, as explained in the previous chapter, demand-protest was a primary mode of black activity in the 1960s, while the election of blacks was more a feature of the 1970s and early 1980s. These two forms of political behavior did not usually occur together to any degree. Thus the less the degree of demand-protest, the greater the tendency to elect blacks to office. Yet if multivariate relationships are explored solely for the 1960s (1960–1970), black demand-protest is found to be significantly, directly, and *positively* related to black employment, especially in recreation. In fact, this variable is much more important statistically than the percentage of black officials for this earlier period. It was during the early 1970s and after that black elected officials assumed prominence in the employment process. This finding indicates the important role of protest during the 1960s, when that was the dominant mode of political activity among blacks.

Looking beyond the issue of employment to the actual delivery of public services, factors related to paved streets and neighborhood park acreage for blacks were investigated. Figures 5.3 and 5.4 present the path model results. For these services it was important to look at not only the absolute level of service provision for blacks (percent of streets paved and amount of park acreage per population) but also the *relative distribution* of such services. This is calculated as the ratio of the absolute level of service for blacks to the absolute level for whites. Such an indicator of relative distribution suggests how blacks are doing, compared to whites, in garnering a share of available services. As mentioned previously, this is an important measure of the relative progress of blacks.

Once again the presence of *black elected officials is consistently the most significant independent variable, although more so for parks than for paved streets.*[68] This is not surprising. The provision of street paving and recreational facilities was often very political in the sense that it was one way in which council members could "bring home the bacon," or provide constituents with tangible rewards for their votes. These services were always a primary topic of concern among those who paid taxes, since they are among "the most visible signs of tax dollars at work."[69] Thus parks and streets often improved noticeably, even relative to white services, after blacks were elected to office. White officials and citizens were generally more tolerant of changes in capital-intensive, rather than labor-intensive, services,[70] since capital services could be altered by simply reallocating money, while adjustments in human services, especially those which called for racial integration, necessitated changes in white attitudes and values. As a result, even the election of black officials did not assure success in desegregating municipal

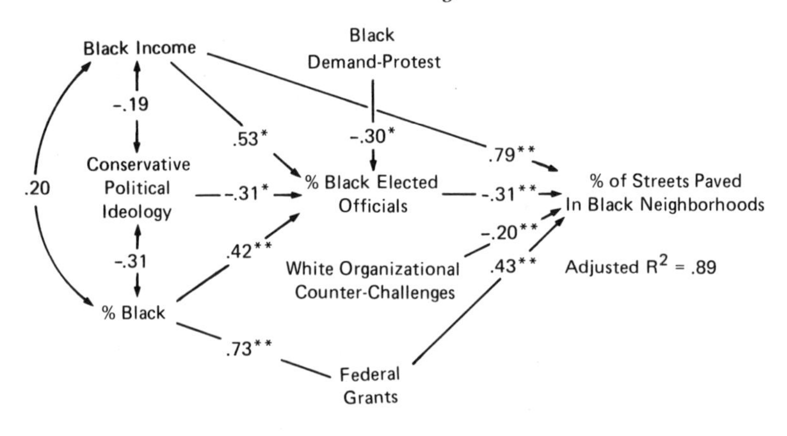

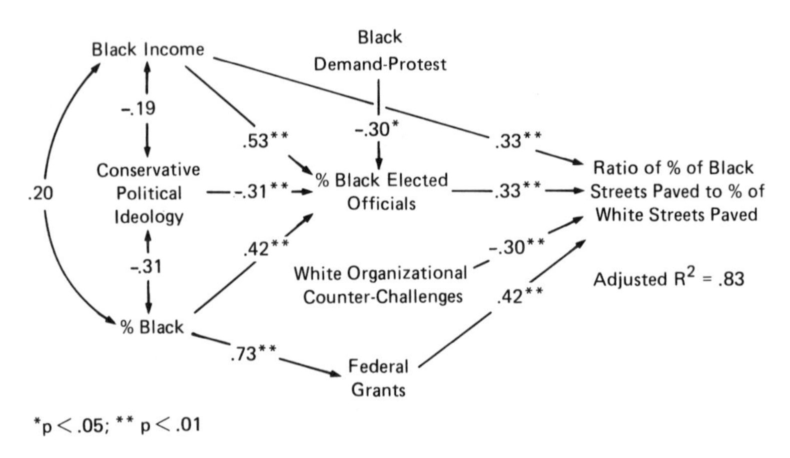

FIGURE 5.3
Path Models of Paved Streets for Blacks (1960–1985)

beaches and pools. Moreover, black citizens often had high expectations that their black representatives would improve their streets and parks quickly and measurably; when they did not, these officials were sometimes not reelected, as is the case of black incumbents in Riviera Beach (1974) and Crestview (1977).[71]

Black officials were more important in the distribution of some services than others. They were seemingly less influential, for example, in getting streets paved than in developing parks for blacks. Indeed, street paving was affected more by federal grants[72] than by locally elected officials. Beginning with urban renewal dollars in the 1960s,

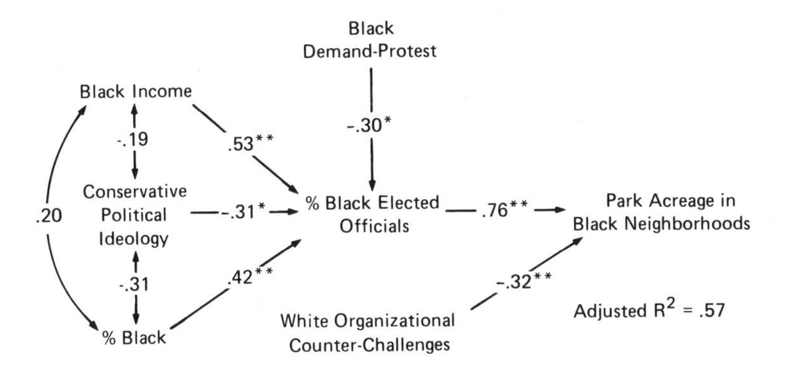

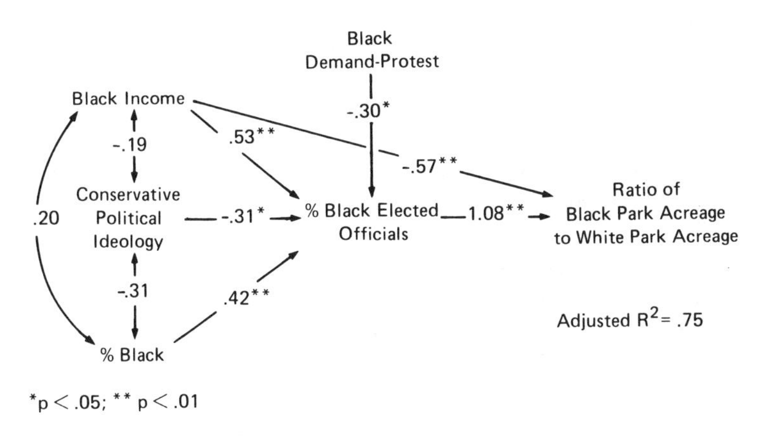

*p < .05; ** p < .01

FIGURE 5.4
Path Models of Neighborhood Park Acreage for Blacks (1960–1985)

federal dollars were crucial to the renovation of black neighborhoods, especially in the Old South. By the mid-1970s, all of these communities had obtained federal Community Development Block Grants targeted primarily for black areas, with substantial proportions of the funds earmarked for street paving and drainage. No doubt the deplorable conditions of housing and public services in black neighborhoods enhanced the eligibility of these cities for such grants. Moreover, between 1974 and 1980, four of the six communities also allocated portions of their federal revenue-sharing monies for street paving in black sections. Due in large part to these various federal grants, almost three times as many streets were paved in black neighborhoods during the 1970s as in the previous decade.

The final political factor that was directly and significantly related to street and park services for blacks was white organizational counter-challenges. As in the case of protective service employment, white counter-organizations had a negative impact, mobilizing in this case to reduce the flow of capital-improvement dollars to black neighborhoods. This phenomenon was especially significant in the Old South where white counter-groups were most visible. There, the role of these white organizations was more visible, and, along with the negative but typically indirect influence of a conservative political culture, it helps to explain why improvements for blacks in streets, parks, and recreation have been considerably slower and more difficult to achieve. White neighborhoods in the Old South, for instance, were much more likely than those in the New South to have unpaved streets and were therefore in competition with blacks for scarce dollars allocated for paving.

These path models, like the previous ones, explained a high proportion of the variation in public services. Moreover, essentially the same contextual variables were indirectly related to these levels of services through their influence on the percent of black elected officials. Black median family income, however, is a black resource variable that entered as a significant influence, one that is both direct and indirect. In the case of street paving, where city assessment plans were common, the level of black income would seem a particularly important factor in the delivery of such services. Black income was also highly related to federal grants, since the more affluent New South cities were usually more successful in procuring grant monies.

Once again black demand-protest is shown to be indirectly and negatively related to the dependent variables. As we have seen, however, protests were sometimes instrumental in improving recreational facilities for blacks. Demonstrations played a key role, for instance, in desegregating the beaches in Daytona and in helping to improve black parks in Riviera. Thus in the more liberal cities of the New South, protest served to awaken public officials to important black grievances. It also, as in the case of Daytona Beach, threatened to disrupt the local economy, and thereby exact unacceptable costs upon business leaders; in this instance, protest became a political bargaining tool of sorts for blacks, and expedited the difficult process of integration. The role of demonstrations and other forms of political protest in facilitating integration will become more apparent when we look at certain changes in the private sector.

While these political variables were statistically significant in determining the extent of black street and recreational services, several other factors not included in the models seemed to have been of moderate importance in some of the communities. The local press in Daytona Beach and Lake City, through feature articles and editorials, publicized the generally deplorable conditions, lack of paved streets, and inadequate parks in black neighborhoods. While embarrassing some city officials, this publicity tended to increase the level of awareness of service inequities and generated some support among officials for improved streets and recreation.

Private organizational efforts by blacks were often helpful in effecting improvements in parks and recreation, and sometimes compensated for lack of public initiative. As we have seen, parks for blacks (and often for whites as well) were originally developed by private groups, particularly in the Old South. In the black neighborhood of Lake City, for example, all but two acres of Annie Mattox Park continues to be privately operated and improvements to it have been primarily the result of fund-raising efforts by black organizations. Fairview Park in Crestview, although deeded to the city some time ago, is supervised and partially maintained by black citizens. Additional donations of labor and money by blacks have been responsible for the development of a small museum of local black history at Fairview.[73] In Titusville, Citizens Backers, a black group organized when Sylvan Park was closed for the first time in 1977, was instrumental in getting the park reopened, even volunteering its own members to help supervise recreation there.[74]

As other studies have suggested, bureaucratic decision rules have also been important determinants at times of the distribution of street paving and even of recreation. In Crestview in the late 1970s, priority was given to paving roads with the highest maintenance costs. This decision was seemingly made in order to reduce maintenance expenses, yet its effect was to favor white neighborhoods in the northern part of the city, where the streets were more heavily traveled and where a mostly clay soil composition and hilly terrain meant frequent road washouts.[75] In other cases, bureaucratic rules tended to favor blacks. In the late 1960s Titusville faced the problem of paving some forty miles of dirt streets, much of them in outlying areas that had recently been annexed. To help remedy this situation, the city decided to split evenly with property owners the costs of paving; formerly, property owners had had to pay the total cost of paving their streets. In addition, the city extended the time period for property assessment billing for paving from five to ten years.[76] These new rules made it easier for property owners, including many low-income blacks, to afford to have their streets paved. In the area of parks and recreation, financially strapped Titusville decided to close Sylvan Park in the late 1970s because it was in the poorest condition and had the highest maintenance costs of any park in the community.

Although these bureaucratic decisions were ostensibly made on the basis of rational, nonpolitical criteria, such rules had the effect of favoring certain groups and depriving others and were often politically motivated. This was usually the case with rules concerning the assessment of property owners for some of the costs of street paving. For poor blacks, such assessment decisions were of particular importance, but because these regulations usually had strong institutional support, had often been in effect for long periods of time, and were based (according to city officials at least) on rational, objective considerations and not class or race, they were difficult to change. Nonetheless, in the less traditional New South, white officials were more willing to reconsider bureaucratic rules in light of their possible racial (and sometimes class) consequences. Normally such reconsideration did not occur without blacks first pressing the issue.

Summary

Streets and recreation are important municipal services for most citizens. This is especially true for southern blacks since they have been denied such basic services for so long a time. Blacks value improvements in these services not only because of their functional importance but also because of their psychological and symbolic significance. The inadequate provision of streets, parks and recreation, as well as other services, had long denoted the inferior status of blacks in the South.

In the late 1950s and early 1960s, the condition of streets in most black neighborhoods was very poor, especially in the Old South. Relatively few streets were paved, and black areas typically lacked street drainage, sidewalks, streetlights, and street signs. Blacks also lacked adequate parks and recreation facilities. In the relatively poor, Old South communities there were no developed public parks for blacks or whites. And though blacks in the New South cities enjoyed municipal parks at this time, such parks were relatively small and not as well maintained as those in white neighborhoods. In accordance with southern tradition, moreover, all parks and recreation programs were totally segregated.

During the next two and one-half decades, street services for blacks improved markedly. In every community proportionally more street paving occurred in black neighborhoods than in white areas, especially during the 1970s. As expected, the more affluent New South cities showed the largest improvement in street services for blacks; by 1980 almost all streets were paved in the black sections. Despite increases in street services, by 1985 the impoverished Old South cities still lacked paving for approximately one-third of the roads in black neighborhoods. These changes also tended to contradict Keech's findings about the influence of minority population size on public services.

Park and recreation programs for blacks improved too, albeit modestly, during these years. In almost all communities park acreage as an indicator of recreational distribution showed absolute increases for black neighborhoods, but acreage increases were relatively greater for most white neighborhoods. In support of Keech, blacks fared relatively better in park acreage increases in communities with a black majority, and somewhat worse in cities with a medium proportion of blacks. In terms of quality of park facilities, there were improvements in all black areas, especially in New South cities that could afford qualitative improvements. In the Old South, lingering racism and poverty combined to produce few public improvements, but private, self-help efforts by blacks sometimes resulted in modest recreational development. Perhaps the most significant recreation issue, however, was the desegregation of facilities. Integration usually provoked intense racial anxieties for whites, and thus proceeded slowly and with difficulty, especially at traditionally all-white municipal beaches and swimming pools. Such integration was initiated sooner and achieved more easily in the New South than it was in the Old South. Although most recreational programs were integrated to some degree by the late 1970s, many beaches, pools, and even neighborhood parks were still used almost exclusively by only one racial group.

Black employment in these municipal departments also changed over time. In 1960, blacks were hired only for the most menial positions in public works, and although this pattern continued, by 1985 more blacks were found in supervisory and administrative positions. In recreation, blacks fared somewhat better early on, since most cities preferred to have black supervisors in black neighborhood parks. This was still the case in 1985, but in communities where blacks were a majority, the top-level recreational administrators were also now blacks. Clearly, most cities had hired and promoted more blacks than ever before during these years, with the greatest gains being made in departments of recreation.

What political factors account for these various improvements in streets and recreation? As in the case of black employment in police and fire protection, conventional political strategies, particularly the influence of black elected officials, were most important. Blacks in public office played a crucial role in upgrading services and increasing employment. Of significance, too, were federal grants, at least for street paving, especially Community Development Block Grants and revenue sharing. Black resources, including median income, were also important in the provision of these basic services. On the other hand, black demand-protests tended to have an indirect and somewhat negative impact on service improvements. Nevertheless, in the New South peaceful protests were sometimes an impetus to the integration and upgrading of recreational facilities, especially during the 1960s. A greater and more direct negative influence, particularly in the Old South, resulted from the countermobilization responses of certain white groups. Finally, in some communities other less important factors, including the local press, private efforts by blacks, bureaucratic decisions, also helped to bring about service changes.

It is clear that the civil rights movement had an impact on streets and recreation for blacks, since these services improved more during these decades than in any previous era. In 1960, black streets and parks were so poor compared with those in most white neighborhoods that the issue of equality was merely a dream, yet over the next several decades this issue became a significant one politically. Nevertheless, in the mid-1980s services for blacks still lagged behind those for most whites, especially in the poor, racially conservative Old South. If federal dollars become increasingly scarce, this inequity in services will most likely continue for some time. In recreation, for example, most whites have a choice between municipal and private facilities—a choice most poor blacks still do not have. And in street services, paving and drainage are increasingly provided by private developers, who pass on their costs to relatively affluent whites. As a result, the issue may not be whether black and white parks and streets are equal, but whether the level of public services provided blacks compensates sufficiently for the absence of alternatives.

6

The Private Sector: Social and Economic Progress

> Negroes used to have to sit in a separate area in the theater—in the balcony, and the theater wasn't integrated until the late 1960s when blacks caused a ruckus. —Theater manager, Crestview

> We hired our first colored teller [in this bank], but many customers will still not go to her.
> —Bank personnel manager, Titusville

Perhaps the most important long-range goal of the civil rights movement in the South was not the achievement of fundamental political rights and improved public services, but the betterment of social and economic conditions for blacks. To be sure, the attainment of full and free political participation was a significant legal and status goal, and the resulting improvement in basic municipal services enhanced the living conditions of many blacks. But it was always assumed that the larger and more complex battle would be the quest by blacks for economic equality with whites. As Martin Luther King, Jr., claimed in 1967: "With the Voting Rights Act one phase of development in the civil rights revolution came to an end. A new phase opened. . . . White America was ready to demand that the Negro should be spared the lash of brutality and coarse degradation, but it had never been truly committed to helping him out of poverty. . . . Jobs are harder and costlier to create than voting rolls."[1] Furthermore, although the achievement of basic political goals was probably a prerequisite to the fulfillment of welfare goals, there was skepticism that political advances could affect economic and social conditions for blacks to any great degree.[2] Surprisingly, however, there have been few attempts to assess the impact of the civil rights movement with regard to black social and economic advances.

Before the civil rights movement, public accommodations in the South were almost always segregated racially. The assumption of black social inequality was supported by a rigid caste-like system resting upon both laws and folkways. Blacks were either denied services altogether, restricted to separate facilities, or allowed to use public accommodations on a segregated basis. In addition to state or municipal laws requiring such segregation was the assertion by white businessmen that they had a right to use their property as they saw fit and to refuse service to whomever they chose. Such denial of services was not only degrading to blacks but often very inconvenient, especially for blacks traveling through the South.[3]

By the late 1960s, however, many private-sector services were desegregated, though the degree of integration varied according to the attitudes of the businessmen involved, community context, and other factors. The type of service also seemed to make a difference: more personalized services (such as barber shops and mortuaries), private clubs, and churches usually remained segregated. The immediate causes of integration have been widely debated. Many scholars have suggested that the strong arm of the federal government, primarily in the form of the 1964 Civil Rights Act, coupled with the pressure of black demonstrations and sit-ins, was most important in the desegregation process.[4] Other social scientists, however, have claimed that the increasingly progressive attitudes of many southern white businessmen were fundamental factors.[5] Whatever the reality, there is clearly a lack of precise data both on the extent of racial desegregation of public and private accommodations and on the major forces influencing this process.

Prior to the mid-1960s, the main economic thrust of the civil rights movement was for equal service rather than for equal employment. But once blacks discovered they could successfully demand equal service, they soon extended their demands to the job market. Employment opportunities, of course, are perhaps the best measure of black economic achievement. Yet traditionally in the South blacks have either been denied jobs or been given the most menial jobs. The perception of most southern employers was that blacks were lacking in intelligence, training, and education, and were incapable of performing in high-level jobs. The most consistent stereotype attached to blacks was the concept of "strong back, weak mind"; blacks were usually considered only for jobs which required physical strength or stamina and little intelligence. In addition, employers feared losing white customers and creating friction among white employees if they hired or promoted blacks.[6]

The 1960s and 1970s, nonetheless, seemed to be decades of clearcut advancement in black employment, as nonwhites gained a somewhat greater share of white-collar jobs; blacks were no longer found only in lower-paying service- and farm-worker categories. Partly as a result of these advances, median black family income in the South rose from 46 percent of white income in 1959 to 55 percent in 1972, and this improvement was greater than in any other region of the country (although in the North and West nonwhites continued to have incomes that were greater in both absolute and relative terms).[7]

These changes in black employment were apparently due to several factors. The 1960s was a period of rapid economic expansion in the South, a process including increased urbanization and industrialization, and this economic growth resulted in new job opportunities for blacks as well as whites. The higher educational achievements of blacks, as well as the ferment of the civil rights movement during this period, also promoted black entry into the skilled-job market. Another possible factor was the change in attitudes of many southern businessmen, who partially acceded to new black demands for jobs in order to avert further racial tension and instability, which they believed was "bad for business."[8] Of major importance, too, were the federal efforts to eliminate job discrimination and to train blacks for better jobs. The 1964 Civil Rights Act in particular signaled "a strong and positive commitment by the federal government to the achievement of racial equality," especially in the South, where discrimination and income inequality were greatest.[9]

Attempts to explore the relationship between black social and economic advances in the South and local politics are scarce. In his mid-1960s study, Keech claimed that "Negro votes are less able to secure fair and equal treatment in the private sector of social life than in the public sector" because the government has less legal authority and regulatory influence in the private realm.[10] He suggested that the ideology of free enterprise still strongly resisted government interference in private business. Matthews and Prothro also concluded that the vote was an effective resource in promoting racial change in the private sector only "when the costs of abandoning segregation are relatively low for the white community."[11] However, when whites felt that the costs of integration were too high, as in the areas of employment, housing, and schools, then the black vote seems to have been ineffective. Matthews and Prothro suggested, nevertheless, that other modes of political intervention, such as court litigation, demonstrations, and federal regulation, may have been more fruitful in breaking down racial barriers in the private realm.[12] The importance of federal intervention in the quest for equality by blacks was particularly stressed.

This chapter will look at the impact of the civil rights movement on the private sector in southern communities. Specifically, its focus is on the extent to which private establishments have desegregated, in terms both of serving and, more particularly, of employing blacks. An assessment will also be made of which factors or conditions made a difference in, or helped to explain, the degree of integration, with special attention given to the role of political forces.

Desegregation of Private Establishments

The provision of private services to blacks in these six communities was almost completely discriminatory prior to the 1960s. In many cases blacks were denied a service altogether, such as admission to motels, apartment complexes, and country clubs. In other instances they were served separately from whites, as in the case of restaurants that offered blacks carry-out service in lieu of seating or movie theaters that permitted blacks to sit only in a designated section. With the advent of the civil rights movement and subsequent federal legislation, it was assumed that these walls of discrimination would begin to crumble and eventually disappear. To what extent has this process occurred?

Informed citizens in each of the communities were asked to evaluate the extent and length of time taken for the desegregation of several different kinds of private establishments. The results of these queries are summarized in table 6.1 by establishment and by community groupings. Almost all informants, regardless of race or community, believed that movie theaters, restaurants, bowling alleys, and motels were fully integrated by the late 1970s. They also estimated that these facilities were first desegregated sometime between 1964 and 1967. On the other hand, only a minority of these citizens thought that bars and lounges, apartments, and country clubs were integrated; they believed that the desegregation process had begun somewhat later for these institutions, where integration implied more personalized contacts between whites and blacks. This is a situation that many whites evidently still find threatening. Other more objective sources strongly supported the perceptions of these citizens.[13]

The degree and timing of desegregation varied somewhat depending on the type of community. In the New South cites most private establishments were more fully mixed racially, and were integrated earlier in time, than their counterparts in the Old South communities. This reflects the less rigid and less enduring racial norms that would be expected in the New South. Typical of the more conservative Old South was the comment by a white businessman in Crestview: "Some establishments closed down before they'd integrate. . . . There was the

TABLE 6.1

Evaluations by Community Informants of Degree and Timing of Racial Desegregation of Private Establishments

	Community Groupings[a]											
Type of Establishment	*All Communities*		*Old South*		*New South*		*Low % Black*		*Medium % Black*		*High % Black*	
Movie theaters	99[b]	1964–65[c]	100	1964–65	100	1964–65	100	1964–65	100	1964	97	1965
Bars and lounges	39	1967–68	28	1968–69	49	1966–67	28	1967–68	28	1967–68	62	1969–70
Restaurants	93	1964–65	89	1965–66	97	1964–65	89	1964–65	94	1964–65	96	1965
Country clubs	9	1966–67	0	1971–72	24	1964–65	0	1969	21	1964–65	0	1974
Bowling alleys	100	1965	100	1966–67	100	1964–65	100	1964–65	100	1964–65	100	1965
Motels	97	1965–66	98	1967	96	1964–65	98	1965–66	97	1964–65	97	1964–65
Apartments	28	1969	7	1971	46	1967–68	30	1969	23	1968	36	1971

[a] Variations in numbers of informants interviewed in each community were controlled by weighting each community equally.

[b] Percentage evaluating the establishments as fully integrated as of the late 1970s.

[c] Average estimates as to the time period when such establishments were first desegregated.

fear of having your business ruined if blacks came in. Many whites wouldn't eat in the same place [with a black]."[14]

In general, the proportion of blacks living in a community had little effect on the degree of integration, although in majority-black communities, bars, lounges, and apartments were apparently more thoroughly integrated than in the medium- and low-percent black cities. Yet the first desegregation of these facilities in communities with a majority of black residents probably took place somewhat later than in other cities. It seems during the 1960s that the large number of blacks in these cities was considered by whites to be an immediate threat, thus delaying desegregation. But once blacks in Gretna and Riviera Beach exerted their political strength in the early 1970s, discriminatory barriers began to fall rather quickly and completely.

While most public accommodations are now formally open to blacks and will serve them, the quality of service often suggests something less than complete integration. Blacks are still commonly treated as second-class citizens in many parts of the South, especially in the Old South. "White prejudice still has not disappeared," claimed a longtime Crestview businessman. "In restaurants whites will get waited on first, and blacks will usually get poorer service."[15] Such discriminatory treatment discourages blacks from continuing to patronize some establishments, thus reinforcing segregationist norms. As a restaurant owner in Lake City described it: "We have few black customers. . . . They stick more to their own places. They're made to know where they're not welcome."[16]

Of all private establishments surveyed, the most segregated continued to be country clubs. These exclusively white clubs usually allowed blacks to utilize the facilities only if accompanied by a club member. In the Old South, no country clubs reported having any black members, and even black guests were often made to feel unwelcome. The antagonism toward blacks in those establishments was clearly reflected in the words of the manager of a country club just outside of Crestview: "We don't get many coloreds in here because a lot of them are trash . . . and some might get 'fresh' with the wives [of white members] and we'd have to kick them out. They tend to get drunk, too!"[17]

Although most clubs in the New South had a very small number of black members by the late 1970s, only the municipally owned golf club in Daytona was thoroughly integrated. Even in the New South, admission requirements usually discriminated against most blacks. Typically, membership in these clubs required recommendation or sponsorship by several club members, a careful screening for "social acceptability" by a governing board, and payment of costly initiation fees (as much as $600 or more) plus annual dues. As a result, only a small number of middle-class and professional blacks had a reasonable chance of joining them.

One other area of the private sector where almost total segregation prevails is residential housing and apartments. Such segregation, in fact, continues to be the norm in the Old South.[18] In Lake City in 1980, for instance, more than 90 percent of blacks lived in residential blocks which were eighty percent or more Negro.[19] Part of the problem, according to informed residents, is that many blacks in the Old South are simply too poor to afford housing in white neighborhoods. Black poverty aside, however, the major issue is that most whites have still not accepted interracial housing, and when blacks attempt to move into white areas, they are often either harassed or made to feel unwanted. In some cases white landowners have simply refused to sell to blacks in order to keep them out, and there have been claims that banks have often turned down loans to blacks who wished to build homes outside ghetto areas.[20]

By contrast, modest amounts of housing and apartment integration have taken place in New South cities. In 1970 an average of 90 percent of the blacks in these three communities lived in residential areas that were 70 percent or more black, while by 1980 some 72 percent lived in predominately black neighborhoods.[21] Not only are there more middle-class blacks who can afford higher-priced housing, but more whites are willing to accept (or at least not reject outright) a black family or two in their neighborhood. New South communities, moreover, have been more active in gaining federal rent supplements and housing assistance programs, which have enabled blacks to buy or rent outside of traditional black neighborhoods, and public housing has become somewhat dispersed throughout these communities. City government, too, has been more involved in preventing discrimination in the sale or rental of housing. In Riviera Beach, where there has been a substantial increase in residential integration since 1970, the city council passed and strictly enforced a fair-housing law and an anti–block-busting ordinance during the decade.[22]

Despite a period of increased residential integration, the vast majority of blacks, even in the New South, are still highly segregated from whites. Most black population growth since 1970 has been in white areas adjacent to predominately black neighborhoods; there has been little movement of blacks into white tracts far from traditional ghetto areas.[23] The more affluent sections, especially beachfront areas, remain essentially white. While the cost of housing in these areas is prohibitive for all but a few blacks, there are also informal sanctions against minority encroachment. On occasion, blacks moving into these wealthy enclaves have been openly harassed; the home of the first black resident of Singer Island in Riviera Beach, for example, was splattered by vandals with black paint.[24]

Factors Related to Desegregation

Clearly most public accommodations were desegregated by the late 1960s while most bars, private clubs and housing are still far from being racially mixed. To understand this process of desegregation, it is important to know why and how integration occurred in the private sector. What were the major causal factors related to the integration process? Again, informed residents in the community were queried, and the results are summarized in table 6.2. The factor mentioned most frequently by the interviewees was the 1964 Civil Rights Act, which was followed by extensive federal pressure to desegregate. In fact, this was the only factor cited by 50 percent or more of respondents in each community. In the Old South, a relatively high percentage of well-informed citizens assessed the role of the national government as crucial in changing deeply held racial norms and behavior. As a black teacher in Crestview put it: "Integration here has been due to federal law; otherwise things would be the same way today. Things don't change easily in small, poor, Deep South towns."[25]

Title 2 of the 1964 Civil Rights Act forbids discrimination by a person engaging in business if his customers or a "substantial portion" of the products he uses are involved in interstate travel. This title, subsequently upheld in federal court, clearly broadened and deepened the federal commitment to ending segregation in public accommodations. Compliance with the law in the South was relatively prompt and extensive, although acceptance in rural, Old South areas tended to be "minimal and grudging."[26] The law was successful in helping to end segregation because businessmen perceived that they *had* to comply, that other businessmen would do likewise, and that they could condemn Washington for forcing such compliance. Most whites, in fact, were not threatened by the desegregation of public accommodations, since for the most part few blacks could afford to use such facilities, and those blacks who did were usually middle class and therefore more acceptable to whites.[27]

The second major factor related to desegregation, and one mentioned only slightly less frequently than federal law, was political action by blacks that brought pressure (usually economic) to bear on the owners of private establishments. The kinds of political action referred to

TABLE 6.2

Major Causes of Racial Integration of Private Establishments According to Community Informants

	Community Groupings					
Causal Factors Mentioned	*All Communities*	*Old South*	*New South*	*Low % Black*	*Medium % Black*	*High % Black*
Civil Rights Act (1964) and/ or federal pressure	55%[a]	65%	50%	54%	57%	56%
Black political action pressuring private establishments	47	38	53	30	52	52
Influence of national civil rights trend or mood	15	10	18	11	8	26
Presence of major "outside" forces (military bases, new businesses, etc.) encouraging integration	13	10	17	32	3	4
"Spillover" effects of school integration	11	20	7	24	5	4

[a] Percentage of community informants mentioning the factor. Totals are more than 100 percent due to multiple factors mentioned by some respondents.

here were of the unconventional type, including sit-in demonstrations, marches, boycotts, pickets, and special meetings with businessmen and public officials. Such protests began, as we have seen, in the early 1960s in the New South cities and usually took the form of sit-ins at lunch counters. Somewhat later the black demonstrations, now including boycotts, pickets, and marches, spread to other public accommodations, such as restaurants, movie theaters, motels, and beaches. By the early 1970s even segregated bars and lounges were challenged by blacks in Titusville and Riviera Beach, and lawsuits or threats of legal action had become a favorite tactic.[28]

These protests were generally successful, especially in the New South. Claimed a black leader in Daytona: "We demonstrated to integrate a number of places—Morrison's, Walgreens, and others. We even marched and demonstrated to open the beaches. But we also negotiated with the business community and city officials."[29] Yet in the Old South and in communities in which blacks were a relatively small proportion of the citizenry, unconventional tactics were mentioned much less frequently as factors related to desegregation. In the Old South most whites were unsympathetic to black demands for integration and certainly to tactics such as protests, and blacks usually remained in their subordinate economic and political status. As a Crestview black leader put it: "Many blacks work for whites, and they're afraid to do much. Whites retaliated against some black leaders for demonstrating."[30] In communities with relatively small black populations, blacks often lacked the numbers and organizational strength necessary to carry out significant political actions.

Where black demonstrations were successful, however, such effectiveness was primarily due to the threatened or actual economic impact of protests on local businesses. Black boycotts and picketing were even able to close down some white businesses. In other cases the disruption and chaos created by the demonstrations were seen as potentially harmful to business and to economic progress in general. New South cities, particularly Daytona Beach, were concerned with their image and were fearful that racial protests would reduce tourism, as it had in nearby St. Augustine following the massive 1964 demonstrations there.[31] Occasionally desegregation protests also resulted in racial violence, which endangered community stability. In such situations, businessmen and city officials often joined together to attempt to preserve peace. For example, following the Lake City movie theater incident, in which a minor race riot developed as a result of desegregation challenges, the mayor and local business leaders intervened. The mayor, ever mindful of black votes, helped to desegregate seating in the theater and encouraged the integration of other businesses, arguing that such changes were inevitable and that businessmen should accept them.[32]

In a few cities those businessmen who realized that integration was inevitable actually took leading roles in urging compliance with the law. In Titusville and Daytona, a number of businessmen served on biracial committees that were helpful in gaining community acceptance of integration and in making the transition a relatively smooth and peaceful one. Often businessmen assumed this leadership role because they realized it was in their economic self-interest to do so; that is, integration meant stability and perhaps increased business. "Integration was partly due to the desire of businessmen for the dollar, and it greatly expanded business," observed a Daytona businessman. "There was a real economic incentive to get the black dollar."[33] Failure to achieve integration, on the other hand, meant continued demonstrations, instability, and the creation of a negative climate for business generally and tourism in particular.

While federal legislation and pressure and black civil rights activity were most important in desegregating private establishments, other factors (see table 6.2) were reported as moderately influential in particular communities. One such factor, more important in majority-black and New South cities than elsewhere, was the national mood of approval for equal rights for blacks. The New South was less insulated from national trends than rural areas, and this egalitarian feeling or mood seemed to have a pervasive influence, even a legitimizing effect there. "We haven't had to push too much here. . . . When the civil rights movement came along, if we decided to go somewhere we just went, and we didn't have any problem," commented a black councilman in Riviera Beach.[34]

Another factor of some importance was the presence of nonindigenous or "outside" forces that tended to favor integration. As we have seen, the proximity of Eglin Air Base to Crestview served as a moderating influence on race relations in that city. Black soldiers from the base were often the first to challenge segregated facilities. Some local businesses began to serve blacks because they were afraid of being placed off-limits to all military personnel if they did not.[35] In Titusville, Cape Kennedy and the new aerospace industries had a similar impact. "The driving force behind integration here was the influence and growth of NASA. . . . It brought a whole bunch of Yankees to the South," claimed a longtime Titusville city official.[36] Such "outside" forces were significant catalytic agents in communities that had no sizable black populations to press for change.

Finally, the effect of public school integration appears to have been a factor influencing desegregation generally, especially in the Old South and in communities where the black population was relatively small. School integration was a long and difficult process in these cities, but once achieved it seemed to have positive spillover effects. Not only did it seem to ameliorate racial attitudes over time, but as racial integration began to take place in public schools, the expectation grew that the desegregation of public accommodations and other institutions was inevitable and would soon follow. As a black respondent in Lake City put it: "Once the school system desegregated, it opened up everything else."[37]

Blacks and the Job Market

As soon as blacks achieved substantial equality of service in most public accommodations, they tended to turn their attention to employment. Improved jobs were seen not only as the major way for blacks to escape economic impoverishment, but also as a means of enhancing black pride and self-esteem. Traditionally, of course, blacks were relegated to the most menial and lowest-paying jobs. In 1960, blacks made up 19 percent of the work force in the South but claimed only 6 percent of the professional and managerial positions and 5.6 percent of the jobs as craftsmen and in clerical and sales. Blacks, were vastly overrepresented in such unskilled-labor positions as nonfarm laborers (47 percent), private household workers (79 percent), and other service workers (37 percent).[38] Yet in a comprehensive review of the changing social and economic status of blacks in the United States during the 1960s, Levitan, Johnston, and Taggart concluded that "in the labor market, blacks have probably made more progress than in any other socioeconomic dimension, though their status is still far from equal."[39] How and to what extent blacks in these southern communities have been able to improve their condition of employment are thus important questions.

The main method of analysis of black employment in these communities consisted of the random selection of a variety of private establishments and an interview with the owner or manager of each to gain information on hiring practices for blacks. Businesses were purposely chosen to provide variety in terms of size and service offered. The kinds and numbers of establishments selected were restaurants (31); industrial or manufacturing businesses (25); retail stores and banks (56); motels and apartments (35); and recreational establishments (16) including movie theaters, bowling alleys, and country clubs.

The total sample size was 163, with relatively more establishments randomly selected in the larger communities; the range varied from 39 establishments in Daytona Beach to 11 in the Gretna area. (Appendices 1 and 3 contain a more complete description of the methodology employed and the interview schedules.) In addition, informed citizens in each community were also asked a series of questions concerning black-employment practices, and as always, local newspapers provided some useful information on this issue. For the most part, however, the analysis here relies on data gleaned from interviews with local businessmen.

Results of the surveys of private establishments indicated that most businesses first began to employ blacks in the mid-sixties, but that only 12 percent of businesses had hired any prior to 1960. By the late 1970s, however, 81 percent had hired one or more blacks. Thus, the vast majority of businesses in the communities studied have employed blacks, and they have done so since the mid-1960s. This dramatic change has occurred in a relatively brief period of time.

By the late seventies the average percentage of black employees for all private establishments was 19 percent (table 6.3). However, there were some interesting variations. Blacks were seriously underrepresented in proportion to their availability in the labor market in professional and managerial occupations (2 percent) and in skilled and semiskilled positions (12 percent). Yet blacks had achieved—or exceeded in some cases—proportional equality in unskilled or menial jobs, with an overall average of 31 percent.[40] With regard to variations in employment by type of establishment, only industries and retail stores hired any blacks in professional or managerial positions, and both at the professional and skilled occupational levels the employment record of industries was consistently better than that of nonindustrial establishments. Other private businesses still tended to hire the vast majority of their black employees as menial workers—as dishwashers and cooks in restaurants, maids in motels, and janitors.

Looking at the data by community suggests, first of all, that there was a positive relationship between the proportion of blacks in the population and black employment. Although interview results with informed residents confirmed this relationship, it was apparent only at the skilled and unskilled level; at the professional level there was little or no variation with the proportion of blacks. Among professionals, blacks were poorly represented in every community. There was also a relationship between size of the black population and the average length of time since blacks were first hired: the greater the percentage

TABLE 6.3

Reported Mean Percentage of Employees Who Are Black in Various Private Establishments

	Community Groupings[a]					
Kinds of Establishments	*All Communities*	*Old South*	*New South*	*Low % Black*	*Medium % Black*	*High % Black*
All establishments	19[b] (2,[c]12,[d]31[e])	24 (3,16,42)	14 (1,7,21)	11 (2,6,21)	19 (2,9,31)	28 (1,20,42)
Restaurants	25 (0,13,41)	30 (0,13,48)	21 (0,13,33)	11 (0,6,20)	25 (0,5,48)	41 (0,35,54)
Industries	21 (5,20,29)	27 (10,16,45)	15 (2,15,12)	22 (7,18,40)	20 (5,25,15)	20 (4,18,21)
Retail stores and banks	16 (3,10,27)	22 (3,14,43)	7 (2,2,11)	6 (3,3,16)	13 (6,9,25)	27 (0,17,47)
Motels and apartments	17 (0,2,24)	14 (0,0,18)	18 (0,3,30)	14 (0,3,22)	24 (0,4,33)	12 (0,0,18)
Movie theaters, bowling alleys, country clubs	23 (0,18,32)	32 (0,25,48)	11 (0,10,16)	8 (0,8,16)	12 (0,10,19)	42 (0,38,67)

[a] All community samples were weighted equally in this analysis so as to control for variations in number of businesses sampled from one community to another.
[b] Mean percentage of all employees who are black.
[c] Mean percentage of professional or managerial employees who are black.
[d] Mean percentage of skilled or semiskilled employees who are black.
[e] Mean percentage of unskilled or menial employees who are black.

of blacks in the population, the earlier blacks were first employed in the private sector.

Second, and quite surprisingly, the community grouping data show that *Old South establishments employed somewhat greater proportions of blacks than those in the New South communities*, and this pattern was consistent for all levels of employment and for all kinds of establishments except motels and apartments. The literature had suggested that just the opposite would be the case, with faster-growing, economically more prosperous, and racially moderate New South cities, whose businesses were generally larger and more rapidly expanding than those in the Old South, compiling a better black employment record. Yet the findings indicate that the Old South has actually been more active in black hiring than the New South.

Nevertheless, several caveats must be mentioned with regard to these unexpected findings. For the professional and managerial occupations, community informants disagreed with these survey findings, indicating that New South businesses had achieved a somewhat better black employment record than those in the Old South, where promotions of blacks, it was claimed, occurred less frequently. Census data for 1980 also presented a differing picture of black occupational status in these Old and New South communities. These data corroborated the survey findings that higher proportions of working blacks were employed in unskilled or menial positions in the Old compared to the New South. But at the higher levels of occupational status (semiskilled, skilled, professional, and managerial), the census found that blacks had achieved somewhat greater proportional employment in the New South cities, a finding that is contrary to the results here.[41]

Two other explanations for these somewhat contradictory findings are variations in sampling procedures and dissimilarities in the black-majority communities. In addition to possible normal sampling errors, there was a tendency to oversample motels and apartments in the New South. These businesses were much more prevalent in the tourist-oriented economies of the New South, but they consistently exhibited the poorest black-employment records of all establishments surveyed. Hence any oversampling of motels and apartments would distort the overall results for the New South cities. The disparity in black employment between Old and New South communities can also be attributed to significant differences in black hiring between Gretna (40 percent average black employment) and Riviera Beach (15 percent average black employment). As we have seen, by 1980 Gretna was nearly an all-black town (88 percent black), while Riviera Beach had a smaller black population (67 percent). Gretna, moreover, is located in a majority-black county (60 percent Negro), while Riviera is situated in a county with a relatively small percentage of blacks (14 percent). Hence the community pressures to hire blacks were considerably greater in the Gretna area, where employers had available a predominantly black labor force.[42] When these two communities are omitted from the survey analysis, the results show that Old South businesses employed only slightly greater proportions of blacks than did establishments in the New South (16 percent versus 14 percent). Yet even with these caveats, the findings still indicate that the Old South has had a better black-employment record, at least at the lower and middle occupational levels, than was expected. Some of the reasons for this phenomenon will be explored later in this chapter.

Factors Affecting Black Employment

In addition to being asked for data on levels of black employment, businessmen were also queried about a variety of factors that may have influenced the hiring process. These factors included the nature, size, and age of establishment; general recruitment and hiring procedures; the employer's general attitude toward blacks; affirmative action practices; size of black clientele; and possible problems resulting from serving and employing blacks (see questionnaires, appendix 3).

To explore the relationships between these independent variables and the dependent variable of black employment, I first looked at simple bivariate correlations. The results are depicted in table 6.4. The correlations indicate that several independent variables are significantly related (in a statistical sense) to black employment, and that the variable most highly related by far is the proportion of black applicants: the greater the percentage of black job applicants, the greater the proportion of employees who were black, at least at the skilled and unskilled levels. The relationship of the proportion of black applicants to black employment at the professional or managerial level is insignificant. Of course, the proportion of black applicants reflects to some degree the percentage of blacks in the population—and therefore in the potential work force—of the community.

Another factor moderately associated with black employment is the length of time since initial black hiring (measured in terms of the number of years ago that blacks were first hired). This finding lends support to the hypothesis that once the racial barrier was broken, it was easier for a business to hire additional blacks subsequently. Once again, however, this relationship is significant only at the menial-job level, suggesting that initial employment of blacks at unskilled levels

TABLE 6.4
Relationship between Private Establishment Characteristics and Proportion of Black Employees

Characteristics of Establishment	Proportion of Employees Who Are Black, by Occupational Level			
	Total	*Professional or Managerial*	*Skilled or Semiskilled*	*Unskilled or Menial*
Total number of employees	−0.02	0.18	0.09	−0.02
Type (local or state; national)	0.02	0.05	0.05	0.10
Age (length of time in city)	0.05	0.06	0.10	0.15
Proportion of applicants who are black	0.60*	0.11	0.56*	0.59*
Number of years ago blacks first hired	0.30*	0.12	0.16	0.45*
Presence of affirmative action program[d]	0.13	0.38*	0.35*	0.09
Rate of black applicant refusals[d]	−0.08	0.02	−0.05	−0.05
Proportion of customers who are black[a]	0.14	0.00	0.02	0.17
Lack of qualified black applicants[b,d]	−0.07	−0.03	−0.12	0.02
Presence of black-white employee problems[b,d]	0.19*	0.04	0.16	0.12
Negative employer attitude toward blacks[a,c,d]	0.05	0.00	−0.17	0.09

[a] Data were collected only from establishments other than industries and retail stores (N=82).
[b] Data were collected only from industries and retail stores (N=81).
[c] The attitudinal question employed here was as follows: "Some managers of establishments complain that Negroes are more likely to be involved in shoplifting and vandalism than whites, and therefore it is necessary to keep a watchful eye on them when they are in the establishment." (Peter H. Rossi, Richard A. Bert, and Bettye K. Eidson, *The Roots of Urban Discontent* [New York: John Wiley and Sons, 1974], p. 462.) Responses were coded as follows: 0 = strongly disagree; 1 = disagree somewhat; 2 = agree somewhat; 3 = strongly agree.
[d] Measure of association reported for this ordinal-level variable is Kendall's Tau-B; all other variables are interval-level and the reported correlation statistic is Pearsonian.
* $p < .01$. All community samples were weighted equally in this analysis.

did not necessarily lead to employment of blacks at higher levels later on.

The reported existence of black-white employee problems was also moderately correlated with black employment. Friction between black and white employees is positively related to black employment (not negatively as predicted), but the relationship may be the reverse of what it was thought to be. That is, instead of racial friction among employees having influenced black hiring, it seems more likely that increases in black employment, especially at skilled positions where whites felt most threatened, may have resulted in some racial conflict. This was particularly true in the Old South, where some whites clearly resented working with blacks. For example, the owner of a department store just outside Gretna claimed that after his hiring of black clerks for the first time, several white employees complained about having to share rest-room facilities with them.[43] In Lake City, the manager of an industrial firm stated: "Some of our white ol' country boys hate blacks and have asked not to have to work with them, so they don't have to."[44] The result in that firm was a segregated work force.

Interracial employee problems were most highly correlated with black employment in industrial firms, at least at the professional or managerial level. More than any other type of establishment in these communities, industries had hired proportionately more blacks at this high level, a finding that clearly suggests the degree of conflict that occurred whenever blacks initially entered an area of employment previously reserved for whites.

Although the proportion of customers who are black was not significantly associated with black employment, this variable was highly and positively related to the length of time since blacks were first hired. Breaking the color barrier in hiring may have encouraged the growth of black clientele, or the potential size of the black clientele may have prompted the earlier hiring of blacks. The proportion of black customers was also highly correlated, but in a negative direction, with the reported rate at which black employees were fired from or quit their jobs. This suggests that having relatively large numbers of black clientele has perhaps served to insure better treatment for black employees; fearful of losing or alienating black customers, employers may think twice before dismissing or displeasing black workers.

Although employer attitudes toward blacks, as measured here, were not significantly correlated with black employment, other evidence suggests that such attitudes did have some influence. The attitudinal question utilized for employers (see table 6.4) may not have been successful in tapping racial orientations, or may have elicited mainly socially acceptable responses. In any case, unsolicited comments by a number of employers indicated that they had a primarily negative view of black workers. This view was especially prevalent in the Old South and among owners or managers of relatively small businesses in the New South. Some typical comments expressing this negative orientation were the following:

"Most blacks are ignorant and uneducated, and you can smell them a mile away."[45]

"The problem is that colored people don't want to work—they'd rather sit around and collect welfare."[46]

"Coloreds steal a lot—we've caught them stealing bottles of whiskey."[47]

"Blacks are destructive—they won't take care of other people's property or of what they have."[48]

"Most blacks are not very qualified. . . . They lack initiative, absenteeism is high, and they have terrible habits."[49]

"Blacks don't show respect anymore. The young ones especially have a lack of courtesy. . . . They're afraid to say 'yessir,' 'nosir.' "[50]

Thus a number of white businessmen associated blacks with lack of proper hygiene, ignorance, laziness, untrustworthiness, undependability, disrespect, excessive drinking, and an unwillingness to help themselves. While most employers would not openly admit that these attitudes influenced their hiring practices, such views could not help but affect employment and promotion patterns. These businessmen also claimed that many of their white customers shared their negative attitudes toward blacks and frequently objected to being served by a black employee. Indeed, pressure from white clientele was often cited as a reason for not hiring or promoting many blacks. An incident recalled by a restaurant owner in Lake City is illustrative: "We tried a black waitress for two days, but the police and some other people called the manager and told him they wouldn't eat in this place until she left. She was a high school honor student, but we had to fire her."[51]

Role of Affirmative Action

The final factor significantly correlated with black hiring, at least at the skilled and professional levels, was affirmative action. Affirmative action means any government-fostered and/or voluntary action by a private business "going beyond the cessation of formal discriminatory practices."[52] Fifteen percent of the sample of businesses (all but one were industries or large retail stores) responded positively when asked if they were going out of their way to hire blacks and therefore had a formal or informal affirmative action program. Most of these firms admitted that they fell under the federal affirmative action guidelines. Unlike most other establishments in the sample, these businesses claimed to be actively recruiting black employees for skilled managerial positions through local high schools, predominantly black colleges, the state employment agency, newspaper advertising, and in several cases, through the establishment of special job-training programs for minorities. Thus the significant positive correlation here indicates the importance of affirmative action programs in insuring blacks greater access to high-level positions in which they have been and continue to be seriously underrepresented.

Affirmative action was the only variable moderately associated with black employment at the professional level, yet its influence was limited by opposition from various sources. Opposition was especially strong in the Old South communities, where affirmative action practices were not significantly correlated with the hiring of blacks at *any* occupational level. Old South newspaper editorials, an indicator of popular opinion, tended to strongly criticize affirmative action programs for infringing on individual rights and for producing "racial animosity."[53] At KKK rallies in the late 1970s and early 1980s in Crestview and Lake City, affirmative action was bitterly denounced for allegedly "giving unqualified blacks the jobs that belong to whites."[54] Old South businessmen, too, tended to resent federal regulations and federal pressure relating to affirmative action. One Lake City banker claimed openly that he kept his total number of employees below a certain level in order to avoid being covered by federal equal-employment regulations.[55] A businessman in Gretna stated this resentment even more forthrightly: "If I don't wanna employ niggers, I shouldn't have to, and no government is going to tell me I have to. Next step I gotta send my kids to school with 'em and then I'll have to entertain them. I've got my rights too!"[56]

In the New South, affirmative action was moderately associated with black professional employment, and the program was more widely accepted than in the Old South. This was especially true among the larger, nationally affiliated firms. A 1971 local-newspaper survey of major businesses in Daytona, for example, showed that blacks were increasingly being hired and promoted into such prominent positions as telephone operators, bank tellers, and hospital technicians. Formerly blacks were limited in these businesses to menial positions such as maids, laundry workers, and porters. According to Daytona businessmen, a major cause of this change in black employment status was the advent of federal affirmative action programs.[57] Larger, New South firms were also more likely to be guided in their hiring practices by a sense of social responsibility. "Every company has an obligation to help a community which provides it a home . . . and to put aside personal prejudices," stated the manager of a Daytona manufacturing business. "It is our responsibility to hire a qualified black no matter what other workers think."[58]

Yet even in the New South, many businessmen expressed criticism of or at least reservations about affirmative action. Some were concerned that it might jeopardize the merit principle in hiring. "We don't make jobs for blacks, but we give them an opportunity and they must be *qualified*. . . . We don't try to fill quotas," claimed the owner of a Titusville manufacturing firm.[59] Other businessmen criticized affirmative action for allegedly promoting reverse discrimination against whites. "Some white workers feel blacks are being given preferential treatment, and this creates ill feelings," stated one Titusville storeowner.[60] In other instances businessmen claimed that their affirmative action efforts on behalf of blacks were being diluted by federal pressure to hire other minorities, such as women, Hispanics, and the handicapped. For all these reasons, affirmative action in the New South did not affect black employment as much as expected.

Variations among Communities

There were several important variations among the communities in the factors influencing black employment. Grouping the communities according to the black proportion of the population indicates that in the low-percent black cities, there was only a moderate correlation between the proportion of black applicants and employment at the skilled and menial levels. For medium- and high-percent black cities, these same correlations were much higher, especially in communities where blacks were the majority. Similarly, the presence of affirmative action programs in the low-percent black cities was not significantly associated with black hiring at the professional or managerial level, but in the medium- and high-proportion black communities, such programs were highly related to hiring professional blacks. In addition, the reported rate of firings or dismissals of black workers from jobs was highly associated with black employment in those two cities with relatively small black populations, only moderately related to black employment in the medium-percent black cities, and insignificantly associated with black hiring in the majority-black communities. These findings suggest that the greater the proportion of blacks in the community and in the available labor pool: 1) the larger the percentage of black applicants in the private sector who were hired (although only at the skilled and menial levels); 2) the greater the influence of affirmative action programs on black employment at the professional level; and 3) the less evident the tendency to fire black employees. Hence, relative size of the black population seems to exert an important independent effect on several aspects of the black employment process.

As for New and Old South communities, there were few major differences in the correlations of independent variables with black employment. In the New South, the type of firm (national affiliate as opposed to state or local affiliate) was moderately associated with black hiring at all occupational levels; these results suggest the importance of nationally based businesses for minority employment in the expanding New South. In the Old South cities, where there were fewer national firms, the type of firm was not significantly related to black hiring. Finally, as previously mentioned, affirmative action programs were insignificantly associated with hiring of blacks on the professional level in the Old South, while moderately correlated with such employment in New South communities.

Nevertheless, these few differences in the factors associated with black employment fail to explain the somewhat superior employment record of Old South, as opposed to New South, businesses. Indications by Old South businessmen that they received a higher proportion of black applicants and began hiring blacks considerably earlier than most of the recently developed New South businesses account for some of the disparity.[61] These are the two variables most highly correlated with black employment generally. Yet there is another important factor: one of the reasons most frequently mentioned by business owners or managers in the Old South for employing blacks was that it was "good for business." This response referred usually to the positive impact black employees might have on attracting increased black clientele. Fully 30 percent of Old South businesses considered the presence of black employees to be a positive factor, while the comparable figure for New South firms was only 14 percent.

Even though Old South businessmen claimed to have had more unqualified black applicants and more black-white employee problems, and exhibited a more negative attitude toward blacks than New South businessmen, they still employed blacks in higher proportions, in part for economic reasons. Indeed, *it seems that these economic incentives may have finally superseded certain racial fears*, or perhaps, at least in employment, these fears have declined over the last two decades. In Gretna, where whites were traumatized by a black political takeover, a white businessman asserted that "it's just good business to hire some blacks. . . . It would hurt business not to integrate, since many blacks buy from me."[62] In addition, a few businessmen claimed it was economically feasible to employ blacks as menial laborers because they could pay them less than they would other workers. Many blacks were, in fact, willing to work for low wages. Yet the main economic motivation for most businesses seemed to be not the reduction of wages but the possible increase in black customers.

Multivariate Analysis

Moving beyond simple correlations, multiple regression and path analysis were used to explore more fully the relationships among the variables when in combination with other factors. In addition to characteristics of the employment process and attributes of the various businesses, basic political and contextual variables were also entered into the analyses. These variables, most of which were used in path models in the previous two chapters, include indicators of community political ideology, the percentage of blacks among local elected officers, the number of black political organizations, and the number of black protests and riots. It was hypothesized that, although political variables would be more influential in the public than in the private sector, at least some of these political factors might affect private employment. One new contextual variable, the percentage of blacks aged sixteen and over in the labor force in 1980, was also added to this analysis. The assumption here was that the proportion of blacks in the potential labor market of the area would be an important ingredient in the employment process.[63]

Testing various paths of influence,[64] I was able to arrive at a parsimonious model which explained more than 40 percent of the variation in the total proportion of blacks employed (figure 6.2). Other models of employment by occupational level explained less variation, except at the menial-job level. Generally the results of the path analyses lended support to the findings suggested by simple correlations, but there were several exceptions. As expected, the proportion of black applicants was the factor most highly and directly related to black employment, and this was true for all occupational levels except the professional or managerial level. Blacks in elected office, the existence of affirmative action programs, and the policies of nationally based (as opposed to local or statewide) firms significantly increased

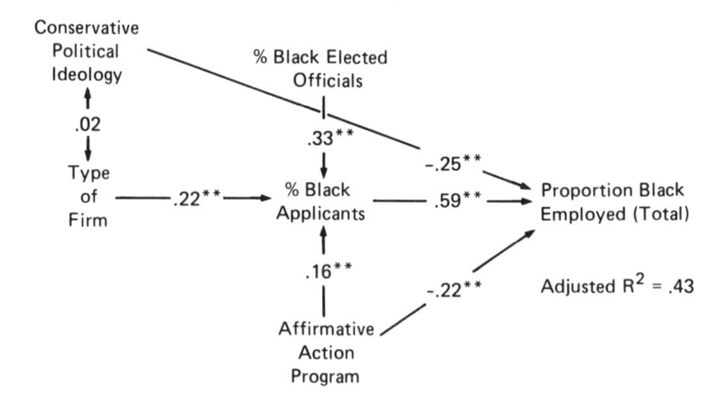

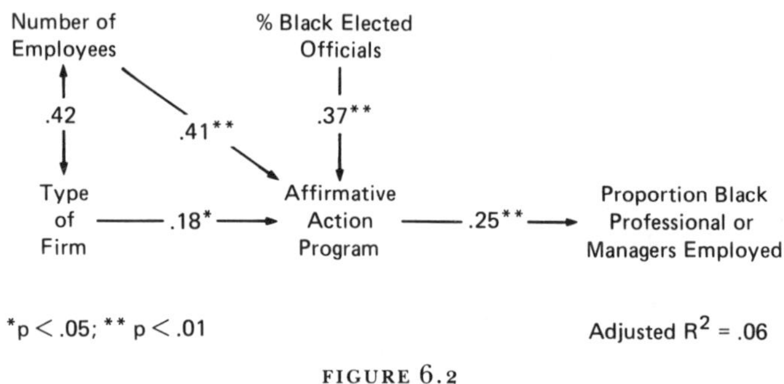

FIGURE 6.2
Path Analyses of Black Employment

the percentage of black job applicants and thus had important indirect effects.

Path analyses also indicated that the presence of affirmative action programs had the single greatest direct effect on professional black employment, although they explain only 6 percent of the variation. In addition, this variable had a positive, indirect influence on black applicants at other employment levels. Affirmative action thus seems to have encouraged more blacks to apply for jobs, perhaps because equal-opportunity employers recruit and advertise more actively than other firms, and perhaps too because blacks are more likely to apply to establishments they know have an affirmative action program and are therefore clearly looking to hire minorities. At the menial-job level and for black employment generally, however, such programs had a moderately negative direct effect, suggesting that affirmative action

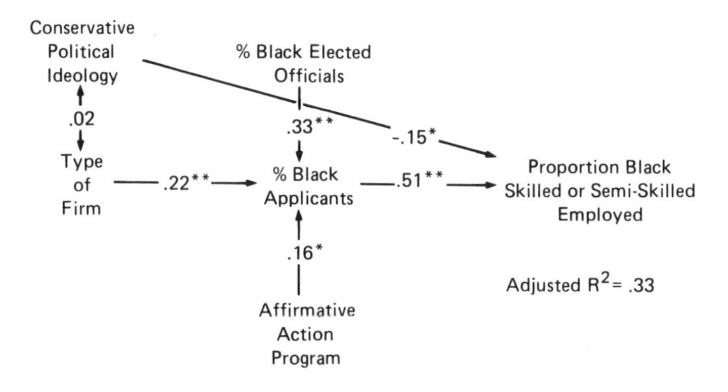

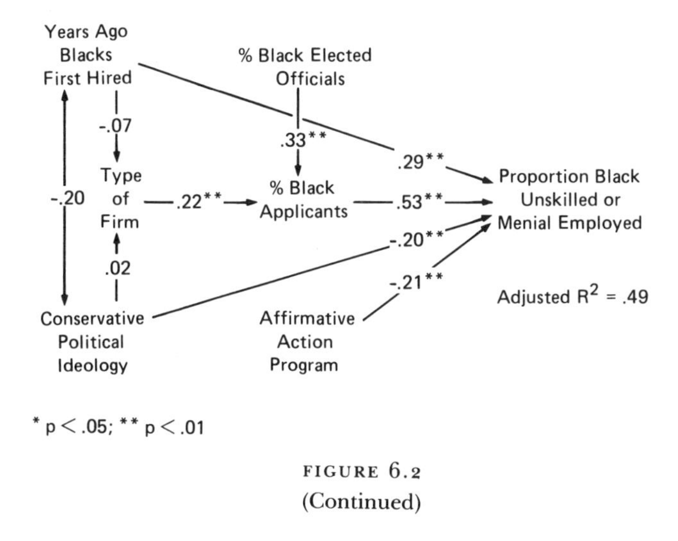

* $p < .05$; ** $p < .01$

FIGURE 6.2
(Continued)

may have actually discouraged or depressed black hiring at the unskilled-job levels, where blacks are usually overrepresented. While this depressing effect may have been an intended goal of some affirmative action programs in order to encourage the movement of more blacks into higher positions, this finding also indicates the occasionally negative impact of a program that is intensely disliked by some employers.

Several other political variables had a significant impact on black employment. Political ideology in the form of racially conservative voting patterns had a consistently direct and negative effect on black hiring at almost every level. This finding indicates that even when business owners' or managers' racial attitudes had little or no direct impact on the employment of blacks, the conservative norms of the community tended to depress the level of black hiring, thus suggesting that the general political and racial orientations of the community do influence private-sector decisions.

As in the case of public employment, black elected officials were again a significant factor in the hiring of black citizens. Unlike their role in the public sector, however, the role of black officials here was only moderate and indirect. Blacks in local office have apparently influenced employment in two ways. First, black officials have inspired members of their race to apply for jobs: a black councilmember or a mayor is a signal to many blacks that the community is open to and accepting of racial changes. Black officeholders have also directly promoted the hiring of minorities by encouraging black citizens to apply for and pursue private-sector jobs. Second, black officials are normally supportive of affirmative action efforts. Although, as we have seen, affirmative action requirements have had mixed results in the private sector, black elected officers have often encouraged local businesses to develop and implement equal-opportunity programs.

According to these analyses, other political factors did not play a significant role in broadening opportunities in the private sector. A few black interest groups, particularly the NAACP, were active in some communities in encouraging black hiring and improving work conditions. In addition, black protests and riots were sometimes directed at employment conditions for blacks, although these unconventional activities occurred mainly during the late sixties or early seventies. While it is difficult to assess the impact of interest-group activity, black protests and violence often proved to be efficacious, at least in the short run.

Southern businessmen generally feared that local turmoil was bad for business and tended to work to promote orderly change as a way of averting chaos.[65] Hence, as a way of reducing disorder, employers often responded to black disturbances with increased black hiring. Even more than peaceful protests, black riots shocked and frightened many businessmen into greater employment of blacks. This economic response was apparent following riots in Riviera Beach (1967), the Gretna area (1970), and Daytona Beach (1970). In the Gretna area, for example, the major black violence in nearby Quincy resulted in several substantive responses by the white community, including increased hiring of blacks by local businesses. "We hired blacks as salesclerks for the first time in the early 1970s after the riot," stated a department store owner. "The riot spurred businesses to create more jobs for blacks."[66] Another white businessman claimed: "The riot shocked the community into thinking that blacks had to participate more."[67] Many establishments throughout the county began to employ blacks above positions as common laborers, but how extensive and long lasting these economic responses proved to be was difficult to determine. General indications were, however, that business reactions to such disturbances were typically short-term, and that once the protests and violence declined and the pressure was off, business leaders were less willing to make significant changes in their minority hiring practices.

Economic Development in the 1980s

By the 1980s blacks had made considerable progress toward fulfilling most political goals and began to focus on securing additional economic resources. Cutbacks in federal monies and a reduced federal emphasis on affirmative action made blacks aware that assistance from Washington was no longer dependable. Local resources and opportunities for public employment were also limited. As a result, blacks increasingly shifted their attention toward finding more and better jobs in the private sector and to promoting greater opportunities for black businesses. Clearly the emphasis in the 1980s, particularly in the New South, was on "economic empowerment" for blacks.[68]

Major efforts in most communities were directed at gaining increased employment and improved working conditions for blacks. The NAACP was especially active in this regard, negotiating with local businesses in Titusville to resolve alleged job-discrimination cases and actively encouraging Lake City businesses to hire more blacks.[69] In Daytona, as part of a "fair share" for blacks campaign, the NAACP canvassed businesses to see if they were making an effort to hire and promote blacks. When businesses refused to accept the "fair share" principle, the NAACP threatened them with boycotts and selective buying.[70] Similarly, the NAACP court suit filed against Eglin Air Force Base near Crestview, claiming discrimination in hiring and promotions of black civilian employees, won a favorable judgment in 1981. The resulting consent agreement brought about a substantial increase in black employment (from 4 to 10 percent) among the base's 4,800 civilian workers within a five year period.[71]

Other initiatives emphasized long-term economic development and more permanent job opportunities. Several communities actively sought to bring in more industry to provide additional jobs for blacks, and black councilmembers and administrators were usually very involved in such ventures. Lake City officials, for example, applied for and received from the CDBG program a grant for economic development that enabled the city to expand water services enough to attract a manufacturing plant to the area. The relocated firm created 150 new jobs, 135 of which were filled by low-income persons, primarily blacks.[72] The most ambitious projects, however, included plans in Riviera Beach for major commercial and residential harbor development and in Gretna for an industrial park. These major undertakings, it was thought, would not only fuel economic growth but would significantly improve long-term employment opportunities for blacks. Unfortunately, political scandals and instability, along with the fears potential backers have of investing in a predominantly black community, have seriously eroded the viability of these projects.

Besides attempting to increase employment, blacks in the New South also directed efforts at boosting minority-owned businesses. Black businesses began to decline following desegregation in the 1960s, as blacks increasingly ventured outside their neighborhoods to shop. In addition to having to confront greater competition, black-owned businesses tended to suffer from lack of investment capital, poor management and marketing skills, and occasionally from urban renewal's "restructuring" of downtown areas.[73] A variety of approaches was used to rejuvenate these faltering businesses and to provide an impetus to the development of more minority firms. Riviera Beach, for example, passed a bonus-density ordinance that allowed developers to build more units per project if they utilized minority contractors. The Daytona Council adopted an affirmative action strategy, approving a 10-percent bidding preference for minority firms on city projects. The incentive system and the set-aside approach were moderately successful in bolstering black businesses. Helpful, too, were city low-interest loans to a limited number of minority-owned businesses in Riviera and Daytona.[74]

Perhaps the most unique and eclectic attempt at furthering black-owned businesses, however, was Daytona's Community Development Corporation (CDC). Established in 1982 as a public-private nonprofit agency, CDC was managed and directed by community members. The corporation proved helpful in securing loans from area banks for local businesses and in providing technical assistance to minority businessmen. CDC also strongly encouraged blacks to shop locally by publishing and promoting a directory of minority businesses and by sponsoring annual fairs or "expos" to display the products of local firms.[75] These supportive activities were beneficial as black-owned businesses increased by 12 percent (from 169 to 189 firms) in three years.[76] Lack of capital, however, was reportedly still a major problem for such businesses, and many continued to relocate outside the black community to gain areawide patronage.[77]

Summary

Changing the social and economic conditions for blacks in the South has been a slow and difficult process. Yet as we have seen, several political factors were instrumental in helping blacks to improve their status in the private sector. Once the barriers of strict segregation were removed in the mid-1960s, most private establishments began to integrate. This process occurred somewhat earlier and was more fully achieved in the New rather than Old South. Nevertheless even in the mid-1980s racial discrimination is still the norm in such private facilities as country clubs, apartments, and bars and lounges. Residential housing, too, is almost totally segregated, although less so in the New South.

The forces behind the desegregation of private establishments were the 1964 Civil Rights Act, subsequent federal pressure, and collective action by blacks that served to coerce businessmen into opening their doors to minorities. Federal pressure was particularly important in Old South communities, where integration was relatively slow and difficult and where black demonstrations were less effective. As Wirt claimed in his study of desegregation of public accommodations in Mississippi, compliance with the federal law was relatively prompt even in the Deep South because the conditions of the law were seen as "explicit and inescapable."[78] Thus, most businessmen felt that all private establishments would have to comply, that they could blame Washington for it, and that they would not lose business as a result. In the larger, more pluralistic New South communities, and in cities where blacks were found in sizeable proportions (30 percent or more), black mobilization and protest were seen as effective forces in desegregation. Such protests were successful because many businessmen feared their disruptive qualities would harm them economically. Other less important factors that also encouraged integration included the national mood favoring civil rights, outside forces influencing the community, and the "spillover" effects of school desegregation.

Greater equality of service was always believed by social scientists to be easier to achieve than equality in employment, and the findings here strongly support this contention. More than a decade after the 1960s civil rights movement, blacks were rarely found in professional or managerial positions and were still underrepresented at skilled and semiskilled levels. In proportion to their numbers, blacks still found themselves just as overrepresented in menial jobs as they had been in the 1960s. Results of the survey of businesses indicated that black employment and promotions have been retarded both by friction between black and white employees and by politically conservative community attitudes. On the other hand, there are several factors that have generally served to encourage increased black employment at skilled or professional positions, including a larger number of black job applicants; an increase in the number of businesses that have begun to hire blacks and thus have taken that important initial step of breaking the racial barrier; the presence of affirmative action programs; and the increase in the percentage of blacks among local elected officials.

Demographic characteristics of communities were also related to black employment. The relative size of the black population was directly and linearly related to black employment at the skilled and menial levels. In addition, the greater the proportion of blacks, the greater the number of black job applicants, and the level of applicants was in turn significantly associated with the level of black employment. A number of businessmen also mentioned that they believed it was "good for business" to hire blacks; this attitude was especially strong in the majority-black communities, where the potential for increasing black clientele was the greatest.

One of the more surprising findings of the survey was that black employment was somewhat greater in the Old South than in the New South, at least at the menial and skilled occupations. This suggests that some of the greatest changes in private-sector employment since the civil rights movement may have taken place in the communities where racial progress was considered most difficult. Certainly the focus of much civil rights effort was in the Old South. Furthermore, a number of Old South businessmen thought it was "good for business" to employ more blacks, and in these relatively poor communities cheap labor and the possibility of drawing a larger clientele were economically attractive. Indeed, it seems that these economic incentives may have finally supplanted certain racial fears. In the New South, on the other hand, the advanced technology of some of the newer businesses may have significantly decreased demand for unskilled labor and increased the demand for highly skilled manpower, thus putting many blacks at a disadvantage.[79]

Finally, it was found that black political activity was an important factor in bringing about social and economic change in the private sector, but that its effect varied depending on the communities and the kinds of changes being assessed. Previous studies have suggested that electoral behavior has not usually had an important influence on the private sector, and this investigation tends to support that contention. Black elected officials, however, did exert a moderate influence on black employment, a finding that suggests that when blacks are able to elect their own representatives to office the policy ramifications go beyond the public sector. Other political factors, though, had more impact on private-sector changes. Collective action by blacks, including protests, sit-ins, boycotts, and private negotiations with businessmen, were considered one of the two most important factors in the desegregation of private establishments in the 1960s. To a lesser extent, these same political tactics, as well as black violence, sometimes served to motivate businessmen to hire more blacks in communities where blacks made up a sizeable proportion of the population. By the late 1970s, however, these unconventional activities were no longer a significant factor in the employment process.

Even more important than black political action was the role played by the federal government in private sector change. The 1964 Civil Rights Act and subsequent federal pressure were crucial in the desegregation of public accommodations, especially in the Old South. In addition, Title 7 of that act, certain executive orders, and the Equal Employment Opportunity Act of 1972 all encouraged the development of affirmative action programs, and these programs have had a modest but significant impact on black employment at the skilled and professional levels.

Clearly the social and economic condition of blacks in the South has improved since the civil rights movement. Most public accommodations now serve blacks, and minority employment in skilled and semiskilled positions has increased, particularly in the Old South, where race relations were most precarious. As expected, conventional modes of black political participation—except for the influcence of black elected officials—were not important in effecting such changes; black protests and federal pressure were found to be more influential political forces. Yet blacks in the South are still far from achieving economic parity with whites. Racial segregation continues to be the norm in most apartment and residential housing and in private clubs, and blacks are seriously underrepresented in professional and managerial positions in the private sector. The quest of blacks for political equality is much more complete, but the struggle for economic and social equality is still far from over.

7

The Civil Rights Movement and Social Change

> In the early 1960s white officials wouldn't even acknowledge blacks. . . . They almost totally ignored them. But today whites sit and talk with blacks about all sorts of things.
>
> —White elected official, Riviera Beach

The southern civil rights movement, born in the aftermath of the *Brown* decision, represented a potent challenge to white hegemony and signaled the beginning of a long, intense struggle to allow blacks to participate more fully in all aspects of American life. Except for a brief period during Reconstruction, blacks in most of the South had been denied basic political and economic rights. Although the emphasis of the movement was on political equality for blacks, it was assumed that political power could eventually be converted into improved economic and social conditions, and that the yoke of oppression and discrimination against blacks would thereby be removed forever. To what extent the movement has fulfilled these expectations, and exactly how such changes have occurred, are the basic questions addressed in this book.

Thus far most of the literature concerning the civil rights movement in the South has focused on its more dramatic aspects, especially its crises and its often heroic struggles for change.[1] Few scholars, however, have investigated closely the impact or results of the movement at the community level. Such local changes have often taken place rather calmly and slowly and thus have been removed from the spotlight of publicity. Political scientists, deeply concerned with the problems of change and "modernization" in third-world countries, have strangely ignored the transformations occurring in our own underdeveloped areas.[2] With a focus more on consensus than on conflict, and on institutions rather than on social movements, American political scientists have generally held "a very static view" of our society, with little understanding of change or the roots of change.[3]

In hopes of at least beginning to fill this void in social science research, this study has attempted to assess the process and consequences of black political participation in several carefully selected southern communities by charting political and economic changes over time and by exploring the linkages with various modes of political participation. In this conclusion I would like to summarize the findings of previous chapters and then discuss the implications of these findings for political participation and social change more generally in the United States.

The Nature of The Movement

The civil rights movement in the South has generally been characterized as a rather monolithic development, a major mobilization of blacks (and a few whites) that, with the invaluable support of the federal government, successfully challenged white dominance. Indeed, it is often considered the most profound social movement of the century and one of the most significant in our history. This political mobilization and challenge took place largely between the mid-1950s and mid-1960s, and it was assumed that by the late sixties or early seventies most discriminatory barriers to black progress had been toppled. With traditional white elites no longer in complete control, and with blacks having gained a share of political power, popular legend suggests that blacks proceeded to make vast strides in improving their plight. While duly noting that most southern blacks have still not achieved complete economic or social equality with whites, such sanguine accounts inevitably trumpet the great success of the movement.[4]

The results of this investigation of the black movement in various communities fail to support such an optimistic view; nor do the findings agree with the more pessimistic conclusions that black mobilization has had little or no significant impact on the South, especially in the economic realm, and that power has not really changed hands to any degree. What this study has found is that the movement, at least at the local level, was not as simple and uniform as many believed, that the way it began and the form it took varied to a degree throughout the South, and that its results have been rather mixed. On the whole, southern blacks have achieved marked gains in the political arena in most communities, but improvements in the economic and social sectors have been more difficult and less apparent. Nevertheless some economic change has occurred, even in the most traditional settings, and political forces, especially black activism, have often been important in forging gains in various aspects of society.

The civil rights movement has not been as monolithic or uniform as commonly conceived, and the developmental patterns and sequences of black mobilization differed from community to community. Most noticeably, the time period of the initial stirrings of independent political activity by blacks varied a great deal. Political culture obviously influenced these variations: the New South communities experienced significant black politicization during the 1950s and early to mid-1960s, but such activities were rarely found in the Old South prior to the late sixties and seventies. Thus Gretna and Lake City faced no independent black political initiatives until the 1970s, whereas in Daytona Beach such political activity had begun approximately two decades earlier.

One way of classifying these developmental political patterns is to look not only at the degree of black politicization but also at the nature of the political relationships between the white and black subcommunities. Quite clearly the predominant kind of white-black political relationship that develops affects black political activity, and vice versa, so that what is usually found is a reciprocal and dynamic interaction. In suggesting such a conceptual framework for southern communities, Clubok, De Grove, and Farris constructed a typology of five possible patterns: 1) the *non-voting community*, where blacks generally do not register or vote either because of active hostility by whites or because of fear or indifference; 2) the *low-voting, unorganized community*, where the white power structure allows only a few "safe" blacks to vote and there is no attempt to organize blacks politically to any great degree; 3) the *manipulated community*, where blacks are politically organized and many do vote, but their participation is controlled for the most part by white political leaders; 4) the *independent bargaining community*, where blacks are organized and vote independently of the white political structure, and black leaders bargain with white politicians for gains for the black neighborhoods; and 5) the *officeholding community*, which is similar to the independent bargaining pattern except that black gains have resulted in the appointment or election of blacks to public offices.[5]

Each of these patterns reflects both the degree of black political participation and the primary structural relationship between the black and white political communities. To some degree these five categories represent ideal types; in addition, the typologies are not all-inclusive and patterns may overlap at any particular point in time. But this framework does enable one to conceptualize black politicization as a changing, evolving pattern that is dependent to a certain extent on the nature of the relationship between the two subcommunities. Thus if the pattern of structural relationship and the level and nature of black political involvement in a town or city change noticeably, we say that it has undergone a transformation from one type to another. The typology also allows one to chart more clearly the timing and developmental sequences of black political change from one community to another. Finally, one additional pattern has been suggested by this study—that of *political control*—to denote the situation in which blacks hold a clear majority of elected city or town offices and thereby dominate a community politically. This pattern, perhaps unforeseen by Clubok, De Grove, and Farris in the 1960s, developed during the seventies in both majority black communities.

Lack of precise historical data, especially on the informal patterns of relationship between blacks and whites, makes it difficult to categorize these communities for certain time periods. Nor is it always clear when a transformation from one type to another has in fact occurred. Nevertheless, I have suggested the general patterns of black political change for each of the six communities (figure 7.1). As depicted in the figure, the stages of political development in each varied greatly from the early fifties through 1985. As we have seen, most of the New South cities experienced the independent-bargaining and officeholding patterns long before most Old South communities did. Only in Titusville, with a small minority population, did blacks fail to gain elected office, although several blacks were appointed to important positions in its city hall by the latter 1970s. This early achievement of relatively independent political status by blacks in the New South was due to a variety of factors, including the superior political organization there of blacks, a high degree of black economic independence, a reservoir of middle-class black leaders, and a high rate of registration and voter turnout by blacks. Typically, a period of direct black challenge to white dominance, usually in the form of protest or violence, was also necessary to free blacks from the bonds of white control. Also important in the New South were the relatively liberal racial attitudes of most whites and the largely pluralistic and fluid power structures both of which allowed entrance to emerging groups.

Blacks in the Old South communities, in contrast, were confronted with primarily conservative white racial views and a more elitist power structure. Nonetheless, the key elements necessary for transformation to independent-bargaining status and beyond were similar to those required in the more progressive New South. But blacks in the Old South normally needed the additional support of both the federal government, including federal courts, and outside black leaders or groups. External leaders often played the crucial initial role of mobi-

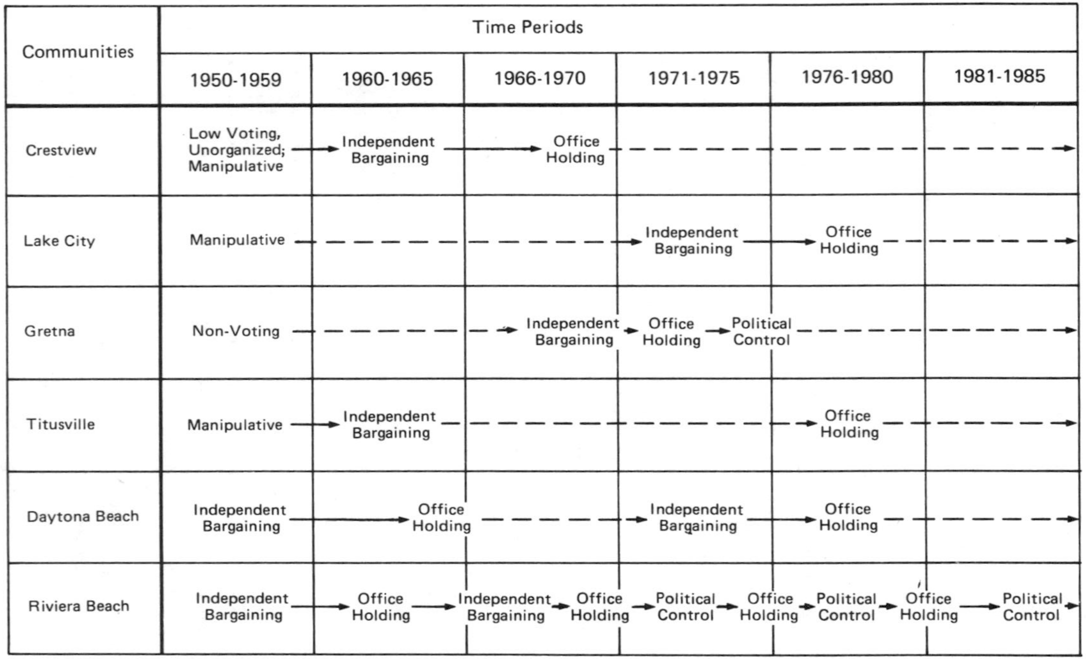

Communities	Time Periods					
	1950-1959	1960-1965	1966-1970	1971-1975	1976-1980	1981-1985
Crestview	Low Voting, Unorganized; Manipulative	Independent Bargaining	Office Holding			
Lake City	Manipulative			Independent Bargaining	Office Holding	
Gretna	Non-Voting		Independent Bargaining	Office Holding; Political Control		
Titusville	Manipulative	Independent Bargaining			Office Holding	
Daytona Beach	Independent Bargaining	Office Holding		Independent Bargaining	Office Holding	
Riviera Beach	Independent Bargaining	Office Holding	Independent Bargaining; Office Holding	Political Control; Office Holding	Political Control; Office Holding	Political Control

FIGURE 7.1

Stages of Black Political Development

lizing local blacks, providing political experience and savvy, and raising important racial issues. Blacks in the Old South also required at least some assistance from more moderate whites, and usually some reduction in opposition from extremist whites, in order to successfully challenge elites in power.

While political culture had a definite influence on patterns of development, the proportion of blacks in the population was apparently a less important factor. Only in communities with a black majority, like Gretna and Riviera Beach, was there some basic congruity in development, as each community experienced patterns first of black officeholding and then of political control during the 1970s. This was not surprising, given the fact that blacks made up more than 50 percent of the citizenry in these locales and that by the seventies blacks were politically active almost everywhere. Yet even these two communities underwent very disparate processes of change during the fifties and sixties.

Aside from the general similarities in political development among some New South cities, there were no other obvious trends in the stages of black political activity. This suggests that at the local level the civil rights movement did not evoke a unilinear process of change. Indeed, the path of political development proved to be markedly different for each of the six communities. While most of the communities moved through several stages during this thirty-five-year time period, progress was much slower for some than others. Titusville, for example, was not able to advance beyond the independent-bargaining pattern, which it achieved to a great degree by the early 1960s, until the late 1970s. Lake City and Gretna also experienced no significant political change for approximately two decades or more, and then each community underwent major transformations in the 1970s. In contrast, Crestview progressed through several stages of development in succession in the 1950s and 1960s, a pattern unlike other Old South communities and somewhat similar to the types of changes taking place in Daytona and Riviera Beach. Yet blacks in Crestview, due to dire poverty and lack of organizational strength, never gained the degree of political independence or officeholding which blacks enjoyed in the New South cities. Thus the process and degree of racial change differed even within specific stages of development.

Not only did the rates of political change vary greatly, but occasionally a community skipped a stage or two and in other instances the path of development was interrupted at times by setbacks, or reversals to prior patterns. Gretna, for example, progressed quickly, once blacks were mobilized, from the nonvoting pattern to independent bargaining and beyond and apparently never experienced the low-voting, unorganized, or manipulated patterns. By contrast, Daytona and Riviera Beach experienced setbacks when blacks lost crucial election races. These temporary reversals in black political development were sometimes the results of a short-lived white backlash following intense black violence, as in Riviera Beach in the late 1960s and Daytona in the early 1970s. In another instance, blacks lost political control in Riviera when whites were able to countermobilize effectively for elections while blacks displayed moderate indifference by not going to the polls.

Despite the lack of uniformity in the process and rates of political change, it is clear that in most communities the civil rights movement played a major role in accelerating the pace of black political development. In a relatively brief period of time, these six cities and towns passed through an average of three stages of development. There is also evidence that if this study had extended back in time just one more decade, we would find that several of these communities experienced transformations in racial and political patterns during the 1940s equivalent to at least one or two more stages of change.[6] This suggests that the years immediately preceding the period of most intense civil rights activity, that is the years of prelude to the movement, were also important in setting the stage for the process of community change. It is still apparent, however, that the most extensive political changes for these communities took place during the years from the late 1950s to 1980, during the apogee and aftermath of civil rights activity.

In addition to hastening the rate of political change, the civil rights movement also served as a crucial impetus to transforming white dominance in the traditional black-white political pattern. Although passage through the first three stages of political development—nonvoting, low-voting, unorganized, and manipulated—signaled "progress" for blacks, none of these transformations threatened the nature of white political hegemony to any great degree. Even in these early stages, when blacks began to organize and vote, their nascent political activities were controlled by whites and utilized to serve white interests. However, at the point in time when blacks were able to make the shift to an independent-bargaining stage, and to subsequent stages, the traditional political pattern of black-white relationships was called into question and altered. White politicians no longer dominated black political activity, and many blacks moved from a "subject" to more of a "participant" political status. Moreover blacks began to utilize the political system and to bargain effectively with whites in order to gain advantages for themselves. As a result, they not only achieved much greater control over their own destiny, but they also managed to modify, and perhaps change forever, white political dominance at the local level.

This transformation of political power relationships was perhaps the most important contribution of the civil rights movement. In all six communities, blacks were able to progress to an independent-bargaining stage or beyond mainly as a result of intense civil rights activity that usually involved protest or violence. In fact, this political mobilization had its greatest impact on power relationships in the Old South communities where white elites were most firmly entrenched. Thus each of the Old South communities experienced significant political changes between 1950 and 1980, progressing from patterns of nonvoting (Gretna), low-voting (Crestview), or manipulation (Lake City) to officeholding and even political control. These major transformations were unparalleled in most of the New South cities during this period. As we have seen, the civil rights movement was initiated relatively early, and changes occurred rather easily, in the New South, so that by the latter 1950s or early sixties all three of these cities had already achieved independent-bargaining patterns of power. As a result, the focus of the movement thereafter, at least from the standpoint of the federal government and national civil rights organizations, was on the Old South, where change was perceived to be slower and more difficult. This emphasis on the Old South appears to have paid off for blacks, for it ultimately loosened the stern yoke of white political oppression.

The Political Effects of Black Mobilization

While the nature and influence of the civil rights movement varied a great deal from one community to another, all of these cities and towns were able to transform traditional white-black political patterns to some degree during this period of revolutionary fervor. This successful challenge to white hegemony, along with the concomitant increase in black political power, were the immediate goals of the movement. It is clear that these short-run goals have essentially been fulfilled; blacks have gained a degree of independence from the white political structure, and in every community blacks are relatively active participants in the political process. Indeed, blacks have won significant elected or appointed political positions in each of these cities and towns. Achievement of such positions of power has been a highly visible and a very substantive indication of black political success; yet it is important to ask whether these gains have been more symbolic than real for black citizens. Has political success resulted in significant improvements for blacks, and if so, in what particular areas or aspects of life?

It is a common assumption that political power can easily be translated into gains in the public sector. This study has explored that assumption closely, examining changes over time in a variety of municipal services including police and fire protection, streets, parks and recreation, and employment. Such services were of paramount importance to blacks, who were generally less able to afford the basic amenities of life. Indeed, much civil rights activity at the local level focused on inadequacies in the provision of these services for blacks. As we have seen, the civil rights era from 1960 to 1985 marked a period of improvement in each of these services, although the level of improvement varied somewhat from one community and kind of service to another.

Southern blacks had long endured inequalities in both the distribution and employment of protective services. With many poor black areas suffering disproportionately high rates of crime and fire, the need for protective services was often greater for blacks than it was for whites. Yet adequate police and fire protection were often lacking in black neighborhoods, and police brutality toward black people was a common practice. In addition, the employment of black police and firemen was rare or nonexistent.

During the decades from the 1960s to the 1980s, police and fire protection for blacks improved in every community. Fire service was enhanced by increases in street paving and streetlighting, improved water service, housing rehabilitation, and the addition of fire hydrants and substations in black neighborhoods. These capital improvements, along with increased professionalism and more modern equipment, were most evident in the wealthier New South cities. Police protection for blacks also improved. Patrols were eventually integrated, black officers were allowed to arrest whites—not just blacks—and patrols in some black neighborhoods were increased. Moderately effective police-community relations programs and minority recruitment efforts, both suggesting an increased sensitivity to black concerns, were initiated in some New South communities. Perhaps most important, in almost all the communities incidents of police violence against blacks decreased.

In the area of employment, the numbers and proportion of black firemen and police officers increased, but only moderately, in most of the municipalities. The hiring of black firefighters was an especially significant change, since fire departments had been extremely resistant to integrating their personnel. Promotions of blacks in the protective services, however, have been relatively infrequent although there has been some improvement since the late seventies. Despite these overall improvements in black employment, progress generally has been rather minimal since the mid-1970s for several reasons. Low pay, better job opportunities in the private sector, discriminatory application requirements, continued white racism among some employees, and few promotional opportunities all served to discourage potential black applicants and to encourage blacks to leave jobs in police and fire departments. In addition, local freezes on public hiring, cutbacks in the CETA program, and modifications in affirmative action tended to diminish black employment opportunities.

Although the number of available municipal jobs is limited, these posts have proven to be of great importance to blacks. Jobs in the public sector often provide steadier work and better pay than comparable tasks in the private sector. In addition, government work offers a number of blacks the opportunity to learn managerial skills that can translate into high-level private-sector positions.[7] Finally, as we have mentioned, the black community as a whole often gains improved services when there are more blacks in positions of authority in the municipal bureaucracy.

Besides police and fire protection, other important municipal services include streets, parks, and recreation. As they were in the case of protective services, southern blacks had almost always been denied equitable streets and recreation. Typically streets in black neighborhoods were unpaved or poorly maintained, making access difficult as well as providing a vivid reminder of blacks' second-class status. Public parks and recreation were totally segregated, with blacks receiving inferior facilities and programs or, sometimes, none at all. When blacks were hired in these departments, it was only for the most menial and physically demanding jobs. And though they fared somewhat better in recreation departments than they did in public works, blacks were only allowed to work within the black community.

Since 1960 street services—primarily paving—for blacks have improved significantly, even relative to street improvements in white areas. Indeed, changes here have been greater than in any other municipal service. As anticipated, improvements were most evident in the more affluent New South, where by 1980 almost all streets were paved in the black sections. In parks and recreation, change was more modest. Although the number and size of parks in most black neighborhoods increased, park acreage grew even more rapidly in most white areas. Qualitatively, black recreational facilities and programs also showed improvement, but primarily in the New South cities. But high vandalism rates and greater park use in black areas and local budget cutbacks in the late 1970s meant greater park deterioration and somewhat reduced recreation programs for blacks.

The most controversial issue concerning recreational services for blacks, was of course the desegregation of facilities, especially municipal beaches and swimming pools. This issue almost always provoked racial anxiety among whites, and as a result, integration proceeded slowly and with considerable opposition. As in the case of other service improvements, progress here was achieved earliest and most easily in the New South. Yet the 1980s still found most beaches, pools, and neighborhood parks frequented almost exclusively by only one race, even though this practice was now a matter of choice, not law.

It was expected that political culture, captured by the contrast between the Old and New South, would be an important contextual variable in any study of the civil rights movement and its impact. Clearly the pattern of changes in municipal services for blacks strongly supports this contention. In almost all cases black public services improved most, sometimes quantitatively but almost always qualitatively, in the New South. Whether it was the first hiring of black police (and usually black firemen as well), the paving of streets, housing rehabilitation, school integration, police-community relations programs, or desegregation of parks and pools, most New South cities achieved changes sooner and to a greater degree than most Old South communities. Lacking the strong cultural strain of racism that was prevalent in the Old South, the New South found it relatively easy to integrate public facilities and employment. In addition, the greater industrialization and affluence of the New South provided a more lucrative tax base, thus giving local governments there a much better opportunity to make costly capital improvements in minority areas.

The other major contextual variable that was expected to affect the pattern of community change was the relative proportion of blacks in the population. Here, too, the findings tend to support previous expectations. Where blacks constituted a majority of the voting population and gained political control, as they did in Gretna and Riviera Beach by the early 1970s, they were able to redistribute basic public services by bringing about relative changes. This was especially the case in Gretna, where blacks were the overwhelming majority and where they completely dominated local government. In such instances of black political hegemony there was sometimes service discrimination by blacks against whites. This reverse discrimination was most clearly evident in public employment, as blacks sought immediate redress, and perhaps revenge in some cases, for past inequities.

As Keech suggests, however, a linear relationship cannot be found between the size of the black population and relative service gains. Thus, where the black proportion of the voting population increased but still constituted less than a majority, blacks did not necessarily secure a more equal share of municipal services. As we have seen, improvements in services for blacks in Daytona Beach and Lake City, both with moderate-sized black populations, were about the same as most services gains in Titusville and Crestview, each with relatively small numbers of blacks. This finding supports Keech's claim that there is a middle range of relative black population size at which whites feel most threatened and resist black service demands. However, where blacks constitute a small minority (approximately 5 to 20 percent) of the population, they are not perceived as a significant threat by whites and change can occur relatively easily. This helps to explain why blacks in Titusville and Crestview experienced greater improvements in services than their politically active numbers would have predicted. Nonetheless, it is also clear that Keech's claims were more valid for the Old South where the influence of race was and still is most apparent. Yet by the 1980s, even in the Old South, racial norms seem to have eased somewhat and whites now feel less threatened by black demands.

Although not related to contextual variables, one other conclusion is apparent from a review of changes in municipal services for blacks. It is easier to change the policies of public services that are primarily capital-intensive, such as parks, street paving, and water and sewage, than those of the primarily human services of police and fire protection; in almost all cases, capital-intensive services showed greater relative change than did the human or labor-intensive services. The reasons for this seem clear. Creating change in capital goods requires only a reallocation of funds or the alteration of plans for capital projects; a decision can be made to pave one street rather than another, or build a park on one side of town instead of another, in order to create greater service equality for blacks. Of course these decisions, too, can be controversial as well as politically difficult. However, they are easier and generally involve far fewer political costs than decisions that call for reallocation of human resources, which often require painful readjustments in behavior and attitudes. Providing greater levels of police and fire protection for the black community may require taking policemen from the white section of town and deploying them in the black section, for example, or forcing white firemen to begin eating and living with black firemen. These are obviously dramatic steps, ones that cannot be implemented as readily as plans for the construction of a sewer or playground. In black-majority cities, however, where blacks eventually controlled policy development, and in New South cities, where more tolerant racial attitudes existed, these human resource services did evolve more easily.

Changes in the Private Sector

While blacks achieved marked gains in the political arena in most communities, improvements in the economic and social sectors have been more difficult and less apparent. Not only have whites generally been more resistant to changes in the private sector, but also blacks focused most of their attention, at least initially, on inequities in the public realm. Nevertheless some economic and social change has occurred, albeit slowly and grudgingly, even in traditional settings.

The most obvious and clear-cut changes in the private sector have been in public accommodations. Totally segregated in most communities through the 1950s, establishments such as movie theaters, restaurants, and motels began to desegregate in the early and mid-1960s. Almost all such public accommodations are open to blacks today. However, in private establishments and in areas where more personal contact between blacks and whites might occur—in country clubs, bars and lounges, apartments, and residential housing—there has been relatively little desegregation. Here whites clearly feel more threatened and racial anxiety is apparent even today. On the other hand, for economic and other reasons, blacks in the Old South have generally not sought entrance into these exclusive white domains.

Desegregation of all types of private establishments began earlier and has advanced further in the New South than it has in the Old South. Not only is racial fear among whites today less apparent in the New South, but blacks there have been more politically assertive in gaining entrance to various private clubs and residential areas; and more blacks in the New South are financially qualified to move into these white enclaves. In the Old South (and sometimes in the New South as well) white racism is still a factor in many establishments, although only rarely does it completely bar blacks from admission. Racism today seems to operate in a more subtle manner, but one that still denies many blacks complete equality of service. In addition, relative poverty, especially in the Old South, deprives blacks of the opportunity to enjoy certain private facilities. "Blacks can go to Morrison's [cafeteria] to eat now, but they don't always have the money to do so, and sometimes they feel uncomfortable there—some don't even know what silverware to use," claimed a Titusville black leader.[8]

Although changes in public accommodations proved to be relatively easy and swift, improvements in black employment opportunities, perhaps the best indicator of black economic progress, have remained difficult and slow. Traditionally, of course, southern blacks were either denied employment or given only the most menial, low-paying jobs. The findings here indicate that most businesses began to integrate their employees sometime during the mid-1960s, but that this initial achievement was followed by only marginal progress in black employment. By the latter 1970s, blacks made up a very small proportion of professional and managerial positions and only a moderate proportion of skilled and semiskilled labor; most businesses that employed blacks still hired them as unskilled or menial laborers. Although the data over time are less than adequate, they suggest that most of the improvements in black employment have been limited to the gradual shifting of more blacks into skilled-labor positions.

As expected, employment opportunities for blacks increased with the rising proportion of blacks in the community, except at the professional level where blacks fared poorly everywhere. Unexpectedly, however, it was found that black employment rates were somewhat better in the Old South than in the New South, even when controlling for other community factors that might have influenced such differences. This surprising finding seemed to be due primarily to economic considerations, as businessmen in the poverty-ridden Old South perceived that increased black employment would attract more black customers and generally would be good for business. Thus, a fundamental reordering of priorities has apparently taken place among many businessmen in the Old South. As historian Elizabeth Jacoway, in a study of southern businessmen, explains it, "Although the maintenance of white supremacy remained a cherished objective, somewhere along the way it slipped from its traditionally dominant position and the primary objective for the South's business leaders became economic growth."[9]

Even in the Old South overt racial discrimination is no longer seen as a major barrier to black employment, and this change has been no small triumph for the civil rights movement. Job impediments now for blacks have more to do with institutional constraints, economic considerations, and levels of education. As a black informant in Crestview put it: "Blacks need to get educated—they need to help themselves and qualify themselves. Too many simply don't put forth the effort."[10] This is not to suggest that discrimination is no longer a factor, but to surmise that it is often operating more subtly. The history of racial discrimination in education and training, the fear of having a black supervise whites, and the presence of formal and informal seniority systems, which have been used to thwart the entry of blacks into white-collar positions, are all forces that have made it difficult for blacks to penetrate higher levels of employment. The greater emphasis by blacks on economic empowerment in the 1980s offers hope for improved job opportunities.

Despite the removal of blatant barriers of discrimination in employment and the integration of other private-sector institutions, black economic progress has not been as great as some analysts had predicted. Table 7.1 summarizes the socioeconomic situation of blacks in 1979–1980 in each of the communities. The table also presents comparable data for whites. As we can see, the economic plight of blacks in most of these communities was still quite dismal, especially in the Old South. In 1979, black per capita annual income averaged only $3,559, or 48 percent of the white income average of $7,430. In the Old South communities, black per capita income was just $3,210, and the average poverty rate of blacks loomed large at 46.1 percent. Black incomes were higher in most New South cities (an annual average of $3,908) and rates of black poverty were generally lower, except for

TABLE 7.1
Socioeconomic Status of Whites and Blacks

	Per Capita Income (1979)		% of Persons Below Poverty (1979)		% High School Graduates (1980)	
Community	*Whites*	*Blacks*	*Whites*	*Blacks*	*Whites*	*Blacks*
Crestview	$5,363	$2,901	19.8%	49.1%	53.0%	38.6%
Lake City	$7,158	$3,997	10.9	42.3	68.0	40.0
Gretna	$6,320[a]	$2,731[a]	6.0	43.9	63.6	29.0
Titusville	$7,427	$3,665	8.1	49.8	74.3	51.6
Daytona Beach	$7,186	$3,264	15.1	38.6	69.6	50.6
Riviera Beach	$11,126	$4,796	7.1	20.5	68.4	49.2

SOURCES: U.S. Bureau of the Census, *1980 Census of Population*, Vol. 1, *Characteristics of the Population*, chapter C (General Social and Economic Characteristics), part 2 (Florida), sections 1 and 2 (July 1983); and Census of Population and Housing, 1980: Summary Tape File 3A (Florida) [Machine/Readable Data File]/prepared by Bureau of the Census, 1982.

[a] Such data for cities and towns of less than 2,500 in population are unavailable; therefore county-level figures are used here and are approximations of income data for Gretna.

Titusville, where the economic recession of the 1970s and cutbacks at the space center seemed to affect blacks disproportionately. Yet even in the New South, black incomes averaged only 46 percent of the relatively high incomes of whites. Moreover, in Daytona Beach and Riviera Beach, where black poverty is relatively low, it was still two to three times higher than the poverty figure for whites.

Formal education is usually an important ingredient for economic success, yet the level of education achieved by most blacks still lags well behind that of most whites. As shown in table 7.1, only a little more than one-third of adult blacks aged twenty-five or over have graduated from high school in the Old South communities, while in the New South the comparable figure is one-half. Yet some 66 percent of white adults have a high school diploma, and this percentage is even higher in the New South. By the 1980s, when a college education had become an increasingly important requirement in the job market, fewer than 7 percent of adult blacks in these communities had four or more years of college; the comparable figure for whites is 14 percent.[11]

Other indicators reinforce this view that, on the whole, blacks are still an impoverished and deprived race. The official unemployment rate among blacks in 1980 was 11.3 percent; in the Old South communities it was more than 14 percent. This jobless rate was almost two and one-half times the rate for whites. As a result, blacks were still very dependent on public welfare as a source of income. More than 25 percent of all black households received public assistance other than Social Security in 1979, while the white assistance level was only 6 percent. As expected, the black welfare rates were considerably higher in the Old South (31 percent) than in the New South (20 percent). Even though a relatively large number of blacks were on public welfare, the average annual level of assistance was low—only $1,973 per household.[12] Hence a large number of blacks were still mired in poverty, with little education, no jobs or only low-paying jobs, and little public assistance. This seemingly hopeless situation was summarized most poignantly by a black administrator in Titusville: "Many blacks still need economic help. We have moved from a stage of economic exploitation to one of economic uselessness, and we need to get out of this."[13]

However, this negative assessment of the contemporary plight of blacks in these communities presents a somewhat distorted picture. For many blacks in both the Old and New South the last two decades have been marked by some economic progress. While comparable census data over time are nonexistent or sparse for most of these communities, there is at least some longitudinal information available for three of the six locales: Daytona Beach, Riviera Beach, and Gretna (Gadsden County).[14] Assuming that socioeconomic changes in these communities are similar to those in the other cities, it is possible to point out several indicators of economic improvement for blacks. In terms of annual income, median black family earnings in 1979 were only about one-half those of white families. Nonetheless between 1959 and 1979 black family median income *quadrupled* on the average in these three communities, and this is a significant increase even after controlling for inflation. Moreover, despite the economic recession of the late 1970s, the gap in per capita income between blacks and whites narrowed somewhat in most of these communities between 1969 and 1979.[15] Not surprisingly, in the 1970s blacks' per capita incomes relative to whites increased the most in the Old South, where, as we have seen, employment opportunities for blacks were somewhat better than in the New South. With rising incomes, the rate of poverty among black families declined by some 25 percent between 1959 and 1979, a rate of decline that was somewhat higher than that for white families. In education, too, blacks made important progress. Since 1960 there has been a 27 percent increase in black high school graduates in these three communities, and the white-black gap in graduation rates has declined markedly in the New South cities.[16]

Perhaps most noticeable, however, has been the development and growth of a viable black middle class. In 1979, thirty-one percent of black households in these three communities had annual incomes of $15,000 or more, and almost 20 percent earned more than $20,000 a year. By contrast, in 1959 only 2 percent of black families had reported annual incomes of $10,000 or more.[17] As anticipated, this emergent black middle class was most prevalent in the New South. Thus for a sizeable number of black families, the sixties and seventies were a period of unparalleled economic mobility. Yet this middle-class phenomenon also brought about deep class divisions in the black communities, since fully another one-third of black families still live in poverty. In contrast to the growing middle class, this black underclass appears to have been relatively unaffected by the civil rights movement. No doubt these economic divisions are already having ramifications for local politics, as blacks of differing classes increasingly disagree as to the appropriate goals and strategies of political action.

The Role of Black Political Participation

As we have shown, the civil rights era and its aftermath were periods of significant change for blacks in the public sector but only moderate transformation in the private realm. Yet knowing precisely what changes have occurred for southern blacks raises the important question of how and why such improvements took place. The other major goal of this study has been to assess the relative efficacy of various black political activities, as well as the role of other major factors, in this process of change.

One of the most widely-debated issues in American politics has been the relative "openness" and "responsiveness" of the political system to minority group demands. This issue has often been couched in the form of a debate between pluralists and elitists. Proponents of pluralism contend that the system is relatively open to a variety of groups and that conventional politics, especially the electoral process, is effective in the process of change. On the other hand, the camp that views the political system as elitist sees politics as relatively closed to minorities and argues that conventional strategies are therefore usually unproductive. More radical theorists claim that only certain unconventional modes of participation, such as protest and even violence, can bring about change for those who are excluded from political power. Although the results of this study will not resolve this debate, they do shed some light on the utility of various forms of minority political participation.

Conventional Strategies

The political strategies employed by any minority group are affected by several factors, including goals, circumstances, and resources. A group's goals, in particular, shape its strategies, since ends and means are inextricably intertwined. Political, economic, and demographic conditions also influence minority tactics, as do the capabilities of the group, yet within these limitations, most minorities still have an array of strategies available to them.

Conventional political strategies, consisting primarily of electoral and interest-group efforts, assume that the political system is sufficiently accessible to allow minorities to gain a fair share of power. Conventional strategies have always been considered the most "acceptable" forms of political action. Voting, lobbying, and other orthodox forms of participation are viewed as the essence of democracy, and this "American way" is a basic assumption of most civics courses offered in our public schools. How valid these normative prescriptions are for racial minorities, however, is a question not often addressed.

The basic mode of conventional politics, and certainly the core of the American democratic creed, is the act of voting—more broadly defined as electoral participation. Civil rights leaders tended to perceive the ballot as the most important right southern blacks could obtain. It was strongly believed that the vote would pave the way for other basic changes, including improvements in education, employment, and public services. Besides having this instrumental value, the franchise was also seen as providing politically powerless blacks with a new sense of self-worth.

When blacks first began to register and vote, whites usually responded with threats, harassment, and even physical violence. These responses were initially successful in thwarting the black vote, but as the black electorate increased in numbers white tactics began to change. At this point, white politicians actively sought black voters through various manipulative strategies, including the co-optation of some black leaders. This period of electoral manipulation resulted in few real benefits for most blacks other than token satisfactions in the form of moderately improved public services and the appointment of small numbers of blacks to low-level municipal jobs. Nevertheless, the larger the relative size of the black electorate, and the less amenable black voters were to easy manipulation, the greater the level of benefits blacks derived from voting.

As blacks achieved a more independent economic and political status, their vote was less easily controlled by whites, and the franchise became still more effective as an instrument of real change. This shift was most clearly seen in the election of blacks to public office for the first time; it was also demonstrated in the election of more moderate whites, especially in the New South, where liberal candidates were more plentiful, and in bond issue elections on capital improvements. Although blacks were not always successful in these elections, their tendency to engage in bloc voting nevertheless served as a vivid expression of black demands.

In the private sector, however, black voting was not important—at least not directly—in affecting changes either in public accommodations, employment, or residential housing. Indeed, by the early 1980s black voter registration rates had dipped in the New South (Daytona and Riviera Beach showed the lowest rates in more than two decades), suggesting a new political apathy among many blacks. The primary goals of blacks in the New South were no longer in the public realm but in the private sector and consisted of better jobs and improved housing. When the achievement of these goals proved to be immune to direct electoral challenge, black political strategies apparently began to adapt to the changed circumstances.

While black voting was moderately effective as an instrument of change, black organizational efforts proved to be less significant. Of course, organizational efforts were not always totally distinct from electoral strategies, since black interest groups usually played a role in mobilizing blacks to register, vote, and even compete for public office. Yet interest-group tactics extended well beyond the electoral arena and often included voicing black demands at public meetings, lobbying public officials and businessmen, initiating lawsuits, filing complaints with the federal government, and planning and organizing for direct action. In almost every community, each of these forms of group activity was important at one time or another.

While the modes of organizational activity varied a great deal, so did the kinds of groups. Black interest groups ranged in nature from neighborhood associations and local voter leagues to nationally affiliated civil rights organizations such as the NAACP, CORE and SCLC. The former, community-based groups tended to be single-issue oriented and relatively short-lived, usually focusing on a particular grievance or form of discrimination. The latter organizations, the more familiar civil rights groups, were more often involved in a broad range of issues and endured over a longer period of time in these communities; this was especially true of the NAACP, as we have seen. In general, because the New South communities were more urbanized and pluralistic in structure, they produced a greater number and variety of black organizations. These New South groups were usually indigenous; that is, they were initiated and financed primarily by local leaders and citizens. In the smaller, more elitist, and poorer Old South communities, black interest groups were less numerous and more exogenous in nature. Such groups were often established by leaders from outside the community, were based elsewhere, and received more external funding. This outside support was essential, at least initially, to the development of black organizations in the Old South, since local blacks often lacked the necessary experienced leadership and resources, and whites were likely to thwart or co-opt any indigenous organizational attempts.

Black interest groups were not important, at least not directly, in the improvement of municipal employment and services for blacks. As we have seen, other political factors were much more strongly associated with changes in local public resources. Organizational efforts did prove somewhat more effective in the private sector. Black groups, especially the NAACP, played a key role in desegregating public accommodations and, to a lesser extent, in attempting to improve employment opportunities and working conditions for blacks.

While black organizations were often essential as a base and support for blacks in local politics, the nature of these groups, their goals, and their tactics tended to alter over time. The earliest associations were usually local voter leagues or traditional NAACP organizations, whose goals included the mobilization of blacks as an independent political force, the encouragement of electoral participation, the confronting of segregation in public accommodations, and the improvement of public services. By the mid and latter 1970s, however, these traditional groups had declined and other kinds of black organizations often emerged to replace them. In these new organizations, composed primarily of younger, better-educated, and more middle-class leaders and members, the protest leaders and traditional ministers of the earlier period played a less prominent role. By this time the goals of the movement had become more economic in nature, and its organizational tactics were less confrontationist and more conventional. The new black leaders, often college educated and generally professional, were well equipped to work "within the system"; many of them were employed alongside whites and lived in predominately white residential neighborhoods. These new groups were sometimes criticized for being out of touch with poor blacks and for being too moderate in their goals and tactics. They also symbolized the growing class divisions among blacks, and their emergence sometimes led to increased fragmentation and ideological controversy. This organizational transition was much more apparent in the New South than in the Old South, where the goals and nature of many black groups continued to reflect the struggle to achieve more basic political changes.

Black Elected Officials

The most important form of all conventional—and unconventional—political activities was electing blacks to local office. This political mode proved to be more significant than organizational efforts or any other mode of political behavior. Although black officials were usually elected as the result of black electoral participation (often with the help of some white votes), the presence of such officials went beyond the scope and general influence of voting alone. Black representation "on the inside" was a direct and effective conduit for political input from black citizens and, more than any other conventional mode, gave them easy, constant, and relatively quick access to the decision-making arena and to white leaders, both public and private. In addition the aura of legitimacy that generally surrounds elected representatives gave black officials a degree of influence and power in the public realm that other black leaders and organizations rarely had. Nonetheless, it was not clear whether black elected officials were more effective when they were part of a larger liberal coalition that was dominant in city politics.

In the black-majority communities, of course, black officeholders were able to develop their own dominant ruling groups, but in the other cities either liberal coalitions were rarely dominant or black officials had difficulty gaining access to such groups.

In the struggle for improvements in municipal services, black officials were the single most important political factor. This was true for most capital and labor-intensive services. But black representatives were more effective in changing employment opportunities than they were in affecting capital-based services such as street paving, even though, as has been shown, capital-oriented services were almost always more amenable to change. Moreover, blacks in public office were able to affect *relative* (not just absolute) *changes* in services; that is, to a degree their impact was of a redistributive nature. Redistribution of public services is often difficult to achieve because it usually requires that goods or services be denied to one group (whites in this case) in order to be granted to another group (blacks). Thus attempts at redistributing services have almost always been resisted by white officials. Black representatives were most easily able to effect relative changes in services in communities in which blacks were in the majority and ultimately in political control, but they were also moderately effective in redistributing services in cities with medium-sized and even small black populations.

Black officials tended to utilize a variety of tactics in order to improve public services. Most commonly, they encouraged and even pressured local officials to employ more blacks in positions other than menial ones and to upgrade municipal services in minority neighborhoods. Sometimes successful "encouragement" required little more than enlightening white officials about the vastly inferior conditions of city services in some minority areas. Often black representatives persuaded city officials to seek federal grants more aggressively, especially grants that were earmarked for low-income neighborhoods.

Besides working on the inside to improve conditions, black elected officials were frequently instrumental in promoting increased political participation by black citizens. Not only were blacks much more likely to register and vote when a member of their race competed for public office, but in numerous other ways minority citizens were more attentive to and involved in local politics when a black assumed office. "With black elected officials, blacks know they're being represented—as a result they come to city council meetings more now and bring their complaints to their councilmen. Previously blacks were afraid to go before all-white councils," claimed a black Riviera Beach official.[18] Furthermore, black representatives often played an educational role by helping to make minority citizens more aware of how the political system works and by showing them how to be effective in local politics. For many blacks who had been totally shut out of "the white-man's politics" for generations, this educational experience was invaluable.[19]

Black officeholders also proved instrumental in having blacks appointed to citizen advisory boards and committees.[20] While black appointments tended to be concentrated on committees dealing primarily with minority interests (like human relations or commmunity development), black officials were typically able to achieve black representation on other, more important boards as well, including planning and zoning, personnel or civil service, housing, and tax adjustment. Such appointments enabled elected officials to reward those who supported them and to provide at least symbolic representation to minority citizens.[21] However, analyses indicate that black representation even on the more important committees had no significant impact either on the distribution of basic city services or minority employment patterns.[22]

While black officials were effective agents of change in the public sector, they proved to be less significant in improving conditions in the private realm. For the most part, the private sector was simply beyond the pale of black public officials as well as most other conventional political strategies. Black representatives sometimes attempted to encourage more industries and retail businesses to relocate in their communities in order to improve the tax base and provide additional jobs, but these efforts were rarely very successful. Such attempts were most pronounced in communities with sizeable black populations. However, the lack of basic public services, as in Gretna, and the racial makeup of these locales tended to deter industrial and commercial growth. Black elected officials were more effective in encouraging blacks to apply for jobs and in supporting affirmative action efforts in the private sector.

Even in the public sector, however, blacks in elected office were limited in their ability to influence change. This was most apparent in communities where blacks numbered less than a majority and where black officials were a decided minority on elected bodies. One important limitation was and continues to be the general lack of public financial resources, especially in the more impoverished Old South communities. Basic capital improvements in black neighborhoods that have few municipal services are expensive, and federal funds for such improvements are diminishing. Moreover, conservative whites have been extremely unsympathetic to the demands of black representatives, especially when those demands have entailed a redistribution of resources and services from white neighborhoods to black areas.

A number of black officials also faced the problem of being elected in an at-large system and were therefore dependent on a sizeable white vote for victory at the polls. This was the case in Crestview, Titusville, and Daytona Beach, where blacks constituted a minority of the population. This "dual legitimacy," or cross-pressuring from two different subcommunities, has usually forced black candidates to moderate their views so as not to alienate whites, and as a result, black candidates make fewer demands on behalf of their constituents.[23] In Crestview, this dilemma was reflected in the statement of a long-time black councilman, an official elected largely by white votes: "I never worked exclusively for blacks, even though their services are the worst. I tried to help the entire city equally, blacks as well as whites."[24]

Somewhat surprisingly, many black representatives reported that conflict within and lack of cooperation from the black community itself was often a major impediment to more effective public service. While the black community was usually united and provided full support for the first black candidates for office, this unity and support often factionalized and dwindled after the goal of electing the first blacks was achieved and more black candidates began to contest for power. These political splits sometimes denied minority candidates and incumbents the unified racial support necessary for election victory. In addition, black officials were frequently criticized by their black constituents for not fulfilling more of their political promises. In the words of a black councilman in Riviera Beach: "Black expectations are high when a black is elected. They want us to change the world in one day, and when we don't do this they brand us as 'Uncle Toms.' "[25] Such initially high expectations inevitably led to disillusionment and ultimately to a decrease in political involvement.

In some cases abuse of political power by black officials themselves lessened their effectiveness and reduced their political support. Being accused and convicted of criminal offenses while in office, as was the case with the mayor of Gretna and the police chief in Riviera Beach, or of misusing political power, as in the public-housing scandal in Riviera Beach, made it difficult for black officials to hold the trust and support of their constituents. No doubt the activities of blacks first elected to office were more closely scrutinized than other local officials, and this constant attention sometimes created additional tensions for black officeholders. Perhaps most importantly, such offenses tended to reinforce the attitude held by some whites that blacks cannot be trusted and are unqualified to serve in public office.

CHAPTER 7

Unconventional Strategies

Clearly conventional black politics and especially black elected officials were very important in the process of change; yet conventional approaches suffered from several serious limitations. First, such strategies had little effect in altering conditions in the private, nongovernmental sector. Housing and private-sector employment, for example, were clearly beyond the pale of most conventional politics. In addition, though blacks gained political resources, they still lacked the economic resources that are so crucial to governing and building a new community power-base. As the late Stein Rokkan once observed, "The vote potential constitutes only one among many different power resources—votes count in the choice of governing personnel but resources decide the actual policies."[26] Thus in most communities, white business leaders control vast amounts of money, major credit sources, and most significant organizations. White businessmen also have a favorable standing with the media and enjoy a high degree of social status. This concentration of resources gives business leaders a position of power that goes well beyond the much more limited political power of even a well-organized black community.[27] Finally, conventional minority strategies produce changes that take place only slowly and gradually, if at all. Because electoral politics is controlled and structured to some degree by those in power, the impetus for reform is blunted and change usually occurs in a very deliberate, incremental manner.[28] While this process maintains stability and allows orderly social change, it also explains why conventional political approaches have only a limited and very gradual impact on policy.

Although the focus of much of the civil rights movement was on conventional politics, particularly the vote, much attention was also given by blacks to the use of more unconventional strategies. Consisting primarily of various kinds of collective protests and occasionally violence, unconventional approaches were often viewed, at least from the pluralist perspective, as rare and "extreme" forms of action that were unnecessary, irrational, and sometimes counterproductive to political change. On the other hand, other social scientists argued that unconventional strategies were relatively common and normal in politics and were often necessary ingredients for real change to take place. Until recent times, little scholarly attention was devoted to these more unconventional political approaches, and the pluralist assumptions dominated American politics. With the advent of the civil rights movement, however, these widely believed pluralist notions were called into question, and a variety of groups struggling for power began to utilize unconventional tactics. Yet the efficacy of these tactics, especially violence, remains very much in question. Unexplored even more is the relationship, if any, between conventional and unconventional strategies in the process of social change.

Most prevalent among the nontraditional approaches used by southern blacks were various kinds of peaceful protest. Sit-ins, boycotts, marches, pickets, and other public demonstrations were first employed on a relatively large scale in attempts to desegregate public accommodations. Beginning in the early 1960s, each of these communities experienced some degree of black protest directed at integrating lunch counters, restaurants, movie theaters, and motels. Such protests were quite successful, especially in the New South and in communities where blacks were a significant proportion of the population. Buttressed by the 1964 Civil Rights Act, black desegregation demands were perceived by many whites as generally legitimate and relatively limited in scope. Moreover, the protests themselves dramatized the injustice of segregated facilities as no conventional political activity could. Indeed, the peaceful nature of civil disobedience stirred the national conscience and attracted favorable media attention. At the community level, the demonstrations were effective primarily due to their real or threatened economic and political sanctions. Some white businesses suffered financially as a result of the sit-ins and boycotts, and community stability and peace were often imperiled by the chaos and occasional violence which developed.

Once the demands of black protesters moved beyond the desegregation of public accommodations, however, these unconventional techniques became less effective. Protests did have a short-term impact on some municipal services for blacks, particularly during the 1960s and before blacks were elected to office. By the late sixties and early seventies, however, black demonstrations were less common and directed more toward improving black employment and work conditions, increasing municipal services, and occasionally opening private clubs such as bars and lounges to blacks. Black protesters also focused a great deal of attention on school desegregation issues, especially "second-generation" forms of discrimination.[29] While these later protests were moderately effective in altering some conditions, whites were clearly more threatened by such proposed changes and less willing to respond to the new black demands. Once blacks shifted their attention to institutions of employment, education, and private clubs, whites generally became more fearful of the perceived interracial ramifications and more aware of the redistributive nature of the policy demands. As a result, white support decreased, especially in the more conservative Old South. Moreover, the protest strategies themselves had grown somewhat routine in most communities and by the mid-1970s were no longer as effective. White policymakers had become immune to the dramatic aspects of demonstrations and developed various counterstrategies for muting their effectiveness.[30]

While peaceful protest was the most frequent form of unconventional activity during this period of civil rights struggle, black violence was also relatively common. Consisting primarily of riots and some interracial fighting, reported episodes of violence occurred in every one of the communities except Crestview. Indeed, full-scale riots took place in most of the communities, marking the radical phase of the movement and often producing a watershed in black-white relations. Although black violence usually coincided with protest activity, either directly preceding or following peaceful demonstrations, it was often the act of violence, more than protest or any other political strategies, that catalyzed the transition to black independence. Such violence, or at least major and prolonged protest, was usually necessary to break the stranglehold of white political control and hasten the process toward meaningful social change.

At the very least, black violence proved to be a powerful vehicle for expressing political grievances. Lack of public services, problems of school desegregation, lack of jobs, and police brutality were the major issues that sparked most of the riots and interracial conflicts. The violence was not only dramatic, and attracted the attention of whites far more than conventional political activity, but it also served as a clear and unambiguous warning that blacks were no longer willing to tolerate certain conditions. By flooding the media with information about the seriousness of various problems faced by blacks, such actions also helped to transform their grievances into public issues. As a result, black violence often stimulated immediate, although short-term, change. In the wake of rioting, police and other city services were often increased, more blacks were appointed to citizen advisory boards, school desegregation issues were confronted, black employment rose, and working conditions sometimes improved. Such changes, of course, were most likely to take place in the more liberal New South and in the black-majority communities, where the black population represented, potentially, a destabilizing force of significant size.

In addition to creating the crisis conditions often necessary for change, rioting, as well as major protests, seemed to give blacks—particularly younger blacks—a more positive image of themselves and their potential for power. Thus the act of directly confronting whites, especially the police, who were often viewed as the symbols of oppression, gave blacks more confidence to assert themselves politically. Violence also tended to bring blacks together, and thereby provided an impetus to organizational efforts that typically followed in its wake.

Yet because the costs of severe violence were sometimes high for blacks and the resources necessary for prolonged conflict were lacking, this form of political action rarely continued for any length of time, and blacks were unable to keep continued pressure on those in power through interracial conflict. Moreover, black violence, like a double-edged sword, had negative as well as positive effects. Rioting frequently led to increased white alienation toward blacks and a strong wave of political backlash. Elements of this white backlash included electoral reprisals toward black candidates at the polls, increased pressure for resegregation (especially of schools), an emphasis on "law and order," some increased harassment of blacks, and a reduced response to black demands from public officials. These negative consequences resulted from the strong belief shared by most white citizens that domestic violence by outgroups is immoral and unjustified.[31]

Nevertheless this backlash, while virulent at times in the immediate aftermath of black violence, was usually itself a short-term response. In the long run it temporarily slowed, but did not halt, racial progress. This was probably because the most severe form of racial violence, large-scale rioting, generally took place in the communities in the late sixties or early seventies and rarely reoccurred thereafter. This one-time occurrence, over a relatively brief period of the civil rights era, not only reduced the policy impact of conflict, but also seemed to ameliorate backlash reactions. Sociologist William Gamson, who has made historical studies of numerous protest groups, claims that "successful groups almost never used it [violence] as a primary tactic. . . . Violence, in short, is the spice of protest, not the meat and potatoes."[32]

Thus it is evident that nontraditional strategies were generally necessary for meaningful community change. But the relative success of these various strategies depended on a variety of conditions, including the political culture of the community, the relative size of the black population, the goals of the protesters, and the type of strategy employed. In most instances, too, unconventional approaches evolved in cadence with various conventional strategies; at some point it was necessary for protest to be translated into electoral mobilization. The employment of both approaches, usually not simultaneously but in relatively close sequence, raises the unanswered question of the relationship between these general modes of participation.

The results of this study suggest that, contrary to speculation, conventional and unconventional strategies did not usually negate or interfere with each other, but tended rather to complement and reinforce each other.[33] Protest and violence complemented conventional black politics in several ways, including 1) reducing white control and manipulation, which had often muted the effectiveness of conventional approaches; 2) effecting a degree of private sector change, a process outside the influence of most conventional strategies; 3) helping to further mobilize blacks, thus reinforcing the organizational efforts which were often a necessary ingredient for change; and 4) creating destabilizing, crisis conditions that were essential to accelerate the pace of social change beyond the relatively slow, gradual shifts associated with electoral politics.

On the other hand, conventional approaches were often more useful than unorthodox methods in 1) affecting changes in Old South and low-proportion black communities, where protest and violence were sometimes less effective; 2) providing a steadier and more consistent pressure for change, which was lacking in the more unpredictable, ephemeral, unconventional techniques; and 3) serving as a moderate influence that appealed to whites in power and tended to assuage the backlash to black violence. This latter advantage of conventional politics was especially important in the process of forging and consolidating black gains. As Jack Walker put it in a case study of racial change in Atlanta: "The liberal [black] group's function is, literally, to start fights they are unable to finish. They are able to create a crisis, but are frequently unable to resolve it because they have no basis for contact with the dominant white leaders."[34] Walker went on to say that it is the role of the moderate black leaders, with "their reputations and the connections they have built up with the white community through the years," to then resolve the crisis and negotiate institutional changes.[35]

What this suggests is that neither conventional nor unconventional politics alone has usually been sufficient for meaningful change to occur with any degree of alacrity. Indeed, most often some combination of both approaches has been necessary for real and relatively rapid change. As we have seen, those communities experiencing the greatest racial transformations—Riviera Beach, Daytona Beach, and Gretna—clearly utilized just such a combination of strategies. Blacks achieved less success in the other three communities in part because of the lack or underutilization of one or both of these essential political approaches.

Other Forces of Change

Black political participation has clearly been one of the most important factors in the process of social change. While the developmental/

modernization thesis suggests that natural economic growth over time is primarily responsible for change, the findings here indicate otherwise. In the public sector, and occasionally in the private area as well, the rate of change in the level of services for blacks usually outstripped that for whites. Developmental theory predicted approximately equal rates of change for blacks and whites; or where racially discriminatory norms still dominated, it predicted that whites would continue receiving more and better services. The fact that this theory cannot explain the kinds of policy changes that have occurred in most of these communities indicates that other forces must have been operating to counter these "natural" trends. Moreover, the passage of time, as measured in the path models, did not alone have any direct impact on public or private policies of concern to blacks.

This is not to say, however, that socioeconomic variables are insignificant. As we have seen, the relatively liberal racial atmosphere and rapid economic development of the New South clearly eased the way for black progress, while the conservative orientation of the Old South has served to retard such progress. Similarly, demographic variables, such as the black proportion of the population, have often influenced the degree and rate of racial transformation. But, these contextual factors alone were not sufficient to explain changes. Here, black politicization, in several of its forms, and certain other political factors were of critical importance.

Chief among these other political forces of community change was the federal government. From the federal courts to various laws, regulations, and grants, the national government played a key role in promoting racial equality. Most school desegregation issues, as well as a number of other local conflicts, were ultimately resolved in federal district courts, which often proved to be a counterforce to white intransigence. National civil rights laws, especially the 1964 Civil Rights Act, and to a lesser extent affirmative action regulations, also served as an important impetus to racial change, especially in the private sector. In addition, federal grants, including revenue sharing, Community Development Block Grants, and CETA, provided a share of the necessary dollars to finance local public service improvements and increased employment opportunities, and the civil rights guidelines that accompanied these grants sometimes proved to be the "sticks" attached to the "carrots" of federal funds. In all these ways, Washington played a very influential role, particularly in the Old South, where poverty and white racism were such insurmountable barriers to progress.

While the impact of the federal government was often major enough to dwarf the effects of other agents of change, other forces nevertheless performed vital roles. The emergence of a number of moderate and liberal white leaders and white citizens often provided the balance of support necessary to convert black demands into policy. Of special importance were politically moderate city managers, council members, municipal department heads, and businessmen who were able to serve as liaisons with the black community, help forge policy changes to meet black needs, and in general, create a climate of racial understanding. But the black movement also spawned white organizational counter-challenges. Ranging from extremist—like the KKK—to moderate in ideology, these white groups had a significant depressing effect on public services for blacks, especially in the Old South.

In addition to these influences, there were specific outside forces and factors that served to challenge community traditions, including race relations. Intervening political forces were especially significant in the Old South, where racial norms were most firmly entrenched. For example, the entrance of outside organizers into Lake City and Gretna from nearby areas was crucial to the successful political mobilization of blacks in these communities; lacking a reservoir of independent, middle-class citizens and indigenous political leaders, local blacks were initially forced to rely on outsiders to provide the necessary ingredients for change. At times certain other factors were instrumental as well in transforming race relations. Although difficult to measure, the national civil rights movement and the generally egalitarian mood of the country in the 1960s tended to reinforce the views of local moderate whites that racial discrimination was morally wrong and that black political mobilization, including protest, was legitimate. Obviously this influence, conveyed primarily through the national media, was most pervasive in the New South. Similarly, the development of the Kennedy Space Center near Titusville and the growth of Eglin Air Base just outside of Crestview had a tremendous impact on each of these cities. By attracting more liberal, middle-class citizens—both white and black—into these communities and by spurring the stricter enforcement of federal laws, including school desegregation, these enormous federal installations tended to encourage the civil rights movement and hasten racial progress. Along with the federal government directly, these projects played an essential role in the process of change.

Implications for Theories of Democracy and Social Change

Clearly the results of this study shed some light on the debate between the plural and elite views of democracy in the United States and on theories of social change. The pluralist perspective, as we have discussed, tends to interpret American politics as an extremely open system with relatively free and easy access for all competitors. According to this model, change occurs somewhat slowly but in an orderly manner due to the generally strict adherence to the "rules of the game." These rules stress conventional strategies, especially electoral politics, as the proper means of affecting change, and they interpret unconventional approaches as essentially abnormal and unproductive.

Quite obviously this study of the black movement in the South contradicts pluralist assumptions in a number of significant ways. First, groups poor in resources, leadership, and organization do not have easy access to the political system, nor do these prerequisites to power always develop simply or naturally. Often "outside" or external assistance is crucial for such outgroups to even begin to compete in the political arena. Moreover, some linkage with "advantaged" groups (in this case, moderate or liberal whites) is generally important. Without these forms of external support, seriously disadvantaged groups will usually find it impossible to play the game with any degree of success.

Second, the pluralist contention that conventional politics alone are sufficient to bring about major changes for outgroups is flawed. Those in power are able to structure and manipulate the conventional political actions of minorities, especially voting, and can thereby minimize the impact of such strategies. Indeed powerholders often develop countergroups that act to limit the demands of the disadvantaged. As a result, changes due to conventional politics are normally limited in scope and relatively slow to occur. Under these conditions modest transformations may take place in the public sector but few or none in the private, nongovernmental realm.

Third, the pluralist view of unconventional forms of participation is in error. Protest and even violence, rather than being self-defeating, are often necessary for change. Unconventional politics tend to complement and reinforce conventional modes by serving as important means of attention-getting and mobilization. Such functions are conducive to transformations not only in the short run, in the provision of some services, but in the longer-run distribution of power.

These criticisms lend support to the elite interpretation of American politics. Yet the conclusions of this study counter elite theory in several important ways as well. Elite theorists' contention that conventional political strategies are typically useless in bringing about fundamental change is not completely correct, for while it is true that such strategies have proved to be generally inefficacious in the private realm, conventional approaches have often produced incremental changes in public services; over time, such piecemeal improvements can amount to rather substantial change. Moreover, electoral mobilization and the resulting increase in the number of minorities elected to political office have clearly bolstered the impact of conventional strategies, at least for blacks. This development, a direct product of the civil rights movement, has resulted in a marked revision (but not yet a rejection) of the claim that "politics as usual" will not work for disadvantaged groups.

Radical critics of elitism are also in error when they suggest that only unconventional strategies (if any) can be successful for outgroups. Such an assertion ignores the double-edged nature of violence and to a lesser extent, of protest. Under certain circumstances violence is counterproductive, bringing about political backlash and further repression. In addition, unconventional approaches in general lack continuity and the ability to implement reform. Hence, unconventional politics alone are no more successful than conventional strategies alone; all these perspectives—the elitist, the radical, and the pluralist—ignore the importance of the reciprocal, mutually supportive relationship between these two approaches to change.

Lastly, this look at the civil rights movement and community change challenges the elite view that since outgroups possess little or no significant political influence, real social change can only result from the actions of those in power. As we have seen, black groups in a variety of settings have played important roles in the process of change despite attempts by elites to block or at least manipulate the activities of these groups. As sociologist Doug McAdam, in a history of recent black insurgency in this country, describes it: "In place of our image of an elite comfortably in control of the political environment, it would seem more accurate to see the elite as a harried group scrambling to manage or contain numerous challenges that arise to threaten the fundamental prerogatives of class rule."[36] This is not to argue that elites are vulnerable to challenges from any or all outgroups, or that pluralist theory offers a more accurate portrayal of change. Instead, it is to suggest that elite groups are not always so dominant or invincible, and that insurgents can, with the necessary mobilization and the proper combination of strategies, influence significant change.

What bearing do these findings have for sociological theories of social movements and change? Quite clearly the results here support the resource mobilization theory of the development and impact of collective action. This theory, one may recall, emphasizes the political orientation of social movements and focuses on the factors that lead to the accumulation of resources. Such resources are considered crucial to the process of organizing to bring about change. The emphasis of this study has not been, however, on why and how social movements begin, but on what strategies for change are most effective and on the political outcomes of such movements. Thus the focus here has been on aspects of outgroup insurgency that have been seriously neglected in most previous studies.

In attempting to call attention to the dilemma of tactics, I have found that the political strategies of insurgents are important. Those in power can be influenced and changes effected, but the nature of the tactics employed is often crucial to success. Furthermore, the choice of strategies depends on the goals of the minority group, the political culture and openness of the system, and the relative size of the insurgent group. It has been suggested that there is often a complementary relationship between conventional and unconventional strategies, and that this seems to be the essential mix for optimum success and change. While disruptiveness can lead to immediate and relatively short-term benefits and can take place without formal organization, such organization is usually necessary for long-term, more permanent change and is not incompatible with the mobilization process. Thus it is not just the massing of resources, but how those resources are employed strategically, that is important.

In terms of the political outcomes of social movements, I have indicated the significance of exploring both the public and private sectors and of looking at such changes in the immediate time frame as well as over the longer term. It was found that gains in political power are usually translatable into improved public benefits, yet these changes vary to some degree depending on the kind of service and the nature of the community. Enhanced political power has much less influence, however, in the private arena. While collective action can effect some social and economic change, such improvements are typically slower to occur and much more difficult to bring about than public-sector changes. Improved socioeconomic conditions are also dependent on such factors as the type of community, the relative size of the insurgent group, and the nature of the benefit.

In addition to exploring several relatively uncharted areas of theoretical concern, this study has provided new evidence for some of the continuing debates among social-movement scholars. One such debate concerns the function of internal organization versus outside resources in the generation of social movements. This close investigation of the civil rights movement has indicated that external resources were important, indeed crucial, at times. The federal government, outside political leaders, and certain environmental factors were often critical to the initiation and continuance of collective action. This was particularly the case in closed, elite-dominated societies and in situations where the outgroup was relatively small in numbers and poor in resources. Under such conditions, external forces served as a necessary catalyst for change. Even under more favorable circumstances, outside resources provided an important supportive structure that tended to ease and quicken the process of change.

Nevertheless, I do not intend to deny the significance of internal organization and resources. Not only in the initiating phase but particularly in the long-term activities of the movement, the internal organization of insurgents was a key variable. The clear shift in federal-government assistance to the black movement by the early 1980s is a good illustration of how outside groups may eventually lose interest or feel threatened by the movement and withdraw their support. Thus the level of minority organization and the generation of internal resources are important for the long-run success or even just the continuation of the movement. The ability of insurgent leaders and organizations to adapt internally to changing goals, local political conditions, and reduced outside support is also a significant factor. Minority-group relations with the local media, with business leaders, and with local public officials are other valuable resources for the movement. Hence improving local conditions depends greatly on the degree of support or resistance from those in power at the community level, especially those with economic resources. In the period studied this was apparent even when the insurgents constituted a majority of the population and held political control, but still lacked vital economic power.

In the end what does all this suggest about the future of the black movement in southern communities? No doubt the decline of the national civil rights movement and the decrease in support from the federal government have made it more difficult for blacks to mobilize and achieve change at the local level. The development and growth of a black middle class has resulted in class divisions and increased internal conflict within the movement. Whites in power, moreover, are willing to allow only moderate changes in basic institutions, especially in the economic sector. Even after the most active years of the civil rights movement, these elites still maintain an inordinate amount of control over local decisions, particularly in the Old South. It seems, by the mid-1980s, that white powerholders have gone about as far as they are willing to go to accommodate black demands. Similarly white elites, along with many middle-class blacks, have implicitly accepted the existence of a sizeable underclass of poor blacks who seem beyond the reach of most government programs and even of the self-help efforts of minority organizations. Hence it appears that liberal-democratic thought has been overly optimistic about social change in this country, at least in the South, and about the role of insurgent groups in the process of change.

Yet it is apparent that the civil rights movement engendered a sense of racial pride, confidence, and cohesiveness that was only rarely found previously in black political culture in the South. These enhanced qualities, along with important electoral gains, have insured that the results of the Second Reconstruction will be more permanent than the First. These significant changes have provided blacks with more control over their own destiny than they ever enjoyed before. Although any dramatic new phase in the movement must await the proper social conditions, it is clear that the role played by blacks and the political strategies they employ will be extremely important.

Appendix 1

Methodology

A variety of research approaches have been employed in this investigation of black politics and community change. The study of social and political phenomena, even at one point in time, is an extremely complex matter; attempting to analyze changes in these phenomena and the factors related to such changes compounds the task immensely. No single methodological approach seemed adequate. As a result, I utilized a battery of research techniques, each having certain advantages and disadvantages, as a way of confirming or contradicting the basic findings of any single approach. Although this multiple indicators' strategy was time-consuming and labor-intensive, it allowed me to report my ultimate conclusions with a much greater feeling of confidence.

As suggested earlier, the most useful of the research methods was the in-depth interviews with well-informed citizens. I used a reputational approach as the primary means of nominating citizens who were considered most cognizant of local politics and race relations since the late 1950s. Initially, names of knowledgeable residents were solicited from newspapers, public officials, and prominent private citizens. Before an individual was interviewed, however, he or she had to be nominated by at least two other persons. At the end of each interview, respondents were asked to nominate other well-informed citizens. While a few nominees in each community refused to be interviewed, more than 80 percent of those nominated two or more times, and more than 90 percent of those receiving at least three nominations, were interviewed in each community. The total number of interviewees was 113 and was almost equally divided by race. The smaller communities naturally contained a shorter list of nominees and therefore fewer interviewees. The number of interviewed citizens in each community was as follows: Crestview, 17; Lake City, 18; Gretna, 12; Titusville, 22; Daytona Beach, 22; and Riviera Beach, 22.

These respondents were broadly representative of the political, economic, and social spheres of each of these communities. Their occupations were diverse: 42 percent were involved in some aspect of business and included small farmers, morticians, realtors, bankers, newspaper editors, car dealers, store owners, and others; 20 percent were in the field of public education, primarily teaching or administration; another 20 percent had careers in public service (other than education) at the county or city level; 6 percent were lawyers, doctors, or dentists; 4 percent were ministers; another 4 percent held blue-collar occupations; and 4 percent were involved in other various careers including nursing, the military, and homemaking. The questions asked of these respondents dealt with a range of social and economic issues, but the emphasis was on political matters. In this regard these interviewees were well qualified; one-half had or did hold local public office, most often the post of city-council member. A number of others, not public servants by career nor elected to municipal office, had served on citizen-advisory boards.

The longitudinal dimension of this study, an exploration of race relations and politics over approximately twenty-five years dating from the late 1950s, means that these citizens were usually adult residents of these communities over this entire time period. Indeed, this was one of the stated criteria for nomination. Thus, 78 percent of the interviewees had lived in their respective communities since the late 1950s or before, while most others assumed residency by at least the early or mid-1960s. In the Old South communities most interviewees had been lifelong residents. Respondents in the faster growing New South, however, were much less likely to have spent their entire lives in these cities, yet even here some 64 percent had been continuous residents since at least 1960.

The privacy of these knowledgeable citizens was respected, and all respondents cooperated with the clear understanding that they would not be quoted directly or even acknowledged as a source of information. Where particularly salient quotes have been used in this book, I obtained permission to do so from the respective interviewee if the attribution of the statement might in any way jeopardize his or her privacy. It seemed important to assure anonymity not only to encourage more honest and candid responses, but also to protect the respondents (especially blacks) from any harm that might arise because they expressed their views. Although racial issues no longer evoke the intense fears and emotions they once did in many southern communities, strong race-related feelings have not disappeared by any means, especially in the Old South.

The interviews with these informed citizens were carried out between July 1976 and September 1978. Shorter follow-up interviews with smaller numbers of respondents were conducted in each community in 1980–1981 and again in 1986–1987. These follow-up interviews were performed in order to validate certain prior claims as well as to update the study through the mid-1980s. The original interviews were conducted by the author, a fellow professor, and specially trained graduate and undergraduate students from the University of Florida. All follow-up interviews were carried out by the author. Although almost all of the interviewers were white and half of the respondents were black, race differences did not present a serious problem. Virtually all of the black respondents were middle class or lower-middle class and, while many lived in segregated communities, most of them worked with whites and most had daily conversations with whites. Perhaps for these reasons, being interviewed by a middle-class white appeared to generate very little constraint among the respondents in the interview process.

The actual interviews averaged approximately ninety minutes in length, although a significant number of them went beyond two hours. Interviewers were asked questions about general political issues in the community, various aspects of race relations, public and private services in the white and black neighborhoods, and political participation of blacks (see appendix 2 for the interview instrument). The questionnaire was pretested and consisted of both open-ended and closed-ended items. In every case probing by the interviewer was encouraged and items were cross-checked for internal consistency. How ever, it was not difficult to get most citizens to talk. Indeed, once word got around about the nature of the study (which did not take long in the smaller communities), a number of respondents expressed an eagerness to present their views. The validity of these views was always a matter of concern, but I was careful to cross-check accounts of actual events against the stories of other respondents or persons involved in the event, and when possible, against newspaper reports or public records.

Measurement of Public Services

One of the most formidable, yet important, goals of this study was to chart indicators of a variety of municipal services over time. As mentioned, six service areas in the public sector were investigated: police protection, fire protection, streets, water and sewage, parks and recreation, and employment. For each service a variety of both quantitative and qualitative indicators was gathered. Moreover, such data were retrieved for both the predominately white and predominately black areas of each community. While it has been commonly asserted that there is little information available about urban service distributions, I, as well as several other social scientists, find this claim to be generally untrue.[1] Municipal records, city planning agencies, departmental records, and federal grant applications usually contain detailed data on the quantity and quality of many city services. Additional evidence was derived from interviews with department heads and selected personnel, respondent interviews, and local newspapers.

Certainly the most difficult municipal service data to obtain were those for the earlier years, particularly the late 1950s and much of the 1960s, and those for certain Old South communities where public records in general were sparse. Many of these cities, both in the Old and New South, had lost or destroyed many detailed data for the period prior to the 1970s. As a result, I was forced to rely for the earlier periods on newspaper reports and more subjective sources of evidence. Once again the most reliable source generally was the retrospective perceptions of knowledgeable citizens. As mentioned previously, these informants were longtime residents, had observed changes in public services over time, and in many cases had actually participated in the processes of change. The communities studied were relatively small, and even modest changes were rather easily discerned; respondents were often able to recall specific streets that had remained unpaved for some time and to name the first black employees who were hired during the earlier years. Therefore it seemed reasonable to assume that these respondents' perceptions of municipal services were fairly accurate, and some of the objective data on various services over time tended to confirm this belief.[2]

Although evaluations by well-informed citizens were an important method of measuring municipal services over time, I also relied heavily on three other sources of evidence. One reliable and very useful source was the local newspaper. By perusing each issue of a community's newspaper since the late 1950s, I was able (with the assistance of many helpful students) to chart specific changes in various city services. Examination of local newspapers provided detailed information over the entire time frame of this study, an especially important contribution for the earlier years where human recollection sometimes proved to be hazy. As for kinds of data, city or county newspapers often provided lists of streets paved or repaired, specific improvements made in neighborhood parks and recreation programs, the names and races of those hired and promoted in the police and fire departments, and much other specific information.

Department heads and various departmental personnel provided another important source of evidence about city services. They not only gave me access to useful departmental records and memos, but were usually willing to submit to interviews in which I probed their memories. In the smaller Old South communities where records were particularly lacking, the recollections of long-time city personnel were often the best source of information. In addition to current personnel, we solicited the names of retired departmental employees, especially former heads of departments, who were considered particularly knowledgeable, and we interviewed these persons in order to gain better data for the early years. Besides providing basic information on the quantity and quality of services, department heads (and sometimes other high-level personnel) were also able to give valuable insights into the politics of city services, including why certain services changed—or did not change—over time.

In order to gain a more racially balanced perspective on municipal services, all local black elected officials not already queried as community informants were interviewed. Some of this interviewing was completed as part of another study in 1975–1976,[3] but all subsequently elected blacks were also queried. These in-depth interviews focused primarily on the possible impact, especially in the public sector, of having blacks in local office, but attention was also given to other areas in which black officials may have attempted to promote change, to possible constraints faced by such officials, and to electoral and in-office strategies employed by blacks. These interviews provided not only a much better understanding of the roles of black elected officials, but also enhanced my comprehension of how and why improvements occurred in various city services.

On a few, very rare, occasions when these various sources failed to provide the detailed evidence necessary, I carried out my own data-gathering ventures.

These consisted of on-site observations of services, such as detailed descriptions, including photographs, of parks; or of windshield surveys of paved and unpaved streets. Such ventures were usually necessary only in the Old South, but were sometimes performed in other communities where data were sparse or very inconsistent. In all cases I sought to achieve a general consistency of evidence from a variety of sources, with the idea that repeated corroboration would enhance the credibility of findings. In most instances this consistency was achieved; when serious discrepancies emerged, however, I continued the investigation with additional sources and with on-site inspections.

Measurement of Private Sector Services

In addition to examining basic public services, this study investigated changes in the private, nongovernmental sector. The emphasis here was on black advances in the social and economic realms, particularly the nature and degree of black integration and employment. As in the case of the study of municipal services, I again employed a variety of research methods.

The most important sources for information about the private sector were the interviews of the owners or managers of a variety of private establishments in each community. These establishments were randomly selected across a wide range of businesses and services, were of various sizes, and included restaurants (31), industrial or manufacturing firms (25), retail stores and banks (56), motels and apartments (35), and movie theaters, bowling alleys and country clubs (16). The total sample size was 163, with relatively more establishments selected in the larger communities: Crestview, 23; Lake City, 23; Gretna, 11; Titusville, 37; Daytona Beach, 39; and Riviera Beach, 30. Manufacturing or industrial firms, retail stores, and banks were chosen randomly from lists supplied by the Florida Department of Commerce and local Chambers of Commerce, while all other establishments were randomly selected from listings in the Yellow Pages of the local telephone directory.

The interviews with owners or managers of these private establishments were structured in form (see appendix 3 for the interview schedule), with queries about their treatment of and attitudes toward black employees and customers. More specifically, questions were posed concerning a number of factors which may have influenced integration in the private sector, including nature, size, and age of establishment, general recruitment and hiring practices, affirmative action programs, possible problems resulting from serving and employing blacks, and attitudes toward blacks. Many of the questions were adapted, or in a few instances borrowed directly, from Rossi, Berk, and Eidson's *The Roots of Urban Discontent,* part of which entailed interviews with ghetto businessmen concerning their treatment of blacks.[4]

The interview instrument was pretested in a nearby city, and the interviews were carried out in 1976–1978 by myself and trained graduate and undergraduate students. The refusal rate of interviewees averaged only two per community and not more than four in any community. Refusals by owners or managers were primarily due to an alleged lack of time, although the interviews averaged only twenty to thirty minutes and prospective interviewees were advised of this. What became apparent in the pretesting and early interviews, however, was that the issue of race was clearly more controversial in the private sector than it was in the public sector, and that in certain kinds of establishments and in the Old South the issue was a particularly sensitive one. For example, attempts to carry out interviews with managers of bars and lounges proved to be impossible; two student interviewers were literally thrown out of one bar, and a fellow-professor and myself were warned on several occasions in the Old South not to even attempt to enter certain "hometown" bars for reasons of physical safety. As a result, bars and lounges were omitted from the list of private sector establishments in which interviews would be performed, and I decided to carry out most of the private sector research in the Old South communities myself, along with one graduate student.

A second approach to gauging black progress in the private realm relied on the interviews with informed citizens. Besides being asked about public services, these citizens, both black and white, were queried extensively about private sector changes, including desegregation of public accommodations, employment, and housing. Section C of the interview schedule (appendix 2) lists the specific questions asked. These respondents proved to be very aware of racial conditions in the social and economic arenas; since many of them had full-time occupations in the private sector, this was not unexpected. As in the case of responses about public services, there was a general consistency in the responses of these citizens about the private sector. This pattern suggested a common perception of reality within each community, and served to confirm and clarify the results derived from the sampling of private establishments.

Another method of gaining information about the private sector consisted of the careful reading of the local and regional press. This method proved less helpful than other approaches simply because local newspapers gave less attention to the private than to the public realm. Nonetheless, newspapers were often valuable sources of information for the late fifties and sixties, periods for which personal recollections were less consistent. Only in Crestview and Gretna, where local news coverage consisted of a weekly countywide newspaper, was this source less than adequate, forcing me to rely more on oral histories.

In studying all these communities we perused not only the major local and regional presses, but also local and statewide black-operated newspapers, in order to gain a more racially balanced perspective. Local black presses were rare (only Daytona and Riviera Beach had them, but only for brief periods) and back issues were difficult to obtain. However, we did examine issues of two statewide black newspapers, the *Miami Times* and the *Florida Star*, for the entire time period of this study, and their coverage of major racial issues in these communities was useful.

A final source of information, not just for the private sector but for race relations more generally in each community, was the local library. Although most city or town libraries contained little on local black-white relations, especially in the Old South, we did make occasional discoveries that proved helpful. Sometimes a master's thesis, a county or city history, or even a personal diary or scrapbook provided a piece of information that enabled me to better understand and explain changes and stability in race relations. In every community, of course, we interviewed local historians and longtime news reporters in order to gain a better historical perspective and a sense of the community's racial patterns. Our goal was always to gain a good understanding of the community, both past and present, as a context within which to place the dynamics of race and politics.

Multivariate Analysis

In order to explain levels of public services and employment for blacks in both the public and private sector, this study utilized a variety of political and contextual independent variables in a multivariate analysis. As mentioned in chapter 1, various forms of black political participation were important elements in the movement. Paramount among these conventional political variables was electoral participation. Electoral mobilization is multifaceted, but black voter registration is considered one important aspect and a good indicator of potential black voters.[5] It is also an electoral mode for which data are readily available over time. I operationalized this variable in two ways: as the proportion of adult blacks registered to vote, and as the black percentage of all voter registrants. This latter figure provides an indicator of both the black registration rate relative to that of whites and the relative size of the potential black voting population.

Another significant aspect of electoral politics is the actual election of candidates to office. A considerable volume of literature suggests that, as mentioned previously, black elected council members and especially mayors do tend to influence local policies on behalf of blacks. This variable is measured in several ways. The first and simplest way is the black percentage of all city elected officers (councilpersons and mayor). This is a standard measure and provides an indicator of black representation in local office. Second, I created a measure of black representational equity by dividing the percentage of elected seats held by blacks by the percentage of blacks in the city's population.[6] This ratio indicates how closely the percentage of posts won by blacks reflects the black proportion in the community.

Finally, it was found by Browning, Marshall, and Tabb that the degree of incorporation of minorities into the political system, rather than representation alone, increases the probability of outcomes favorable to such groups.[7] By political incorporation they refer to the extent to which blacks are able to become members of coalitions that dominate city policy-making on minority-related issues. This factor is measured as a scale based on three elements of black influence in the city council: the number of black council members, black participation in the dominant coalition, and black control of the mayor's office.[8] I replicated this measure here to test whether black incorporation in the dominant liberal coalition had a greater influence on policy than did simple minority representation in elected office.

In addition to forms of electoral participation, blacks used group-based tactics to pursue their goals; it is apparent that such black political organizations were important at times in affecting local policy. Ranging in nature from nationally based organizations like the NAACP and CORE to such local groups as municipal voter leagues, black interest groups articulated demands on a variety of issues. This variable was operationalized in two ways: as the number of formal black political organizations in the community, and as the reported number of group-articulated demands made of city policy-makers.

Nonviolent protest tactics by blacks also may have influenced policy changes. These unconventional political acts were most prevalent in the 1960s and tended to focus on desegregation issues. Black violence, another unconventional tactic, was also viewed as politically important in the civil rights movement. Riots and other relatively spontaneous forms of group violence have sometimes brought about both tangible and symbolic changes. Protests and riots were measured in terms of the number of occurrences of each such phenomenon.

Beyond various forms of black political participation, other political variables were important in local decision making.[9] Certainly the role of the federal government loomed large as a supportive force in the movement. Federal initiatives were measured in three ways. First, the number of direct federal interventions, in the form of court suits and formal investigations, was calculated.[10] Excluded here were school-oriented interventions, such as desegregation court cases, since these were seen as having little relevance beyond educational institutions. Second, I indicated the municipal adoption (or not) of a federally enforced affirmative action plan to govern employment procedures. While affirmative action requirements did not begin for local governments until the mid-1970s, not all cities and towns actually implemented such a plan. Third, the number of federal grants obtained primarily for the purpose of improving black neighborhoods was computed. The sources of such grants included the Community Development Block Grant program (and its predecessor urban renewal) and various public works, housing, and sometimes revenue sharing allocations.

While black politics and the federal government attempted to modify the status quo, white opponents of the movement often mobilized to maintain it or to reverse whatever progress had been made. In this way the tactics and power of the white countermovement may have reduced or even in some areas negated the policy impact of the black movement.[11] As indicators of countermovement strength and efforts, I used the number of formal white counter-organizations and the number of counterchallenges by such organizations. White countermovement groups consisted typically of extremist organizations like the Ku Klux Klan, but more moderate groups, such as the Singer Island Civic Association in Riviera Beach, were also included. The countermovement challenges of these organizations took a variety of forms, including mass rallies and demonstrations, electoral mobilization, and direct demands of public officials.

These intervening political variables were mediated, of course, by the context in which they occurred. Context is a complex factor, but it is important to represent, at least in general form, the environment within which the movement took place. I have suggested that two basic contextual variables were potentially significant. First is the relative size (percentage-wise) of the black population in the community. Since Key's seminal work, most major studies of southern politics have examined this factor and found it to be important. The other major contextual variable is political culture. The Old South–New South dichotomy is one standard means of depicting the unique cultural characteristics of diverse regions within the South. This typology, however, is somewhat static and perhaps oversimplified. An improved measure, I believe, is one that presents the political and racial ideology of the community. According to Colby, a good indicator of the degree of racial conservativism is the percentage of votes cast for segregationist-supporting or anti–civil rights presidential candidates (Barry Goldwater in 1964, George Wallace in 1968, and Ronald Reagan in 1980).[12] In the absence of public-opinion data for the communities, these voting results provide the best available evidence of the degree of racially conservative political ideology. Moreover, this indicator is relatively highly correlated ($r = .68$) with Old South (as opposed to New South) communities and is therefore considered a valid measure of political culture.

In addition to these contextual variables, some studies have suggested that black socioeconomic resources may be an important factor in policy changes.[13] Such resources, in addition to having a direct impact on the policy process, are necessary for sustaining black mobilization efforts. Socioeconomic resources are measured as black median family income, a fairly standard indicator.

The final contextual factor considered was the time dimension. As mentioned, there is some indication that natural growth and progress over time may be sufficient to account for changes in policy. This study's longitudinal approach, looking at the dependent and independent variables at six evenly spaced intervals between 1960 and 1985, permitted an analysis of the time factor. To do so I set up a "dummy" time variable (1960–1970 = 0; 1975–1985 = 1) and entered it in the multivariate analysis as an independent variable. This indicator provided a test of whether the passage of time alone explained improvements in services for blacks.

The data on these independent variables were gathered from many of the same sources as the information on the dependent variables. Local public records, newspaper reports, and the U.S. Census provided most of the data, but interviews with informed residents were also helpful when these more formal sources were lacking. Mid-decade demographic and socioeconomic data were retrieved from census estimates or interpolated from regular census information.

As mentioned, this study took a time-series approach, utilizing measures taken over a twenty-five-year period (1960–1985), in order to determine the effects of political participation. Too short a time sequence, for example five to ten years, would make it impossible to assess the longer-term impact, whereas too long a period might wash out the more immediate effect of certain factors.[14] To remedy this, I analyzed the relationships between the independent and dependent variables both over shorter, ten-year time periods as well as over the entire twenty-five-year time frame. The shorter periods consisted of two theoretically important time spans: 1) 1960–1970, a period within which demand-protest and riots were more dominant and electoral mobilization was just emerging in most communities; and 2) 1975–1985, the time sequence wherein electoral modes, especially black elected officials, were preeminent. Because data on some variables were not available for every year (especially the early years), measures were taken every five years beginning with 1960 and ending in 1985. This approach provided six points in time and assured that there would be little missing data. For independent variables with measures available for each year, I took the average over the five years as the best indicator for the period.

All of the independent variables were examined for multicollinearity. In a factor analysis with varimax rotation, the fourteen political variables created five basic factors or dimensions (table A.1): electoral mobilization, organization and protests, the federal role, the white countermovement, and riots. While the resulting factor scores could have been used as scales when more than one variable loaded highly on a factor, I decided against this technique for the reason of interpretability. This was especially a problem for the electoral mobilization factor (factor 1), where a number of different aspects of political participation loaded together. Moreover, the use of scales explained no more variation in the multivariate analyses than did the employment of individual variables. Thus I chose to select the variable with the highest loading on each factor to represent that dimension. In the case of factor 2 (organization and protest), Browning, Marshall, and Tabb suggest combining these variables in an additive manner into what is termed "demand-protest".[15] To compute this new variable I simply added together the number of organizational challenges and the number of protests.

Among the four contextual variables there was little collinearity except for the indicators of black income and time, which were relatively highly intercorrelated ($r = 0.82$). For theoretical reasons, and because it loaded most highly on the factor in a factor-analytic routine, the time variable was selected to rep-

APPENDIX 1

TABLE A.1

Factor Analytic Results for Political Independent Variables

Variables	*Factor 1*	*Factor 2*	*Factor 3*	*Factor 4*	*Factor 5*
			Factors[a]		
% Blacks registered to vote	0.67				
Black % of registrants	0.96				
% Black elected officials	0.97				
Black representational equity	0.85				
Black political incorporation	0.94				
# Black organizations		0.81			
# Black organizational demands		0.93			
# Black protests		0.90			
# Black riots					0.84
# Federal interventions			0.60		
Federal affirmative action plan			0.93		
# Federal grants			0.74		
# White counter-organizations				0.93	
# White organizational counter-challenges				0.95	

[a] All factor loadings of 0.60 or more are reported.

resent this dimension. However, when trying to explain levels of capital-intensive services, like street paving, black income was the preferred variable, since it seems to have more theoretical relevance.

The multivariate analysis utilizing these independent variables attempted to show how forms of black political behavior interacted with other independent variables to explain levels of public services for blacks. Knowledge of the temporal sequences among variables, as well as some basic theoretical justifications for the relationships among the variables, allow one to hypothesize certain paths of influence.[16] The basic path model here is essentially a two-step recursive (unidirectional) model with three contextual independent variables, five

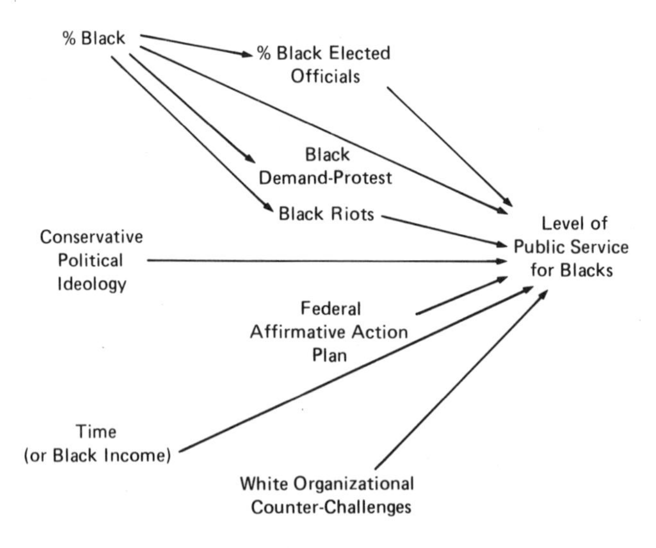

FIGURE A.1
Hypothesized Path Model

intervening political variables, and a dependent variable. Once these relationships have been hypothesized, it is possible to estimate the magnitude of the linkages between variables in the model through the use of multiple regression analyses. The hypothesized path model for these variables is shown in figure A.1.

Appendix 2

Questionnaire for Community Informants

This is a study, conducted through the University of Florida, to investigate changes in Florida cities over the last 15 years. We will be looking at six cities in depth (including this one), concentrating on public services, private (or non-governmental) services, and race relations. As part of this study, we are interviewing well-informed citizens in each city. We would like to stress that the results of this interview will be reported *anonymously*; that is, no names will be mentioned in the final report. Thus, we hope that you will feel free to respond to our questions in an open and candid manner.

Section A—First of all, we would like to ask you a few general questions about yourself and this city.

1. How long have you lived in ______________ ? ______________
2. What is your present occupation? ______________
3. Have you had other major occupations? If so, what jobs? ______________
____
4. Have you ever held public office in this city? If so, what public office(s) and when? ______________
____
5. Every city faces some serious problems. Thinking back over the last 10 to 15 years, what do you think have been the two or three most serious problems this city has faced? ______________
____

Section B—In the next section, we would like to ask you several questions about city services and what you think about them.

6. The city government provides a number of public services to the citizens of this city. Which public services do you think are *most* important?
____
Which public services do you think are *least* important?
____
7. Which public services do you think the city has increased or improved the *most* over the last 15 years or so? Why?
____
Which public services have been increased or improved the *least* over the

last 15 years or so? Why?

____

____

8. In some cities in Florida, there appear to be differences in the quantity or quality of public services provided to the black community compared to the white community. Do you think there have been any *differences* in this city over the last 15 years or so (since 1960) in public services provided to the black community compared to the white community? If so, which public services?

____

Why have there been these differences?

____

____

Do these differences still exist today as they did 15 years ago?

____

9. Have there been any *changes* over the last 15 years in any of the public services provided to the *black* community? If so, which public services have been changed?

____

Why were these changes undertaken?

____

____

Do you think the city should take further actions to reduce or eliminate these differences or not? Why or why not?

____

____

How about the county, state or federal governments—should any or all of them take action or not? Why?

____

____

10. Have there been any *changes* over the last 15 years or so in any of the public services provided to the *white* community? If so, which public services have been changed?

____

Why were these changes undertaken?

____

____

11. Which public service do you think are most important to most blacks? to most whites?

____

____

12. The following is a list of public services provided by this city. Please rate how effective you think the city was 15 years ago or so (that is, in 1960) in providing each of the following public services to the black community:

	Very Effective	Somewhat Effective	Not Effective	Don't Know
Police protection	____	____	____	____
Streets and roads	____	____	____	____
Parks and recreation	____	____	____	____
Library	____	____	____	____
Fire protection	____	____	____	____
Water and sewage	____	____	____	____
Public employment	____	____	____	____

13. Please rate how effective you think the city is today in providing each of these public services to the black community:

	Very Effective	Somewhat Effective	Not Effective	Don't Know
Police protection	____	____	____	____
Streets and roads	____	____	____	____
Parks and recreation	____	____	____	____
Library	____	____	____	____
Fire protection	____	____	____	____
Water and sewage	____	____	____	____
Public employment	____	____	____	____

14. Please rate how effective you think the city was 15 years ago or so (that is, in 1960) in providing each of the following public services to the white community:

	Very Effective	Somewhat Effective	Not Effective	Don't Know
Police protection	____	____	____	____
Streets and roads	____	____	____	____
Parks and recreation	____	____	____	____
Library	____	____	____	____
Fire protection	____	____	____	____
Water and sewage	____	____	____	____
Public employment	____	____	____	____

15. Please rate how effective you think the city is today in providing each of these public services to the white community:

	Very Effective	Somewhat Effective	Not Effective	Don't Know
Police protection	____	____	____	____
Streets and roads	____	____	____	____
Parks and recreation	____	____	____	____
Library	____	____	____	____
Fire protection	____	____	____	____
Water and sewage	____	____	____	____
Public employment	____	____	____	____

Section C—In this next section, we would like to ask you some questions about private, or nongovernmental, services like private businesses, restaurants, movie theaters, and housing.

16. There are a number of private businesses or industries in this city. To your knowledge, do any of these businesses refuse to employ blacks? If so, which one(s)?

____

Do most businesses or industries in this city presently employ blacks? If so, since when?

____

Are any blacks in *supervisory* positions in any of these businesses? Which one(s)?

____

____

17. The following is a list of private (nongovernmental) services in this city. Please indicate whether each of the following *private* (nongovernmental) service areas in this city is racially integrated or not in terms of the services each provides:

	Integrated (since when?)	*Nonintegrated*
Movie theaters	______	______
Bars and lounges	______	______
Restaurants	______	______
Country club(s)	______	______
Bowling alley(s)	______	______
Lunch counters	______	______
Motels and hotels	______	______
Apartments	______	______

18. If any of the above are integrated, why and how did this occur?

____

____

____

____

19. *In the past*, have blacks been penalized or threatened in any way for using any of these services? How about today?

____

____

____

____

20. Please rate how good or poor you think each of these private (nongovernmental) services were 15 years ago or so (1960) for blacks, compared to whites:

	Better than Whites	Same as Whites	Worse than Whites	Don't Know
Movie theaters	___	___	___	___
Bars and lounges	___	___	___	___
Restaurants	___	___	___	___
Country club(s)	___	___	___	___
Bowling alley(s)	___	___	___	___
Lunch counters	___	___	___	___
Motels and hotels	___	___	___	___
Apartments	___	___	___	___

21. Please rate how good or poor you think these private services are *today* for *blacks*, compared to whites, in each of the following service areas:

	Better than Whites	Same as Whites	Worse than Whites	Don't Know
Movie theaters	___	___	___	___
Bars and lounges	___	___	___	___
Restaurants	___	___	___	___
Country club(s)	___	___	___	___
Bowling alley(s)	___	___	___	___
Lunch counters	___	___	___	___
Motels and hotels	___	___	___	___
Apartments	___	___	___	___

22. Do many blacks live outside of the traditionally black areas of the city?

___

___

23. Do you think that racial discrimination in private, nongovernmental areas should be eliminated or not? If so, why and in white areas?

___

Who do you think should take action to eliminate discrimination in private areas—the city, private citizens, the federal government, or whom? What action should be taken?

___

___

___

Section D—In this last section, we would like to ask you a few questions about how people take part in politics—things like voting, talking about politics, protesting, and so on.

24. Are there any difficulties people tend to have in registering to vote in this city? How about blacks?

___

___

___

25. Why don't more white people vote in city elections?

Why don't more black people vote in city elections?

26. Have you ever heard of anything happening to blacks who have voted or taken some part in politics here? If so, what? How about 15 years ago or so?

27. Do you ever talk about city government or local problems with any white people? Who? How often (a lot, some, not much)?

With any black people? Who? How often (a lot, some, not much)?

28. You've had both black and white candidates run for office here. Do white candidates do anything to get black votes in local elections? If so, what?

Do black candidates do anything to get white votes? If so, what?

Do black candidates do anything to get *black* votes? If so, what?

29. Do you think having (had) a black in elected city office would (has) made a difference in this city or not? Why?

How about having had blacks appointed to boards or commissions—has this made a difference or not? Why?

30. Which black political organizations have been most important here over the last 15 years or so? Why?

31. Have there been any black protests, sit-ins, boycotts, or riots in this city in the last 15 years? If so, what were the issues involved? What were the effects?

Do you think such protests (or riots) were justified or not?

____

____

32. If blacks wanted to improve public services in the black community, what do you think they should do? Why?

____

____

____

33. If blacks wanted to improve private (nongovernmental) services, what do you think they should do? Why?

____

____

____

34. In terms of blacks gaining what they feel to be equality, do you feel that blacks in this city have tried to move much too fast, too slow, or has it been about right? Explain.

____

____

35. There are many different methods that people use to try to get things changed. Please indicate the *effectiveness* of each of the following methods by which blacks may have tried to influence changes in this city:

	Very Effective	Somewhat Effective	Not Effective	Not Used or Don't Know
Voting	____	____	____	____
Petitions	____	____	____	____
Attendance at public meetings	____	____	____	____
Demonstrations and protests	____	____	____	____
Rioting or violence	____	____	____	____
Court action	____	____	____	____
Outside political pressure from federal or state government	____	____	____	____
Blacks holding public office	____	____	____	____
Securing federal grants	____	____	____	____
Other (specify):	____	____	____	____

36. Which *one* of the above methods do you think has been *most effective*? Why?

____

____

Least effective? Why?

____

____

37. What other knowledgeable citizens, or people who know a lot about politics and race relations in this city over the last 15 years or so, do you think we should interview?

____

____

38. Which three or four do you think would know the most about such events in this community?

____

____

Appendix 3

Questionnaire for Businesses and Industries

1. How long has this business been here? ______________ As an employer in this city, what have been your major problems?

____

____

2. How many employees does your company have? ______________
3. How does your company usually go about getting new workers?

____

____

4. In choosing new employees from among applicants, what characteristics do you usually regard as *most important*? What characteristics are most important for *promotion* of employees?

____

5. Do you get any black applicants for jobs here? What proportion do you think you hire?

____

6. What would you estimate the proportion of blacks to be among your employees in professional and white-collar positions? ________ in skilled labor? ________ in unskilled labor? ________
7. When were blacks first hired in this company? If so, why?

____

8. Have blacks ever been refused jobs in this company? If so, when? Why?

____

____

Have any blacks been fired from, or quit, their jobs here? When? Why?

____

____

9. Some companies have been going out of their way lately to hire blacks. Is this true or not true of this company? Why?

____

____

10. Many companies who have tried to hire blacks have given up because their workers objected so strongly to working with blacks. How have your employees reacted to blacks working here?

____

____

11. Other companies which have tried to go out of their way to hire blacks have found that there were very few qualified blacks to hire. Have you found this to be true here? Explain.

____

____

12. Do you think that companies in this city have a social responsibility to make strong efforts to provide employment to blacks, or not? Why or why not?

____

____

13. Have any federal, state, or local groups urged you to hire more blacks? Explain.

____

____

APPENDIX 3

QUESTIONNAIRE FOR RESTAURANTS, BOWLING ALLEYS, COUNTRY CLUBS, MOVIE THEATERS, MOTELS, HOTELS AND APARTMENTS

1. How long has this establishment been here? __________ As an establishment in this city, what have been your major problems?
   ____

   What is the approximate annual gross income of this establishment? ____
2. How many employees does your company have? ______________
3. How does your establishment usually go about getting new workers?
   ____
   ____
4. In choosing new employees from among applicants, what characteristics do you usually regard as *most important*?
   ____
5. Do you get any black applicants for jobs here? What proportion do you think you hire?
   ____
6. What would you estimate the proportion of blacks to be among your employees?
   ____
7. When were blacks first hired in this establishment? When were most black employees hired?
   ____
8. Have blacks ever been refused jobs in this establishment? If so, when? Why?
   ____
   ____

   Have any blacks been fired from, or quit, their jobs here? When? Why?
   ____
9. Some companies have been going out of their way lately to hire blacks. Is this true or not true of this establishment? Why?
   ____
   ____
10. About what percent of your customers are blacks? ______________
11. Over the last 10 to 15 years, have blacks ever been refused service in this establishment? If so, when and why?
    ____
    ____
12. Some managers of establishments complain that blacks are more likely to be involved in shoplifting and vandalism than whites, and therefore it is necessary to keep a watchful eye on them when they are in the establishment. How do you feel about this? Explain.
    ____
    ____
13. Some managers of establishments say blacks are less likely to complain if

they feel they are not treated fairly; and therefore, they are less likely to be treated as fairly as whites. Do you agree with this or not? Explain.

____

____

____

NOTES

The following abbreviations are used throughout the notes for newspapers:

DBEN	*Daytona Beach Evening News*
GCT	*Gadsden County Times*
LCR	*Lake City Reporter*
ONJ	*Okaloosa News Journal*
PBP	*Palm Beach Post*
TSA	*Titusville Star Advocate*

CHAPTER 1
THE CIVIL RIGHTS MOVEMENT AND ITS CONSEQUENCES

1. *New York Times*, February 2, 1965, p. 1, as quoted in David Campbell and Joe R. Feagin, "Black Politics in the South: A Descriptive Analysis," *Journal of Politics* 37 (February 1975): 129.

2. William C. Havard, "The South: A Shifting Perspective," in William C. Havard, ed., *The Changing Politics of the South* (Baton Rouge: Louisiana State University Press), 1972, p. 11.

3. As quoted in Neal R. Peirce, *The Deep South States of America* (New York: W. W. Norton, 1974), p. 24.

4. *New York Times: Weekly Review*, November 7, 1977, p. 3.

5. William H. Chafe, *Civilities and Civil Rights: Greensboro, North Carolina, and the Black Struggle for Freedom* (New York: Oxford University Press, 1980), pp. vii–viii. See also Earl Black and Merle Black, *Politics and Society in the South* (Cambridge, Mass.: Harvard University Press, 1987), pp. 126–51.

6. Major works here include: Thomas R. Brooks, *Walls Come Tumbling Down: A History of the Civil Rights Movement, 1940–1970* (Englewood Cliffs, N.J.: Prentice-Hall, 1974); Clayborne Carson, *In Struggle: SNCC and the Black Awakening of the 1960s* (Cambridge, Mass.: Harvard University Press, 1981); Chafe, *Civilities and Civil Rights*; David J. Garrow, *Protest at Selma: Martin Luther King, Jr., and The Voting Rights Act of 1965* (New Haven, Conn.: Yale University Press, 1978); Steven Lawson, *Black Ballots: Voting Rights in the South, 1944–1969* and *In Pursuit of Power: Southern Blacks and Electoral Politics, 1965–1982* (New York: Columbia University Press, 1976 and 1985, respectively); Donald R. Matthews and James W. Prothro, *Negroes and the New Southern Politics* (New York: Harcourt, Brace and World, 1966); Doug McAdam, *Political Process and the Development of Black Insurgency, 1930–1970* (Chicago: University of Chicago Press, 1982); August Meier and Elliott Rudwick, *CORE: A Study in the Civil Rights*

Movement, 1942–1968 (Urbana: University of Illinois Press, 1975); Pat Watters and Reese Cleghorn, *Climbing Jacob's Ladder: The Arrival of Negroes in Southern Politics* (New York: Harcourt, Brace and World, 1967); and Juan Williams, *Eyes on the Prize: America's Civil Rights Years, 1954–1965* (New York: Viking, 1987).

7. Although there has been a good deal of confusion in terms of defining policy outputs, Ira Sharkansky's policy distinctions come closest to formulating the postconversion process I have in mind here. He differentiates between public policy, policy outputs, and policy impacts. According to Sharkansky, "public policy represents actions taken by government; policy outputs represent the service levels which are affected by these actions; and policy impacts represent the effect which the service has on a population." My primary concern in this study is public policy and most especially policy outputs, as Sharkansky defines them, but I shall also explore certain nonpublic, or private sector, outputs as well. See Ira Sharkansky, "Environment, Policy, Output and Impact: Problems of Theory and Method in the Analysis of Public Policy," in Ira Sharkansky, ed., *Policy Analysis in Political Science* (Chicago: Markham, 1970), p. 63.

8. See Norman R. Luttbeg, ed., *Public Opinion and Public Policy: Models of Political Linkage* (Homewood, Ill.: Dorsey Press, 1968); Gerald Pomper, *Elections in America: Control and Influence in Democratic Politics* (New York: Dodd, Mead and Company, 1968); and Sidney Verba and Norman H. Nie, *Participation in America: Political Democracy and Social Equality* (New York: Harper and Row, 1972).

9. Matthews and Prothro, *Negroes and the New Southern Politics*, p. 11. See also Brooks, *Walls Come Tumbling Down*, p. 292; and Havard, ed., *The Changing Politics of the South*, p. 20.

10. See Garrow, *Protest at Selma*, pp. 238–40, footnote 1.

11. August Meier and Elliott Rudwick, *From Plantation to Ghetto* (New York: Hill and Wang, 1970), pp. 251–73.

12. Leon Friedman, "The Federal Courts of the South: Judge Bryan Simpson and His Reluctant Brethren," in Leon Friedman, ed., *Southern Justice* (New York: Random House, 1965), pp. 187–88. See also Watters and Cleghorn, *Climbing Jacob's Ladder*, p. 76.

13. Campbell and Feagin, "Black Politics in the South," pp. 149–56; McAdam, *Political Process and the Development of Black Insurgency*, pp. 169–71; and Minion K. C. Morrison, *Black Political Mobilization: Leadership, Power and Mass Behavior* (Albany, N.Y.: SUNY Press, 1987), pp. 248–52.

14. Alan I. Abramowitz, "The United States: Political Culture under Stress," in Gabriel A. Almond and Sidney Verba, eds., *The Civic Culture Revisited* (Boston: Little, Brown and Co., 1980), pp. 198–201.

15. Ladd, *Negro Political Leadership in the South*, p. 47; Matthews and Prothro, *Negroes and the New Southern Politics*, pp. 433, 475; and Watters and Cleghorn, *Climbing Jacob's Ladder*, p. 76.

16. Meier and Rudwick, *From Plantation to Ghetto*, pp. 256–69. See also Chafe, *Civilities and Civil Rights*, pp. 340–42.

17. Jerome H. Skolnick, *The Politics of Protest* (New York: Ballantine, 1969), pp. 8–24.

18. Bryan T. Downes, "A Critical Reexamination of the Social and Political Characteristics of Riot Cities," *Social Science Quarterly* 51 (September 1970): 349–60.

19. Robert A. Dahl, *Pluralist Democracy in the United States: Conflict and Consensus* (Chicago: Rand McNally, 1967). See also Earl Latham, *The Group Basis of Politics* (Ithaca, N.Y.: Cornell University Press, 1952); Arnold M. Rose, *The Power Structure* (New York: Oxford University Press, 1967); and David B. Truman, *The Governmental Process* (New York: Knopf, 1960).

20. Andrew M. Greeley, *Why Can't They Be Like Us?* (New York: E. P. Dutton, 1971), p. 14; and Mark R. Levy and Michael S. Kramer, *The Ethnic Factor* (New York: Simon and Schuster, 1972).

21. Hugh D. Price, "The Negro and Florida Politics, 1944–1954," *Journal of Politics* 17 (May 1955): 218–19.

22. Frederick Wirt, *Politics of Southern Equality: Law and Social Change in a Mississippi County* (Chicago: Aldine, 1970), pp. 166–75.

23. Huey L. Perry, *Political Participation and Social Equality: An Assessment of the Impact of Political Participation in Two Alabama Localities* (unpublished doctoral dissertation, University of Chicago, 1976), chapters 5–6.

24. William R. Keech, *The Impact of Negro Voting: The Role of the Vote in the Quest for Equality* (Chicago: Rand McNally, 1968).

25. Campbell and Feagin, "Black Politics in the South," p. 139; and Joint Center for Political Studies, Washington, D.C., *Black Elected Officials: A National Roster* 15 (1986).

26. James Button, "Southern Black Elected Officials: Impact on Socioeconomic Change," *Review of Black Political Economy* 12 (Fall 1982): 29–45; James David Campbell, *Electoral Participation and the Quest for Equality: Black Politics in Alabama Since the Voting Rights Act of 1965* (Ph.D. diss., University of Texas at Austin, 1976); Mack Jones, "Black Officeholding and Political Development in the Rural South," *Review of Black Political Economy* 6, no. 4 (1976): 375–407; and Albert K. Karnig and Susan Welch, *Black Representation and Urban Policy* (Chicago: University of Chicago, 1980), chapter 6. For a review of the literature in this area see James W. Button and Richard K. Scher, "The Election and Impact of Black Officials in the South," in Harrell R. Rodgers, Jr., ed., *Public Policy and Social Institutions* (Greenwich, Conn.: JAI Press, 1984), pp. 183–218.

27. David C. Colby, "Black Power, White Resistance, and Public Policy: Political Power and Poverty Program Grants in Mississippi," *Journal of Politics* 47 (May 1985): 579–95.

28. Neil R. McMillen, *The Citizens' Council: Organized Resistance to the Second Reconstruction, 1954–64* (Urbana: University of Illinois Press, 1971); and Francis M. Wilhoit, *The Politics of Massive Resistance* (New York: George Braziller, 1973).

29. James W. Button, *Black Violence: Political Impact of the 1960s Riots* (Princeton, N.J.: Princeton University Press, 1978), pp. 126–46; Joe R. Feagin and Harlan Hahn, *Ghetto Revolts: The Politics of Violence in American Cities* (New York: Macmillan, 1973), chapter 5; and Susan Welch, "The Impact of Urban Riots on Urban Expenditures," *American Journal of Political Science* 19 (November 1975): 741–60.

30. Thomas R. Dye and Harmon Zeigler, *The Irony of Democracy* (North Scituate, Mass.: Duxbury, 1978); Floyd Hunter, *Community Power Structure: A Study of Decision-Makers* (Chapel Hill: University of North Carolina Press, 1953); S. J. Makielski, Jr., *Beleaguered Minorities: Cultural Politics in America* (San Francisco: W. H. Freeman, 1973), pp. 126–35; and Harrell R. Rodgers, Jr., "Civil Rights and the Myth of Popular Sovereignty," *Journal of Black Studies* 12 (September 1981): 53–70.

31. Matthews and Prothro, *Negroes and the New Southern Politics*, p. 481.

32. Lester M. Salamon and Stephen Van Evera, "Fear, Apathy, and Discrimination: A Test of Three Explanations of Political Participation," *American Political Science Review* 67 (December 1973): 1288–1306; and Douglas St. Angelo and Paul Puryear, "Fear, Apathy, and Other Dimensions of Black Voting," in Michael B. Preston, Lenneal J. Henderson, Jr., and Paul Puryear, eds., *The New Black Politics: The Search for Political Power* (New York: Longman, 1982), pp. 109–30.

33. "Barriers to Minority Political Progress in the South" (Atlanta, Ga.: Voter Education Project, 1976); Chandler Davidson, ed., *Minority Vote Dilution* (Washington, D.C.: Howard University Press, 1984), chapters 4–7; U.S. Commission on Civil Rights, *The Voting Rights Act: Unfulfilled Goals* (Washington, D.C.: U.S. Government Printing Office, 1981), chapters 3–5; and Watters and Cleghorn, *Climbing Jacob's Ladder*, pp. 28, 121–24.

34. Hanes Walton, Jr., *Black Politics: A Theoretical and Structural Analysis* (New York: J. B. Lippincott, 1972), p. 200. See also Kenneth S. Colburn, *Southern Black Mayors: Local Problems and Federal Responses* (Washington, D.C.: Joint Center for Political Studies), 1974.

35. Button, "Southern Black Elected Officials," pp. 35–37; William E. Nelson and Philip J. Meranto, *Electing Black Mayors* (Columbus: Ohio State University Press, 1977), pp. 335–78; and Michael Preston, "Limitations of Black Urban Power: The Case of Black Mayors," in Louis H. Masotti and Robert L. Lineberry, eds., *The New Urban Politics* (Cambridge, Mass.: Ballinger, 1976), pp. 118–25.

36. Keech, *Impact of Negro Voting*, pp. 80–92. See also Lawrence J. Hanks, *The Struggle for Black Political Empowerment in Three Georgia Counties* (Knoxville: University of Tennessee Press, 1987), pp. 157–58.

37. Chandler Davidson, *Biracial Politics: Conflict and Coalition in the Metropolitan South* (Baton Rouge: Louisiana State University Press, 1972), p. 140.

38. Larry Isaac and William R. Kelly, "Racial Insurgency, the State, and Welfare Expansion: Local and National Level Evidence from the Postwar United States," *American Journal of Sociology* 86 (May 1981): 1356–58; and

Frances Fox Piven and Richard A. Cloward, *Regulating the Poor: The Functions of Public Welfare* (New York: Pantheon, 1971).

39. Dye and Zeigler, *The Irony of Democracy*, pp. 190–91, 384–403. See also William A. Gamson, *The Strategy of Social Protest* (Homewood, Ill.: Dorsey, 1975), pp. 72–88; Skolnick, *The Politics of Protest*, pp. 329–46; and Richard E. Rubenstein, *Rebels in Eden: Mass Political Violence in the United States* (Boston: Little, Brown, 1970).

40. Garrow, *Protest at Selma*, pp. 212–36. See also Paul Schumaker, "The Scope of Political Conflict and the Effectiveness of Constraints in Contemporary Urban Protest," *Sociological Quarterly* 19 (Spring 1978): 168–84.

41. McAdam, *Political Process and the Development of Black Insurgency*, pp. 163–79, 221.

42. Ladd, *Negro Political Leadership in the South*, p. 47; Harrell R. Rodgers, Jr., and Charles S. Bullock, III, *Law and Social Change: Civil Rights Laws and Their Consequences* (New York: McGraw-Hill, 1972), p. 60; and Matthews and Prothro, *Negroes and the New Southern Politics*, p. 433.

43. David C. Colby, "A Test of the Relative Efficacy of Political Tactics," *American Journal of Political Science* 26 (November 1982): 741–53.

44. Piven and Cloward, *Regulating the Poor.*

45. Michael Betz, "Riots and Welfare: Are They Related?" *Social Problems* 21, no. 3 (1974): 345–55; Isaac and Kelly, "Racial Insurgency, the State, and Welfare Expansion," pp. 1348–86; and Edward T. Jennings, Jr., "Urban Riots and Welfare Policy Change," in Helen M. Ingram and Dean E. Mann, eds., *Why Policies Succeed or Fail* (Beverly Hills, Calif.: Sage, 1979), pp. 59–82.

46. Frances Fox Piven and Richard A. Cloward, *Poor People's Movements: Why They Succeed, How They Fail* (New York: Vintage, 1979).

47. Ibid., p. 29.

48. Button, *Black Violence: Political Impact of the 1960s Riots*; Gamson, *Strategy of Social Protest*, pp. 72–88; and Paul Schumaker, "Policy Responsiveness to Protest-Group Demands," *Journal of Politics* 37 (May 1975): 488–521. For an excellent review of the literature on the impact of black violence see Ted Robert Gurr, "On the Outcomes of Violent Conflict," in Ted Robert Gurr, ed., *Handbook of Political Conflict: Theory and Research* (New York: Free Press, 1980), pp. 268–80.

49. Principal proponents of classical collective behavior theory include Kurt Lang and Gladys Lang, *Collective Dynamics* (New York: Crowell, 1961); Neil Smelser, *Theory of Collective Behavior* (New York: Free Press, 1962); and Ralph Turner and Lewis Killian, *Collective Behavior* (Englewood Cliffs, N.J.: Prentice-Hall, 1957).

50. McAdam, *Political Process and the Development of Black Insurgency*, p. 6.

51. Chief formulations of resource mobilization theory include Gamson, *Strategy of Social Protest*; John D. McCarthy and Mayer Zald, *The Trend of Social Movements in America: Professionalism and Resource Mobilization* (Morristown, N.J.: General Learning Press, 1973), and idem, "Resource Mobilization and Social Movements: a Partial Theory," *American Journal of Sociology* 82, no. 6

(May 1977): 1212–41; Anthony Oberschall, *Social Conflict and Social Movements* (Englewood Cliffs, N.J.: Prentice-Hall, 1973); and Charles Tilly, *From Mobilization to Revolution* (Reading, Mass.: Addison-Wesley, 1978).

52. McAdam, *Political Process and the Development of Black Insurgency*, p. 20.

53. See J. Craig Jenkins, "Resource Mobilization Theory and the Study of Social Movements," *Annual Review of Sociology* 9 (1983): 527–53; McAdam, *Political Process and the Development of Black Insurgency*; and Aldon D. Morris, *The Origins of the Civil Rights Movement: Black Communities Organizing for Change* (New York: Free Press, 1984), and idem, "Black Southern Student Sit-In Movement: An Analysis of Internal Organization," *American Sociological Review* 46 (December 1981): 744–67.

54. Morris, "Black Southern Student Sit-In Movement," p. 746.

55. Jenkins, "Resource Mobilization Theory and the Study of Social Movements," pp. 543–44; David Snyder and William R. Kelly, "Strategies for Investigating Violence and Social Change: Illustrations from Analyses of Racial Disorders and Implications for Mobilization Research," in Mayer N. Zald and John D. McCarthy, eds., *The Dynamics of Social Movements: Resource Mobilization, Social Control, and Tactics* (Cambridge, Mass.: Winthrop, 1979), pp. 224–33; and Charles Tilly, *Big Structures, Large Processes, Huge Comparisons* (New York: Russell Sage Foundation, 1984), pp. 33–42.

56. Carole Pateman, "The Civic Culture: A Philosophic Critique," in Almond and Verba, eds., *The Civic Culture Revisited*, pp. 95–96.

57. Isaac and Kelly, "Racial Insurgency, the State, and Welfare Expansion," pp. 1351–54.

58. Perry, *Political Participation and Social Equality*, p. 41.

59. Campbell and Feagin, "Black Politics in the South," p. 139.

60. Alfred B. Clubok, John M. DeGrove, and Charles D. Farris, "The Manipulated Negro Vote: Some Pre-Conditions and Consequences," *Journal of Politics* 26 (February 1964): 112–29.

61. Matthews and Prothro, *Negroes and the New Southern Politics*, p. 117. See also V. O. Key, Jr., *Southern Politics* (New York: Vintage, 1949), p. 9.

62. Keech, *Impact of Negro Voting*, pp. 99–101.

63. Harry Holloway, *The Politics of the Southern Negro: From Exclusion to Big City Organization* (New York: Random House, 1969), pp. 26–28; Matthews and Prothro, *Negroes and the New Southern Politics*, pp. 173, 219; and Price, "The Negro and Florida Politics," p. 204.

64. See Walter A. Rosenbaum, *Political Culture* (New York: Praeger, 1975), pp. 3–8.

65. Matthews and Prothro, *Negroes and the New Southern Politics*, p. 219.

66. Manning J. Dauer, "Florida: The Different State," in Havard, ed., *The Changing Politics of the South*, pp. 92–164.

67. Key, *Southern Politics*, p. 83.

68. Earl Black, *Southern Governors and Civil Rights: Racial Segregation as a Campaign Issue in the Second Reconstruction* (Cambridge, Mass.: Harvard University Press, 1976), pp. 91–92; McMillen, *The Citizens' Council: Organized Resistance*

to the Second Reconstruction, pp. 99–101; and H. D. Price, *The Negro and Southern Politics: A Chapter of Florida History* (Westport, Conn.: Greenwood Press, 1957), pp. 36–38.

69. Button, "Southern Black Elected Officials."

70. Clubok, De Grove, and Farris, "The Manipulated Negro Vote."

71. Price, *The Negro and Southern Politics*.

72. Rufus P. Browning, Dale Rogers Marshall, and David H. Tabb, *Protest Is Not Enough: The Struggle of Blacks and Hispanics for Equality in Urban Politics* (Berkeley: University of California Press, 1984); and Matthews and Prothro, *Negroes and the New Southern Politics*, pp. 219, 239–61.

73. Keech, *Impact of Negro Voting*, pp. 40–79; and Gunnar Myrdal, *An American Dilemma: The Negro Problem and Modern Democracy* (New York: Pantheon, 1944), pp. 333–63.

74. Keech, *Impact of Negro Voting*, pp. 95–99.

75. Eugene J. Webb, et al., *Unobtrusive Measures: Nonreactive Research in the Social Sciences* (Chicago: Rand McNally, 1966), p. 3.

Chapter 2
The Old South and the Politics of Race

1. Price, *The Negro and Southern Politics*, pp. 36–37.

2. Holloway, *Politics of the Southern Negro*, pp. 26–27.

3. Key, *Southern Politics*, p. 671.

4. Black, *Southern Governors and Civil Rights*, pp. 91–92; and Dauer, "Florida: The Different State," pp. 136–39.

5. Holloway, *Politics of the Southern Negro*, p. 26.

6. Interview, community informant, Crestview, November 4, 1977.

7. Jerry M. McDonald, *Okaloosa: A History of Okaloosa County and Parts of Her Neighboring Counties to the 1940s*, research paper, Robert Sikes Library, Crestview, 1968, p. 36.

8. Henry Allen Dobson, *A History of Okaloosa County, Florida* (M.A. thesis, Southeastern Louisiana University, 1974), pp. 91–107; McDonald, *Okaloosa: A History*, pp. 59–61; *Pensacola News-Journal*, November 14, 1976, p. 3B; and *Pensacola Journal*, November 17, 1976, p. 2B.

9. Interviews, three community informants, Crestview, November 4, 1977; September 7, 1978; and September 8, 1978.

10. *ONJ*, July 8, 1954, p. 4.

11. *ONJ*, May 20, 1954, p. 1.

12. *ONJ*, October 17, 1957, p. 1B; and *Pensacola Journal*, October 11, 1957, p. 6B.

13. Interviews, longtime black resident, Crestview, December 18, 1980, and black community informant, Crestview, July 28, 1975.

14. Interview, longtime black resident, Crestview, December 18, 1980.

15. *Pensacola Journal*, July 21, 1953, p. 1; *West Florida Daily Globe*, July 20, 1953, p. 1; and July 28, 1953, p. 1.

16. Interviews, three community informants, Crestview, November 3, 1977; November 4, 1977; and September 7, 1978.

17. Interview, community informant, Crestview, September 7, 1978.

18. *Pensacola Journal*, December 1, 1962, p. 5B; December 7, 1962, p. 2C.

19. *ONJ*, May 20, 1954, pp. 1, 6; and *DBEN*, September 9, 1959.

20. *ONJ*, March 11, 1965, p. 1; July 22, 1965, p. 1; and August 25, 1966, p. 1.

21. U.S. Department of HEW, Office of Civil Rights, Directory of Public Schools in Large Districts (Elementary and Secondary), Enrollment and Staff by Racial/Ethnic Group, Fall 1967, p. 157.

22. Nancy M. Kenaston, *From Cabin to Campus . . . A History of the Okaloosa County School System* (Crestview, Fla.: Okaloosa County School Board, 1977), pp. 127, 194–95, 243; and *ONJ*, August 24, 1967, p. 1.

23. *ONJ*, September 1, 1960, pp. 2–3B.

24. Interview, black policeman, Crestview, September 7, 1978; *ONJ*, August 10, 1961, p. 1.

25. City Budget, Crestview, June 1, 1964 to June 30, 1965; *ONJ*, June 15, 1961, p. 1; June 14, 1962, p. 3A; and January 28, 1965, p. 6.

26. *ONJ*, October 6, 1960, p. 1; January 19, 1961, p. 1; June 10, 1965, p. 1; February 15, 1968, p. 1; and December 11, 1969, p. 1.

27. U.S. Commission on Civil Rights, *Political Participation* (Washington, D.C.: U.S. Government Printing Office, 1968), p. 216.

28. Interview, black elected official, Crestview, July 28, 1975; *ONJ*, August 18, 1966, p. 4B; September 15, 1966, p. 1A; and September 29, 1966, p. 1A; and Voter Registration Records, City Hall, Crestview.

29. *ONJ*, September 5, 1968, p. 1A; September 26, 1968, p. 1; July 16, 1970, p. 1A; *Pensacola Journal*, September 25, 1968, pp. 1–2A; and Voter Registration Records, City Hall, Crestview.

30. *ONJ*, March 24, 1960, p. 1B; July 18, 1963, p. 1; May 12, 1965, p. 1.

31. *ONJ*, February 13, 1964, p. 4A.

32. *ONJ*, April 9, 1964, p. 5A.

33. *ONJ*, November 7, 1968, p. 3A.

34. *ONJ*, March 24, 1960, pp. 1, 4A; and June 2, 1960, p. 1.

35. *ONJ*, June 23, 1960, p. 1.

36. Florida Development Commission, *Comprehensive Development Plan for Crestview, Florida*, Part 1, 1966, pp. 91, 111–12.

37. City Election Results for Bond Election of June 9, 1965, City Clerk's Office, City Hall, Crestview; and *ONJ*, June 3, 1965, p. 1; June 10, 1965, p. 1; and October 12, 1967, p. 1.

38. *ONJ*, April 14, 1966, p. 6A; and January 19, 1967, p. 1.

39. *ONJ*, May 16, 1968, p. 1; January 29, 1970, p. 1; February 12, 1970, p. 1; and January 7, 1971, p. 1A; *Pensacola News*, May 14, 1968, pp. 1–2A.

40. *ONJ*, October 6, 1966, p. 1A; October 6, 1967, p. 1; and May 6, 1971, p. 8.

41. *ONJ*, February 24, 1966, p. 4A.

42. ONJ, March 27, 1969, p. 1.

43. Kenaston, *From Cabin to Campus*, p. 198.

44. ONJ, June 27, 1968, p. 6A; and January 4, 1973, p. 1.

45. *Pensacola Journal*, June 13, 1972, p. 1C.

46. ONJ, June 28, 1973, p. 7; August 9, 1973, p. 1; February 14, 1974, p. 3; and December 12, 1974, pp. 1–2A.

47. *Mims* v. *Wilson*, 514 F. 2d 106 (U.S. Court of Appeals, 1975); and *Pensacola Journal*, June 13, 1972, p. 1C; and October 20, 1973, p. 1A.

48. Interview, community informant, Crestview, November 2, 1981; *Pensacola Journal*, November 11, 1976, p. 1B; September 17, 1980, pp. 1, 14A; and December 17, 1980, p. 3C.

49. Interview, Samuel Allen, Crestview, July 28, 1975; and ONJ, August 30, 1973, p. 5.

50. ONJ, January 17, 1974, pp. 1–2.

51. ONJ, February 15, 1973, p. 4; January 24, 1974, p. 1; October 3, 1974, p. 1; February 18, 1979, p. 1A; and March 1, 1979, p. 2A.

52. Interviews, three community informants, Crestview, September 15, 1977; November 3, 1977; and January 12, 1978.

53. ONJ, October 30, 1975, p. 1; and *Pensacola Journal*, January 24, 1978, p. 1B.

54. Interview, Samuel Allen, Crestview, December 18, 1980.

55. Center for Community Development and Research, Florida A&M University, Data Base for Okaloosa County, 1976, p. 11; "Okaloosa: A County Wed to an Air Base," *Florida Trend* 17 (December 1974): 49–52; and West Florida Regional Planning Council, Land Use Plan for the West Florida Region, Vol. 2 (July, 1977), p. 131.

56. ONJ, August 28, 1975, p. 2; and September 29, 1977, p. 1.

57. Interviews, two community informants, Crestview, November 4, 1977.

58. Community Development Block Grant Application, City of Crestview, Fla., 1980; and ONJ, July 29, 1976, p. 1; September 29, 1977, p. 1; and August 16, 1979, pp. 1–2A.

59. ONJ, September 30, 1976, p. 1; October 6, 1977, p. 6A; and September 25, 1980, p. 1.

60. Equal Employment Opportunity Commission, State and Local Government Information (EEO–4), City of Crestview, July 29, 1980.

61. ONJ, March 9, 1972, p. 4; March 16, 1972, pp. 1–2A; and March 11, 1976, pp. 1–2A.

62. ONJ, January 25, 1973, pp. 1–2; and September 19, 1974, p. 1; *Pensacola Journal*, February 6, 1973, p. 1B; and February 13, 1973, p. 1D.

63. ONJ, February 7, 1974, p. 1; August 15, 1974, p. 1; and October 10, 1974, p. 1; *Pensacola News*, August 27, 1974, pp. 1–2A; *Pensacola Journal*, October 16, 1974, p. 1B.

64. ONJ, February 3, 1977, pp. 1–2; February 10, 1977, p. 1; and February 16, 1978, p. 1; and *The Bulletin* (local newspaper), October 14, 1976, pp. 1–2.

65. *Gainesville Sun*, May 26, 1975, p. 1C.

66. *ONJ*, July 6, 1978, p. 2A; July 13, 1978, pp. 1–2A; July 27, 1978, p. 1; and August 17, 1978, pp. 1–2A; *Pensacola Journal*, August 15, 1978, p. 1; August 16, 1978, p. 1.

67. Interviews, community informants, Crestview, September 8, 1978; and local newspaper reporter, Crestview, December 18, 1980.

68. *ONJ*, July 27, 1978, p. 3A.

69. *ONJ*, June 17, 1976, p. 9; and June 24, 1976, p. 6A.

70. *ONJ*, February 1, 1979, pp. 1, 4A; July 12, 1979, p. 2A; and March 13, 1980, p. 1.

71. *ONJ*, January 29, 1976, p. 1; January 13, 1977, p. 3; and December 25, 1980, pp. 1, 10A.

72. Affirmative Action Plan for the City of Crestview, Fla., November, 1977, annex # 1 (B).

73. Interview, community informant, Crestview, September 7, 1978.

74. U.S. Bureau of the Census, *1980 Census of Population*, Vol. 1, *Characteristics of the Population*, Chapter C, "General Social and Economic Characteristics," Part 11, Florida, Section 2, July 1983, p. 648.

75. Community Development Block Grant Application, 1980, pp. 2–3.

76. *Pensacola Journal*, April 30, 1978, p. 1.

77. Interviews, three community informants, Crestview, September 7, 1978, and December 18, 1980.

78. Voter Registration Records for 1973, City Hall, Crestview.

79. Interview, black elected official, Crestview, August 7, 1986; *ONJ*, September 10, 1981, p. 1; September 14, 1983, pp. 1–2; September 4, 1985, pp. 7–8; and September 11, 1985, pp. 1–2.

80. *ONJ*, January 24, 1980, p. 1; February 7, 1980, p. 1; April 10, 1980, p. 1; April 17, 1980, p. 1; and May 15, 1980, p. 1.

81. *Pensacola Journal*, May 24, 1980, p. 1C.

82. Interview, community informant, Crestview, January 13, 1978.

83. Interviews, two community informants, Crestview, November 4, 1977, and January 12, 1978. Also, in our random survey of twenty-three business managers in Crestview, eight (35%) volunteered views that blacks in general were not willing to work or were too dependent on welfare.

84. U.S. Bureau of the Census, *1980 Census of Population*, Florida, Section 2, p. 648.

85. Interview, public official, Crestview, August 7, 1986; *ONJ*, January 5, 1982, p. 1; June 10, 1982, p. 1; February 2, 1983, p. 1; March 14, 1984, p. 1; March 13, 1985, p. 1; and January 22, 1986, pp. 1–2.

86. EEO–4 Form, City of Crestview, 1986.

87. Interview, city clerk, May 28, 1987; and *ONJ*, February 6, 1985, p. 1.

88. Lake City–Columbia County Chamber of Commerce, "Lake City and Columbia County, Florida," pamphlet, 1973, pp. 1–9.

89. Edward F. Keuchel, *A History of Columbia County, Florida* (Tallahassee, Fla.: Sentry Press, 1981), p. 186.

90. Interview, white community informant, Lake City, August 11, 1976.

91. Keuchel, *A History of Columbia County*, pp. 26–60; and Lake City–Columbia County Chamber of Commerce, "Lake City and Columbia County," p. 11.

92. Allen W. Trelease, *White Terror: The Ku Klux Klan Conspiracy and Southern Reconstruction* (New York: Harper and Row, 1971), p. 242.

93. Fran Hesser, "Carpetbaggers Were Not Welcome," LCR, December 13, 1974; Joe M. Richardson, *The Negro in the Reconstruction of Florida, 1865–1877* (Tallahassee, Fla.: Florida State University, 1965), pp. 172–73; and Trelease, *White Terror*, pp. 242–45, 310.

94. Hesser, "Carpetbaggers Were Not Welcome," no page.

95. "The First Hundred Years, 1874–1974," LCR, December 13, 1974; and *Gainesville Sun*, April 2, 1978, p. 3C.

96. Interviews, two black community informants, Lake City, February 11, 1977, and June 10, 1976.

97. Clubok, De Grove, and Farris, "The Manipulated Negro Vote," p. 128. The community referred to as Tobacco Hill is Lake City.

98. Ibid., pp. 115–18; and LCR, May 1, 1959, p. 1; and May 8, 1959, p. 1.

99. Clubok, De Grove, and Farris, "Manipulated Negro Vote," p. 119.

100. Ibid., p. 126; and interviews, community informants, Lake City, June 8, 1976; August 3, 1976; August 11, 1976; November 4, 1977; and December 1, 1977.

101. Clubok, De Grove, and Farris, "Manipulated Negro Vote," p. 128; and interview, community informants, Lake City, December 1, 1977.

102. LCR, April 14, 1961, p. 3; December 7, 1966, p. 1; and September 8, 1971, p. 2.

103. *Florida Times-Union*, April 8, 1964, p. 27; and May 18, 1965, p. 20; LCR, April 3, 1964, p. 1; April 10, 1964, p. 1; May 20, 1965, p. 1; and Supervisor of Elections Office, Lake City, Official City Election Results, April 22, 1964.

104. LCR, January 8, 1965, pp. 1–2.

105. Keuchel, *A History of Columbia County*, pp. 208–10; LCR, February 18, 1965, p. 1; June 3, 1965, p. 1; April 14, 1966, p. 1; June 15, 1967, p. 1; July 4, 1968, p. 1; January 8, 1969, p. 1; August 27, 1969, pp. 1–2; January 2, 1970, p. 1; February 13, 1970, p. 1; and U.S. Department of HEW, Office of Civil Rights, *Directory of Public Elementary and Secondary Schools, Enrollment and Staff by Racial/Ethnic Group*, Fall 1968, p. 239.

106. Interviews, five community informants, Lake City, June 10, 1976; August 3, 1976; August 11, 1976; February 11, 1977; March 7, 1977; March 15, 1977; and December 1, 1977; and Keuchel, *A History of Columbia County*, pp. 207–8.

107. LCR, November 13, 1964, p. 1; and November 6, 1968, p. 1.

108. LCR, June 5, 1964, p. 3A; see also LCR, July 26, 1963, p. 2A; August 2, 1963, p. 2A; and March 13, 1964, p. 2A.

109. LCR, September 12, 1958, p. 1; August 30, 1963, p. 1; and November 1, 1963, p. 1.

110. *Gainesville Sun*, September 6, 1981, p. 12A; and September 28, 1981, p. 3B.

111. Clubok, De Grove, and Farris, "Manipulated Negro Vote," pp. 128–29; interviews, two black community informants, Lake City, August 11, 1976, and March 7, 1977; and LCR, December 27, 1974, p. 1.

112. Interview, white leader, Lake City, by Professor Keith Legg of the University of Florida, 1975.

113. U.S. Bureau of the Census, 1970 Census of Population, Vol. 1, *Characteristics of the Population,* Part 11, Florida, Section 1, 1973, pp. 373, 401, 408, 423.

114. Clubok, De Grove, and Farris, "Manipulated Negro Vote," p. 129.

115. LCR, November 26, 1974, pp. 1–2; and November 27, 1974, p. 1.

116. LCR, January 13, 1975, p. 1.

117. *Florida Star,* April 12, 1975, p. 1; *Florida Times-Union,* March 27, 1975, p. 4B; and LCR, March 27, 1975, p. 1; and March 28, 1975, pp. 1–2.

118. LCR, April 24, 1974, p. 1; April 24, 1975, pp. 1–2; May 14, 1975, p. 1; June 2, 1975, p. 1; March 23, 1976, p. 1; and June 8, 1976, p. 1.

119. Interview, city commissioner, Lake City, March 13, 1981; and LCR, April 6, 1977, pp. 1, 10.

120. Interview, Columbia County Administrator, Lake City, October 21, 1977; and LCR, March 24, 1975, p. 1; September 4, 1975, p. 1; and April 18, 1976, p. 1.

121. LCR, July 23, 1975, p. 1B; January 12, 1976, p. 1B; and June 30, 1976, p. 1B.

122. Interview, community informant, Lake City, October 21, 1977.

123. LCR, June 8, 1976, p. 1.

124. LCR, July 20, 1976, p. 1.

125. LCR, March 7, 1977, pp. 1, 10; May 3, 1977, pp. 1, 10; June 28, 1979, p. 1; and June 29, 1979, p. 2.

126. Interviews, two local newspaper reporters, Lake City, October 15, 1977, and February 21, 1981.

127. LCR, April 27, 1967, p. 1A; April 7, 1971, p. 1; April 9, 1975, p. 1; and November 16, 1977, p. 1.

128. *Florida Times-Union,* June 19, 1978, pp. 1A, 6A; June 22, 1978, p. 3B; and LCR, October 13, 1976, pp. 1, 12; April 5, 1978, p. 1; April 18, 1978, p. 1; June 21, 1978, p. 1; and August 30, 1978, p. 4.

129. LCR, October 5, 1977, p. 1; October 19, 1977, p. 1; April 17, 1978, p. 1; February 7, 1979, pp. 1–2; and February 21, 1979, pp. 1–2.

130. *Florida Times-Union,* February 26, 1981, pp. 1B, 4B; LCR, April 26, 1978, p. 1; November 16, 1979, pp. 1–2; February 26, 1981, p. 1; April 6, 1981, p. 1; May 19, 1981, pp. 1–2; April 21, 1982, pp. 1–2; and letters from director, Office of Revenue Sharing, Department of the Treasury, to city manager, Lake City, February 9, 1981, and June 5, 1981.

131. LCR, November 23, 1976, p. 1; April 26, 1978, pp. 1–2; May 2, 1978, p. 1; May 24, 1978, pp. 1–2; June 27, 1978, p. 1; and July 12, 1978, p. 1.

132. *Gainesville Sun,* March 21, 1979, p. 3A; *Florida Times-Union,* March 20,

1979, p. 3B; and LCR, March 14, 1979, pp. 1–2; March 15, 1979, pp. 1–2; March 16, 1979, pp. 1–2; and March 19, 1979, pp. 1–2.

133. LCR, March 20, 1979, pp. 1–2; March 28, 1979, pp. 1–2; March 29, 1979, p. 2; April 11, 1979, pp. 1–2; and letter from chairperson, Community Affairs Fair Action Committee, to chairman, Columbia County School Board, March 19, 1979.

134. LCR, April 12, 1979, pp. 1–2.

135. LCR, April 3, 1979, pp. 1–2; April 5, 1979, pp. 1–2; April 6, 1979, p. 2; April 9, 1979, p. 2; and April 16, 1979, pp. 1–2.

136. LCR, June 27, 1979, pp. 1–2; July 27, 1979, p. 2; September 7, 1979, p. 2; September 14, 1979, pp. 1–2; October 4, 1979, p. 2; and October 18, 1979, p. 1.

137. *Florida Times-Union*, February 15, 1980, p. 5B; and Columbia County supervisor of elections, Registered Voters By Race, Columbia County (by precinct), October 4, 1980.

138. LCR, October 9, 1980, pp. 1–2; and November 6, 1980, pp. 1–2.

139. LCR, February 26, 1980, p. 1.

140. LCR, June 6, 1980, p. 1; and July 23, 1980, pp. 1–2.

141. LCR, December 21, 1979, pp. 1–2; July 23, 1980, pp. 1–2; and November 19, 1981, pp. 1–2.

142. *Florida Times-Union*, April 12, 1980, pp. 1B, 5B; and LCR, January 11, 1979, pp. 1–2; January 24, 1979, pp. 1–2, 4; and April 28, 1980, p. 1.

143. Interview, black elected official, Lake City, February 13, 1981.

144. LCR, September 29, 1976, pp. 1, 8; September 8, 1978, p. 1; and September 13, 1978, p. 2.

145. LCR, December 15, 1981, p. 1; and letter to mayor of Lake City from Councilman Samuel Thompson, December 14, 1981 (copy).

146. *Gainesville Sun*, September 5, 1981, p. 1C; and September 6, 1981, p. 12A; interview, black elected official, Lake City, December 18, 1981; and LCR, August 1, 1977, pp. 1–2; August 28, 1981, pp. 1–2; September 7, 1981, pp. 1–2; and September 11, 1981, p. 1B.

147. Interviews, two public officials, September 15, 1986; LCR, August 2, 1982, p. 2; September 8, 1982, pp. 1–3.

148. LCR, November 10, 1981, pp. 1–2; September 8, 1982, pp. 1–3.

149. LCR, June 19, 1984, pp. 1–2; July 11, 1984, pp. 1–2; January 15, 1986, pp. 1–2; and September 3, 1986, pp. 1, 3.

150. LCR, January 4, 1982, pp. 1–2; March 15, 1984, pp. 1–2; September 18, 1984, pp. 1–2; and July 22, 1985, pp. 1–2.

151. Interview, public official, Lake City, January 29, 1987; LCR, May 24, 1984, pp. 1–2; June 4, 1984, p. 2; and May 5, 1986, pp. 1–2.

152. Interview, Recreation Department official, Lake City, January 29, 1987; LCR, May 19, 1982, p. 1; January 6, 1983, pp. 1–2; and February 16, 1984, p. 3.

153. Interviews, two city officials, September 15, 1986, and September 17, 1986; LCR, April 24, 1985, pp. 1–2; January 27, 1986, pp. 1–2.

154. Much of this section is drawn from Paige A. Parker and James W. Button, "The Civil Rights Movement in the Rural South: Black Revolt in a Florida Town," March, 1978, unpublished paper.

155. Richardson, *The Negro in the Reconstruction of Florida*, pp. 188, 194.

156. Center for Rural Development, *People and Jobs for Gadsden County* (Gainesville, Fla.: Institute of Food and Agricultural Sciences, University of Florida, 1977), p. 1; Dudley Clendinen, "Dead End on a Tobacco Road," *The Floridian* (Sunday supplement to the *St. Petersburg Times*), March 28, 1971, pp. 11–19; and J. Randall Stanley, *History of Gadsden County* (Quincy, Fla.: Gadsden County Times, 1948), p. 61.

157. Office of Economic Opportunity, *Gadsden County Community Profile* (Washington, D.C.: Office of Economic Opportunity Information Center, 1966), pp. 2–3.

158. Center for Rural Development, *People and Jobs*, p. 5.

159. GCT, September 13, 1956, p. 1; December 27, 1956, p. 1; March 28, 1957, p. 1.

160. U.S. Commission on Civil Rights, *Report* (Washington, D.C.: U.S. Government Printing Office, 1959), p. 56. See also U.S. Commission on Civil Rights, *Report, Voting*, Vol. 1, 1961, pp. 162–64.

161. Meier and Rudwick, *CORE: A Study in the Civil Rights Movement*, pp. 92, 99, 106–7, 259–61; and Watters and Cleghorn, *Climbing Jacob's Ladder*, p. 143.

162. GCT, April 16, 1964, p. 1; and *Tallahassee Democrat*, August 5, 1964, Section 2, p. 11.

163. GCT, August 6, 1964, p. 1; December 10, 1964, p. 1; July 1, 1965, p. 1; August 19, 1965, p. 1; Meier and Rudwick, *CORE*, pp. 260–61, 270; and *Tallahassee Democrat*, August 5, 1964, p. 11; August 17, 1964, p. 9; and June 26, 1965, p. 2.

164. *New York Times*, May 18, 1964, p. 25.

165. GCT, December 10, 1964, p. 1; December 3, 1964, p. 1; and Watters and Cleghorn, *Climbing Jacob's Ladder*, p. 144.

166. GCT, April 4, 1965, p. 1; March 17, 1966, p. 1; May 5, 1966, p. 1; and May 26, 1966, p. 1.

167. Interview, black elected official, Gretna, July 26, 1975.

168. GCT, July 9, 1964, p. 1; July 15, 1965, p. 1; August 1, 1968, p. 1; and July 30, 1970, pp. 1, 16.

169. GCT, May 21, 1970, p. 1; May 28, 1970, p. 1; June 4, 1970, p. 1; and February 4, 1971, p. 1.

170. GCT, October 15, 1970, p. 1; *New York Times*, October 13, 1970, p. 49; *Tallahassee Democrat*, October 11, 1970, p. 1; October 12, 1970, p. 11; October 13, 1970, p. 13; and October 14, 1970, p. 13.

171. Interview, white community informant, Gretna, November 17, 1977.

172. Interview, black elected official, Gretna, November 18, 1977.

173. GCT, October 22, 1970, p. 1; December 10, 1970, p. 1; January 28, 1971, p. 1; February 4, 1971, p. 2; interviews, two black public officials, Quincy, November 18, 1977, and December 19, 1977.

174. GCT, February 11, 1971, pp. 1–2; *Tallahassee Democrat*, February 8, 1971, section 2, p. 11; February 9, 1971, section 2, p. 11; and February 10, 1971, section 2, p. 9.

175. *Tallahassee Democrat*, February 10, 1971, Section 2, p. 9.

176. GCT, March 4, 1971, p. 1; and *Tallahassee Democrat*, February 28, 1971, pp. 1, 14.

177. GCT, February 18, 1971, p. 1; and March 25, 1971, p. 1; interviews, two officers, Sheriff's Department, Quincy, July 22, 1976.

178. *Tallahassee Democrat*, February 14, 1971, Section C, p. 3.

179. GCT, April 13, 1978, p. 7B; and Miles K. Womack, Jr., *Gadsden: A Florida County in Word and Picture* (Quincy, Fla.: Taylor Publishing Co., 1976), pp. 281–87.

180. GCT, August 13, 1959, pp. 1, 8.

181. Interviews, three community informants, Gretna, July 26, 1975; August 15, 1976; and November 18, 1977.

182. Interviews, two black community informants, Gretna, July 26, 1975.

183. Interviews, two black community informants, Gretna, December 20, 1977.

184. GCT, December 2, 1971, p. 1; interviews, two black community informants, Gretna, December 20, 1977, and March 19, 1981; *Tallahassee Democrat*, December 6, 1971, p. 13; *Florida Star*, December 18, 1971, p. 1.

185. GCT, December 9, 1971, p. 1; and December 7, 1972, p. 1; interviews, two black community informants, Gretna, July 26, 1975, and December 20, 1977; *Tallahassee Democrat*, December 8, 1971, p. 30.

186. Florida A&M University, School of Business and Industry, *Comprehensive Development Plan, Phase One, Town of Gretna, Florida*, June, 1974, pp. 2, 27.

187. Paige Alan Parker, *Political Mobilization in the Rural South: A Case Study of Gadsden County, Florida* (unpublished doctoral diss., University of Florida, 1980), p. 113.

188. Interviews, two black community informants, Gretna, July 26, 1975.

189. GCT, May 8, 1975, p. 1; June 5, 1975, p. 1; and interview, community informant, Gretna, July 26, 1975.

190. Interview, white community informant, Gretna, August 13, 1976.

191. GCT, July 24, 1975, p. 1; August 3, 1978, p. 1; interviews, four community informants, Gretna, July 26, 1975; and August 13, 1976.

192. Interview, white community informant, Gretna, August 13, 1976.

193. GCT, December 8, 1977, p. 1; December 22, 1977, pp. 1, 16; interviews, four community informants, Gretna, August 13, 1976; December 20, 1977; December 21, 1977; and December 29, 1977.

194. GCT, December 13, 1973, p. 4; *Tallahassee Democrat*, December 3, 1973, p. 19; December 4, 1973, p. 9; December 5, 1973, p. 15; and October 16, 1974, p. 26.

195. GCT, March 21, 1974, p. 1; September 26, 1974, p. 1; December 15, 1974, p. 1; and February 20, 1975, p. 1; *Tallahassee Democrat*, September 25,

1974, p. 17; September 26, 1974, p. 16; October 16, 1974, p. 26; and February 19, 1975, p. 15.

196. GCT, August 10, 1972, p. 1; interviews, two community informants, Gretna, July 26, 1975; and August 13, 1976.

197. GCT, August 26, 1976, p. 1; October 28, 1976, p. 16; June 2, 1977, p. 1; July 7, 1977, p. 1; November 3, 1977, p. 1; August 3, 1978, p. 1; September 27, 1979, p. 3; October 25, 1979, pp. 1,3; and November 1, 1979, p. 1; *Tallahassee Democrat*, January 11, 1979, p. 1D.

198. Interviews, two white community informants, Gretna, March 12, 1981 and March 19, 1981.

199. *Tallahassee Democrat*, January 19, 1978, pp. 1, 3A.

200. GCT, April 13, 1978, p. 7B.

201. GCT, December 22, 1977, pp. 1, 16; Parker, *Political Mobilization in the Rural South*, pp. 87–90.

202. GCT, February 9, 1978, p. 1; May 4, 1978, p. 1; January 10, 1980, pp. 1, 3; January 31, 1980, p. 1; February 7, 1980, pp. 1, 3A; May 22, 1980, pp. 1, 3A; *Tallahassee Democrat*, January 31, 1980, pp. 1, 10A; May 24, 1980, pp. 1, 2B.

203. GCT, October 25, 1979, p. 1; November 8, 1979, p. 1.

204. GCT, February 7, 1980, p. 4A; *Tallahassee Democrat*, November 15, 1979, pp. 1, 8A; November 21, 1979, pp. 1, 2B.

205. Community Development Block Grant Application, *Small Cities' Program, Town of Gretna, Florida, 1979–1980*, pp. 1–2; and 1980 Census of Population and Housing, Summary Tape File 3A (Florida) [machine/readable data file], Prepared by Bureau of the Census, 1982.

206. GCT, May 11, 1978, p. 1B; October 18, 1979, p. 1; April 16, 1981, pp. 1, 3A; and August 20, 1981, pp. 1, 3A.

207. Interview, town administrator, Gretna, March 19, 1981; GCT, August 7, 1986, p. 1.

208. GCT, August 18, 1983, p. 3; July 3, 1986, p. 1; December 4, 1986, p. 5A; *Tallahassee Democrat*, August 20, 1983.

209. *Tallahassee Democrat*, February 26, 1985, pp. 1–2B; April 22, 1985, pp. 1–2C.

210. GCT, July 12, 1979, pp. 1–3; November 1, 1979, p. 1; January 3, 1980. p. 3; and interview, town administrator, Gretna, March 19, 1981.

211. Interview, town administrator, Gretna, March 26, 1987; GCT, February 4, 1982, p. 3.

212. GCT, September 6, 1984, p. 5; *Tallahassee Democrat*, January 27, 1985; May 3, 1987, pp. 7–8A.

213. GCT, April 18, 1985, p. 4; May 2, 1985, p. 4; *Tallahassee Democrat*, May 5, 1987, p. 4A; interview, town administrator, Gretna, March 26, 1987.

214. GCT, October 4, 1984, p. 2; February 14, 1985, p. 3; April 10, 1986, p. 3; *Tallahassee Democrat*, December 28, 1984, pp. 1–2C; May 5, 1987, pp. 1, 5A; interviews, two town officials, Gretna, March 26, 1987, and April 3, 1987.

215. GCT, February 13, 1975, p. 1; February 20, 1975, p. 1; March 13, 1975, p. 1; March 27, 1975, p. 1; and April 21, 1977, p. 1.

216. GCT, November 3, 1977, p. 1; and December 8, 1977, p. 16.

217. GCT, September 14, 1978, p. 1; September 11, 1980, pp. 1, 18A; and October 9, 1980, pp. 1, 8.

218. GCT, October 16, 1980, p. 4A.

219. GCT, September 16, 1982, p. 4; October 7, 1982, p. 1; February 9, 1984, p. 1; and November 6, 1986, p. 1.

220. Interview, black elected official, Gretna, July 26, 1975.

Chapter 3
The New South and Political Change

1. Elizabeth Jacoway, "An Introduction," in Elizabeth Jacoway and David R. Colburn, eds., *Southern Businessmen and Desegregation* (Baton Rouge, La.: Louisiana State University Press, 1982), p. 11.

2. David R. Colburn and Richard K. Scher, *Florida's Gubernatorial Politics in the 20th Century* (Tallahassee, Fla.: University Presses of Florida, 1980), p. 224.

3. Philip J. Trounstine and Terry Christensen, *Movers and Shakers: The Study of Community Power* (New York: St. Martin's Press, 1982), pp. 40–47.

4. Holloway, *Politics of the Southern Negro*, p. 28.

5. Ibid., p. 28.

6. City of Titusville, Planning Section, *City of Titusville Comprehensive Plan, Population Element*, May 8, 1980, pp. 1–2; and DeWitt McGee and Associates, *Land Use Survey and Analysis: Titusville, Phase I*, 1961, pp. 5–6.

7. Ibid. See also Titusville Centennial Commission, *Countdown In History: Historical Booklet and Program*, 1967; and TSA, September 24, 1980, p. 26.

8. Interview, community informant, Titusville, April 30, 1981.

9. *New York Times*, December 27, 1951, pp. 1, 22; December 28, 1951, p. 13; Price, *The Negro and Southern Politics*, pp. 57, 117–18; and TSA, December 28, 1951, pp. 1–2, 4.

10. TSA, September 24, 1980, p. 57.

11. Interview, black informant, Titusville, November 18, 1976.

12. Price, *The Negro and Southern Politics*, p. 45.

13. TSA, June 8, 1954, p. 2.

14. TSA, May 21, 1954, p. 2; and May 28, 1954, p. 1.

15. City (Titusville) Government, "First Annual Report to the Citizens," June 1953, pamphlet; and Titusville Centennial Commission, *Countdown In History*.

16. Interview, community informant, Titusville, February 10, 1977.

17. TSA, February 29, 1960, p. 1; March 12, 1962, p. 7; July 16, 1962, p. 1; January 18, 1963, p. 1; and March 4, 1963, p. 1.

18. TSA, February 24, 1960, p. 1; and May 23, 1962, p. 1.

19. TSA, July 12, 1961, p. 1; June 5, 1963, p. 1; and June 17, 1963, p. 1.

20. Interview, black informant, Titusville, September 9, 1977; and TSA, December 8, 1961, p. 7; June 29, 1965, p. 3; August 18, 1965, p. 3; September 2, 1965, p. 3; and January 26, 1966, p. 3.

21. TSA, June 12, 1963, p. 1; June 17, 1963, p. 1; and June 14, 1965, p. 3.

22. TSA, May 30, 1960, p. 1; July 6, 1962, p. 1; February 15, 1963, p. 4; and March 23, 1964, p. 3.

23. Interview, black informant, Titusville, September 9, 1977; and TSA, June 12, 1963, p. 1; July 10, 1964, p. 1; and April 12, 1965, p. 3.

24. TSA, January 2, 1961, p. 1; October 13, 1961, p. 1; June 26, 1964, p. 1; and July 31, 1964, p. 1.

25. TSA, July 18, 1967, p. 1B; and January 8, 1968, p. 1; U.S. Department of HEW, Office of Civil Rights, *Directory of Public Elementary and Secondary Schools, Enrollment and Staff by Racial/Ethnic Group*, Fall 1968, pp. 236–37.

26. "A New Brevard Economy Emerging," *Florida Trend* 15 (April 1973), pp. 101–2; and "Brevard Makes a Comeback," *Florida Trend* 16 (December 1973), pp. 62–63.

27. TSA, August 5, 1964, p. 2B; and April 13, 1965, p. 3.

28. Interview, black informant, Titusville, November 4, 1976.

29. Interview, community informant, Titusville, October 14, 1976; see also *Annual Report*, Human Relations Commission, Titusville, December 1969.

30. TSA, December 20, 1963, p. 4; see also TSA, January 27, 1964, p. 2; April 1, 1964, p. 4; and June 29, 1964, p. 4.

31. TSA, June 8, 1966, p. 4; and June 16, 1966, p. 4.

32. TSA, April 30, 1968, p. 20C; and July 29, 1968, p. 4A.

33. TSA, January 26, 1966, p. 3; June 6, 1966, p. 1; and January 19, 1967, p. 13.

34. Interview, community informant, Titusville, September 8, 1977; and TSA, January 3, 1967, p. 1; January 9, 1967, p. 1; January 19, 1967, p. 1B.; February 8, 1967, p. 1; and November 24, 1967, p. 1B.

35. TSA, May 16, 1969, p. 3A; and May 19, 1969, p. 1; see also *Annual Report*, Human Relations Commission, December 1969.

36. TSA, June 29, 1967, p. 1; February 13, 1968, p. 1B; June 20, 1968, p. 1A; and September 30, 1968, pp. 1–2A.

37. TSA, November 6, 1968, pp. 1, 6A.

38. TSA, September 6, 1966, pp. 1–2.

39. TSA, May 24, 1967, p. 1B; June 21, 1967, p. 1; June 28, 1967, p. 1B; and July 28, 1967, p. 1.

40. TSA, June 20, 1967, p. 1; June 29, 1967, p. 1; November 27, 1967, p. 1B; and February 17, 1969, p. 1.

41. TSA, February 29, 1968, p. 1A; August 12, 1968, p. 1A; September 20, 1968, p. 1B; February 21, 1969, p. 1; February 27, 1969, p. 1B; and March 24, 1969, p. 1.

42. TSA, September 11, 1967, p. 5; January 11, 1968, p. 1B; January 15, 1968, p. 1B; October 21, 1968, p. 1A.

43. (Cocoa) *Evening Tribune*, September 25, 1968, p. 4A; TSA, September 24,

1968, p. 1A; September 25, 1968, pp. 1, 5A, 1B; and September 30, 1968, pp. 1–2A.

44. *Florida Today*, July 1, 1984, p. 10.

45. TSA, July 5 and 6, 1971, pp. 1, 12A; and July 8, 1971, p. 1A; (Cocoa) *Today*, July 6, 1971, pp. 1, 10A; July 7, 1971, pp. 1–2B; and July 8, 1971, pp. 1–2B.

46. *Annual Report*, Human Relations Commission, Titusville, 1972; TSA, December 30 and 31, 1971, pp. 1, 8A; and January 4, 1972, p. 1A; and (Cocoa) *Today*, December 31, 1971, pp. 1–2B.

47. TSA, November 27 and 28, 1968, p. 3A; July 14, 1971, p. 1A; and March 15, 1972, p. 1A; and (Cocoa) *Today*, July 15, 1971, p. 2B.

48. TSA, April 30, 1968, p. 20C.

49. Interview, black informant, Titusville, March 10, 1977; see also interviews, two black informants, Titusville, November 18, 1976, and September 9, 1977.

50. Interviews, two black informants, Titusville, November 18, 1976, and September 9, 1977; and (Cocoa) *Today*, August 8, 1971, pp. 1–2B.

51. *Annual Report*, Human Relations Commission, Titusville, 1970–71, p. 6; and TSA, December 24 and 25, 1970, p. 1A+.

52. Telephone interview, black real estate developer, May 7, 1981; and (Cocoa) *Today*, January 24, 1973, pp. 1–2B.

53. TSA, July 31, 1968, p. 1A.

54. TSA, November 3, 1965, p. 20.

55. TSA, September 4, 1970, p. 3A; September 9, 1970, pp. 1, 3A; and September 30, 1970, pp. 1, 10.

56. Interview, black informant, Titusville, November 18, 1976; and TSA, September 8, 1972, pp. 1, 10A; September 13, 1972, pp. 1A, 1B; and October 4, 1972, pp. 1A, 1B.

57. TSA, March 17, 1970, pp. 1, 3A; and (Cocoa) *Today*, January 23, 1970, p. 1B.

58. Interview, black informant, Titusville, October 14, 1976; and TSA, November 24, 1976, p. 3A.

59. Interview, former president of Citizens Backers, Titusville, May 1, 1981; and TSA, March 2, 1977, p. 1A; April 27, 1977, p. 8A; March 15, 1978, p. 2A; April 18, 1979, pp. 1, 3A; and November 5, 1980, p. 3A.

60. Interview, president of Progressive Action Society, Titusville, April 30, 1981.

61. Ibid.; interview, white informant, Titusville, April 30, 1981; and TSA, April 18, 1979, pp. 1, 3A.

62. Interviews, president of Progressive Action Society, Titusville, April 30, 1981; and former president of Citizens Backers, Titusville, May 1, 1981.

63. City of Titusville Planning Department, *Neighborhood Housing Improvement Study, Phase 1*, June 1971, pp. 27–30, 36, 64–67.

64. U.S. Bureau of the Census, *1970 Census of Population*, Vol. 1, *Characteristics of the Population*, Part 2, Florida, Section 1, 1973, pp. 377, 405, 410, 425.

65. "A New Brevard Economy Emerging," pp. 101–102; and TSA, July 30, 1975, pp. 1–2A; and September 8, 1976, p. 1A.

66. *Annual Report*, Human Relations Commission, Titusville, 1969; City of Titusville Planning Department, *Neighborhood Housing Improvement Study*, p. 85; and interview, white informant, Titusville, November 18, 1976.

67. City of Titusville Planning Department, *Neighborhood Housing Improvement Study*, pp. 87–89; and TSA, April 15, 1969, p. 1A; April 24, 1969, p. 1B; September 11, 1970, p. 1; and May 21, 1971, p. 1A.

68. TSA, August 11, 1971, pp. 1, 12A; March 13, 1974, p. 4A; and September 25, 1974, p. 1.

69. City of Titusville, Community Development Block Grant Application, Titusville Improvement Program, May 14, 1980; and TSA, June 11, 1975, p. 13A; April 12, 1978, p. 1A; and April 18, 1979, p. 3A.

70. TSA, May 26, 1976, p. 3A; and September 1, 1976, p. 2A.

71. City of Titusville, Affirmative Action Program, November 1974; and TSA, May 19, 1976, p. 4A.

72. TSA, July 27, 1977, p. 5A.

73. Telephone interview, Titusville chief of police, May 4, 1981; and TSA, October 22, 1980, pp. 1, 3A.

74. TSA, May 14, 1974, pp. 1, 4A; May 15, 1974, p. 3A; May 16, 1974, pp. 1, 3A; May 17, 1974, pp. 1, 3A; January 10, 1975, p. 1A; January 27, 1975, p. 1A; April 30, 1975, pp. 1–2A; and August 22, 1985, pp. 1, 3A; and interview, black informant, June 17, 1987.

75. TSA, December 19, 1979, pp. 1–2A.

76. TSA, May 14, 1974, pp. 1, 4A.

77. TSA, May 16, 1985, p. 3A.

78. Interview, former president of Citizens Backers, Titusville, May 1, 1981; and TSA, August 26, 1981, pp. 1–2A.

79. Interview, city manager, Titusville, April 30, 1981; and TSA, March 19, 1976, p. 4A; February 28, 1979, p. 1A; March 7, 1979, pp. 1–2A; September 26, 1979, pp. 1, 3A; and May 21, 1985, pp. 1, 3A.

80. *Florida Today*, July 11, 1982, pp. 1, 3B; July 12, 1983, pp. 1, 3B; and September 11, 1983; TSA, September 14, 1983, p. 4A; Interview, NAACP official, Titusville, November 20, 1986; and Voter Registration Totals, Supervisor of Elections Office, Brevard County, October 11, 1986.

81. Interview, black candidate for local office, Titusville, November 21, 1986; TSA, March 3, 1982, p. 2A; March 10, 1982, p. 1A; March 17, 1982, p. 3A; and September 15, 1982, p. 2A.

82. Interviews, two community informants, Titusville, November 20, 1986; *Florida Today*, November 6, 1985, pp. 1–2A; TSA, April 4, 1985, p. 1A; and November 7, 1985, p. 1A.

83. Interviews, two community informants, Titusville, April 30, 1981.

84. U.S. Bureau of the Census, 1980 Census of Population, Vol. 1, *Characteristics of the Population*, Chapter C, "General Social and Economic Characteristics," Part 11, Florida, Section 1, July 1983, pp. 261, 303, 310.

85. Interview, black informant, Titusville, May 1, 1981.

86. Federal Writers' Project in Florida, Works Progress Administration, *Daytona Local Guide*, 1973, p. 5; Ernest W. Hunt, *From the Timucuans to the Land Boom—A History of the Daytona Beach Area, 1513–1930* (M.A. Thesis, Stetson University, 1971), pp. 4–5; and Jeffrey Tucker, "It's Daytona Beach v. the Fickle Tourist," *Florida Trend* 20 (June 1977), pp. 46–55.

87. Lewis Killian and Charles Grigg, *Racial Crisis In America: Leadership In Conflict* (Englewood Cliffs, N.J.: Prentice-Hall, 1964), pp. 30–31. The Florida community surveyed herein is Daytona Beach. See also Price, *The Negro and Southern Politics*, pp. 260, 262.

88. Fred Booth, "Early Days in Daytona Beach, Florida; How a City Was Founded," *Journal of the Halifax Historical Society* 1, no. 1 (1951); Federal Writers' Project, *Daytona Local Guide*, pp. 33–43; Ianthe Bond Hebel, ed., *Centennial History of Volusia County, Florida, 1854–1954* (Daytona Beach, Fla.: College Publishing Co., 1955), pp. 92, 149–85; and Hunt, *From the Timucuans to the Land Boom*, pp. 41–82.

89. Jesse Walter Dees, Jr., "Bethune-Cookman College (1904–1954)," in Hebel, ed., *Centennial History of Volusia County*, pp. 57–60; Ianthe Bond Hebel, *Daytona Beach, Florida's Racial History*, 1966, unpublished manuscript; and Hunt, *From the Timucuans to the Land Boom*, pp. 89, 102–3.

90. *DBEN*, August 8, 1967, p. 9; September 13, 1984, p. 1C; Dees, Jr., "Bethune-Cookman College," pp. 59–60; Hebel, *Daytona Beach, Florida's Racial History*; and Rackham Holt, *Mary McLeod Bethune: A Biography* (Garden City, N.Y.: Doubleday, 1964), pp. 120–23.

91. Interview, community informant, Daytona Beach, April 14, 1977; see also interviews, two community informants, Daytona Beach, April 14, 1977, and April 15, 1977.

92. *DBEN*, November 19, 1948, p. 1; November 23, 1948, p. 1; and December 7, 1948, p. 1; *Daytona Beach News-Journal*, December 5, 1948, pp. 1, 7; and December 8, 1948, p. 1; interview, black community informant, Daytona Beach, October 13, 1977.

93. Hebel, *Daytona Beach, Florida's Racial History*, p. 4.

94. *DBEN*, February 16, 1950; February 26, 1950; March 30, 1950; May 2, 1950; May 5, 1950; and August 12, 1950; telephone interview, black community informant, May 4, 1982.

95. *DBEN*, November 14, 1956; and Killian and Grigg, *Racial Crisis In America*, p. 30.

96. *DBEN*, March 16, 1950; June 30, 1955; July 6, 1955; and September 30, 1963, p. 13; and telephone interview, black community informant, May 4, 1982.

97. *DBEN*, August 19, 1949; August 24, 1949; and August 25, 1949.

98. *DBEN*, July 16, 1957; August 22, 1957; August 24, 1957; August 28, 1957; August 29, 1957; and January 12, 1960, p. 9.

99. *DBEN*, December 8, 1955; December 11, 1956; December 13, 1956; December 18, 1956; and December 20, 1956.

100. *DBEN*, May 18, 1954, p. 4.

101. *DBEN*, June 1, 1955, p. 3.

102. *DBEN*, January 3, 1956; and April 7, 1959.

103. *DBEN*, August 22, 1956; October 23, 1956; and October 24, 1956.

104. *DBEN*, February 25, 1960, p. 2; March 3, 1960, p. 9; March 4, 1960, Section 2, p. 11; April 8, 1960, p. 6; April 28, 1960, p. 9; and August 16, 1960, p. 8; *Florida Star*, March 5, 1960, p. 1.

105. *DBEN*, May 30, 1963, p. 1; June 4, 1963, p. 4; June 7, 1963, pp. 1–2; June 10, 1963, p. 1; June 4, 1963, p. 13; and September 30, 1963, p. 13; *Florida Star*, June 8, 1963, p. 1; and *New York Times*, June 7, 1963, p. 17; and June 8, 1963, p. 10.

106. *DBEN*, August 4, 1964, p. 9; August 6, 1964, p. 13; October 23, 1964, p. 11; November 11, 1964, p. 9; and November 13, 1964, p. 11.

107. *DBEN*, November 9, 1960, p. 9; November 25, 1960, p. 30; January 3, 1961, p. 9; January 4, 1961, p. 1; November 7, 1961, p. 9; November 16, 1961, p. 1; May 8, 1962, p. 9; March 10, 1965, p. 9; and November 9, 1965, p. 9; and *Florida Star*, July 16, 1960, p. 1.

108. *DBEN*, June 21, 1960, p. 9; and June 27, 1960, p. 13; *Florida Star*, June 25, 1960, p. 1.

109. *DBEN*, January 4, 1961, p. 1; April 15, 1964, p. 1; and December 18, 1964, p. 3; and Killian and Grigg, *Racial Crisis in America*, pp. 29, 44–80.

110. *DBEN*, April 12, 1960, pp. 1–2; April 28, 1960, p. 9; June 3, 1960, p. 1; August 17, 1961, p. 19; *Florida Star*, June 11, 1960, p. 1; and June 18, 1960, p. 1; *Miami Times*, August 19, 1961, p. 1.

111. *DBEN*, August 24, 1962, p. 9; October 29, 1962, p. 1; September 8, 1964, p. 11; and June 15, 1965, p. 9.

112. *DBEN*, November 18, 1960, p. 13.

113. *DBEN*, October 27, 1960, p. 9; November 30, 1960, p. 1; and December 7, 1960, p. 11.

114. *DBEN*, December 7, 1960, p. 4.

115. *DBEN*, April 10, 1964, p. 9; April 13, 1964, pp. 1–2; July 6, 1964, p. 13; July 15, 1964, p. 9.

116. *DBEN*, January 13, 1965, p. 1; January 14, 1965, p. 9; and January 27, 1965, pp. 1, 3.

117. *DBEN*, October 6, 1965, pp. 1–2; October 20, 1965, p. 1; and Office of the City Clerk, Daytona Beach, General Election Results by Precinct, October 19, 1965.

118. *DBEN*, December 7, 1962, p. 1; November 20, 1963, p. 13; February 4, 1964, p. 9; April 7, 1964, pp. 1–2; and March 31, 1966, p. 15.

119. Institute for Social Research, Florida State University, *An Inventory of Community Living Conditions and Attitudes in Daytona Beach, Florida*, no. 4, January 10, 1962, pp. 14–25.

120. *DBEN*, January 7, 1960, p. 4; February 29, 1960, p. 4; October 10, 1960, p. 4; and September 10, 1964, p. 4.

121. *DBEN*, November 23, 1960, p. 4.

122. Interview, community informant, Daytona Beach, July 14, 1977; see also interviews, community informants, Daytona Beach, April 14, 1977, and July 14, 1977; and Killian and Grigg, *Racial Crisis in America*, p. 30.

123. Killian and Grigg, *Racial Crisis In America*, pp. 33–34.

124. DBEN, November 6, 1968, p. 7; and Office of the City Clerk, Daytona Beach, Results of the General Presidential Elections by Precinct, November 3, 1964, and November 5, 1968.

125. DBEN, April 18, 1962, p. 11; May 2, 1962, p. 1; and July 31, 1967, p. 9.

126. DBEN, December 19, 1962, p. 13; and January 10, 1964, p. 13; *Miami Times*, June 28, 1968, p. 9.

127. DBEN, July 8, 1964, p. 11; and August 30, 1966, p. 9.

128. Interview, community informant, Daytona Beach, April 28, 1977; see also interview, community informant, May 13, 1977.

129. DBEN, April 18, 1967, p. 2; April 19, 1967, p. 11; October 18, 1967, p. 9; and October 22, 1969, p. 7; and *Miami Times*, July 28, 1967, p. 24.

130. DBEN, October 9, 1964, p. 9; January 22, 1968, p. 13; October 5, and 1970, p. 15.

131. DBEN, July 19, 1967, p. 1; August 3, 1967, p. 15; and November 11, 1969, p. 10.

132. DBEN, June 21, 1965, p. 11; and September 16, 1966, p. 9.

133. DBEN, April 8, 1969, p. 3; December 19, 1969, p. 1.

134. DBEN, March 29, 1967, p. 11; June 17, 1969, p. 11; June 23, 1969, p. 7; July 10, 1969, p. 9; August 7, 1969, p. 9; and November 7, 1969, p. 1.

135. DBEN, January 5, 1970, p. 1; January 8, 1970, p. 9; January 15, 1970, p. 9; January 28, 1971, p. 9; and February 1, 1971, p. 9.

136. U.S. Bureau of the Census, *1970 Census of Population*, Vol. 1, *Characteristics of the Population*, Part 11, Florida, Section 1, 1973, pp. 372, 400, 407, 417, 422.

137. DBEN, July 17, 1970, p. 11; and Mike Bowler, "Southern Regional Council Report on Daytona Beach," reprinted in *Daytona Beach News-Journal*, December 13, 1970, p. 2C.

138. Bowler, "Southern Regional Council Report," pp. 2–3C; DBEN, October 7, 1970, p. 11; October 16, 1970, p. 11; November 2, 1970, p. 9; November 3, 1970, p. 1; November 4, 1970, pp. 1, 12; November 5, 1970, p. 9; November 6, 1970, pp. 1–2; November 9, 1970, p. 11; November 10, 1970, p. 9; and November 11, 1970, p. 13; *Miami Times*, November 13, 1970, p. 1; and *New York Times*, November 10, 1970, p. 51.

139. Bowler, "Southern Regional Council Report," pp. 2–3C; and DBEN, July 2, 1970, p. 9; and September 29, 1970, p. 1.

140. Bowler, "Southern Regional Council Report," pp. 2–3C; and DBEN, November 13, 1970, p. 2; and November 16, 1970, p. 1.

141. Bowler, "Southern Regional Council Report," pp. 2–3C; and DBEN, September 19, 1969, p. 12; November 16, 1970, p. 1; November 17, 1970, p. 9; November 24, 1970, p. 10; February 18, 1971; and August 5, 1971, p. 9.

142. DBEN, August 3, 1971, p. 10; September 17, 1971, p. 7; October 6, 1971, pp. 4, 9; and October 20, 1971, p. 9.

143. DBEN, January 11, 1972, p. 3; June 22, 1972, p. 3; August 4, 1972, p. 13; March 8, 1973, Section 2, p. 12; March 20, 1973, Section 2, p. 13; December 6, 1973, p. 1B; and October 3, 1974, p. 1B; and interview, local newspaper reporter, Daytona Beach, August 31, 1977.

144. DBEN, February 6, 1974, p. 9B; and July 25, 1974, p. 1B.

145. DBEN, November 10, 1972, p. 4; and October 17, 1973, p. 1B.

146. DBEN, July 9, 1971, p. 13; November 7, 1975, p. 1B; December 18, 1975, p. 1B; March 1, 1976, p. 1B; May 5, 1977, p. 1B; June 11, 1980, p. 1B; May 17, 1983, p. 1B; May 23, 1983, p. 1B; May 24, 1983, p. 1B; and September 12, 1984, p. 1B; and telephone interview, black elected official, Daytona Beach, July 2, 1982.

147. DBEN, February 9, 1976, p. 1B; February 18, 1976, pp. 1–2B; February 24, 1976, p. 1B; and March 4, 1976, p. 2B.

148. DBEN, November 3, 1977, p. 2B; and December 8, 1977, p. 1B.

149. DBEN, July 7, 1977, p. 1B; September 8, 1977, p. 1B; September 20, 1977, p. 4A; August 2, 1979, p. 1B; and April 17, 1980, p. 1B.

150. DBEN, January 9, 1975, p. 1D; and October 17, 1977, p. 1B.

151. DBEN, October 8, 1979, p. 1B; and October 17, 1979, pp. 4A, 1–2B; interviews, two black elected officials, Daytona Beach, October 16, 1981; and Office of the Supervisor of Elections of Volusia County, General Election Results by Precinct, October 17, 1979.

152. DBEN, January 15, 1975, p. 1; January 14, 1976, p. 1B; January 24, 1977, p. 1B; April 10, 1979, p. 1B; and January 25, 1981, p. 3E; *Daytona Beach News-Journal*, January 27, 1985, pp. 3–6I.

153. DBEN, April 2, 1974, p. 1B; January 24, 1977, p. 1B.

154. DBEN, December 2, 1976, pp. 1, 10A; April 11, 1977, p. 1B; and February 13, 1978, p. 1B; letter from director, Federal Office of Revenue Sharing, to city manager of Daytona Beach, April 6, 1977 (copy).

155. DBEN, March 2, 1977, p. 1B; October 12, 1977, p. 1B; January 10, 1979, p. 1B; July 2, 1979, p. 1B; and July 23, 1979, p. 1B.

156. Interview, black community informant, Daytona Beach, August 14, 1981.

157. DBEN, April 10, 1980, p. 4A.

158. DBEN, August 10, 1981, p. 1B; September 8, 1981, p. 1B; October 12, 1981, p. 1B; and October 21, 1981, p. 1B; Interviews, two black elected officials, Daytona Beach, October 16, 1981.

159. DBEN, July 15, 1982, p. 1C; August 2, 1983, p. 1B; September 13, 1984, p. 1C; and October 16, 1985, p. 6C.

160. Interviews, two black elected officials, Daytona Beach, October 16, 1981, and a city administrator, Daytona Beach, August 14, 1981; also, Office of City Clerk, Daytona Beach, Official List of Citizen Advisory Board Members, June 1, 1981.

161. Affirmative Action Report to the city manager from the employee relations director, Daytona Beach, June 16, 1981.

162. DBEN, July 23, 1979, p. 1B; and interview, city administrator, Daytona Beach, August 14, 1981.

163. *Daytona Beach Morning Journal*, May 10, 1984, pp. 1, 3B; and interview, city department head, Daytona Beach, February 26, 1987.

164. DBEN, June 6, 1980, p. 2B; and interviews, police officer, Daytona Beach, October 16, 1981, and the city manager, Daytona Beach, August 14, 1981.

165. U.S. Bureau of the Census, *1980 Census of Population*, Vol. 1, *Characteristics of the Population*, Chapter C, "General Social and Economic Characteristics," Part 11, Florida, Section 1, July 1983, pp. 259, 301, 308.

166. *Daytona Beach Morning Journal*, April 23, 1983; September 15, 1983, p. 4B; and October 8, 1984, p. 9A.

167. *Daytona Beach Morning Journal*, April 23, 1983.

168. DBEN, January 9, 1984, p. 4A; May 15, 1984, p. 1B; October 16, 1985, p. 1C; and February 2, 1984, p. 7A; *Daytona Beach Morning Journal*, March 5, 1985; November 5, 1985; and December 18, 1986.

169. *Daytona Beach Morning Journal*, February 8, 1983; September 15, 1983, p. 4B; and October 8, 1984, p. 9A.

170. *Daytona Beach Morning Journal*, February 26, 1986; interview, black community informant, Daytona Beach, February 25, 1987.

171. Office of the Supervisor of Elections of Volusia County, City Voter Registration by Precinct, April 15, 1981. See also the 1980 Census of Population and Housing, Block Statistics, Florida, Selected Areas, PHC 80–1–136, 1981.

172. Interviews, two black community informants, Daytona Beach, April 28, 1977, and July 14, 1977.

173. DBEN, July 8, 1975, p. 1A; and January 23, 1980, p. 1C.

174. Killian and Grigg, *Racial Crisis In America*, p. 31.

175. Bicentennial Commission, *A History of Riviera Beach, Florida*, City of Riviera Beach, Fla., 1976, pp. 1–24; City of Riviera Beach, *Comprehensive Development Plan for the City of Riviera Beach, Florida*, 1974, pp. 26–28; PBP, March 31, 1968, p. B11; and J. Wadsworth Travers, *History of Beautiful Palm Beach*, West Palm Beach, Fla.: Palm Beach Press, 1928, pp. 40–43.

176. Bicentennial Commission, *A History of Riviera Beach*, pp. 9–10, 25, 45; and Vivian Reissland Rouson-Gossett, ed., *Like A Mighty Banyan: Contributions of Black People to the History of Palm Beach County* (Palm Beach Co.: Palm Beach Junior College, 1982), pp. 14–15.

177. *A History of Riviera Beach*, pp. 27–41; and City of Riviera Beach, *Comprehensive Development Plan*, pp. 28–31.

178. City of Riviera Beach, *Comprehensive Development Plan*, pp. 39–40.

179. U.S. Bureau of the Census, *Census of Housing Characteristics*, Florida, Vol. 11, 1960, p. 124.

180. Interview, political scientist, Florida Atlantic University, Boca Raton, March 3, 1977.

181. Price, *The Negro and Southern Politics*, pp. 46, 56.

182. Bicentennial Commission, *A History of Riviera Beach*, pp. 57–58; City of Riviera Beach, *Comprehensive Development Plan*, p. 29; PBP, July 31, 1967, p. 7; *Palm Beach Post-Times*, April 1, 1956, p. 49; and Rouson-Gossett, ed., *Like a Mighty Banyan*, pp. 36–38.

183. PBP, April 4, 1956, p. 1; April 18, 1956, pp. 1, 10.

184. As quoted in Julian Bond, *Black Candidates: Southern Campaign Experiences* (Atlanta, Ga.: Voter Education Project, 1968), p. 25.

185. Interview, political scientist, Florida Atlantic University, March 3, 1977; see also Bond, *Black Candidates*, p. 26.

186. Interviews, three community informants, Riviera Beach, November 4, 1976; November 5, 1976; February 4, 1977; and PBP, September 21, 1972, pp. C1, 3.

187. *Miami Times*, August 5, 1961, p. 1; and PBP, February 18, 1960, p. 1; January 11, 1961, p. 2; January 18, 1961, p. 13; January 25, 1961, p. 13; April 11, 1961, p. 13; and March 6, 1962, p. 13.

188. Clubok, De Grove, and Farris, "The Manipulated Negro Vote," pp. 113–16. Lisa City is Riviera Beach.

189. Bond, *Black Candidates*, pp. 25–26; *New York Times*, April 19, 1962, p. 63; Office of City Clerk, Riviera Beach, Official Election Results by Precinct, April 17, 1962; and PBP, April 2, 1962, p. 15; April 4, 1962, p. 1; and April 18, 1962, p. 1.

190. Bicentennial Commission, *A History of Riviera Beach*, p. 58; and PBP, May 26, 1962, p. 13; November 5, 1962, p. 23; April 7, 1963, p. 1; February 25, 1965, p. 7; July 9, 1965, p. 7; and January 21, 1966, p. 7.

191. *Miami Herald*, January 5, 1967; and PBP, June 7, 1966, p. A7; June 8, 1966, p. A7; December 22, 1966, p. A7; and January 5, 1967, p. A7.

192. Interview, black informant, Riviera Beach, May 3, 1977; Meier and Rudwick, *CORE: A Study in the Civil Rights Movement*, pp. 90–91, 108; and PBP, April 12, 1960, p. 1; July 2, 1960, p. 1; September 22, 1960, p. 2; and July 5, 1964, p. A4.

193. PBP, September 6, 1962, p. 1; September 4, 1963, pp. 1–2; September 5, 1963, p. 1; and February 28, 1965, p. 1; and *Palm Beach Post-Times*, July 15, 1973, p. 1B.

194. PBP, April 8, 1964, p. 1; April 7, 1965, p. 7; April 6, 1966, p. A7; April 5, 1967, p. 7; and April 19, 1967, p. 7.

195. Interviews, two black elected officials, Riviera Beach, December 5, 1975, and August 3, 1976; PBP, February 19, 1970, p. D1; and *Palm Beach Post-Times*, March 24, 1968, p. A4.

196. Interview, black informant, Riviera Beach, May 2, 1977.

197. *Miami Herald*, August 1, 1967, pp. 1, 4A; and August 2, 1967, p. 2; *New York Times*, August 1, 1967, p. 17; PBP, August 1, 1967, p. 1; and August 2, 1967, pp. 1–2.

198. *Report of the National Advisory Commission on Civil Disorders* (New York: Bantam), pp. 112–13, 158–59.

199. PBP, August 1, 1967, p. 1.

200. PBP, August 2, 1967, p. 2.

201. PBP, August 2, 1967, p. 6.

202. Interview, white informant, Riviera Beach, May 2, 1977.

203. PBP, April 3, 1968, p. 2; November 7, 1968, p. 2A; and April 2, 1969, p. 1.

204. PBP, June 24, 1969, p. 2; and September 23, 1969, p. B1.

205. PBP, September 16, 1969, p. 1; and October 16, 1969, p. D1; and U.S. Department of HEW, Office of Civil Rights, *Directory of Public Elementary and Secondary Schools, Enrollment and Staff by Racial/Ethnic Group*, Fall 1968, pp. 252–53.

206. Interview, white informant, Riviera Beach, May 2, 1977.

207. Interview, black informant, Riviera Beach, May 2, 1977.

208. PBP, June 29, 1969, p. C4; July 18, 1969, p. 9; July 29, 1969, p. 14; and October 10, 1969, p. B12.

209. Interview, black informant, Riviera Beach, August 16, 1976; and PBP, May 8, 1969, p. A2; July 18, 1969, p. B1; August 8, 1969, p. A2; September 18, 1969, p. B6; September 21, 1969, p. B9; October 16, 1969, p. D3; and January 25, 1970, p. D11.

210. *Miami Herald*, August 31, 1969; September 18, 1969; November 6, 1969; and November 7, 1969; PBP, August 21, 1969, p. D1; and November 11, 1969, p. A11.

211. PBP, February 11, 1970, p. A9; and February 15, 1970, p. B1.

212. City of Riviera Beach, *Comprehensive Development Plan*, pp. 60–63; and PBP, April 7, 1971, pp. 1, 4A.

213. U.S. Bureau of the Census, *1970 Census of Population*, Vol. 1, *Characteristics of the Population*, Part 2, Florida, Section 1, 1973, p. 424.

214. PBP, April 8, 1970, p. C1; April 9, 1970, p. F1; and April 22, 1970, p. C1.

215. PBP, February 26, 1971, p. A1; March 2, 1971, p. B1; March 4, 1971, pp. A1, 12, 14; March 5, 1971, pp. A1, 12; March 6, 1971, p. B1; March 7, 1971, pp. A1, 16; and March 8, 1971, pp. A1, 5.

216. PBP, March 4, 1971, p. A12.

217. *Miami Times*, April 30, 1971, p. 1; and PBP, April 7, 1971, pp. A1, 4; April 21, 1971, p. A1; April 22, 1971, p. A1; and April 24, 1971, p. A10.

218. PBP, June 3, 1971, p. D1; and October 2, 1971, p. C2; *Palm Beach Post-Times*, September 12, 1971, p. B5.

219. *Miami Herald*, April 2, 1972, p. 4B; and PBP, June 2, 1971 p. C1; July 8, 1971, p. D1; July 27, 1971, p. B2; April 2, 1972, p. B2; and July 27, 1973, p. C2.

220. PBP, September 2, 1971, p. D4; November 10, 1971, p. C1.

221. Interviews, two black elected officials, Riviera Beach, December 29, 1975, and November 4, 1976; *Miami Herald*, July 6, 1971, pp. 1–2B; and April

2, 1972, p. 4B; *PBP*, November 4, 1971, p. A1; November 11, 1971, p. C1; November 12, 1971, p. C3; November 25, 1971, p. E3; January 5, 1972, p. C1; March 29, 1972, p. C1; April 11, 1972, p. C3; and June 20, 1973, p. C2.

222. Interview, black city official, Riviera Beach, August 6, 1980.

223. *PBP*, April 19, 1972, pp. A1, 9; April 20, 1972, pp. A1, 4; April 25, 1972, p. B1; and May 11, 1972, p. D1.

224. *PBP*, April 21, 1972, p. A18.

225. *PBP*, September 16, 1972, p. C1; November 9, 1972, pp. C1–2; and November 12, 1972, p. B2.

226. *PBP*, April 4, 1973, p. C1; and April 3, 1974, p. C1.

227. *PBP*, April 1, 1975, p. C1; and April 16, 1975, p. C1.

228. *PBP*, February 22, 1973, p. C1; March 1, 1973, p. C1; April 19, 1973, p. C1; and April 22, 1973, p. B2.

229. *Miami Herald*, June 8, 1977, p. 1B; and *PBP*, June 28, 1972, p. C1; August 16, 1972, p. C1; September 30, 1972, pp. C1–2; December 30, 1977, p. C2; January 5, 1978, p. C2; March 1, 1978, p. C2.

230. *PBP*, February 1, 1976, p. B1; January 5, 1978, p. C2; November 16, 1978, p. C2; December 20, 1978, p. D1; and November 2, 1979, p. C2; and *Palm Beach Post-Times*, December 29, 1974, pp. B1–2.

231. Interview, black elected official, Riviera Beach, December 29, 1975; and *PBP*, May 7, 1975, p. C1; June 25, 1975, p. C1; and October 2, 1975, p. E1.

232. *Miami Herald*, March 20, 1977, pp. 1, 8D; and *PBP*, March 4, 1977, p. C2; March 17, 1977, pp. A1, 13; March 19, 1977, pp. C1–2; and April 25, 1977, p. C1.

233. *PBP*, April 5, 1978, p. C1; April 6, 1978, p. C1; April 19, 1978, p. C1; June 8, 1978, p. C2; and April 4, 1979, p. C1.

234. *PBP*, February 22, 1974, p. C2; November 11, 1976, p. C1; and November 18, 1976, p. C2.

235. *Miami Herald*, February 1, 1975, p. 2B; *PBP*, May 2, 1979, p. B2; and U.S. Department of HUD, Annual Community Development Programs, Palm Beach County, 1975–1985.

236. Interview, black community informant, Riviera Beach, August 6, 1980; and *PBP*, December 29, 1976, p. C2; and September 18, 1978, p. C1.

237. Memo of budget director, Riviera Beach, "Uses of Federal Revenue Sharing by Entitlement Period," January 2, 1981; and *PBP*, December 18, 1978, p. C2; May 21, 1979, p. C2.

238. *PBP*, July 25, 1982, p. B2; and February 6, 1986, p. B1.

239. Office of Supervisor of Elections, Palm Beach County, "Voter Registration by Precinct," July 21, 1980.

240. Interviews, two city officials, Riviera Beach, March 11, 1987; and *PBP*, January 3, 1986, p. B3.

241. *PBP*, April 4, 1979, p. C1; April 5, 1979, p. A20; and April 2, 1980, p. C1.

242. Interviews, two community informants, February 4, 1977, and August 6, 1980; and *PBP*, November 24, 1986, pp. 1, 4A.

243. *Miami Herald*, April 6, 1980, pp. 1–2B; *PBP*, June 7, 1979, p. C2; September 6, 1979, pp. C1–2; September 26, 1979, p. A14; April 1, 1980, p. A18; April 3, 1980, p. C1; January 25, 1981, p. B2; and January 28, 1981, p. A14.

244. Interview, black informant, Riviera Beach, May 2, 1977.

245. *PBP*, April 8, 1981, p. C1; April 6, 1983, p. 1C; April 3, 1985, p. B1; April 2, 1986, p. B1; and November 23, 1986, pp. 1, 12A.

246. *PBP*, January 1, 1984, p. 1D; July 15, 1984, pp. A1–2; July 17, 1985, pp. 1–2B; and November 24, 1986, p. 4A; (Fort Lauderdale) *Sun-Sentinel*, August 10, 1983, pp. 1, 14A.

247. Interview, black city official, June 26, 1987; and *PBP*, June 19, 1986, p. 4B; June 23, 1986, p. 2B; November 23, 1986, pp. 1, 12A; November 25, 1986, p. 4A.

248. *PBP*, February 2, 1983, p. 1C; March 21, 1983, pp. B1–2; August 17, 1983, p. B3; February 6, 1985, pp. 1, 7B; and November 24, 1986, p. 4A.

249. Interview, city manager, Riviera Beach, August 6, 1980; and *PBP*, July 15, 1984, pp. A1–2; and November 25, 1986, pp. 1, 4A.

250. Interview, black mayor, Riviera Beach, December 5, 1975; see also *Miami Herald*, April 2, 1972, p. 4B.

Chapter 4
Black Political Participation and Changes in Police and Fire Protection

1. David L. Cingranelli, "Race, Politics and Elites: Testing Alternative Models of Municipal Service Distribution," *American Journal of Political Science* 25 (November 1981), pp. 680–86; Robert L. Lineberry, *Equality and Public Policy: The Distribution of Municipal Public Services* (Beverly Hills, Calif.: Sage, 1977), p. 117; and Kenneth R. Mladenka and Kim Quaile Hill, "The Distribution of Urban Police Services," *Journal of Politics* 40 (February 1978), pp. 127–28.

2. Keech, *Impact of Negro Voting*, p. 48; and U.S. Commission on Civil Rights, *Law Enforcement: A Report on Equal Protection in the South* (Washington, D.C.: U.S. Government Printing Office, 1965), pp. 92–97.

3. Myrdal, *An American Dilemma*, pp. 535–43; U.S. Commission on Civil Rights, *Law Enforcement*, pp. 92–97; and U.S. Commission on Civil Rights, *Report, Justice*, Vol. 5 (Washington, D.C.: U.S. Government Printing Office, 1961), pp. 5–44.

4. Keech, *Impact of Negro Voting*, p. 63.

5. Keech, *Impact of Negro Voting*, pp. 49–50; Matthews and Prothro, *Negroes and the New Southern Politics*, pp. 479–80; Price, "The Negro and Florida Politics," p. 218; and Wirt, *Politics of Southern Equality*, p. 168.

6. Matthews and Prothro, *Negroes and the New Southern Politics*, p. 480.

7. U.S. Department of Labor, *Negro Employment in the South*, Vol. 3; *State and*

Local Governments, Washington, D.C.: U.S. Government Printing Office, 1973, p. 3; and Browning, Marshall, and Tabb, *Protest Is Not Enough*, pp. 174–78.

8. Davidson, *Biracial Politics*, pp. 121–38.

9. U.S. Commission on Civil Rights, *For All the People . . . By All the People: A Report on Equal Opportunity in State and Local Government Employment* (Washington, D.C.: U.S. Government Printing Office, 1969), p. 12.

10. Equal Employment Opportunity Commission, *Minority and Women in State and Local Governments* (Washington, D.C.: U.S. Government Printing Office, 1974), p. 12.

11. Matthews and Prothro, *Negroes and the New Southern Politics*, p. 480; and U.S. Department of Labor, *Negro Employment in the South*, p. 3.

12. U.S. Commission on Civil Rights, *For All the People*, p. 13.

13. Ladies Auxiliary "Firebells," Crestview Fire Department, pamphlet, 1977, n.p.; and *ONJ*, October 26, 1961, p. 1.

14. Myrdal, *An American Dilemma*, p. 535.

15. Interview, community informant, Lake City, January 30, 1977.

16. *PBP*, May 26, 1962, p. 13.

17. William M. Bishop, Consulting Engineers, Inc., *Facilities Plan for a Sanitary Sewerage Project for Gretna, Florida*, April, 1975, Tallahassee, Fla., pp. 2–3.

18. North Central Florida Regional Planning Council, Community Development Block Grant Application, Lake City and Columbia County, May 1, 1976, p. 3.

19. Philip B. Coulter, Lois MacGillivray, and William Edward Vickery, "Municipal Fire Protection Performance in Urban Areas: Environmental and Organizational Influences on Effectiveness and Productivity Measures," in Elinor Ostrom, ed., *The Delivery of Urban Services: Outcomes of Change* (Beverly Hills, Calif.: Sage, 1976), pp. 243–56.

20. Florida A&M University, School of Business and Industry, *Comprehensive Development Plan—Phase One, Town of Gretna, Florida*, June, 1974, pp. 44–46; and *GCT*, May 11, 1972, p. 1.

21. Interview, city fireman, Lake City, February 27, 1976.

22. Interviews, three community informants, Gretna, November 17, 1977, and December 29, 1977.

23. Interviews, two longtime police officers, Lake City, February 12, 1976, and March 9, 1976; and interview, community informant, Lake City, December 1, 1977.

24. Bowler, "Southern Regional Council Report on Daytona Beach," *Daytona Beach News-Journal*, December 13, 1970, p. 3C; and Clubok, De Grove, and Farris, "The Manipulated Negro Vote," pp. 117–26.

25. Interview, community informant, Lake City, December 1, 1977.

26. Interview, community informant, Daytona Beach, April 14, 1977.

27. *DBEN*, November 10, 1960, p. 9; November 25, 1960, p. 30; December 5, 1960, p. 9; and January 25, 1961, p. 9.

28. Interview, news reporter for *DBEN*, Daytona Beach, April 14, 1977.

29. Interview, community informant, Crestview, January 13, 1978.

30. DBEN, November 11, 1970, p. 13; and TSA, November 21, 1968, pp. 1, 3A; November 22, 1968, pp. 1, 5A; and May 6, 1969, p. 1.

31. Clubok, De Grove, and Farris, "Manipulated Negro Vote," p. 121; Interviews, two black community informants, Lake City, February 11, 1977; March 3, 1977.

32. Clubok, De Grove, and Farris, "Manipulated Negro Vote," pp. 118–28.

33. PBP, April 2, 1972, p. B2.

34. ONJ, October 19, 1978, p. 3A.

35. DBEN, May 12, 1960, p. 9; Interviews, two police officers, Lake City, March 9, 1976, and March 12, 1976; and interview, police officer, Crestview, September 7, 1978.

36. Interview, community informant, Titusville, April 22, 1977.

37. *Palm Beach Post-Times*, January 1, 1972, pp. 1, 10C; and TSA, March 5, 1975, p. 1.

38. DBEN, August 3, 1970, p. 13; and interviews, four police officers, Titusville, August 3, 1976; August 11, 1976; and August 12, 1976; interview, police officer, Daytona Beach, February 11, 1977.

39. Interview, police officer, Daytona Beach, February 4, 1977; and TSA, November 29, 1968, p. 1A; April 28, 1969, p. 8A; September 23, 1970, p. 1; January 25, 1972, p. 1A; and June 4, 1973, p. 12A.

40. The proportion, rather than simply the number of blacks, provides a good indicator of black penetration, relative to whites, into these departments. Absolute gains in numbers alone, for example, may not mean much for blacks if white numbers are increasing even more rapidly and blacks are therefore falling further behind in a relative sense. In addition, a look at the percentage of blacks in higher ranks is perhaps the best indicator of progress, since resistance from whites would normally be greater at this level than at lower levels.

41. The primary indicator of the incidence of police brutality was the local press reportings of such events. Where the local newspaper was less than adequate in its coverage of racial incidents, such as in some Old South communities, greater reliance was placed on interviews with community informants and public officials to provide information about these incidents.

42. Most community informants also ranked black officials and/or the black vote as the most important method by which blacks had attempted to improve services in their community. Regression models, however, show that when an indicator of the black vote (the percentage of blacks among registered voters) is substituted for the proportion of black elected officials, it is a less statistically significant variable than black officials in almost every equation. Moreover, when a measure of minority incorporation into a dominant liberal coalition is substituted for the proportion of black officials, it too is somewhat less significant in every model. The reason for this seems to be the absence of a dominant liberal coalition in most of these southern communities, the exception being the majority-black communities in which blacks have established their own ruling coalition.

43. When outlier and influential data points are removed from these regression equations, the proportion of black officials is reduced in its level of significance but is still one of the top two most important variables in every model except one. Removal of these data points, however, yields a much lower R^2 for each equation and therefore creates a much less robust model. For information on how to identify outlier and influential points and whether such points should be removed from the data set, see Sangit Chatterjee and Frederick Wiseman, "Use of Regression Diagnostics in Political Science Research," *American Journal of Political Science* 27, no. 3 (August 1983), pp. 601–13.

44. PBP, April 23, 1971, p. D1; January 1, 1972, pp. 1, C10; October 7, 1974, p. B1.

45. Interviews, city manager, Daytona Beach, August 14, 1981; black elected official, Daytona Beach, October 16, 1981; black elected official, Lake City, February 13, 1981; city manager, Lake City, February 6, 1981; and black elected official, Crestview, September 15, 1977.

46. DBEN, December 28, 1970, p. 9; August 5, 1971, p. 9.

47. Interviews with chief executive officers and affirmative action directors for all communities.

48. Interview, city official, Lake City, October 21, 1977.

49. GCT, November 1, 1979, p. 1; and interview, town official, Gretna, May 20, 1981.

50. DBEN, March 19, 1970, p. 11.

51. DBEN, October 16, 1975, pp. 1, 3B.

52. Interview, city official, Daytona Beach, February 10, 1977.

53. Lawrence W. Sherman, "After the Riots: Police and Minorities in the United States, 1970–1980," in Nathan Glazer and Ken Young, eds., *Ethnic Pluralism and Public Policy* (Lexington, Mass.: D.C Heath, 1983), pp. 226–29.

54. Interviews, two community informants, Gretna, November 17, 1977; and December 29, 1977.

55. GCT, October 25, 1979, pp. 1, 3.

56. Other policy outputs of police services, such as police response-time to calls for assistance, were also important to blacks. However, such data by neighborhood were difficult to obtain generally and non-existent in the smaller communities.

57. Sherman, "After the Riots," pp. 225–26.

58. Ibid., p. 221.

59. Interview, city official, Riviera Beach, August 6, 1980; see also *Miami Herald*, June 8, 1977, p. 1B.

60. Letter from director, Federal Office of Revenue Sharing, to city manager, Daytona Beach, April 16, 1977 (copy).

61. Carol A. Pigeon, "Police, Fire, and Refuse Collection and Disposal Departments: Manpower, Compensation, and Expenditures," *Municipal Year Book 1979* (Washington, D.C.: International City Management Association, 1979), pp. 176–231; and City Budgets for 1977–78.

62. Advisory Board, Inc., Report to Riviera Beach Fire Fighters Association, November 10, 1975, p. 19.

63. Interview, city official, Riviera Beach, August 6, 1980.

64. Interview, fire department officer, Riviera Beach, August 6, 1980.

65. Interviews, city official, Titusville, April 30, 1981, and black leader, Titusville, May 1, 1981; and *Florida Today*, June 10, 1985, pp. 1 and 3B.

66. Interview, black city official, Lake City, February 13, 1981.

67. Interviews, four fire department officers, Daytona Beach, February 4, 1977.

68. Interview, fire department officer, Crestview, December 18, 1980.

69. Interview, fire department officer, Riviera Beach, August 6, 1980.

70. Interview, black city official, Lake City, February 13, 1981; see also interview, black city official, Crestview, December 18, 1980.

71. Interview, black fireman, Lake City, February 24, 1976.

72. Bowler, "Southern Regional Council Report," p. 3C.

73. Interview, community informant, Titusville, May 1, 1981.

74. *Florida Today*, June 10, 1985, pp. 1 and 3B.

75. Interviews, two city officials, Daytona Beach, August 14, 1981.

76. *Daytona Times*, January 8–14, 1987, pp. 1 and 3A; and *PBP*, November 4, 1984, p. C2.

77. Interviews, three fire department officers, Daytona Beach, February 4, 1977, and February 22, 1977.

78. Interview, city official, Daytona Beach, August 14, 1981; see also *DBEN*, October 21, 1980, p. 1B.

79. Interview, community informant, Titusville, May 1, 1981.

80. Interview, community informant, Crestview, December 18, 1980.

81. *LCR*, March 30, 1979, pp. 1–2.

82. *LCR*, April 2, 1979, p. 6; and September 18, 1979, p. 1.

83. Interview, black leader, Titusville, May 1, 1981.

84. Interview, community informant, Daytona Beach, May 13, 1977.

Chapter 5
Other Public Services and the Politicization of Blacks

1. Susan B. Hansen, "Participation, Political Structure, and Concurrence," *American Political Science Review* 69 (December 1975), p. 1199.

2. Floyd J. Fowler, Jr., *Citizen Attitudes Toward Local Government, Services, and Taxes* (Cambridge, Mass.: Ballinger, 1974), pp. 53–54.

3. *Report of the National Advisory Commission on Civil Disorders* (New York: Bantam, 1968), pp. 143–45.

4. *Hawkins* v. *Shaw*, 437 F. 2d (5th Circuit 1971).

5. Myrdal, *An American Dilemma*, vol. 2, p. 347.

6. Ibid.

7. George E. Antunes and John P. Plumlee, "The Distribution of an Urban Public Service: Ethnicity, Socioeconomic Status, and Bureaucracy as Determi-

nants of the Quality of Neighborhood Streets," in Robert L. Lineberry, ed., *The Politics and Economics of Urban Services* (Beverly Hills, Calif.: Sage, 1978), pp. 51–70; and Frank S. Levy, Arnold J. Meltsner, and Aaron Wildavsky, *Urban Outcomes: Schools, Streets, and Libraries* (Berkeley, Calif.: University of California Press, 1974), Chapter 2.

8. Antunes and Plumlee, "Distribution of Urban Public Services," p. 65.

9. Steven D. Gold, "The Distribution of Urban Government Services in Theory and Practice: The Case of Recreation in Detroit," *Public Finance Quarterly* (January 1974), pp. 107–30; and Lineberry, *Equality and Urban Policy*, pp. 108–9.

10. Lineberry, *Equality and Urban Policy*, pp. 108–17 and 142.

11. Keech, *The Impact of Negro Voting*, pp. 53–54; Myrdal, *An American Dilemma*, Vol. 1, pp. 497–500; and Price, "The Negro and Florida Politics," p. 219.

12. Keech, *The Impact of Negro Voting*, pp. 53–54.

13. Ibid., pp. 58–61. See also Price, "The Negro and Florida Politics," p. 219.

14. Ibid. pp. 62–63.

15. *ONJ*, March 24, 1960, p. 4A.

16. *ONJ*, July 20, 1961, p. 1.

17. Interview, black community informant, Gretna, March 19, 1981.

18. Community Development Block Grant Application, Gretna, Florida, 1979–1980, p. 4; and William M. Bishop, Consulting Engineers, Inc., *Facilities Plan for a Sanitary Sewerage Project for Gretna, Florida*, April 1975, pp. 3, 8.

19. Most of the decisions concerning the distribution of street paving were made by municipal or town officials, except for those involving state roads, which were paved and maintained by the state Department of Transportation. County government did finance some paving, especially in the rural Old South, but even here municipal officials usually determined which roads were to be paved.

20. *ONJ*, December 13, 1979, p. 1A; August 4, 1977, p. 1; April 3, 1980, p. 1.

21. Memo, Public Works Department of Daytona Beach, "Street Resurfacing by Geographical Area and Race," August, 1981.

22. Interview, community informant, Titusville, April 30, 1981.

23. Interview, black community informant, Crestview, September 15, 1977.

24. *DBEN*, November 23, 1960, p. 4.

25. Interview, community informant, Crestview, November 4, 1977.

26. Interview, community informant, Lake City, June 17, 1976.

27. Myrdal, *An American Dilemma*, Vol. 1, pp. 335–36.

28. Lineberry, *Equality and Public Policy*, pp. 110–11.

29. Caroline Allen, "Fairview Park History Recorded," *North Okaloosa Bulletin* (newspaper), no date; interview, black recreation supervisor for Fairview Park, Crestview, January 12, 1978.

30. Interview, community informant, Lake City, April 27, 1981.

31. Interview, community informant, Crestview, January 13, 1978.

32. PBP, December 18, 1960, p. 1; January 11, 1961, p. 2; January 18, 1961, p. 13; and December 15, 1961, p. 29.

33. DBEN, May 9, 1949.

34. Arthur D. McVoy and The City Planning Board, *The Master Plan for the City of Daytona Beach, Florida*, March 1, 1942, pp. 37, 41.

35. Institute for Social Research, *An Inventory of Community Living Conditions and Attitudes in Daytona Beach, Florida*, pp. 17–18.

36. ONJ, April 13, 1961, p. 1; June 15, 1961, p. 1; June 14, 1962, p. 3A; January 28, 1965, p. 6; and June 29, 1967, p. 1.

37. ONJ, January 17, 1974, pp. 1–2; September 19, 1974, p. 1; January 29, 1976, p. 1; *Pensacola Journal*, February 6, 1973, p. 1B; February 13, 1973, p. 1D.

38. Interviews, two community informants, Gretna, August 14, 1976, and March 7, 1983.

39. TSA, January 5, 1973, p. 1B; April 12, 1978, p. 1A.

40. DBEN, March 14, 1978, p. 1B; *Daytona Beach News-Journal*, January 25, 1981, p. 5E; January 27, 1985, p. 5I.

41. E. Franklin Frazier, as quoted in Myrdal, *An American Dilemma*, Vol. 1, p. 1274 (footnote 41).

42. Interview, black community informant, Lake City, May 15, 1981; black supervisor of recreation, Lake City, April 27, 1981; also LCR, December 22, 1966, pp. 1–2; June 12, 1970, p. 1; September 8, 1971, p. 2.

43. Killian and Grigg, *Racial Crisis in America*, p. 63.

44. Ibid., pp. 62–65.

45. Ibid., pp. 63–65 and 75; Telephone interview, black community informant, Daytona Beach, May 4, 1982.

46. Interviews, two community informants, Lake City, December 1, 1977, and May 15, 1981; LCR, April 14, 1961, p. 3; June 2, 1961, p. 1; November 24, 1966, p. 1; September 8, 1971, p. 2.

47. Interviews, Director of Recreation, Lake City, March 7, 1983; black public official, Lake City, March 9, 1983; and a recreation supervisor, Lake City, January 29, 1987; LCR, March 15, 1984, pp. 1–2; and March 12, 1985, pp. 1–2.

48. DBEN, April 20, 1965, p. 9; July 18, 1972, p. 9; interview, public official, Daytona Beach, February 21, 1978; TSA, July 6, 1962, p. 1; and July 10, 1963, p. 1.

49. ONJ, January 29, 1976, p. 1; December 25, 1980, pp. 1, 10A; January 15, 1981, p. 1.

50. Interview, black community informant, Crestview, December 18, 1980.

51. Interviews, two black informants, Crestview, August 7, 1986; ONJ, June 10, 1982, p. 1; and September 10, 1986, pp. 1–2.

52. Interview, director of Recreation, Riviera Beach, July 30, 1976.

53. Interview, director of Parks and Recreation, Titusville, April 30, 1981; TSA, October 10, 1979, p. 2A.

54. PBP, June 15, 1982, p. 1B.

55. TSA, October 21, 1981, p. 2A.

56. Interview, public official, Lake City, March 13, 1981; LCR, March 28, 1979, p. 16E.

57. "Evidence and Proposed Remedies, Lake City, Florida," attachment to letter to the city manager of Lake City from director of Federal Office of Revenue Sharing, February 9, 1981, p. 8.

58. Ibid., pp. 6–7.

59. Interview, director of Parks and Recreation, Titusville, April 30, 1981; TSA, July 16, 1980, p. 1A; October 21, 1981, p. 2A.

60. Myrdal, *An American Dilemma*, Vol. 1, p. 335; and Rodgers and Bullock, *Law and Social Change*, pp. 122–23.

61. Interviews, director of Public Works, Gadsden County, August 6, 1976; and supervisor in Streets Division of Public Works, Titusville, August 16, 1976.

62. DBEN, July 3, 1961, p. 11; interview, director of Recreation, Daytona Beach, February 12, 1978; PBP, April 11, 1961, p. 13.

63. Equal Employment Opportunity Commission, State and Local Government Information (EEO-4) Forms for each community, 1980.

64. Ibid.

65. Interview, director of Recreation, Daytona Beach, July 14, 1977.

66. The author also investigated water and sewage service changes, and political factors associated with such changes, for these six communities. Since the findings were similar to those reported here for streets and recreation, I saw no need to report in detail the results for one more capital-intensive service. See James Button and Richard Scher, "Impact of the Civil Rights Movement: Perceptions of Black Municipal Service Changes," *Social Science Quarterly* 60 (December 1979), pp. 497–510.

67. Neither indicators of the black vote or of black incorporation into the dominant coalition explain as much variation in most of these models as does the proportion of blacks in elected city office. Nonetheless, when not in the majority, black officeholders were predictably less influential in boosting employment of blacks.

68. Even when the dependent variable is "changes" from one 5-year time period to the next in park acreage or paved streets, the proportion of black elected officers is still statistically significant and the most important independent variable in the regression models. Black officials, however, are not significant in models of "changes" in black employment in public works and recreation. In addition, when outlier and influential data points are removed from each of the equations depicted in figures 5.1 to 5.4, there are no alterations in the relative influence of the independent variables and the explained variation is slightly higher in all models except for black park acreage.

69. ONJ, March 26, 1986, p. 1A.

70. Keech, *The Impact of Negro Voting*, p. 96.

71. ONJ, September 15, 1977, pp. 1–2; and September 29, 1977, p. 1; PBP, February 22, 1974, p. C2; and April 3, 1974, p. C1.

72. The measure of federal involvement preferred in these models is the number of federal grants rather than the presence of affirmative action, since the dependent variables represent capital-intensive (not employment) services.

73. *Pensacola News-Journal*, September 24, 1978, pp. 1–2C.

74. TSA, April 27, 1977, p. 8A; and March 15, 1978, p. 2A.

75. Interview, director of Public Works, Crestview, November 3, 1977; ONJ, June 30, 1977, p. 1.

76. TSA, January 22, 1969, p. 1B.

CHAPTER 6
THE PRIVATE SECTOR

1. Martin Luther King, Jr., *Where Do We Go From Here: Chaos or Community?* (New York: Bantam, 1967), pp. 4 and 6.

2. Davidson, *Biracial Politics*, pp. 123–40; Keech, *The Impact of Negro Voting*, pp. 96–99; and Thomas Sowell, *Race and Economics* (New York: David McKay Co., 1975), pp. 127–28.

3. Myrdal, *An American Dilemma*, Vol. 2, pp. 605–39; and Rodgers and Bullock, *Law and Social Change*, pp. 55–59.

4. Donald J. McCrone and Richard J. Hardy, "Civil Rights Policies and the Achievement of Racial Economic Equality, 1948–1975," *American Journal of Political Science* 22 (February 1978), pp. 1–17; Rodgers and Bullock, *Law and Social Change*, pp. 60–64; and Watters and Cleghorn, *Climbing Jacob's Ladder*, pp. 75–76.

5. Jacoway and Colburn, eds., *Southern Businessmen and Desegregation*, pp. 1–14.

6. Steven M. Gelber, *Black Men and Businessmen: The Growing Awareness of a Social Responsibility* (Port Washington, N.Y.: Kennikat Press, 1974), pp. 57–72; and Herbert R. Northrup, et al., *Negro Employment in Southern Industry: A Study of Racial Policies in Five Industries* (Philadelphia: University of Pennsylvania Press, 1970), pp. 6–17.

7. Sar A. Levitan, William Johnston, and Robert Taggart, *Still a Dream: The Changing Status of Blacks Since 1960* (Cambridge, Mass.: Harvard University Press, 1975), p. 21.

8. Watters and Cleghorn, *Climbing Jacob's Ladder*, pp. 350–52. See also Gelber, *Black Men and Businessmen*, pp. 3–5; and Ladd, *Negro Political Leadership in the South*, p. 23.

9. McCrone and Hardy, "Civil Rights Policies and the Achievement of Racial Economic Equality," p. 2. See also Paul Burstein, *Discrimination, Jobs, and Politics: The Struggle for Equal Employment Opportunity in the United States Since the New Deal* (Chicago: University of Chicago Press, 1985), Chapter 6.

10. Keech, *The Impact of Negro Voting*, p. 96.

11. Matthews and Prothro, *Negroes and the New Southern Politics*, p. 479.

12. Ibid.

13. The results of interviews with owners or managers of randomly selected private establishments in the six communities (see below in text) confirm these findings. The reported average percentage of customers who were black for all establishments was 20%, but for apartments the figure was 3%, and for country clubs less than 1%.

14. Interview, community informant, Crestview, January 13, 1978.

15. Ibid.

16. Interview, businessman, Lake City, October 21, 1977.

17. Interview, businessman, Crestview, September 16, 1977.

18. Black housing data by tract and block through the U.S. Census are unavailable for most smaller communities, but 1980 precinct voter registration by race in Crestview and in Lake City indicated that very few blacks lived outside of the traditional black sections of these cities. In Gretna, the town administrator provided a map of data on residential housing by race, and this too indicated almost complete segregation.

19. 1980 Census of Population and Housing, Block Statistics, Florida, Selected Areas, PHC 80–1–11, 1981 (microfiche).

20. Interviews, community informants, Lake City, June 4, 1976; and Crestview, January 13, 1978.

21. U.S. Bureau of the Census, Census of Housing: 1970, Block Statistics, Final Report HC(3)–53 and –54, Florida, 1971; and 1980 Census of Population and Housing, Block Statistics, Florida, Selected Areas, PHC 80–1–136, 1981. No such data are available for these cities for 1960.

22. *Miami Herald*, August 9, 1974, pp. 1–2B; September 6, 1974, p. 1B; *PBP*, November 10, 1971, p. C1.

23. See Morton D. Winsberg, "Changing Distribution of the Black Population: Florida Cities, 1970–1980," *Urban Affairs Quarterly* 18 no. 3 (March 1983), pp. 361–70.

24. *PBP*, July 20, 1971, p. B1.

25. Interview, black community informant, Crestview, January 12, 1978.

26. Wirt, *Politics of Southern Equality*, pp. 275–76.

27. Rodgers and Bullock, *Law and Social Change*, pp. 63–65; and Wirt, *Politics of Southern Equality*, p. 275.

28. *Cocoa Today*, August 8, 1971, pp. 1–2B; *PBP*, October 24, 1975, p. C1.

29. Interview, black community informant, Daytona Beach, October 13, 1977.

30. Interview, black community informant, Crestview, January 12, 1978.

31. Bowler, "Southern Regional Council Report," p. 3C; and David R. Colburn, *Racial Change and Community Crisis: St. Augustine, Florida, 1887–1980* (New York: Columbia University Press, 1985), pp. 143–58.

32. Interviews, white community informant, Lake City, December 1, 1977; black community informant, Lake City, March 8, 1977.

33. Interview, community informant, Daytona Beach, October 13, 1977.

34. Interview, black community informant, Riviera Beach, November 4, 1976.

35. Interview, community informant, Crestview, November 4, 1977.

36. Interview, community informant, Titusville, February 10, 1977.

37. Interview, black community informant, Lake City, November 4, 1977.

38. U.S. Bureau of the Census, U.S. Census of Population: 1960, Nonwhite Population by Race, Final Report, p. 102.

39. Levitan, Johnston, and Taggart, *Still a Dream*, p. 333.

40. The 1980 census data on black occupational status for these communi-

ties tend to confirm these findings in terms of level of employment. See U.S. Bureau of the Census, *1980 Census of Population*, Vol. 1, *Characteristics of the Population*, Chapter C, "General Social and Economic Characteristics," Part 11, Florida, July 1983, pp. 294, 296, 524, 628, 633, 814.

41. Ibid. These census data are not wholly comparable to the survey data, however. The census surveyed black citizens, not businesses, and utilized six general categories of occupational status which were unlike the three used here. More importantly, the census included all public employees in its analysis while this survey looked at just the private sector. The inclusion of public employees tended to enhance the occupational status record of the New South in particular, and would explain some of the differences in results between the census and this survey.

42. The geographical confines in which we sampled private establishments most likely affected these results as well. For Gretna, which had only a gas station and a grocery store, we sampled businesses primarily in the Quincy area, the nearest urban area and the place where most Gretna residents reportedly worked. For Riviera Beach, however, we sampled businesses only within the city of Riviera Beach. Although Riviera had a number of private establishments from which to sample, later data informed us that most of this city's residents worked *outside* of Riviera in other parts of the county, especially in the nearby urban area of West Palm Beach. Thus the results of the sampling, limited only to Riviera Beach, may have been misleading. Moreover, other labor force data indicated that black employment rates for Riviera Beach residents were relatively high. See City of Riviera Beach and Urban Planning Studio, *Comprehensive Development Plan for the City of Riviera Beach, Florida*, June, 1974, pp. 60, 63; and U.S. Bureau of the Census, 1980, *Census of Population*, Vol. 1, *Characteristics of the Population*, Chapter C, "General Social and Economic Characteristics," Part 11 (Florida), 1983, pp. 478, 501, 524.

43. Interview, businessman, Quincy, November 17, 1977.

44. Interview, businessman, Lake City, May 28, 1976.

45. Interview, businessman, Lake City, June 17, 1976.

46. Interview, businessman, Crestview, July 28, 1977.

47. Interview, businessman, Crestview, September 16, 1977.

48. Interview, businessman, Lake City, January 30, 1977.

49. Interview, businessman, Titusville, April 19, 1979.

50. Interview, businessman, Lake City, August 3, 1976.

51. Interview, businessman, Lake City, October 21, 1977.

52. Nijole V. Benokraitis and Joe R. Feagin, *Affirmative Action and Equal Opportunity: Action, Inaction, Reaction* (Boulder, Colorado: Westview Press, 1978), p. 1.

53. As an example, see *ONJ*, June 24, 1976, p. 6A.

54. *LCR*, September 7, 1981, p. 1; see also *ONJ*, July 13, 1978, pp. 1–2A.

55. Interview, businessman, Lake City, August 3, 1976.

56. Interview, businessman, Gretna, November 17, 1977.

57. *Daytona Beach News-Journal*, February 14, 1971, pp. 1–2D.

58. Interview, businessman, Daytona Beach, February 18, 1977.

59. Interview, businessman, Titusville, April 20, 1979.

60. Interview, businessman, Titusville, April 19, 1979.

61. Old South businesses reportedly first employed blacks, on the average, thirteen years ago, while the comparable figure for New South businesses was seven years. However, the businesses sampled in New South communities had not existed in these developing areas for as long as had establishments in the relatively stable Old South (the mean years were 14 and 21, respectively).

62. Interview, businessman, Gretna, November 17, 1977.

63. Data for the selected political and contextual variables were for 1980 and were typically an average measure for the 1976–1980 time period. During this time frame, indicators of black political organizations and protests were statistically independent and were therefore entered as separate, not combined, variables. Finally, ordinal-level independent variables from the survey were dichotomized for this analysis in order to meet the assumptions of the linear regression model.

64.

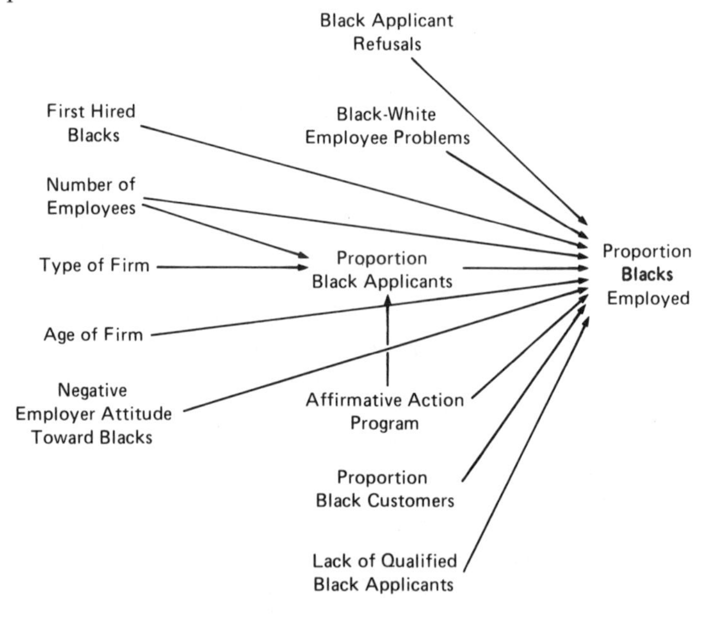

FIGURE 6.1
Path Model of Private Sector Employment

65. Watters and Cleghorn, *Climbing Jacob's Ladder*, pp. 350–51.

66. Interview, businessman, Quincy, November 17, 1977.

67. As quoted in Parker, *Political Mobilization in the Rural South*, p. 38.

68. Hanks, *The Struggle for Black Political Empowerment*, pp. 156–58.

69. Interview, NAACP leader, Titusville, November 20, 1986; and *LCR*, January 6, 1983, pp. 1–2; and February 16, 1984, p. 3.

70. *Daytona Beach Morning Journal*, December 1, 1982; December 28, 1982; and April 23, 1983.

71. *Pensacola Journal*, September 17, 1980, pp. 1, 14A; December 17, 1980, p. 3C; *Daytona Beach Morning Journal*, November 11, 1986.

72. Florida Department of Commerce, *Small Cities CDBG Program, Economic Development Category*, City of Lake City, 1984, p. 3; and interview, CDBG Coordinator, Lake City, January 29, 1987.

73. *Daytona Beach Morning Journal*, September 15, 1983, p. 4B; and October 8, 1984, p. 9A; *Daytona Beach News-Journal*, July 13, 1986, pp. 1–2E.

74. Interviews, city official, Riviera Beach, March 12, 1987; and director of Community Development, Daytona Beach, February 27, 1987.

75. Interview, black community informant, Daytona Beach, February 25, 1987; *Daytona Beach Morning Journal*, February 8, 1983; and September 15, 1983, p. 4B; *DBEN*, January 26, 1984, p. 2B.

76. *Daytona Beach Morning Journal*, October 8, 1985.

77. *Daytona Beach News-Journal*, July 13, 1986, pp. 1–2E.

78. Wirt, *Politics of Southern Equality*, p. 275.

79. See Davidson, *Biracial Politics*, pp. 139–40.

Chapter 7
The Civil Rights Movement and Social Change

1. Steven F. Lawson, "From Sit-In to Race Riot," in Jacoway and Colburn, eds., *Southern Businessmen and Desegregation*, p. 257.

2. Matthews and Prothro, *Negroes and the New Southern Politics*, p. 10; see also Ira Sharkansky, *The United States: A Study of a Developing Country* (New York: David McKay Co., 1975).

3. Jack L. Walker, as quoted in David J. Garrow, "Social Protest Movements: What Sociology Can Teach Us," *PS* (Fall 1985), p. 815.

4. See Bass and De Vries, *The Transformation of Southern Politics*, Chapter 3; Brooks, *Walls Come Tumbling Down*; and Havard, ed., *The Changing Politics of the South.*

5. Clubok, De Grove, and Farris, "The Manipulated Negro Vote," pp. 113–14.

6. Ibid., pp. 115–17.

7. Peter K. Eisinger, "Black Mayors and the Politics of Racial Economic Advancement," in Harlan Hahn and Charles H. Levine, eds., *Readings in Urban Politics: Past, Present, and Future* (New York: Longman, 1984), pp. 258–59.

8. Interview, community informant, Titusville, May 1, 1981.

9. Elizabeth Jacoway, "An Introduction: Civil Rights and the Changing South," in Jacoway and Colburn, eds., *Southern Businessmen and Desegregation*, p. 3.

10. Interview, community informant, Crestview, September 7, 1978.

11. U.S. Bureau of the Census, 1980 Census of Population, Vol. 1, *Characteristics of the Population*, Chapter C, "General Social and Economic Characteristics," Part 11, Florida, Sections 1 and 2, July 1983.

12. Ibid.

13. Interview, community informant, Titusville, March 10, 1977.

14. Detailed census figures are not available for Gretna prior to the 1970s. However, the results of general surveys in Gretna during the 1970s suggest that the socioeconomic status of blacks there is generally similar to that of blacks elsewhere in Gadsden County.

15. No census data on per capita income by race were reported for 1959. The census data summarized here for 1969 and 1979 include all communities except Crestview. Gadsden County again provides surrogate data for Gretna. The differences in white-black per capita incomes declined by an average of 3 percent during this decade. See U.S. Bureau of the Census, *1970 Census of Population, General Social and Economic Characteristics*, Final Report PC(1)–C11, Florida, 1972; and U.S. Bureau of the Census, *1980 Census of Population, General Social and Economic Characteristics, Florida.*

16. U.S. Bureau of the Census, *1960 Census of Population, General Social and Economic Characteristics, Florida*, Final Report PC(1)–C11, 1961.

17. Ibid.

18. Interview, black elected official, Riviera Beach, December 29, 1975.

19. As part of this study, and another of black elected officials in Florida, we interviewed all blacks elected to municipal office in each of these communities through 1980. We also queried our sample of well-informed white and black citizens as to the impact of having blacks serve in elected office in their community. For a more thorough analysis of white citizens' perceptions see Button, "Southern Black Elected Officials", pp. 41–43.

20. Regressing the percentage of blacks on major citizen advisory boards on the independent variables resulted in two significant explanatory factors: the percentage of black elected officials and the number of riots.

21. Browning, Marshall, and Tabb, *Protest Is Not Enough*, pp. 156–58.

22. Adding the percentage of blacks on major citizen boards to the list of independent variables in the regression equations added no statistically significant explanatory power in terms of the distribution of services and black public employment.

23. Paige Alan Parker and Larry R. Jackson, "The Southern Black Candidate in At-Large City Elections: What Are the Determinants of Success?" Paper delivered at the Annual Meeting of the Southern Political Science Association, Atlanta, Georgia, October 28–30, 1982, p. 18.

24. Interview, black elected official, Crestview, July 28, 1975.

25. Interview, black elected official, Riviera Beach, December 29, 1975.

26. Stein Rokkan, as quoted in Clarence N. Stone, "Race, Power, and Political Change," in Janet K. Boles, ed., *The Egalitarian City: Issues of Rights, Distribution, Access, and Power* (New York: Praeger, 1986), p. 220.

27. Stone, "Race, Power, and Political Change," pp. 220–21.

28. Lester M. Salamon, "Leadership and Modernization: The Emerging Black Political Elite in the American South," *Journal of Politics* 35 no. 3 (1973),

pp. 644–46; see also Matthews and Prothro, *Negroes and the New Southern Politics*, pp. 477–79.

29. "Second generation" discrimination in the schools may take several forms, including the overrepresentation of black students in special education classes or low-ability groups as a way of racially isolating them; the disproportionate expulsions and overly harsh punishments of black students; and the demotion or replacement of black teachers and administrators in desegregated school systems. See Charles S. Bullock III and Joseph Stewart, Jr., "Second Generation Discrimination in American Schools," *Policy Studies Journal* 7 (Winter 1978), pp. 219–24.

30. See Michael Lipsky, *Protest in City Politics: Rent Strikes, Housing and the Power of the Poor* (Chicago: Rand McNally, 1970), pp. 175–81.

31. Monica D. Blumenthal, et al., *Justifying Violence: Attitudes of American Men* (Ann Arbor, Mich.: Institute for Social Research, 1972), chapter 2.

32. William A. Gamson, "Violence and Political Power: The Meek Don't Make It," *Psychology Today* (July 1974), p. 39.

33. See Meier and Rudwick, *From Plantation to Ghetto*, pp. 271–72; and Browning, Marshall, and Tabb, *Protest Is Not Enough*, p. 246.

34. Jack L. Walker, "Protest and Negotiation: A Case Study of Negro Leadership in Atlanta, Georgia," in Harry A. Bailey, Jr., ed., *Negro Politics in America* (Columbus, Ohio: Charles E. Merrill, 1967), p. 133.

35. Ibid.

36. McAdam, *Political Process and the Development of Black Insurgency*, p.233.

Appendix 1

1. Robert L. Lineberry and Robert E. Welch, Jr., "Who Gets What: Measuring the Distribution of Urban Public Services," *Social Science Quarterly* 54 (March 1974), pp. 711–12.

2. See Button and Scher, "Impact of the Civil Rights Movement: Perceptions of Black Municipal Service Changes," p. 501.

3. Button, "Southern Black Elected Officials," pp. 29–45.

4. Peter H. Rossi, Richard A. Bert, and Bettye K. Eidson, *The Roots of Urban Discontent: Public Policy, Municipal Institutions, and the Ghetto* (New York: John Wiley and Sons, 1974), pp. 454–68.

5. Joseph Stewart, Jr., and James F. Sheffield, Jr., "Does Interest Group Litigation Matter? The Case of Black Political Mobilization in Mississippi," *Journal of Politics* 49 (August 1987), p. 781.

6. Karnig and Welch, *Black Representation and Urban Policy*, pp. 70–71.

7. Browning, Marshall, and Tabb, *Protest Is Not Enough*, pp. 24–27.

8. Ibid., pp. 272–76.

9. Ibid., pp. 81–84. Local government structure, especially district vs. at-large elections of council members, often has an important effect on black political opportunities in the South, but these cities all have at-large elections (except Lake City for brief periods) and therefore offer little variation in this factor.

10. Stewart and Sheffield, "Does Interest Group Litigation Matter?" pp. 780–98.

11. Colby, "Black Power, White Resistance, and Public Policy," pp. 582–86; and Stewart and Sheffield, "Does Interest Group Litigation Matter?" pp. 784–85.

12. Colby, "Black Power, White Resistance, and Public Policy," p. 585.

13. Browning, Marshall, and Tabb, *Protest Is Not Enough*, pp. 81–82; and Karnig and Welch, *Black Representation and Urban Policy*, pp. 105–6 and 136.

14. Karnig and Welch, *Black Representation and Urban Policy*, p. 118.

15. Browning, Marshall, and Tabb, *Protest Is Not Enough*, p. 280.

16. Herbert B. Asher, *Causal Modeling* (Beverly Hills, Calif.: Sage, 1976).

Index